IN COLOURS GREEN AND WHITE

A Post-War History of Hibs

Volume Two

John Campbell

BIRLINN

First published in 2013 by
Birlinn Limited
West Newington House
10 Newington Road
Edinburgh
EH9 1QS

www.birlinn.co.uk

Copyright © John Campbell

The moral right of John Campbell to be identified as the
author of this work has been asserted by him in accordance
with the Copyright, Designs and Patents Act 1988

All rights reserved.
No part of this publication may be reproduced,
stored or transmitted in any form without the express
written permission of the publisher.

ISBN: 978 1 84158 996 1

British Library Cataloguing-in-Publication Data
A catalogue record for this book is available from the British Library

Typeset by Iolaire Typesetting, Newtonmore
Printed and bound by Bell and Bain Ltd, Glasgow

CONTENTS

Acknowledgements — vii
Foreword — ix

Chapter One	1967/68:	**Napoli Humbled**	1
Chapter Two	1968/69:	**Record Sale**	13
Chapter Three	1969/70:	**'Nijinsky' Signs**	26
Chapter Four	1970/71:	**Managerial Changes**	36
Chapter Five	1971/72:	**Turnbull Takes the Reins**	51
Chapter Six	1972/73:	**Seventh Heaven**	63
Chapter Seven	1973/74:	**Ring Out the Old**	82
Chapter Eight	1974/75:	**So Near and Yet So Far**	96
Chapter Nine	1975/76:	**Derby Dominance**	118
Chapter Ten	1976/77:	**The End of an Era**	141
Chapter Eleven	1977/78:	**'Shades' Departs**	157
Chapter Twelve	1978/79:	**Hampden Heartbreak**	177
Chapter Thirteen	1979/80:	**Relegation – Despite Best Efforts**	200
Chapter Fourteen	1980/81:	**Straight Back Up**	220
Chapter Fifteen	1981/82:	**Death of an Institution**	240
Chapter Sixteen	1982/83:	**A Legend Returns**	263
Chapter Seventeen	1983/84:	**Youngsters Given Their Chance**	285
Chapter Eighteen	1984/85:	**'Juke Box' Arrives**	302
Chapter Nineteen	1985/86:	**'Juke Box' Departs Again!**	317

Index — 335

ACKNOWLEDGEMENTS

Over the period of time taken to write this book I have been helped and encouraged by many friends and I'd like to thank them all for giving me such tremendous backing. Though the list is long I'd like to single out Brian Johnson from the Programme Shop in Albion Road for access to and use of Hibs match programmes and yearbooks for the whole of the period covered as without them the task would have been so much harder; former director of the club Stephen Dunn and fellow Hibernian author Ted Brack both of whom were kind enough to read the whole manuscript and offer hugely appreciated advice and encouragement; and to Pat Stanton for his foreword. Sincere thanks also to Peter Burns, Neville Moir and all at Birlinn publishers.

FOREWORD

I have known John Campbell for a long time and his love of Hibernian Football Club is evident every time I meet him.

I remember going to Athens with John and a few of the lads when Hibs were due to play AEK. I recall us sitting in a bar not far from the Acropolis in this land of the great philosophers, Plato and Socrates (and I don't mean the Brazilian midfield maestro). We were another group of philosophers pondering on the fate of Hibs and how they would do. There was no lack of wisdom in our discussions either.

With his vast experience of writing about Hibs in the match programme, club website, Hibs.Net and the fanzine, *Mass Hibsteria*, John has a vast knowledge of the Hibs and this shows through in his book. I enjoyed the book immensely and it brought back many happy memories for me.

John is ideally placed to write such a book on the fortunes of our great club and I wholeheartedly recommend *In Colours Green and White* to all Hibs fans.

Pat Stanton

Chapter One

1967/68

NAPOLI HUMBLED

Just four weeks after the end of season 1966/67 Hibs set off on a marathon trip to Canada and the USA, where they would play in the North American League. Based in Toronto for 'home' games, the players flew thousands of miles in order to complete their fixture commitments, with the opening tie taking place in New York on 28 May 1967.

Prior to their departure, Hibs had called up Peter Marinello from the youth ranks and brought back John Blackley from Bo'ness United, where the young defender had been farmed out to gain experience, but neither player made it into the tour party.

The North American competition placed Hibs in the Eastern Division along with Aberdeen, Stoke City, Cerro (Uruguay), Glentoran and Shamrock Rovers. The Western Division contained ADO (Holland), Wolves, Sunderland, Dundee United, Cagliari (Italy) and Bangu (Brazil). In that peculiar conference type of arrangement now seen in American football, Hibs found themselves playing teams both within and outwith their own division, and their travels took them to New York, San Francisco, Dallas, Vancouver, Houston and Cleveland.

In that first game in New York, Hibs drew 1-1 with Cerro, thanks to an Allan McGraw thunderbolt. Three days later, it was Aberdeen in Toronto's Varsity Stadium, but Hibs lost to Eddie Turnbull's team by 2-1, with Peter Cormack on target for the Green and Whites. A long flight to San Francisco followed, but the players showed no ill effects, defeating ADO of Holland 2-0 after goals from Joe Davis (pen) and Cormack.

'Home' form deserted Hibs in the next match with Wolves at the Varsity and despite Davis scoring again from the spot the English outfit, eventual tournament winners, ran out 2-1 victors. The unlikely setting of Dallas brought Hibs up against Dundee United and although they were the better team they could only achieve a 2-2 draw, with goals from Cormack and Colin Stein.

It was a punishing schedule, with just three or four days between matches and thousands of miles to travel when playing away, but Hibs seemed to be coping well when they met the crack Italian outfit Cagliari at the Varsity on 18 June. The fans had expected the Italians to play the tight defensive game which was their hallmark. Surprisingly that was not the case, and both sides went for goals, Hibs coming out on top 2-1 with Cormack and Colin Grant on target. Sadly for Cormack he was sent off in highly controversial circumstances as the Italians got more and more physical. The referee was having real problems controlling the players and eventually decided to abandon the game with seven minutes left. There was some satisfaction for Hibs: the score was allowed to stand and the League took action against Cagliari for their unsporting behaviour.

A cross-Canada flight for the next match put Hibs up against Sunderland in the Empire Stadium, Vancouver. Despite going a goal down, the Hibees roared back to win 4-2 with Eric Stevenson getting a double while Scott and Stein also hit the target. One familiar face in the Sunderland team that day was former Hibs striker Neil Martin. A few days later the teams met again, this time in Toronto, and the Black Cats did a little better in securing a 2-2 draw, Stein and a Davis penalty providing the strikes for Hibs after the visitors had gone two goals up.

Game nine took Hibs to Houston for a match against Bangu of Brazil on the famous Astrodome synthetic surface. Cormack got the goal in a 1-1 draw which ensured a continuation of the good unbeaten run over the previous four games. At this stage, Hibs were looking a good bet to top their division, but a 0-2 reversal against Stoke City in Cleveland dented their chances. Cormack (ankle) and Stanton (blistered feet) missed that game and their absence obviously affected the Green and Whites. Two games remained, both in Toronto and both against Irish opposition. Four points were likely to be enough to win the division and therefore a place in the final. They got off to a good start with a fine 6-1 thrashing of Shamrock Rovers, Grant getting a hat-trick and singles coming from Stein, Cormack and Scott (pen), leaving only the requirement to beat Glentoran in the last game at the Varsity. In terrible storm conditions both teams struggled to find any form and an own-goal was all Hibs had to show for their efforts after 90 minutes in a 1-1 draw.

The 12 games in 43 days gave a record of played 12, won four, drawn five and lost three, with 23 goals scored and 17 conceded. Thomson Allan, Joe Davis, John Madsen and Jim Scott were the only players to feature in every game, while Peter Cormack finished top scorer with six goals. A tired Hibs party travelled back to Scotland, where a few short weeks of rest awaited them before they kicked off the new season.

On Tuesday, 8 August, Hibs travelled to the holiday town of Blackpool and it's assumed they entered into the holiday spirit as they were hammered 6-2 with only a Davis penalty and a strike from Stein to bring back as mementos. Four days later it was down to the serious business of competitive football as Hibs visited Dens Park for the first game in a League Cup qualifying group which also included Motherwell and Clyde. First-team regulars Alan Cousin and Eric Stevenson were both missing due to injury and Jim Scott had been transferred to Newcastle, but Hibs dominated for large parts of the game and were unlucky not to take both points, the game finishing goalless.

The fixture list then gave Hibs three home ties in a row, which must have had manager Bob Shankly thinking that qualification was eminently achievable, especially after a good 1-0 win over Motherwell in the first of those games. Just ahead of that match, Hibs offered a trial to a young full-back who turned out for the reserves at Berwick and impressed so much that he was signed. The lad was Mervyn Jones, a product of Edina Hibs and a nephew of the Rangers stalwart John Greig. The game with Motherwell was not as close as the result suggests and Hibs should have had a lot more than a solitary strike from Grant to celebrate.

Around this time the draw for the first round of the Inter-Cities Fairs Cup was made and Hibs were paired with FC Porto of Portugal, the home leg scheduled for 20 September and the return two weeks later.

Prior to that, however, the Hibees had a few other games to play and the first of those was the League Cup tie with Clyde, who had finished third in the League the previous season and so would be no pushovers. In a game tighter than the scoreline suggests, Hibs ran out 3-1 winners with Davis (pen), Cormack and Grant hitting the target and Clyde countering through Hastings. The result kept Hibs at the top of their group but only on goal average over Dundee, who would be next to visit Leith.

In the Dundee programme notes, praise was offered for the record of Joe Davis in his goal attempts from the penalty spot – the full-back had netted 29 out of 34 times since he took the job in September 1965. Joe was to alter the figures to 30 successes in 35 attempts when he scored in that Dundee game, but his goal, together with a strike from Stein, failed to save Hibs from losing 4-2 and relinquishing top spot in the group to the victors. Dundee had been on an incredible run when they had arrived at Easter Road, having gone their previous 25 matches without defeat, and goals from George McLean (2), Jim McLean and Sammy Wilson won the day and both points for Bobby Ancell's men.

Hoping to recover their form in order to stay in with a chance of qualification for the later stages of the League Cup, Hibs travelled to Motherwell needing both points, but returned with none as the Steelmen triumphed 2-1 in a tough match which saw both physios earning their corn. Goals from John 'Dixie' Deans and Lindsay were met by a single response from young John Murphy, scoring on his debut.

By the time Hibs visited Clyde in the final game they already knew that Dundee had won the group and so it was both galling and satisfying that they turned in a fine display at Shawfield in winning 2-0, thanks to goals from Stein and Cormack. Two League games had to be completed prior to the visit of Porto in the Fairs Cup and the first of those saw Hibs heading for Tynecastle to face Hearts.

In what manager Shankly later described as a display of fast, clever football, Hibs thumped their oldest rivals 4-1, Pat Quinn scoring an unforgettable hat-trick and Cormack raising the rafters in the stands with a magnificent diving header which bulleted past the helpless Cruickshank in the home goal. Hearts found small consolation in a Traynor goal. The visiting fans were ecstatic as they poured out on to Gorgie Road. Sadly, a small number took their celebrations a little too far and earned a reprimand from the Hibs chairman, William P. Harrower, who asked that the good name of Hibernian be kept out of the press for any reason other than performing well on the park.

A fine addition to the first-team squad was soon to arrive: prior to the home League match with Raith Rovers, Hibs announced that they had signed Alex Scott, brother of the recently departed Jim, from Everton. Winner of cup medals with Rangers and Everton, Scott also had huge experience of playing in European competition. With the Fairs Cup tie against Porto looming, it was a shrewd piece of business by manager Shankly.

Newly promoted Raith had narrowly lost their opening fixture 2-1 to Dunfermline and with former Hibee Bobby Kinloch and a young Ian Porterfield, who later went on to star for Sunderland and Aberdeen, in their line-up they looked likely to offer Hibs stiff opposition. As it turned out, the home side proved far too strong for the Fifers and a 3-0 scoreline might have been increased but for some fine goalkeeping by Raith's Bobby Reid. The goals came from Cormack, Stein and the unfortunate Kinloch – who for once did not intend to score for Hibs!

European football nights at Easter Road have been very special over the years and the evening of Wednesday, 20 September 1967, was no different as FC Porto arrived in Leith hoping to snuff out the Scottish challenge. With Alex Scott making his debut, Hibs set about attacking the visitors from the off and two first-half goals from Cormack, together with an early second-half strike from Stevenson, secured a 3-0 lead from this first leg. In truth it could have been six as Hibs saw the visitors clear the ball off their line on three separate occasions.

Ten goals in their last three games seemed to prove that the eye was in and when Hibs took on Dundee United at Tannadice just three days later they continued their fine form and raced into a two-goal lead through Stein and the dependable Davis from the penalty spot. It was Joe's 149th consecutive first-team appearance, an admirable record for any player to wish to protect, and so when he took a heavy thigh knock in the second half he made sure he would begin to receive treatment right away and be ready for the punishing schedule of games ahead. Sadly, the two-goal half-time lead was pulled back in the second period by a determined home side and goals from the Scandinavians Seeman and Dossing earned them a point in a 2-2 draw. It might have actually been a defeat for Hibs had Thomson Allan not saved Seeman's penalty, the first Hibs had conceded in nine months.

One more League game remained before Hibs would face Porto in the return leg of their Fairs Cup tie and that was a home match against bottom club Partick Thistle. The Jags arrived and left with no League points on the board as Hibs went nap with goals from Stevenson (2), Davis (pen), McGraw and Quinn. Thistle's consolation goal came from Rae after outside-left Arthur Duncan had been tripped in the home box. Duncan was superb in that losing Thistle outfit, and it was no surprise that a number of Scottish and English clubs, including Chelsea, were keeping tabs on the flying winger.

Following a nine-hour trip to Oporto, Hibs kicked off their return tie with their Portuguese opponents in confident mood, but things soon began to go wrong as Cormack was ordered off in the first half after reacting to a punch thrown at him by Rolando. Two goals by Valdir then made the Hibees jittery, but when the Spanish referee, Antonio Rigo, awarded the visitors a penalty all hell broke loose. First, the home players surrounded and jostled the referee and this went on for three or four minutes before order was restored. Davis finally got to place the ball on the spot. As Joe moved forward to strike his shot, the Porto keeper Americo came charging out towards him in a disgraceful display of poor sportsmanship, but the Hibs skipper stayed cool and fired the ball home to make it 4-2 on aggregate. A late strike by Pinto failed to save Porto, and Hibs were through.

Back in Scotland, the next action arrived against Celtic at Parkhead, as tough a return to League duty as anyone could have expected. While the Hibs men would undoubtedly be weary after their midweek travels to Portugal, there was every chance that the Celtic players, too, would be feeling the effects of their midweek trip to Moscow, where they had crashed out of the European Cup. In a game far closer than the final scoreline would suggest, Hibs gave a decent showing but still lost heavily 4-0 as Murdoch (2), Wallace and Johnstone breached Thomson Allan's goal. At one point, with the score at 1-0, a cracking header by Stein had whizzed past Simpson in the Celtic goal, only to be booted off the line by Gemmell. Had that gone in, things might have been different, but it was not to be.

As fans turned up for the next home game, against Dunfermline at Easter Road, they were met with the news that Hibs had drawn crack Italian outfit Naples (Napoli) in the second round of the Fairs Cup. The first leg was to be played in Italy in late November, delayed by the fact that Italy had some European Nations Cup qualifiers to fit in.

Dunfermline arrived on the back of a good 1-0 win at Pittodrie and so a difficult match was anticipated. Thankfully, Hibs closed the defensive gaps which had been exploited by Celtic and secured a 2-0 win, a Cormack strike and an own-goal from Pars defender Roy Barry keeping both points in Leith.

With new improved floodlights being installed at Easter Road the following weekend Hibs were of course playing away – at Muirton Park, where St Johnstone were going great guns in the League. They were undefeated so far and fresh from a brilliant 4-1 win away to Dundee. Hibs soon set about bursting the Perth side's bubble and two first-half strikes from Stein put them well in control before Saints pulled one back through Gordon. Stevenson restored the two-goal lead and a late goal from McPhee was not enough to save the day for the Perth men.

Hearts were invited to officially 'open' the new Hibs floodlights on the evening of Monday, 23 October, and both sides put out strong line-ups for the East of Scotland Shield 1966/67 final. Derby matches are often tense and this one proved true to form in front of a sizeable crowd, with Hibs narrowly winning 2-1, their goals coming from O'Rourke and Davis (pen). Donald Ford struck for Hearts.

Hibs were going well in the League and keeping in touch with the leaders when Airdrie arrived at Easter Road. With Billy Simpson in for the injured Bobby Duncan, the Hibees demolished the Diamonds 5-0, Stein hitting a hat-trick, his first for the senior XI. Cormack and Airdrie defender Keenan with an own-goal completed the rout.

While the crushing victory over Airdrie undoubtedly helped the goal average, the following game against struggling Stirling Albion at Annfield most certainly had the opposite effect as Hibs contrived to dominate the first half only to go a goal down right on the whistle. They then fell apart in the second to finish the game 4-1 losers. Kerray, Munro, Peebles and Hall each stuck a goal past poor Thomson Allan, while Stein hit a consolation for the hapless Hibees.

They say a week is a long time in football and it seems manager Shankly spent the next seven days sorting out the heads of those players who fell apart at Stirling, because Hibs went to a much harder venue, Dens Park, and won 4-1. But for bad luck and great goalkeeping by John Arrol they could easily have scored eight. Ironically, Dundee had taken the lead through George McLean, but Hibs came roaring back with goals from Stein (2), Cormack and McGraw that kept them in third place in the League behind Celtic and Rangers. Stein's goals took him to the top of the scoring charts in Scotland with 13 in total, of which ten were League goals.

With the trip to Italy to face Napoli looming, Hibs first had a tough match against Aberdeen at Easter Road to contend with. Eddie Turnbull's Dons were going well both domestically and in Europe, and so Cormack's winner in a tight 1-0 match was very satisfying indeed and meant the Hibees could set off for Naples on the back of two good victories.

The officials and supporters of Napoli made the travelling party most welcome and before the game in the San Paolo Stadium his Italian counterpart presented captain Joe Davis with a bouquet of flowers. Joe then passed the flowers to reserve keeper Willie Wilson, who drew huge cheers from the home support when he presented them to a female supporter in the crowd. The Italian players were not, however, in such generous mood as they set about beating the visitors by a 4-1 scoreline. Many observers thought Hibs unlucky on the night as they had made many chances but taken only one, while Cane struck three for the home side with Altafini getting the other. Stein hit the vital away counter for Hibs.

After the game, the Italian officials held a reception for their visitors and generously presented the club with a silver tray to mark the occasion. In addition, each player was given a musical cigarette box – something that today might not be thought wholly appropriate for professional sportsmen!

Back home in Scotland, it was widely suggested that Hibs had blown their chances of progressing, but Bob Shankly was having none of it, his lone voice insisting that the Hibees could still go through. It would not be long before his words were put to the test as the Italians were due in Edinburgh the following Wednesday. In the meantime, Hibs had the small matter of a League match at Ibrox. With Willie Wilson recalled in goals, they were extremely unlucky to lose the match 2-0 after Greig (pen) and Willoughby struck for the home side. Wilson very nearly saved the penalty, but the sheer power of the shot carried it over the line. At the other end, Sorenson in the Rangers goal had a number of inspirational stops from Stein and O'Rourke.

And so the second-leg tie against Napoli finally arrived. And on a misty Edinburgh evening, a miracle was about to unfold. The Italians, renowned for their defensive capabilities, were simply torn apart in a fantastic display of attacking football by Hibs. It all started after just five minutes when fullback Bobby Duncan hammered the ball towards goal from just inside the opposition half and the home support roared as it flew past the bewildered Dino Zoff to put Hibs 1-0 up on the night. Four more goals arrived without reply as Stanton, Quinn, Stein and Cormack all added to Duncan's opener and made Shankly's words come true. The visitors didn't know what had hit them and ended the game with just ten men after referee Antonio Rigo (remember him from the Porto game?) sent one of their players off near the final whistle. Hibs had made footballing history, becoming the first Scottish team to beat Italian opposition over a two-leg European tie. Their reward was to be drawn against the Fairs Cup holders, Leeds United, in the next round.

If the Napoli game provided a euphoric Hibernian support with a night they would never forget, the following Saturday's home League tie offered a game they possibly prayed they *could* forget. In a complete anti-climax of a match, the home team were abysmal and slumped to a 1-0 defeat at the hands of Morton. Winger Bjarne Jensen, who combined his footballing prowess with abilities in the boxing ring, where he had been junior middleweight champion of Denmark, scored the solitary goal. His strike was certainly a sucker punch to the disappointed home fans.

A bad spell of weather kept Hibs out of action for a fortnight and they resumed their League challenge with a visit to Motherwell, where a solitary strike from Stein earned two valuable points. Stein's goal was the first the side had scored in three League games and was a peach into the bargain as he controlled the ball with his right foot before smacking an unstoppable left-foot shot beyond the Motherwell keeper.

The following midweek, Hibs travelled to Leeds to face the English giants in the Fairs Cup. Once again, Stein was in the news – but, sadly, not for any positive reasons. First, he scored what looked like a perfectly good goal. Even referee Russell of Belfast appeared initially to be pointing towards the centre circle but then changed his mind after protests from the home defenders. Within minutes, Stein was involved again, but this time not for any show of skill: he had to be carried off on a stretcher with a badly bruised ankle after a tackle by Norman Hunter. Despite giving a fantastic account of themselves, the visitors ended up losing the game to a solitary strike by Leeds' Scottish winger, Eddie Gray.

Two days before Christmas 1967, Hibs welcomed Falkirk to Easter Road for a League match and had to shuffle their forward line a little because Stein was still injured. As it happened, he would not have been eligible to start in any event because he was under SFA suspension for the game. Once again, post-European-tie blues set in and only a very late strike by McGraw saved a point after Falkirk had led through Watson. In the match programme that day, Hibs announced that they would be making the stand all-ticket for the upcoming Hearts derby, with briefs costing 15s (75p) for the centre stand and 10s (50p) for the wing stands.

A visit to Rugby Park is never easy and in a dull match dominated by defences Hibs left empty handed having conceded a very soft goal to Tommy McLean in going down 1-0. Nevertheless, they were holding on to third place in the League, with Hearts hard on their heels, so when the two sides met on 1 January 1968 there was even more at stake than the joy of beating your oldest rivals. It was not a classic by any means and tackles were flying in from all directions, but the points stayed at Easter Road thanks to a Davis penalty. It was the first New Year's Day win for Hibs for 20 years. There was, however, a price to be paid in the form of injuries, with Duncan, Scott and Stevenson all limping off the park at the end.

Just 24 hours later, Hibs were in Kirkcaldy to face a Raith Rovers side sitting second bottom of the table. Hibs had to make changes because of the injuries and tiredness of some players from the derby match, and this provided an opportunity for 17-year-old right-winger Peter Marinello to make his debut. He turned in a fine performance, helping the visitors to establish a 2-0 half-time lead with goals from Grant and Cormack. The second half was less enjoyable as the plucky Fifers fought back. Goals from Mackie and Wallace earned them a much needed point.

Dundee United at Easter Road provided the final match before the visit of Leeds. The Hibees struck good form in overcoming the visitors by 3-0, with young Marinello sparkling on the right wing. A double for the prolific Stein and a Quinn strike meant that United went home empty handed.

The Leeds team who arrived at Easter Road on Wednesday, 10 January 1968, were positively packed with talent. Like Hibs, they were sitting in third place in their domestic championship, having not lost a match in the previous eight weeks. Any team boasting players such as Bremner, Charlton, Lorimer, Jones, Gray and Giles in their starting line-up would be entitled to expect to win, but a very plucky and determined Hibs side fought out a 1-1 draw, Stein hitting the Hibees' goal. Of course, the draw was not enough and the Yorkshire club progressed to the next round, but they certainly knew they had been in a game that evening.

If the European adventure was over, Scotland's pioneers in that area of football had not disgraced themselves by any means, the Napoli home match in particular proving that Hibernian could still live with and beat the best on occasion.

Back on the domestic front, Hibs next faced up to Partick Thistle at Firhill and goals from Stevenson and a Davis penalty brought the points back to Leith. Once again, the Thistle outside-left, Arthur Duncan, had a fine game and impressed the many watching scouts in the stands.

The visit of League leaders Celtic would provide a stern test to this Hibs side and on the day it turned into a total nightmare for Bobby Duncan, who not only gave the Glasgow team the lead with an own-goal but then tragically suffered both a broken right leg and severe damage to his ankle ligaments. These injuries were sustained in a challenge from the Celtic outside-left, John 'Yogi' Hughes, and the author's distinct recollection is that the tackle was both outrageous and vicious. Much to the disgust of the Hibs support, it went unpunished by the referee. A second goal for Celtic, courtesy of Lennox, gave the visitors a 2-0 win and two points in their race to win the title.

The Scottish Cup third round had presented Hibs with a visit to Firs Park in Falkirk, where they would take on minnows East Stirling. Manager Shankly was not tempted to rest some of his wearier players and he put out his strongest team, which was just as well because the part-timers played out of their skins, losing only 5-3 in a cracking match. Jones (2) and Gillespie for Shire and Stein (3), Cormack and a Davis penalty provided the goals.

Hibs were still sitting third in the League, with Dunfermline snapping at their heels, when they crossed the Forth to face the Pars on a snow-covered East End Park. In the difficult conditions the visitors came out on top, a single strike from McGraw winning the points.

The chance to consolidate third place came along when St Johnstone visited Easter Road and that aim was duly achieved when Hibs completed a League double over the Perth outfit with a 4-2 win. In a very entertaining game, Aitken and Whitelaw scored for the visitors while Cormack (2), Stein and yet another Davis penalty counted for Hibs. A regular advertiser in the match programme in those days was Fairbairns Off Licence in Albert Street. For many years it boasted excellent prices and invariably attracted queues of people around New Year time. Fairbairns no longer exists, but like many of the players and goals recalled in these memories it formed an integral part of Leith in those days.

Round four of the Scottish Cup took Hibs to Broomfield, where Airdrie awaited. Even before the match, many fans were already speculating as to which side Hibs might meet next, but of course the Scottish Cup has been less than kind to the Hibees over the years and in the shock result of the day the hosts won 1-0. The fight to hold third place in the League, thereby qualifying again for Europe, now became the sole target for the players.

Back in November, Hibs had lost a shocker to Stirling Albion at Annfield. They had the chance for revenge as the strugglers arrived at Easter Road in early March. While Peebles and Hughes breached the Hibs defence, Stirling keeper Murray was beaten five times, the goals coming from O'Rourke (2), Stein, McGraw and Stevenson.

The chance to avenge the Scottish Cup defeat by Airdrie came quickly as Hibs arrived at Broomfield on League business and duly turned over their hosts in a 2-1 win with goals from Stein – his 21st in League and Cup for the season – and an own-goal from Jim Black. The ex-Sunderland man Billy McPheat scored for Airdrie. A reshuffled Hibs defence, brought about by illness and injury to Wilson and Madsen, saw the return of Thomson Allan in goal and Alan Cousin at centre-half, both playing their parts in helping secure the points.

Hibs were third in the League after 25 games and holding an eight-point lead over fourth-placed Dunfermline, so that European spot was looking good as Dundee visited Easter Road. The visitors had crashed out of the Scottish Cup to Rangers the previous week, but were still going strong in the Fairs Cup, and in the quarter-finals were set to meet FC Zurich, who had already eliminated Barcelona and Nottingham Forest.

Whether that fact was on the minds of the visiting players or not is open to speculation, but Hibs won 2-0 with goals from Cormack and Stevenson. Many more chances were either missed by the forwards or saved by the excellent Ally Donaldson in the Dundee goal. The game saw the debut of 19-year-old John Blackley, who was drafted in after Pat Stanton had suffered a broken toe in the previous week.

A five-goal thrashing from Aberdeen in the next match brought Hibs down to earth with a bump as the Pittodrie men handed out a lesson in the game of football. While the players might have pointed to the early loss of experienced defender Billy Simpson and Davis's missed penalty as mitigating factors, the truth was that they were simply second best to a very good Aberdeen side, for whom Johnston (2), Smith, Taylor and Buchan got the goals.

With 37 points acquired, the third-place spot was still safe, but nothing that season could match the dominance of the unbeaten League leaders, Rangers. The Ibrox side, 12 points ahead of Hibs with a game in hand, arrived at Easter Road with 23 wins and three draws in 26 starts, a magnificent record. The Hibees had not managed a win over Rangers since season 1964/65 and that remained the case as the champions-elect recorded a 3-1 win in Leith. Despite a great goal from Stevenson, the Hibs defence could not stop Persson, Henderson and Johnston striking for the visitors.

The next scheduled opponents were Morton, but they were down to play Hearts in the Scottish Cup semi-final, so Hibs arranged to visit Newcastle for a friendly match at St James' Park. Young Jimmy O'Rourke scored for the Hibees, and what a thrill that must have been for him, but ex-Hibee stalwarts McNamee and Scott spoiled the party in securing a 2-1 win for the Magpies.

Back on Scottish soil the following week, Hibs travelled to Shawfield on League business. With a team weakened by the absence of the injured Cormack and Stanton, they managed a very creditable 2-2 draw, having gone in at the interval trailing 2-0 through goals from Anderson and Stewart. A second-half recovery allowed Stein and Stevenson to rescue the point.

Another trip through to the west followed as Hibs visited Cappielow to play Morton. In an astonishing first half, the home side hardly managed to get out of their own area as Hibs pummelled them but failed to break through for the vital opening goal. The Easter Road men paid the penalty when, on the stroke of half-time, Allan put Morton ahead from the spot. The second half was a bit more even in terms of possession, but the Greenock defence stood firm and Allan scored a second to seal a 2-0 win.

With four games left in the League, Hibs needed only four more points to be sure of third place. The first of those games brought Motherwell to Easter Road, where Cormack, recovered from injury, and the ever-reliable Stevenson scored in a 2-1 win, Wilson getting a consolation for the visitors.

A visit to Brockville followed, but the Bairns would not make it easy for Hibs as they wanted to ensure staying out of the relegation dogfight at the bottom with Stirling Albion, Motherwell, St Johnstone and Raith Rovers. With O'Rourke in inspired form, Hibs ran out 3-2 winners, thereby achieving their third-place finish with two games still remaining. O'Rourke was a constant thorn in the flesh of the home defence and it was his vicious shot which led to the first goal after keeper Devlin could only parry the ball into the path of the waiting Stein, who gratefully crashed it home. Jimmy scored the second himself with a 30-yard piledriver and then was brought down in the box, allowing Davis to notch his 12th penalty of the season from 14 attempts. Falkirk scored through Graham and Baillie, but in truth the scoreline flattered the hosts who were always second best on the day.

Two home games would see the season completed and the first came against Clyde, with a chance to improve upon the 2-2 draw of a few weeks earlier. The visitors made it difficult for Hibs, but O'Rourke and Davis (pen) gave the home side a 2-1 lead. Hastings scored for Clyde, who pushed hard throughout the second half for an equaliser, but it was not to be. Pat Stanton, fit again, was on the bench, but never got on to the park as manager Shankly decided against any changes during the 90 minutes.

Kilmarnock provided the opposition on the final day of the season, in a game where Joe Davis and Allan McGraw completed a 100 per cent attendance record in the starting line-up. In fact, Joe completed his third such season in a row and what an important player he had proved to be, with his stout defending and superb accuracy from the penalty spot. A great hat-trick from Stein secured a 3-3 draw and Kilmarnock were to be congratulated for contributing to a super game which never lived up to the customary end-of-season tag. A double from Morrison and a solo strike from McLean kept the fans in place until the final whistle.

A good season overall, then, with only the inevitable disappointment in the Scottish Cup offering any real negatives. Third place and qualifying for Europe was a fine achievement and fans would be given another chance to sample the heady nights at Easter Road, witnessed in the fantastic triumph over Napoli and the tactical but entertaining duel with Leeds. A League double over Hearts added to the enjoyment, as did the emergence of a few promising youngsters such as Peter Marinello, John Blackley and Jimmy O'Rourke, although the last named had been around slightly longer on the scene.

Chapter Two

1968/69

RECORD SALE

An intended tour of North America having been cancelled, Hibs set off instead for Africa, where they would play in five games during late May and early June in Nigeria and Ghana. The first game, on 22 May, saw Hibs line up against a Nigerian Olympic XI in Lagos. The temperature exceeded 100 degrees and the home side had already defeated two English touring sides, Sheffield Wednesday and Blackpool. Although the hosts opened the scoring, Hibs secured a draw with a typical Peter Cormack header, the young striker leaping high above his marker to crash home a cross from Eric Stevenson.

Just three days later, the tourists moved to Kaduna to play Northern Lions and ran out 1-0 winners, thanks to another headed goal from Cormack, the cross this time being provided by Alex Scott. The Nigerian part of the trip ended with Hibs meeting Western Rovers in Ibadan and the tourists took the chance to give youngsters Peter Marinello and John Murphy an outing in a game they won 1-0 when a Stein strike was diverted into the net by a defender.

Moving on to Ghana for the final two games, Hibs met a Ghana select in Accra and lost 1-0 against a very strong team in blisteringly hot sunshine. After the game, manager Shankly entered the home dressing room and, in a gesture which was both well received and appreciated by the home team, told them they were a fine bunch of players and had deserved to win.

The fifth and final game was played in Kumasi. Just prior to kick-off there was a terrible storm, and water had to be swept off the playing surface before the start. A North Ghana XI provided the opposition and Hibs cruised home 2-0 with goals from Stein and a Davis penalty. Highlight of the game was the display put on by Marinello on the wing, and it must have been music to his ears hearing the local fans cheering and clapping at each display of his ball wizardry.

As usual, Hibs kicked off their Scottish season with hopes of improvement from the previous campaign and there was plenty of opportunity to do just that with two domestic challenges, the League Cup and of course the Inter-Cities Fairs Cup, to test them. Prior to kicking a ball in anger they arranged two quite difficult friendlies, first against Fairs Cup co-entrants Newcastle at Easter Road and then a quick visit to St Andrews to take on Birmingham City ahead of the League Cup campaign, where they shared a group with St Johnstone, Raith Rovers and Falkirk.

As Newcastle and Hibs lined up on a lovely sunny Saturday in early August, each knew the sides they would face in the opening round of the European competition. Hibs had been drawn Yugoslavian opponents in Olympia Ljubljana, while the Geordies were to face Feyenoord of Holland – both being exceptionally tough ties in their own right.

In a highly entertaining game Newcastle ran out 2-1 winners, big Wyn Davies adding to a Shevlane own-goal and Stein striking for the home side. It was a new-look defence for Hibs after Shevlane had joined from Celtic and the popular John Madsen had decided to return home to Denmark to pursue a career as an architect, Alan Cousin inheriting the No.5 shirt. In that Newcastle game the Scott brothers faced each other: former Hibee Jim was in a Newcastle shirt and Alex wore No.7 for the home side. Alex, as it happens, did not last the full game and was replaced by Peter Marinello.

Three days later, Hibs faced Birmingham City in the Midlands and achieved a very creditable 2-0 win with goals from Cormack and McGraw. In goal for City that day was none other than Jim Herriot, who would later join Hibs.

Now that the friendlies were out of the way it was down to business in the League Cup, and the opening game brought St Johnstone to Easter Road on Saturday, 10 August, to face a Hibs side looking for a decent run in the competition. In the home team was Pat Stanton, newly voted Player of the Year by the Hibs Supporters' Association in their first-ever award of that accolade. Sadly, the game was marred by a nasty injury to Cormack, who damaged ankle ligaments. That incident seemed to upset the home side, who went on to lose the game to a solitary strike from winger Kenny Aird. A chance to scrape a point was lost when the usually dependable Davis missed from the penalty spot.

Midweek saw Hibs at Stark's Park facing Raith Rovers, and a single strike from O'Rourke won the points, despite huge efforts from the home side to force an equaliser. O'Rourke's goal came thanks to his very quick reactions when the Rovers keeper Reid could only push out a cross/shot from McGraw and Jimmy pounced to stroke the ball home.

In those days the reserves were also matched up in a League Cup section of their own with the same opponents as the big team, and it's worth noting that in each of their 5-1 and 5-2 victories over St Johnstone and Raith Rovers a certain 17-year-old by the name of Alex Cropley got his name on the scoresheet.

With only two points from their opening two games, it was important that Hibs got off the mark at home when Falkirk came visiting. Thanks to goals from O'Rourke and Stein, that's exactly what they did in a 2-0 victory. Cormack was still on crutches following the injury to his ankle, so there was a starting place for Marinello, who taunted and teased the Falkirk defence throughout the 90 minutes with a fine display on the right wing. Although Marinello got the headlines, it is worth recalling the situation surrounding O'Rourke's goal. Hibs got a free kick and Pat Quinn touched it to Jimmy, who duly lashed it home, only to have referee Wilson insist it be taken again. A repeat performance ensued – including the referee insisting it be taken again! The next attempt was third time lucky for Jimmy as the goal stood on that occasion.

With the first round of matches now complete, the teams faced each other again in a reverse of the opening fixtures, and Hibs travelled to Muirton Park seeking revenge for their opening-day defeat at the hands of St Johnstone. Two cracking goals from Stein, whose exploits were still drawing admiring glances from other clubs, were not enough to win the day as the visitors had to settle for a 2-2 draw after St Johnstone clawed their way back from being 2-0 down with late goals by Aitken and Aird, both engineered from midfield by Saints' star man, Alex McDonald. Hibs actually finished the game with just ten men after Pat Stanton saw red and was dismissed by referee Tom (Tiny) Wharton.

In game five of the six-game group matches, Raith Rovers arrived at Easter Road in second place behind Hibs and were duly dumped 3-0 by an in-form home side for whom Marinello opened his first-team account with a fine double, Stanton getting the other. Although Rovers arguably did not have any star names in their line-up, with top scorer Gordon Wallace perhaps the exception, they were a very well organised side under the guidance of manager Tommy Walker, and so the 3-0 scoreline was all the more impressive.

Qualification for the later stages was now virtually assured, but Hibs made absolutely certain when they visited Brockville in the final group match and took both points with an impressive 2-0 win, thanks to an own-goal from Doug Baillie and a great headed goal from Cormack, who had miraculously recovered from his recent injury. Over his time at Easter Road, Cormack was to do this repeatedly, confounding the medical men with his quick recovery powers. Making an appearance in the Hibs defence that day was a young John Blackley, who did not look at all out of place as he gave an assured performance at the back.

The draw for the quarter-finals brought Hibs and East Fife together, with the first leg to be played in Methil. Before that, there was the minor matter of the opening League match at Easter Road – against Hearts. The Gorgie men arrived having failed to qualify from their League Cup section, but they were fired up for the game by newly appointed manager John Harvey, who steered them to a 3-1 win. While Stanton struck for Hibs, the visitors took the points with goals from Jim and George Fleming and Danish cap Rene Moller. One 'weel kent' face in the Hearts line-up that day was none other than Willie Hamilton, who had previously thrilled the Hibs support with a number of outstanding performances in a green and white jersey.

In what was proving to be a very busy time for Hibs in terms of fixtures, they next travelled to Methil for the League Cup tie, and their power was too much for the second division side as they romped home 4-1 winners, thanks to Stevenson, Stein, Marinello and a Davis penalty. Nelson hit the consolation for the Fifers in what proved to be a pretty one-sided affair.

Losing a derby match hurt as much then as it does at any time, and the Hibs players were still smarting from that setback when they crossed the Forth again the following Saturday to take on Raith Rovers. The hosts set about exacting revenge for their League Cup defeats by running out 2-0 winners against ten-man Hibs, Stein having been sent off rather harshly for apparently back-chatting the referee. The home team scored through Falconer and former Dunfermline inside-left George Judge. While Stevenson hit the bar and O'Rourke had a goal bound shot kicked off the line, near misses count for nothing and Hibs had to face the fact that they would be travelling to Yugoslavia for the first leg against Olympia with no points on the League board.

In a downpour which lasted the entire 90 minutes, Hibs struck top form and ran out comfortable 3-0 winners with goals from Stevenson and Stein either side of half-time and an own-goal by Soskic when he headed past his own keeper from a Marinello cross. Although only 4,000 fans turned out to watch, Hibs were well treated: there was a civic reception on the morning of the game and each player was presented with a club pennant from their opposite number prior to the kick-off.

The following Saturday it was back to League duty when Falkirk visited Easter Road, and things looked bleak for the Hibees as the Bairns led 2-1 with just minutes left to play. The home side had scored early through Cormack, but strikes from Young and Graham put manager John Prentice's side ahead until Cormack took a hand in proceedings by snatching a late equaliser and soon afterwards charging into the box, only to be pulled down as he looked set to get his hat-trick. A penalty was awarded and Davis did the needful to earn two precious points as the team struggled with their fitness following the tiring trip to Yugoslavia.

Given that they had strolled the first leg against East Fife in the League Cup quarter-final, Hibs looked racing certainties to overcome the Fifers in the second leg. When Stein and Stevenson put them two up it was time to celebrate the semi-final place that the team had won. Even a goal from Waddell to make the score on the night 2-1 to Hibs and 6-2 on aggregate could not dampen the joy in the dressing room.

On the following Saturday, Hibs travelled to Firhill, where a buoyant Partick Thistle side outgunned them 2-1 in a tousy affair on a very wet pitch. The conditions seemed to take their toll on the Hibees, for whom games were coming thick and fast. O'Neill and McKinnon breached the Hibs defence, while Stein struck the consolation for the visitors. Although form in the League Cup and Fairs Cup was good, two points from four starts in the League was pretty poor. Thankfully, Hibs had a three-goal cushion going into the second leg against Olympia, and so panic did not set in when Popidova gave the visitors a shock lead. Two second-half penalties from Davis won the game and Hibs finished with a comfortable 5-1 aggregate victory.

Those two goals had taken Hibs to a total of 48 scored in Europe, and it was fervently hoped that the draw for the next round would give them the chance to hit the half century. Meanwhile, however, domestic competitions took precedence for the next seven matches and that run started with a home League fixture against Airdrie. At this early point in the season, Airdrie were sitting mid-table, having won two and lost two of their games to date. A rampant Hibs side set about them from the first whistle and goalkeeper Roddy McKenzie was a busy man throughout the game, picking the ball out of the net no fewer than five times as Stein (2), Cormack, Scott and Davis (pen) gave Hibs a nap hand. Defender and ex-Hibee Derek Whiteford struck for the visitors, who also had Jim Black in their side – Black later playing in the Turnbull's Tornadoes side of the early 1970s.

With League form taking a lift from the crushing of Airdrie, Hibs were next at Tynecastle to face Dundee in the League Cup semi-final. It was a truly memorable night for players and fans alike, but especially for Allan McGraw.

The game was finely balanced at 1-1 with 15 minutes left, Stein having scored for Hibs and McLean for Dundee, when McGraw took a heavy knock just below the knee and had to limp off. Hibs had already used their one allowed substitute, O'Rourke replacing Quinn, and so McGraw decided to return to the play, heavily strapped up. He was simply trying to ensure that Dundee had to mark him and so would not benefit from the extra man. In the last minute, with the referee readying himself to take the game into extra time, Stevenson swung in a corner and the ball found its way to McGraw some eight yards out. Astonishingly, the Hibs number six somehow managed to thrust his heavily bandaged knee at the ball and knock it past Ally Donaldson in the Dundee goal. Pandemonium broke out both on and off the park as all realised that Hibs were going to the final, and McGraw was carried off the park shoulder-high by his team-mates.

Another point regarding that game is often forgotten in the excitement of recalling McGraw's heroics: Stein's goal in the semi-final was to be his last for the club. Stein was scheduled to appear before the SFA to receive sentence for his sending off at Stark's Park some five weeks earlier. It seemed likely that a suspension would be issued, keeping him out of the League Cup final against Celtic due at the end of October. As it happened, the suspension was duly applied, but a fire at Hampden Park caused the postponement of the final. By the time it was played the following April, Colin Stein was long gone.

After the euphoria of that Tynecastle victory Hibs next travelled to Shawfield to face Clyde. In a game somewhat spoiled by a howling gale, they got a creditable 1-1 draw, Hood scoring for the Bully Wee and Cormack replying for Hibs. A week later, Kilmarnock were the visitors to Easter Road and they arrived in good recent form, having secured a 3-3 draw at Ibrox, so Hibs would have their work cut out to win the points. As it turned out, the Hibees struck good form that day and but for the heroics of the visitors' keeper, Sandy McLaughlin, the home side would have won by more than just the solitary goal scored by Cormack.

When Dundee United arrived at Easter Road the following Saturday they were sitting second behind Celtic in the League, although just three points ahead of Hibs, who were only 11th. It was still early enough in the season for no real gaps to have yet developed, although promoted Arbroath were propping things up at the bottom with just one point from seven starts. For the third game in succession, Cormack struck the only Hibs goal and with Cameron scoring for United the game finished at 1-1.

Scottish football was rocked in the coming week as Rangers raided Easter Road and took top scorer Colin Stein to Ibrox in a record-breaking transfer between two Scottish clubs, the Glasgow side shelling out £100,000 for his signature. The Hibs support was stunned and speculation began as to whether the management might sign a replacement or simply try to bring someone through from the reserves. In the meantime, the Hibees travelled to Love Street and it's possible the players were also affected by the Stein transfer as they turned in a dismal display in losing 3-0 to their hosts, Adamson (2) and Kane punishing slack defending.

The timing of the Stein transfer could not, it seemed, have been worse as Hibs prepared to travel to Ibrox to take on a rampant Rangers side. Lokomotive Leipzig were due at Easter Road just five days later for a Fairs Cup tie. Bob Shankly moved quickly to bridge the gap left by Stein's departure and signed Joe McBride from Celtic for a nominal fee. McBride was an acknowledged goalscorer, but had been troubled with injuries throughout his career and many Hibs fans doubted the manager's wisdom.

The game at Ibrox was a nightmare for Hibs. Although they played relatively well, they crashed 6-1, with salt being rubbed in the wounds when Stein scored a hat-trick. Johnston, Henderson and Persson completed the rout, but at least newcomer McBride got off the mark by scoring Hibs' only goal on his debut.

Hardly the best preparation for Shankly's men as they set about trying to focus on the upcoming tie against their East German opponents – who, as it happens, were struggling a bit domestically, their lack of a proven goalscorer being the main problem. On a crisp November evening, the home support got its first look at new striker Joe McBride. For those present it was the start of a love affair: all thoughts of Colin Stein evaporated as Joe scored all three goals in a cracking 3-1 victory. Naumann scored for the visitors, but even the loss of a precious home goal in Europe could not dampen the enthusiasm of the Easter Road fans as they streamed out after the game discussing their new goalscoring hero.

If McBride thought he had won the hearts of the home fans with his three-goal home debut he must surely have been entitled to add their souls when Morton visited the following Saturday. The former Celt went one better and hit four in the 5-0 win. Three starts and eight goals was a great way to kick off his spell in the green and white of Hibernian, and Shankly deserved credit for recognising that McBride still had goals in him.

The return game with Leipzig was the following midweek. Despite a quite arduous journey in getting there, including an eight-hour delay in Amsterdam and a 125-mile bus trip once they reached East Germany, they recorded a fantastic 1-0 win, with Grant ensuring a 4-1 aggregate victory. The journey back was little better as their intended departure from East Berlin was cancelled due to fog and they had to travel through the border checkpoint into West Germany, where they boarded a flight to London and from there to Edinburgh.

The visit to Arbroath, just two days after arriving back from Germany, saw a tired Hibs team still manage a good 4-3 win, their first away league victory of the season and an easier victory than the scoreline might suggest. Cormack and O'Rourke got one each while that man McBride got a brace, taking his tally to ten in five games. Hibs actually scored six of the seven goals in the game as both Shevlane and Cousin put through their own goal, Sellars getting the other.

The Fairs Cup draw saw Hibs paired with another German team, Hamburg – a much more difficult proposition than Leipzig. In the meantime they had to set about trying to improve their League position as leaders Celtic arrived at Easter Road having won nine and drawn two of their 12 games so far. The would-be champions were in sparkling form, however, and gave Hibs a bit of a lesson in finishing as they ran out 5-2 winners. The two Joes scored for Hibs, McBride against his former team and Davis from the spot – his 50th penalty success for the Hibees – while Hughes (2), Gemmell (pen), Lennox and McNeill countered for the visitors.

A positive note from the Celtic match programme informed the fans that John Madsen had returned from Denmark and was close to a first-team recall after having come through a couple of reserve games unscathed. This was good news on two fronts: not only was Madsen a good player but his return would release Pat Stanton from defensive duties and allow him to play further forward.

Two tough away games had to be fulfilled before the first leg of the Fairs Cup against Hamburg. The first was at Pittodrie, where Hibs recorded a stunning 6-2 win on a frosty pitch. Cormack got a hat-trick while McBride, Scott and Davis (pen) weighed in with one each. Goalscorers for Aberdeen were Buchan and Forrest but, as Hibs had led 5-1 at half-time, there was never any danger of not securing two superb points at a very difficult venue.

The Pittodrie success boosted both the League position and the confidence, so when Hibs travelled north again seven days later, this time to face Dundee, it was a little disappointing to secure only a 0-0 draw. Both sides created chances in a decent game, but neither goal was breached and a point each was a fair result.

On Wednesday, 18 December, Hibs took on Hamburg at their Volksparkstadion in the away leg of their Fairs Cup tie. With a thickish mist in the air and on a frosty pitch, they lost the game to a solitary strike by Honig after just five minutes. Hamburg had the West German internationalist Uwe Seeler playing at centre-forward that night, but he was kept very quiet by the superb performance of John Madsen. A 1-0 reversal away from home in Europe was a good result and Hibs had every right to be confident about the second leg, at Easter Road some four weeks later.

Back in Scotland on the following Saturday, Hibs entertained a strong Dunfermline side, in second spot in the League, just three points behind leaders Celtic. The Pars were also playing in European competition that season and had enhanced the reputation of Scottish football by reaching the quarter-finals of the Cup Winners' Cup. That being the case, a 3-1 win for Hibs was all the more creditable. Stevenson, after just 40 seconds, McBride and O'Rourke were on target for the Hibees, although O'Rourke also managed to deflect the ball past Thomson Allan to give the visitors their goal.

The Edinburgh derby on 1 January 1969 should have been won by Hibs, but even with all of the pressure in the first half at Tynecastle they could not find a way past Jim Cruickshank. The hosts made more of a game of it in the second period without ever troubling Thomson Allan and the game finished 0-0.

Just 24 hours later, Raith Rovers visited Easter Road and went back to Fife empty handed as Hibs strolled to a 3-0 win with goals from McBride (2) and Cormack. This game marked a welcome return to first-team action for right-back Bobby Duncan, almost a full year after breaking his leg in a game against Celtic at Easter Road.

Just two days after beating Raith, Hibs were in action again and a solo strike from McBride won the points in a hard-fought match at Brockville, where Falkirk were struggling to maintain their First Division status. That evening the draw was made for the Scottish Cup and there were loud groans when Hibs were given an away tie against Rangers. Strangely, the draw did not bother Bob Shankly too much as he was aware that, since the end of the Second World War, Hibs had met the Ibrox outfit six times in the Cup and triumphed on four of those occasions. The man was certainly a positive thinker!

The good run over the busy holiday period had seen Hibs win five points out of a possible six and move to seventh place in the League, four points behind St Mirren but with a game in hand. The feelgood factor soon disappeared, however, as Partick Thistle came to Easter Road and left with both points after winning 2-1. Quinn struck for Hibs, but goals from McLindon and ex-Celt Divers spoiled the day for the home support.

Defeat at home is not the best of preparation before a crucial European tie, but the Hibs players were well up for the visit of Hamburg, the Germans bringing a slender 1-0 first-leg lead to Leith. The game would be refereed by Sven Jonsson of Sweden, and for months, if not years, after the event he was a very unpopular individual as far as the home supporters were concerned. Things went wrong early that night when Mr Jonsson allowed Hamburg's Turkish goalkeeper, Arkoc Ozcan, to take to the field wearing a green jersey. Despite protests from the Hibs bench he was not asked to change it. Throughout the whole game thereafter, the linesmen repeatedly called offside when that was not the case – and this could only be down to the fact that they saw that 'green' jersey in an offside position.

In a cracking game, with Hibs well on top, McBride scored twice. Had that been the end result, Hibs would have gone through, but for once Uwe Seeler managed to lose John Madsen in the box to score the goal which took the Germans through on the away-goals rule. Hibs 'scored' three further goals that night, but each was disallowed, and the fans trooped out after the game feeling cheated out of progressing to the next round.

Hung over after that outcome, Hibs travelled to Airdrie on the Saturday and produced a dismal performance in going down 3-1. McGraw found the net for Hibs, but goals from Jonquin, Goodwin (pen) and Fyfe kept the points in Lanarkshire. Almost two-thirds of the season had now passed and Hibs were lying tantalisingly outside a European qualification spot, so the results would have to improve from here on in if they wanted another bash at Europe. First, they had to face that Scottish Cup visit to Ibrox.

The Hibs side which ran on to the park that day must have resembled a collection of extras from the popular TV show of the day, *Emergency Ward 10*, as Thomson Allan, Peter Cormack, Bobby Duncan and Joe McBride were all nursing injuries picked up against Hamburg, the latter three having actually missed the defeat at Airdrie as a result. Although manager Shankly had made great play of the fact that Hibs had a good post-war record against Rangers, it was a disappointing day. Despite playing well throughout, Hibs could not score and lost the game to a controversial goal from that man Colin Stein. Most in the ground, except the officials it seems, felt he was in an offside position when he fired the ball past Thomson Allan.

Clyde at Easter Road provided the next League test and goals from Cormack and McBride won the points, with the visitors scoring through Hastings. It wasn't the greatest of games and Hibs' resources were being stretched as players dropped out injured and youngsters had to be drafted in from the reserves. It was perhaps as well that a horrific spell of weather descended upon Scotland at that time, and Hibs managed just one more game before the end of February.

In the previous five seasons, Hibs had lost by an odd goal on each occasion they visited Rugby Park to play Kilmarnock. Sad to say, they maintained that unwanted record in going down 2-1 on a bitterly cold day. While McIlroy and Queen struck for the home side in the first half, McBride sparked a second-period fightback with his 15th League goal in just 13 starts, but it was not enough and another two vital points were dropped.

Among the challengers for a European finishing place in the League were St Mirren, who visited Easter Road on 1 March 1969 and suffered a comprehensive 3-0 defeat thanks to goals from O'Rourke, Davis (pen) and the inimitable McBride. Wearing the No.11 jersey for the home side that day was a young lad named Alex Cropley and he was very unlucky not to score on this, his debut, when a great piece of skill presented him with a chance which unfortunately came back off the post. At 18, Cropley had all the attributes required to make a name for himself in the game and, as time would prove, that's exactly what he did.

Cropley was the first Hibs player to come through the ranks from Edina Hibs, at that time run by the Supporters' Association. He had been offered the chance to sign for other clubs on both sides of the border, but the youngster only had eyes for Hibs.

The following Wednesday, Hibs hosted Rangers at Easter Road and in typical style they managed to dominate the game and yet lose 2-1. O'Rourke, who gave the big Rangers defenders their hardest 90 minutes in a long while, put the Hibees ahead and for a long spell the home side threatened to double their lead until referee Mr Anderson of East Kilbride awarded the visitors the softest of penalties, which Greig duly converted. The second half saw Hibs pounding the Rangers goal but failing to score. Then, in injury time, they lost the match to a Johnston goal. It was a sickening defeat and one which even the Rangers officials agreed was undeserved.

A visit to Cappielow followed and Hibs' poor away record continued as the hosts won 4-3 in a thrilling match on a soaking wet pitch. Two Hibs players, Willie Hunter and Peter Marinello, scored their first League goals, the third coming from the ever reliable boot of McBride. Nevertheless, the Hibees' defence had a nightmare and could not contain the young Morton forward Joe Harper, who bagged a hat-trick, Bartram getting the other.

Two one-goal defeats in a row did little to enhance the possibility of European football the following season and when the bottom club, Arbroath, visited in mid-March those chances were delivered another sickening blow as the visitors left with both points in a 2-1 victory. Jack and Sellars silenced the home crowd and Cropley's goal was overshadowed by the unexpected defeat.

With the season getting closer to its end, most clubs faced a quite punishing schedule of games because the bad weather in February had decimated the fixtures. Nevertheless, Hibs and Hearts agreed to meet at Tynecastle in the final of the 1967/68 East of Scotland Shield. The match finished 1-1 in front of more than 14,000 fans. While the record books will show that Moller scored for Hearts and O'Rourke for Hibs, perhaps the most significant event during the game was that Peter Cormack played in goal for most of the second half after Willie Wilson was carried off with damaged ankle ligaments. It's true that Moller scored his goal, the equaliser, while Cormack was in goal, but the Hibs star had a number of very good saves while between the sticks.

Just 48 hours later Hibs travelled to Parkhead and took a very well deserved point in a 1-1 draw. This was literally a game of two halves as Wallace scored for a dominant Celtic in the first half while McBride snatched the equaliser after the break in a half dominated by the visitors. Many observers described this as a League Cup final rehearsal, as the sides were scheduled to meet at Hampden two weeks later.

Ahead of that trip, Hibs played hosts to Aberdeen and had to settle for just a point as the Dons left with a 1-1 draw tucked under their belts. Forrest struck the Aberdeen goal while Hibs had to rely on Mr Dependable, Joe Davis, notching their effort from the penalty spot. Davis did well to score, given that the Dons' keeper, Ernie McGarr, had saved two previous efforts taken against him, but thoughts of missing were clearly not in the mind of the Hibs man as he sent the keeper the wrong way.

On the following Monday evening, Hibs faced Dundee United at Tannadice and were soundly beaten 3-0 by a better team on the night. Salt was rubbed in the wounds as former Hibee Davie Hogg nabbed a double, Cameron getting the other. Hogg's time at Easter Road had seen him often dominate the scoring in the reserve side, but he had never quite managed the breakthrough into the first team, so no doubt that made his goals all the sweeter.

At last the day arrived for Celtic and Hibs to contest the League Cup final. The Glasgow side went into the game as clear favourites, leading the League and showing good form, while Hibs had been on a run of very poor results. Still, manager Shankly was in confident mood because Hibs had very much held their own in that recent League clash at Parkhead. But there was to be no repeat of that performance. Although the Easter Road men started the game brightly they were soon overwhelmed and eventually lost 6-2. Goals from Stevenson and O'Rourke were poor consolation for the Hibs supporters as they watched their heroes losing their fifth post-war final. The Celtic sharpshooters that day were Lennox (3), Wallace, Auld and Craig. It is perhaps significant that the top Hibs goalscorer, Joe McBride, was forced to watch from the stand having been cup-tied in an earlier round while still with Celtic.

The defeat held a double blow for Hibs in that they had also lost the last chance they had of winning a place in the Fairs Cup the following season. More misery came on the following Tuesday, when Dundee, who had also had a poor season, visited Easter Road and took both points in a 3-1 win. The Hibees simply looked jaded and played as though the season's end could not come quickly enough. Scott (2) and Kininmonth punished poor defending while spring-heeled Cormack rose high to head a consolation goal for Hibs.

Around this time, Hibs dipped into the transfer market and signed the experienced Gordon Marshall from Nottingham Forest. Although English-born, the goalkeeper had grown up in Edinburgh and had starred in a Hearts side which had won both League and League Cup before he left to join Newcastle United in an £18,000 transfer. Five years at St James' Park saw him a first-team regular before Forest tempted him further south in 1968. The big keeper went straight into the Hibs team and made his debut at Muirton Park where, after just six minutes, he conceded two goals. It has to be said that these were down to shoddy defending, and Marshall was excellent for the rest of the game. Sadly, Hibs could not recover and ended up losing 2-1, thanks to those early goals from McCarry and Hall. Matters were not helped when Marinello was sent off for making comments to a linesman, and in a period where the words 'consolation goal' seemed to appear much too regularly in Hibs' match reports, it was Stevenson who scored for the Green and Whites.

The 1968/69 East of Scotland Shield final took place at Easter Road on Saturday, 26 April 1969, and Hibs won the trophy for the 40th time, thanks to a single goal struck by O'Rourke and a fine home debut from keeper Gordon Marshall, who denied his former club on a number of occasions. O'Rourke certainly seemed to enjoy scoring against the Tynecastle men as that winner was his third in three meetings.

It was to be O'Rourke's name on the scoresheet again the following midweek as Hibs travelled to East End Park and secured a 1-1 draw,

George McLean notching the Dunfermline goal. The Hibees were actually only minutes away from winning, but in truth a draw was a fair result on the night.

A long, hard season came to an end on Wednesday, 30 April, when Hibs welcomed St Johnstone to Easter Road and exacted revenge on the Saints for that defeat at Muirton just 11 days earlier. Cormack (2), McBride and O'Rourke sent the home fans away happy to have seen a few goals to last them through the summer months.

In end-of-season moves, four well-known Hibs players were given free transfers. Goalkeeper Willie Wilson ended his ten-year association with the club, as did inside-forwards Pat Quinn and Allan McGraw, while defender Alan Cousin was also allowed to leave. Called up from the ground staff were youngsters John Brownlie and Willie McEwan.

Having reached a Cup final, it would be wrong to say this had been a poor season for Hibs. But they had performed inconsistently in the League and been knocked out of the Scottish Cup in the first round, as well as losing top scorer Colin Stein to Rangers. True, Joe McBride had stepped in to replace Stein, and had made a marvellous job of doing so, but still there was a sense of disappointment, especially since the coveted qualification for Europe had not been achieved.

Chapter Three

1969/70

'NIJINSKY' SIGNS

Having enjoyed a couple of months off, the Hibs players returned to training before starting the season with a couple of friendlies ahead of the League Cup qualifying group. The first of those friendly matches took Hibs to Highfield Road, Coventry, and they led through a fine solo goal from Stevenson until ex-Hibee Neil Martin crashed in a last-minute equaliser with a powerful header. Making his debut in that game was new signing Jim Black from Airdrie, a centre-half who commanded a then record transfer fee in excess of £30,000.

The following Tuesday, Newcastle arrived at Easter Road as the new holders of the Inter-Cities Fairs Cup. In a quite entertaining game all that was missing was goals as the tie ended 0-0. This was the first time Hibs played in front of their own fans under their new captain, Pat Stanton. The new skipper, who had been with Hibs for around seven years, notching up more than 300 appearances in all games, took over the captain's armband from Joe Davis.

The League Cup had matched Hibs with Aberdeen, Dunfermline and Clyde in what many described as the toughest group, and the Hibees kicked off their campaign with a home tie against Clyde. Preparations for the game were somewhat disrupted when it was learned that in addition to losing Cormack and Marinello through suspension, Hibs would also be without McBride following his injury in the friendly with Newcastle.

The Hibees coped exceptionally well in the absence of that influential trio and ran out 4-1 winners, Grant getting two and Murphy and Stanton (pen) one each. The Clyde goal was scored by new striker Billy Hulston, who had been drafted in after Harry Hood left in the summer to join Celtic for around £35,000.

East End Park beckoned for the second group match, but a poor performance from Shankly's men saw them beaten 3-1 by a decent Dunfermline side. Two goals from Mitchell and a great solo effort from the former Rangers and Dundee striker George McLean counted for the Pars. Young Colin Grant was on target again for Hibs, who had been teased throughout by the midfield wizardry of a young Fifer named Alex Edwards.

One win and one loss made the third game against Aberdeen at Pittodrie all the more vital to any hopes of qualification. When the Dons raced into a two-goal lead, through Hermiston (pen) and Hamilton, it looked as though Cup progression was dead and buried. But Hibs fought back and took the game to Aberdeen in the second half, scoring goals through Grant and McBride to salvage a point. Defender John Madsen missed this game through injury, but an able deputy was found in Ian Wilkinson, while a young Johnny Hamilton replaced the injured Marinello during the game.

The chance to avenge a defeat came quickly in these group qualifying stages and when leaders Dunfermline visited Easter Road that chance was duly taken as Stanton and Marinello each beat goalkeeper Bent Martin in a 2-0 win, taking the Hibees to the top of the group. It was a fine performance from the Hibs boys and special mention goes to skipper Pat Stanton for nullifying the threat from Alex Edwards in midfield.

Having trounced Clyde 4-1 in the opening match and that with a weakened team, Hibs were confident about going to Shawfield and getting a decent result, but they hardly got out of the starting blocks as the Bully Wee exacted revenge with a 3-1 victory, striker Hulston getting all three, including one from the spot. Although McBride got one back it was a case of too little too late.

Qualification from the group had gone to the wire as both Hibs and Aberdeen, who next met at Easter Road, had the chance to progress to a lucrative tie against either Celtic or Rangers in the quarter-finals. Basically, Hibs needed to win by two goals against Aberdeen, who arrived in Edinburgh having won two and drawn three of their five games to date. It turned out to be a dour affair, with the Dons intent on keeping it tight. After 90 pretty dull minutes the game finished without any goals and so the Dons progressed to the next stage.

There was to be no rest for the players as three days later they opened their League campaign by visiting newly promoted Ayr United at Somerset Park. As in the League Cup group matches, their away form was very poor and their hosts rolled them over 3-0 with goals from Ingram, Ferguson and Rough. The star of the show, however, was their young outside-right, Quinton Young, who tormented the Hibs defence throughout.

Back at Easter Road the following midweek, Hibs continued their Jekyll and Hyde impersonation in comfortably beating a good St Mirren side 2-0, thanks to a double from Cormack. Playing number eight for the Buddies that day was Jim Blair, who would join Hibs in the future.

Around this time the news was breaking that manager Bob Shankly was unhappy with the amount of transfer talk surrounding Hibs and his failure to receive any guarantees that his star players would not be sold. Eventually that uncertainty proved too much for the gaffer, and he resigned immediately after the win over St Mirren, much to the shock of the Hibs supporters, who woke up to read the headlines the following morning.

Speculation immediately began over Shankly's possible successor, but the board would not be rushed and Hibs meanwhile played without a manager, firstly in a home tie against Partick Thistle. The strike power of the Hibs front line was all too much for the visiting defence, which had a young Alan Hansen among its number, and a McBride hat-trick, plus two goals from Cormack, had the home fans singing as they left the stadium. Interestingly, the visitors scored through outside-left Arthur Duncan, who would go on to play a record number of games for Hibs in the future.

Hibs next went to Parkhead to face a Celtic team whose form had been uneven. In terms of possession, the first half was dominated by the home side. When Johnstone put them ahead, most observers thought that would be that. But within three minutes of the restart, Hibs were level. After Marinello and then Stevenson carved open the home defence, centre-half McNeill was caught flat-footed and young Johnny Hamilton crashed the ball past Fallon in the Celtic goal.

Celtic, stung by this blow, fought back hard, but the Hibs defence, marshalled superbly by John Blackley, held firm and the big home crowd was stunned into silence when Pat Stanton crashed home a superb late winner to leave the reigning champions to swallow a rare home defeat. The two points gained pushed Hibs up to fourth place behind Motherwell, Dunfermline and Morton and left Celtic and Rangers trailing behind.

Seven days later, Raith Rovers were the visitors to Easter Road and the game was probably most notable for the fact that full-back Chris Shevlane scored in the 3-1 victory. The other goals were taken well by Marinello and McBride. Colin Sinclair netted for the Fifers, whose line-up included the former Rangers stalwart Ralph Brand.

After the opening-day reversal at Somerset Park, Hibs had now gone four games undefeated and in the week leading up to the Edinburgh derby at Tynecastle the board unveiled its new manager, Willie MacFarlane, who arrived from part-time Stirling Albion. MacFarlane had been a Hibs player in the 1950s and had cut his managerial teeth at Gala Fairydean, Eyemouth United and Hawick Royal Albert before taking over at Stirling. Just minutes after his appointment, MacFarlane endeared himself greatly to the Hibs support by declaring that the Easter Road club was the only one in the world that could have persuaded him to give up his secure job as manager of a plant-hire firm.

By 4.45pm on the following Saturday he had endeared himself even further with those same fans by taking Hibs to Tynecastle, guiding them to a 2-0 win and finishing the day with Hibs as League leaders! Hibs never looked like losing at Tynecastle that day and most neutral observers were of the view that the winning margin could easily have been bigger. As it was, a superb Cormack header from a McBride cross just before half-time was added to just on the hour mark when McBride himself notched the second. Gorgie Road was a sea of green and white as the happy visiting fans headed back into town.

Just one place below Hibs the following week when they visited Easter Road were Greenock Morton, Hal Stewart's men having had a super start to the season. Their previous two visits to the capital had produced two wins, against Hearts in both the League Cup and the League, but that sequence was broken when Stanton struck the only goal in a very close-fought contest.

Could Hibs extend their winning run to seven games? That was the question on the lips of every Hibs fan, but most were not overly confident ahead of their visit to Ibrox. As ever, manager MacFarlane was in confident mood and his confidence was rewarded as the Hibees silenced the big Ibrox support with a fantastic display of passing football to record a 3-1 victory. Youngster Peter Marinello did his growing reputation no harm whatsoever with two great first-half goals before Johnston pulled one back for the hosts. When seasoned campaigner Joe McBride took his total for the season to eight there was no way back for Rangers and Hibs remained sitting proudly at the top of the table.

As 1970 was a World Cup year and Scotland had qualified, clubs had the option to postpone any game where their players had been summoned for international duty. When Peter Cormack was included in the international squad, Willie MacFarlane duly requested that the League home match with Airdrie be played at a later date. Conscious that Hibs fans were still anxious to see their heroes at Easter Road, he invited Tommy Docherty to bring his high-flying Aston Villa side to Edinburgh for a friendly match. It was a move which backfired somewhat when the visitors ran out handsome 4-1 winners. Marinello was injured and would miss games as a result, while McBride notched the only Hibs goal from the penalty spot. Villa scored through Rudge, Rioch, McMahon and Hamilton in a game probably best forgotten.

League business next took Hibs to Rugby Park, where they stopped a long run of odd-goal defeats at that venue by securing a 2-2 draw despite Jim Black being sent off. Kilmarnock's goals came from Mathie and Gilmour, while the Hibees countered through McBride and Cormack.

That was eight in a row without defeat in the League, but the next game saw the sequence end as Hibs came a cropper at Muirton Park. Minus both Cormack and Marinello, they struggled to make chances on the big pitch, and St Johnstone stung their visitors when John Connolly put them ahead early in the second half. Hibs then set about pounding the home defence and on three occasions saw goalbound shots kicked off the line. When the final whistle blew the unbeaten run had ended – as had the stay at the top of the League, with Dundee United overtaking the Easter Road men.

Back at Easter Road, Clyde were the next to visit. After having enjoyed a couple of very good seasons in the top flight they now found themselves stuck at the bottom of the League. When you are down there, Lady Luck tends to desert you. That's what happened to the Bully Wee on this occasion as a poor performance by Hibs still saw them gain both points, thanks to an own-goal by Billy Beattie, who deflected a shot from Stanton past his own keeper. That defeat kept Clyde at the bottom, but ironically took Hibs back to the top.

Another home game followed when Airdrie came to play the match postponed a couple of weeks earlier. The Lanarkshire side had not started well and only Clyde were below them in the table as they ran out on to a floodlit Easter Road that night. Despite a goal from Marshall for the visitors they lost 3-1, thanks to a double from debutant Johnny Graham, signed that week from Falkirk, and a fine individual effort from Cormack. Watching Hibs from the stands that day was another new signing, Erich Schaedler, acquired by Willie MacFarlane from his former club, Stirling Albion.

Jim Black's dismissal at Kilmarnock meant he had to sit out the next game, a table-topping clash with Dundee United, who were on the same points total as Hibs but with an inferior goal difference. With Black missing, MacFarlane opted to move Stanton back into the centre of defence rather than to call in John Madsen. The skipper was outstanding in that role as Hibs won a hard-fought game 1-0, thanks to a goal from surprise inclusion Marinello. The fans who travelled that day were stunned to see the youngster play as his ankle injury, sustained in the friendly with Aston Villa, had looked as though it might keep him out for a while.

With Dundee United losing, Dunfermline took the chance to move up to second place and it was they who were next to face the Hibees, at Easter Road on Tuesday, 22 November 1969. Prior to kick-off, manager Willie MacFarlane was presented with a gallon bottle of whisky from Bell's for being named Manager of the Month in October, and there's every chance he cracked it open after the game to celebrate a superb 3-0 home win by his players. In a quite one-sided game, watched by a crowd of nearly 19,000, Graham further endeared himself to the Hibs fans by scoring another double, while McBride grabbed the other.

Another home game followed, against newly promoted Motherwell. Bobby Howitt's side had certainly made an impact in the top League, winning their first four games and reaching the semi-final of the League Cup. The new boys managed to win a point from the League leaders in a 1-1 draw, Graham getting the Hibees' goal and Goldthorpe netting for the visitors. With Joe Davis seemingly out of the picture, young Willie McEwan took over at left-back and turned in an impressive performance.

With a gap in the domestic fixture list, Hibs took on Polish cracks Gornik Zabrze in a friendly match at Easter Road. The Poles, who had beaten Rangers 3-1 at Ibrox two weeks before, were a fine team, leading their domestic League. They managed a second win on Scottish soil when they beat Hibs 2-1 with a double strike by Jan Banas, Cormack pulling one back for Hibs from the penalty spot. Erich Schaedler made his first-team debut when he replaced Hamilton during the game, while the Poles had in their starting line-up Wlodzimierz Lubanski, Alfred Olek and Jerzy Gorgon, all of whom would go on to star for their country in the World Cup.

We were now at the halfway stage in the League championship, and when Ayr United visited Easter Road on 13 December 1969 Hibs were sitting proudly at the top, having suffered only two defeats. One of those defeats had been on the opening day to Ayr United. They gave Hibs another hard game this time around, but the home side won a seven-goal thriller, thanks to a double each from Stanton and McBride (both pens). In turn, Rough and Hood (2) scored for the visitors, who would go on to be the team scoring most goals against Hibs that season.

Two days after Christmas 1969, Hibs travelled to Dundee and lost not only the game but also the League leadership. The hosts triumphed 1-0, thanks to a Houston goal against a visiting defence forced into change both before and during the game because of injury. Hibs gave as good as they got in all but scoring a goal, and neutral observers agreed that late on in the match the visitors should have been awarded a penalty when former Hibee Jim Easton handled not once but twice in the box. Everyone in the ground saw this incident with, it seems, the exception of referee Webster from Falkirk, and so Hibs travelled home empty handed, with an Edinburgh derby to face just five days later.

When the Gorgie side arrived at Easter Road on New Year's Day 1970 they did so on the back of a 5-0 win over Airdrie and a good 2-2 draw against League contenders Dundee United. As is often the case in these games, however, there was more blood and thunder than good football on display and a pretty dismal 0-0 result was the outcome, even though the hosts finished the game with just ten men after Cormack was sent off.

Just two days later, Hibs crossed the Forth and managed a relatively straightforward 3-0 win over struggling Raith Rovers, Graham (2) and Cormack getting the goals. Not present in the Hibs team that day was rising star Peter Marinello who, it became known soon after, had been transferred to Arsenal in a £100,000 deal which greatly disappointed the Hibs support.

In the days that followed, manager Willie MacFarlane made a shrewd move in the transfer market when he swooped for Partick Thistle winger Arthur Duncan. He paid just £35,000 for the man who would go on to play more competitive games for Hibs than any other in history. Duncan, who had been a former team-mate of John Blackley at Gairdoch United, was a qualified chiropodist and had been a part-timer with Thistle.

It would be a tough debut for the new Hibs man as Celtic came to Easter Road leading the League and looking to avenge the defeat Hibs had given them at Parkhead earlier in the season. This they managed to do in winning a very close game 2-1, thanks to goals from McNeill and Hughes. Debutant Duncan grabbed the Hibs goal and Celtic survived a frantic last ten minutes with Hibs pushing hard to equalise.

Tough games were coming thick and fast, so when Hibs were drawn to face Rangers at Ibrox in the Scottish Cup no-one was really surprised. Sadly, it was to be another short stay in the competition for the Hibees as despite a fine goal from Graham the Glasgow side struck three of their own through McDonald (2) and former Dundee stalwart Andy Penman.

Hibs were back in Glasgow seven days later facing bottom club Partick Thistle at Firhill, and they suffered the same fate in going down 3-1 on a day when the team performed very poorly. Graham was again the scorer, but Thistle countered through Bone, Flanagan and Rae to avenge the 5-1 drubbing they'd suffered at Easter Road back in September.

Bad weather forced Hibs to be out of action again until mid-February and this did not suit the unhappy manager Willie MacFarlane, who was keen to see his players turn the tide after three successive defeats. One factor which helped Hibs maintain their third-place spot in the League was that teams below them were beating each other and not really closing the points gap, but when Dundee arrived at Easter Road they were among the chasing pack and so two points were vital.

Unusually, the game was played on a Monday evening and Hibs sparkled under the floodlights with a great 4-1 win, Duncan getting two while Stanton and McBride added a goal apiece. The Dundee goal was scored by Edinburgh lad Jim Steele, the giant defender having joined Dundee from Tynecastle Boys' Club.

Next up was a trip to Cappielow to face a Morton side holding their own in mid-table. As always seemed to be the case in Greenock, the pitch was like a mud bath, which didn't make for good football. On the day, the 1-1 draw was about right with McBride striking his 14th goal of the season while Osbourne hit a scrappy late equaliser for the hosts, whose keeper Nielsen had an outstanding game.

A visit from Rangers loomed and they would arrive in fighting mood and still smarting after Hibs had dumped them 3-1 at Ibrox the previous October. At this point, the League had Celtic at the top with 42 points from 25 games, Rangers second with 38 from 24 games and Hibs third with 32 from 23 games, so a decent match was anticipated. The near 31,000 fans who attended were not disappointed as Graham and McBride crashed home the Hibs goals while Greig and Stein countered for the visitors.

As Hibs headed through to Paisley the following midweek, another former favourite was heading out of the dressing room. Joe Davis, king of the penalty kick, was off to join Carlisle United. He had been a magnificent servant to Hibs since joining them from Third Lanark, and all at Easter Road wished him well at his new club.

The game at Paisley was another high-scoring occasion, with the teams sharing six goals in a bit of a thriller under the lights. Graham, Cormack and young Alex Cropley hit the Hibs goals while the Buddies had Blair (2) and Adamson to thank for the point.

Another away game followed as Hibs faced Airdrie at Broomfield. It was not a good day for the Easter Road men as they went down 3-2 in a stormy match, with McBride scoring before going off injured and Stanton getting the other. The Airdrie goals came from Jonquin and Jarvie (2). Despite the defeat, Hibs were still in third place when they set off on their travels yet again, this time to face Aberdeen at Pittodrie. On a cold Monday evening in early March, Hibs put their short run of poor results behind them by beating the Dons 2-0 as Cormack and the deadly McBride breached a strong defence.

Now, with two home games coming up, it looked as if that third spot was going to be achieved. The Cormack–McBride partnership was looking quite healthy, and that view was reinforced in the next League result achieved by the Greens.

Prior to playing that match, however, Hibs met Hearts at Easter Road in the 1968/69 East of Scotland Shield and the visitors ran out 2-1 winners, McBride hitting the Hibees' goal from the penalty spot. By that time, Hibs were two down after Winchester had opened the Hearts account in just five minutes and Moller had doubled it two minutes into the second half.

Back on League duty, St Johnstone had narrowly lost to Hibs at Muirton Park the previous November and so a close game was anticipated. That is not how it turned out, as Joe McBride smashed home a hat-trick, one of those goals coming from the spot. Another Hibs goal was scored by Cormack – all this after the visitors had gone ahead through Aitken. Things were looking good for Hibs as they prepared for their next match, which brought high-flying Kilmarnock to Leith on Wednesday, 25 March.

Twenty-four hours before that game, the fruitful partnership between Joe McBride and Peter Cormack came to an abrupt end when the latter was transferred to Nottingham Forest. This was a stunning blow to both the supporters and the club. Cormack had become a hero at Easter Road, and his talent was such that he would go on to star for Forest and then Liverpool, both domestically and on the European scene. Contrary to popular belief at the time, the club tried its very best to keep Peter at Easter Road, but the player had wanted to try English football and this was his chance.

Despite the devastating loss of Cormack, Hibs played well in overcoming a strong Kilmarnock at Easter Road, with Hamilton and Cropley, who had inherited Cormack's No.10 shirt for the game, getting the Hibs goals while McLean scored for the visitors. The match programme for the Killie game informed the Hibs support that hopes were high of a friendly match being arranged against Arsenal to allow everybody to see how much progress Peter Marinello had made since moving to Highbury, but for whatever reason that never took place.

Only five League games remained, three away and two at home. Hibs still held third place, with Dundee United, Hearts and Dundee breathing down their necks, when they travelled to Shawfield to face a Clyde outfit flirting with relegation. As on their previous two visits to Glasgow, Hibs came back empty handed, losing 1-0 to the Bully Wee, whose left-half, McHugh, got the only goal. Strangely, Hibs had beaten both Celtic and Rangers in Glasgow but had failed to overcome the city's so-called lesser teams, and the pity was that Rangers were now stuttering in terms of results, so a second place had not been beyond the Hibees until the defeat by Clyde.

Another away fixture followed with a visit to Fir Park, Motherwell, and on the day that Celtic won the championship Hibs failed to take anything from their own game in a 2-1 defeat. Hamilton scored for Hibs, but a double by Dixie Deans kept the points in Lanarkshire. Deans liked scoring against Hibs, it seems, and he went on to do so on many future occasions after he left Motherwell to join Celtic.

Back-to-back defeats did not provide Hibs with the best preparation for the visit of Dundee United three days later. The Tayside club were sitting in fourth place, just four points behind Hibs with three games to play. As it turned out, Hibs were too good for them and ran out comfortable 3-1 winners, the goals coming from McBride (2 pens) and Grant. Former Hibs man Jimmy Stevenson, drafted in to replace the injured Alan Gordon, a future Hibs signing, scored for the visitors.

The last home game of the season brought Scottish Cup winners Aberdeen to Easter Road, the Dons having beaten Celtic 3-1 a week earlier in front of 108,000 fans at Hampden. Winning ways continued for Eddie Turnbull's men as they won a close game 2-1 with goals from Forrest and Robb, Hibs countering through Stevenson. Saying farewell to the Hibs fans that day, although he didn't actually play in the match, was centre-half John Madsen, who would be returning to his native Denmark to rejoin his former club, Esbjerg. Signed by Hibs from Morton, Madsen gave the Hibees more than three years' good service and he left knowing he would be missed at Easter Road.

In spite of the loss to Aberdeen, Hibs knew they had secured third place when they visited Dunfermline in the final League match on 18 April 1970.

With both Stanton and Blackley missing due to international duty, Hibs still managed to win 2-1, with goals from O'Rourke and Murphy.

One last game would be played before the players broke for the close season and that was at Tynecastle on Friday, 1 May 1970, when the two old Edinburgh rivals met for the 1969/70 East of Scotland Shield. Goals from Graham and McBride were not enough as Ford (2) and Wood ensured the trophy would stay in Gorgie.

Finishing the season in a European-qualifying third place was a good effort by Hibs and the fans would be eagerly looking forward to more of those special floodlit evenings in Leith. The disappointment at losing players like Marinello and Cormack was lightened somewhat by the success of Arthur Duncan after his transfer from Partick Thistle and the emergence of young Alex Cropley, who looked a very exciting prospect indeed.

Chapter Four

1970/71

MANAGERIAL CHANGES

By way of preparation for the new season, manager Willie MacFarlane took his squad to Germany and Holland for a series of three friendlies. In the party was new signing Jim Blair from St Mirren, the striker having caught the eye while bagging 18 goals for the Buddies. Smiling as he boarded the plane at Turnhouse Airport was Chris Shevlane, voted Player of the Year for 1969/70 by the Hibs Supporters' Association. That was the third time the award had been made, the previous winners being Pat Stanton and Jimmy O'Rourke, so the ex-Hearts and Celtic man was in good company.

The first tour match had Hibs facing FC Schalke in their Gelsenkirchen Stadium, which would be used for the next World Cup in 1974. The host side contained three German caps in Libuda, Fichtel and Nigbur, so to gain a 1-1 draw was a very creditable outcome. In fact, Hibs were on top in the game when a torrential downpour made things difficult for defenders and Russman sneaked a goal to put Schalke ahead. However, in his 47th first-team start since joining from Airdrie, Jim Black grabbed a last-minute equaliser, which was no more than the Greens deserved.

Although the next game was in Holland, Hibs stayed in their German hotel, which doubled as a sports centre and had the best of facilities. A 90-minute bus journey took them to Nijmegen, where they met NEC on 29 July and earned another 1-1 draw, Joe McBride scoring for Hibs and Oosterweld for the hosts. That game saw John Blackley sitting out while his place alongside Jim Black in the centre of the defence was taken by John Brownlie. The youngster had a fine game in that position.

For the third and final game, Hibs moved their base into Holland and on 2 August they took on MVV Maastricht, winning the game 3-0 in sweltering heat. The Greens were a class apart from start to finish and won with goals from Joe McBride (pen), Arthur Duncan and Johnny Graham. There was excitement, if that's the right word to describe it, on the flight home from Dusseldorf as the plane burst a tyre on take-off and had to circle the airfield burning off fuel before making an emergency landing. All went well, but nerves were somewhat on edge in the Hibs party!

MANAGERIAL CHANGES

The League Cup draw had pitched Hibs into a group alongside St Johnstone, Aberdeen and Airdrie and it was the Perth men who opened the group with a home game against the Edinburgh side. Goals from Johnny Graham, Joe McBride and Arthur Duncan in a good 3-1 win tell part of the story of a game in which Fred Aitken got the Saints goal. When Shevlane was carried off early in the second half suffering from damaged knee ligaments it allowed Brownlie to come off the bench for his competitive debut, and he certainly caught the eye by laying on two of Hibs' three goals. In the corresponding Reserve League Cup fixture, Hibs won 3-0, thanks to a hat-trick from Roddy Georgeson, a former Port Vale and Dundee player who had won a three-month trial at Easter Road.

Match two in the group brought Airdrie to Easter Road and they arrived having held Aberdeen to a draw in their opening match at Broomfield. If Hibs could beat the Diamonds they would lead the group from a strong position and that's what they did when the match finished at 3-2, thanks to a double from Duncan and a single from McBride. Airdrie's goals came from wingers Billy Wilson and Mark Cowan. In the programme that day was confirmation that in the first round of the Fairs Cities Cup Hibs had drawn Swedish opposition in Malmo.

The halfway stage in the group was reached when Hibs faced Aberdeen at Pittodrie. Leading after a Duncan goal, they missed a number of good chances and paid the penalty when Davie Robb headed an equaliser and the game finished all square at 1-1. It was sad to read in the next home programme that Hibs fans on the train north had caused some damage and that while the first team were playing at Pittodrie the reserves, in losing 2-0 to Aberdeen, saw a few of their players subjected to unwarranted verbal attacks from supporters in the enclosure. Manager Willie MacFarlane took no pleasure in voicing his disapproval of both situations.

Five points from three games soon became seven from four when Hibs overturned Airdrie 4-2 at Broomfield in what you might call a very eventful match. The hosts were awarded two penalties inside the first six minutes by referee Dempsey, but Mark Wilson could only convert one as Gordon Marshall brilliantly saved the other. By half-time both goalkeepers had earned their wages and no further goals had been scored. Early in the second half, Stanton equalised and now that their tails were up the Greens went to town, scoring three more through McBride, Stanton again and a screamer from Duncan. While Eric Stevenson had an effort denied for offside, Airdrie's Drew Busby, later of Hearts, managed to score a late consolation for the Diamonds.

It was around this time that Arthur Duncan, the Hibs left-winger and speed merchant, attracted his new nickname in the Easter Road dressing room. So fast was Arthur that his team-mates decided to christen him Nijinsky after a famous winning racehorse.

With Aberdeen in hot pursuit in the race to win the group, Hibs next entertained St Johnstone at Easter Road. The Greens started well, but when keeper Donaldson brilliantly saved Stanton's penalty the visitors seemed to take heart and Henry Hall put them ahead. Pressure from the home team looked like going unrewarded until Johnny Graham finally managed to beat Donaldson in the last minute to salvage a point.

It was crunch time in terms of which team might go forward to the later stages when Aberdeen visited Leith in the final group match. The Dons and Hibs were on the same points mark, but Eddie Turnbull's team had a better goal difference, thanks largely to a 7-3 demolition of Airdrie in a game where Joe Harper scored four goals. In the match programme, manager Willie MacFarlane promised that his players would go all out to win the game, even though in qualifying it would set Hibs up for a gruelling eight games in 25 days.

Whatever the manager said to the Hibs players in the dressing room before the game it certainly worked. In a blistering first 45 minutes, playing down the famous Easter Road slope, Hibs hammered four goals past a bemused Bobby Clark in the Aberdeen goal. Stanton, Graham, McBride and Duncan all hit the mark and although the visitors did try to rally in the second half, by that time the game was well and truly out of their grasp, leaving Hibs to face the prospect of meeting Rangers in a two-leg quarter-final.

With Cup progression sewn up, Hibs turned their attention to League business and travelled to Tannadice on the opening day to meet Dundee United. After the four-goal performance against Aberdeen the travelling fans were hoping for more fireworks. They were disappointed when Hibs produced an indifferent display and managed only a 1-1 draw. A Doug Smith penalty and a goal from Eric Stevenson left honours even. In notching that goal, Stevie equalled his tally for the whole of the previous season, but what the winger lacked in the scoring stakes he more than made up for in the number of assists accredited to him.

September began with the Edinburgh derby at Easter Road and a pretty dour affair it was, although full marks go to the Hearts keeper, Jim Cruickshank, who kept a clean sheet with a number of excellent saves, most notably from McBride and Willie McEwan. Gordon Marshall had a quieter afternoon, but also managed a clean sheet. By drawing both of their opening League matches, Hibs took their unbeaten run in competitive football for the season to eight – not a bad start, all told.

All good things come to an end, however, and when Rangers visited Easter Road for the first leg of the League Cup quarter-final they won 3-1. Losing a goal in the opening minute did not help the Hibernian cause and yet when Duncan scored for Hibs after a second had been conceded there were hopes that a draw might be achieved. Unfortunately, with Hibs pressing hard for that equaliser, the visitors wrapped things up with a third just 20 minutes from time. The Rangers scorers that night were Graham Fyfe (2) and Alfie Conn.

Newly promoted Cowdenbeath provided the next challenge to Hibs at Central Park. Two goals in the opening six minutes paved the way for a good 4-1 win for Hibs, although, ever the perfectionist, manager MacFarlane felt his players were not at their best on the day. Goals from McBride, Hamilton and a double from young Alex Cropley were more than enough to counter the lone strike from John Dickson and see the points returning to Easter Road. Meanwhile, the reserves were winning their game at Easter Road, with 18-year-old Kenny Davidson getting a hat-trick in the 5-3 victory.

The special occasion that is a European tie at Easter Road has a magical quality about it regardless of the opposition, and although Sweden's Malmo were not considered a big name they were dominant in their own League and had a fine European pedigree, their most famous night coming in 1968 when they defeated Italian giants AC Milan 2-1 in front of around 25,000 home fans.

In what was to be their 31st tie in the Fairs Cup and 37th in European competition, Hibs could boast that only one of the 14 home ties had been lost, to Red Star Belgrade in 1961. Bearing in mind that their Fairs Cup opponents had included Barcelona, Roma, Valencia, Porto, Napoli and Leeds United, that was a pretty impressive record, and it remained intact as Hibs demolished the visitors 6-0 with a display of exciting attacking football. McBride led the way with a hat-trick while Duncan got two and Jim Blair notched his first in a Hibs jersey.

It's worth noting that Joe McBride's hat-trick, scored in a 30-minute burst, took him to the top of the scoring charts in terms of Hibs marksmen in Europe, and although it was only mid-September, it took his tally for the season to nine. Add to those impressive facts, having played 85 games for Hibs, Joe had notched 59 goals, and it's easy to see why he was such a huge hero with the Hibernian support.

When Celtic came to Leith on League business they did so leading the championship with full points, nine goals scored and none conceded, but they left wishing they had not met a Hibs team determined to end that run. Two goals from former Celt Joe McBride, the second being of outstanding quality as he swivelled to hit the ball home from 12 yards, will live long in the memories of those Hibs fans fortunate enough to attend. Those goals ended an astonishing 12-year wait for a home win against the Glasgow side, but past performances were forgotten as the Hibs fans streamed out at the end with all the talk of that second McBride goal. It was a great way for the players to gear themselves up for the three testing away matches to follow.

The first of those took Hibs to Ibrox for the second leg of the League Cup quarter-final. Trailing 3-1 from the home game, it was always going to be a very difficult task to progress. Conceding another quick goal was to prove the downfall for Hibs again, and the 3-1 scoreline at Easter Road was repeated, the hosts scoring through Alex McDonald, John Greig and Graham Fyfe, while Johnny Graham countered for the Greens. A missed penalty by McBride may have been unfortunate, but it would have had little or no effect on the outcome.

Pittodrie was the next port of call as Hibs looked to extend their unbeaten League run to five games. Despite the game being quite even in terms of possession and chances, the Dons ran out 3-0 winners with goals from Jim Forrest, Davie Robb and a Joe Harper penalty. Early in the game, Bobby Clark had a wonderful save from a point-blank effort by McBride. Hibs were aggrieved that Robb's goal had been allowed to stand as Johnny Hamilton certainly seemed to have been fouled by Jim Hermiston, but the referee allowed play to continue and, with Hamilton lying on the turf, Robb slotted home the second Aberdeen goal.

Another goal for the reserves, this time against Aberdeen, earned the now full-time Kenny Davidson a place in the party travelling to Sweden for the return leg of the Fairs Cup tie. Indeed, so confident of qualification was manager MacFarlane that he included the youngster in his starting line-up. Kid Kenny played very well and would have enjoyed being in a winning team as Hibs took the game 3-2 on the night and 9-2 on aggregate. Goals from Bobby Duncan (not as spectacular as his strike against Napoli but just as welcome), Stanton and McEwan saw Hibs through, while Bo Larsson and Per Jonsson scored for the hosts.

When the successful Hibs party touched down in Edinburgh there was news that while the players had been busy on the pitch there had been a lot of activity in the boardroom too. In fact, the changes had been brewing for some time but had just not come into the public domain. William P. Harrower passed over control of the club to the East Lothian-based businessman and lifelong Hibs fan Tom Hart. One of the first things Hart did was to appoint former goalkeeper Tommy Younger to the board – a popular move with the fans as Younger had been a hero in his playing days.

After the highs of winning away in Europe, Hibs returned to domestic duty in facing St Mirren at Easter Road in a League match. The Buddies had started the campaign very well after a disastrous League Cup group display, most notably beating Kilmarnock and Morton and drawing with Rangers in the League race. Home fans who did not normally attend reserve games got their first chance to see Kenny Davidson in action when the manager handed him the No.7 shirt, and it was cheers all round for the youngster as he bagged two goals, Duncan getting a third in a demanding 3-3 draw. Saints earned their point with three well-taken goals from Iain Munro, who would later join Hibs, Ian Lister and Ronnie Hamilton.

MANAGERIAL CHANGES

The second round of the Fairs Cup paired Hibs with Portuguese opposition in Guimaraes, but Hibs still had one more League fixture to fulfil ahead of that Easter Road meeting. The trip to Motherwell brought no reward as the hosts literally played Hibs off the park in thumping them 4-0. Jackie McInally (3) and Jim Muir punished some very slack defending from the Greens, who looked a beaten team well before the end of the 90 minutes.

While Hibs had qualified at a saunter for this stage by beating Malmo 9-2 on aggregate, it's worth noting how some of the other British clubs got on in the competition. Arsenal did well to get past Lazio and earn a second-round meeting with Austrian outfit Sturm Graz, while Irish part-timers Coleraine shocked Kilmarnock by dumping them out at the first hurdle and getting the chance to face Sparta Rotterdam next. Leeds United had progressed to meet Dynamo Dresden and Liverpool overcame Ferencvaros to set up a tie with Dinamo Bucharest. Newcastle stunned Italian giants Inter Milan, a win which took them through to face Pecs Dozsa, while Rangers missed out on the chance to face Coventry after falling to Bayern Munich. Finally, Dundee United disposed of Grasshoppers Zurich and now faced Sparta Prague. There were some cracking teams left in the competition if Hibs could overcome the Portuguese.

On a cool October evening, Hibs managed a decent 2-0 win against stuffy opposition, thanks to goals from Duncan and, right at the final whistle, Pat Stanton. On from the start that night was Kenny Davidson, who certainly gave full-back Jorge a difficult night and did not look overawed in any way at playing on such a stage. It was a good win, but would it be enough to see them through? Only time would tell and until Hibs were scheduled to travel to Guimaraes they had some League business to take care of.

When Ally MacLeod brought his Ayr United side to Easter Road they were just two points adrift of Hibs in the middle of the table, but the gap soon widened to four when the home side swept to a fine 4-0 win with goals from McBride, Davidson, Duncan and Graham settling a decidedly one-sided affair. The score could have been even higher, the Greens hitting the woodwork on three separate occasions.

The following week Hibs had been scheduled to meet Rangers, but the Ibrox club were otherwise engaged, playing in the final of the League Cup, and so Hibs and Hearts decided to fill a blank Saturday by meeting at Easter Road in the final of the East of Scotland Shield. Going into the game, Hibs held the edge in terms of wins in this tournament and they extended that lead by winning 1-0, thanks to a penalty coolly converted by John Blackley after Jimmy O'Rourke had been hauled down inside the box.

The Fairs Cup return leg in Guimaraes saw Hibs going down 2-1 on the day, but progressing on aggregate by 3-2. Although they went two behind in Portugal, they dominated the rest of the game and Johnny Graham's goal could easily have been added to. As it was, one goal was enough and Hibs now had the prospect of playing Liverpool home and away in the third round.

November was looming and it arrived with Scotland taking a battering from very heavy rainstorms. Just before the month commenced, Hibs had been to Cappielow to take on Morton, but the game had to be abandoned after just 35 minutes with the pitch holding water and making the surface unplayable. The following Tuesday, Hibs had to call in local referee Eddie Thomson to carry out a lunchtime inspection as Rangers were due at Easter Road that evening in order to play the fixture postponed because of the League Cup final. It did not take long for Mr Thomson to decide the park could not stage the game and a telephone call was made to Ibrox ahead of their team coach leaving for Edinburgh.

Eventually the storms passed over and Easter Road was ready for the visit of Dundee, who arrived in Leith having secured seven points from eight in their previous four games. Whether Hibs were rusty from lack of playing or because of the amount of water that had fallen in Edinburgh they took nothing from the game despite a great goal and performance from scorer Pat Stanton. Dundee breached the home defence twice with a goal from the deadly Gordon Wallace and an unfortunate deflected own-goal off the Hibs full-back, Chris Shevlane. Stanton went on later that week to star for Scotland in a 1-0 Nations Cup win over Denmark, earning plaudits from team-mates and media pundits alike.

Back on the road, Hibs next travelled to Perth to face St Johnstone, who were undefeated so far at Muirton Park. The pitch enjoyed the reputation of being the biggest in Scotland and both Cropley and Duncan, playing on the wings, certainly enjoyed the space. Duncan it was who set Joe McBride up for the only goal of the game, his fifth League goal of the season.

A couple of what might be called quaint adverts appeared in the match programmes around this time, the first of those announcing that all gramophone records played at the game could be obtained from BAND-PARTS at 102 Leith Street! Many a youngster enhanced their record collection with a visit to that store on a Saturday and if you were hungry as you shopped you could always pop into the nearby Deep Sea chippie for a fish supper! The other advert to catch the eye suggested that if you wanted to buy anything Hibernian then you need only nip into the shop run by MORRIS KAYE at 72 Raeburn Place. I'm pretty certain I got my first-ever Hibs top out of there.

The abandoned match at Cappielow some weeks earlier had been rescheduled and Hibs travelled through with a number of players suffering from a flu bug. Indeed, Pat Stanton was so unwell on arrival that he was sent straight back home and Hibs missed his calming influence in midfield as they lost 2-1 despite taking the lead through Duncan. On the hour mark, Roy Baines misjudged a cross and Osborne took advantage to level. The winner by Sweeney extended Morton's undefeated run to seven games. On the same day at Easter Road, the reserves hit St Johnstone for six, but there was a hard price to pay as young winger Kenny Davidson suffered a broken ankle.

When Kilmarnock visited Easter Road towards the end of November 1970 they were in the most unusual position of propping up the League table. How their fortunes had changed, given that just a few seasons earlier they had won the League championship. Their run of poor results was added to thanks to a single-goal victory for the Greens, Jim Blair being the man on target early in the match. With Stanton missing due to injury, the captaincy was handed to Bobby Duncan, the full-back having returned from a lengthy injury which at one time looked to have threatened his career.

In their fifth game of a busy November, Hibs welcomed Rangers to Easter Road in the knowledge that the Ibrox men were smarting at having already fallen seven points behind leaders Celtic, their cause not helped by the fact that they had lost to Ayr United the previous weekend. Hibs did them no favours that night and won a fine game 3-2, with Jim Blair notching a double and Johnny Graham also scoring. This was great news for Blair, who had been struggling to win over the home support, and he certainly left the field a hero that night. Willie Johnston, who was later sent off, and Colin Stein scored for Rangers, but the best team certainly won on the day.

November finally drew to a close in terms of games played when Hibs were at Brockville to face high-flying Falkirk. The Bairns had started the season well and had been in the top four for a few weeks, and although manager MacFarlane was disappointed in his players a 0-0 draw was a pretty fair result.

Hibs stayed on the road the following week, their topsy-turvy season continuing with a poor 2-0 defeat at Broomfield, the scorers for Airdrie being Busby and McKay. This was hardly the best way to go into their next Fairs Cup encounter, where they would face the might of Bill Shankly's Liverpool, but ahead of that Hibs had another arrival at Easter Road when they appointed Dave Ewing as first-team coach. This appointment certainly raised a few eyebrows among the support as such an appointment seemed an odd move by the Hibs board when a manager was already in place. Those suspicions proved well-founded when Willie MacFarlane resigned and Hibs immediately appointed Ewing as the new manager. The timing was frankly appalling, but who knows what was going on behind the scenes?

Wednesday, 9 December 1970, saw Hibs taking on Liverpool at Easter

Road and having to face such players as Ray Clemence, Tommy Smith, Larry Lloyd, Emlyn Hughes, Steve Heighway and John Toshack. This was a mammoth task for Dave Ewing's side, who had an average age of just 22. On the night, things just wouldn't go Hibs' way and Toshack scored the solitary goal of the game to give the Greens only their second home defeat in European competition. Arthur Duncan had actually put the ball in the net at one point but had that effort disallowed after the referee blew for an earlier foul. One thing which rankled with the Hibs support that night was the fact that Joe McBride only started the game on the bench – a decision which meant that the new manager was already having questions asked of him, given Joe's goalscoring ability and his popularity with the Hibs support.

Back on League business, Hibs next played Dunfermline at Easter Road, the Pars having replaced an improving Kilmarnock in bottom spot. John Blackley, newly appointed vice-captain by manager Ewing, put through his own net to give the visitors one of their goals in a 2-2 draw, while Hugh Robertson bagged the other. Thankfully, Blair's double salvaged a point for the Greens, keeping them in the top half of a League being led by Celtic with Aberdeen in hot pursuit.

The December weather was being kind in the west and Hibs found that their next match, at Shawfield, survived the freeze which had caused postponements elsewhere. For those hardy fans making the journey to follow the Greens there was little play of any quality on view from either team in a dour 0-0 draw. Hibs had early chances but missed them and the game turned into a midfield struggle thereafter.

With Christmas just days away, Hibs travelled south to meet Liverpool in the second leg of their Fairs Cup tie and all who went with them knew they faced a monumental task in trying to qualify. At the end of the day they failed in their task, but they had a good old go at the Reds in front of a crowd of nearly 38,000, with Ray Clemence making tremendous saves from Duncan and McBride and Graham hitting the post. The home side had better fortune in front of goal and strikes from Steve Heighway and Phil Boersma gave them a 2-0 win on the night and a 3-0 win on aggregate. Although we did not know it at the time, this game would mark Joe McBride's last appearance for Hibs: after a few more weeks, he left to join Dunfermline. In later years, Joe would reveal that he left Hibs because he had refused to move home from Glasgow to Edinburgh. Why that was suddenly a necessity is unclear, but it cut short Joe's stay and denied Hibs a proven goalscorer.

Boxing Day saw Dundee United come to Easter Road having achieved only five wins from 17 starts, but they left having secured their sixth in a 1-0 win, new signing Jackie Copland getting the goal. Not such a Merry Christmas for the Hibs fans, who watched their side create several chances but fail to take each one.

MANAGERIAL CHANGES

The year 1971 was heralded in with the traditional New Year's Day derby, this time at Tynecastle, and just like the September meeting at Easter Road this one ended without any goals. It was a derby typical of the kind on offer back then – lots of effort and lots of muscle, but very little in the way of creative play and neither side deserving both points.

Scottish football was rocked on that day when 66 supporters lost their lives in what became known as the Ibrox disaster. Rangers fans streaming out of the ground, their team losing to Celtic, heard a huge roar suggesting that the Ibrox club had scored. Hundreds turned to try and get back up the stairs to see what was going on. A crush ensued and fans were trampled as panic set in, resulting in that tragic loss of life.

The following day Cowdenbeath were the visitors to Easter Road and they arrived five points adrift at the bottom, having managed just two wins and one draw in 18 starts. Hibs had beaten them soundly the previous September and the home support arrived looking for their heroes to get things back on track after having failed to score in their previous three League games. The return of the slightly built Kenny Davidson added some firepower and he grabbed a goal, as did Blackley from the penalty spot, but the visitors also bagged two, through wingers Frank Harper and David Ross, making it a pretty dismal start to the year for the Greens, with just two points from two games.

Hibs next travelled to Glasgow to face a Celtic side desperately chasing leaders Aberdeen. The Parkhead men recorded a 2-1 victory, with goals from Callaghan and Hood, while a last-minute strike by Stanton offered no more than consolation to the visitors, who were slowly slipping down the League order.

Eddie Turnbull brought League leaders Aberdeen to Leith the following Saturday and all the talk should have been about their incredible run of 15 League matches without defeat and keeper Bobby Clark's astonishing 1,000-plus minutes without having conceded a goal – or even the fact that just the previous season Clark had been so disillusioned at being unable to dislodge first-choice keeper Ernie McGarr that he actually played a few games outfield. The talk, though, was of none of this. The focus was on the return of the prodigal son to Easter Road. Manager Ewing, his popularity flagging with the home support, pulled off the master stroke of re-signing the legendary Joe Baker.

The Baker Boy had left Leith almost ten years before, but such was his popularity among the support that the crowd was swelled by thousands coming to see their hero again. Joe was made skipper for the day and, wearing an outrageous pair of white boots, he steered Hibs to a truly fantastic 2-1 win over the League leaders. Pat Stanton got the goal to finally end Bobby Clark's shut-out run and Baker notched the other just four minutes later with a bullet header. Joe Harper got one for the Dons, but it was not enough and the huge Hibernian support roared its delight at the final whistle.

The Scottish Cup draw had paired Hibs with Second Division Forfar Athletic at Easter Road. Not having been signed in time to beat the deadline, Baker was ineligible to play in this game and it was perhaps as well for the Angus side: even without Joe, the home side managed to thrash their visitors 8-1. Jimmy O'Rourke struck an impressive hat-trick and Kenny Davidson, making his Scottish Cup debut, grabbed a double while the others came from Duncan, Stevenson and the Forfar left-half and skipper Bobby Hopcroft, who put through his own goal. Forfar's scorer was Jim McNicol.

With that good win tucked under their belts, Hibs hit the road again on League business and took on St Mirren at Love Street hoping to improve upon just the one point gained in their meeting earlier in the season. The visitors started slowly and Ian Lister scored for the Buddies before Hibs had even had a shot at goal. In a better spell of play, however, Duncan pulled one back. Before the visiting fans had time to finish celebrating it, Lister scored again and despite chasing an equaliser Hibs could only concede a third, to Stewart Miller, and so returned home without any points.

Motherwell provided the next challenge and they came to Easter Road just one point ahead of Hibs in eighth place. They left trailing by a point as the home side won the game with a fine strike by Joe Baker. This game marked the welcome return at outside-left of Alex Cropley, who had been missing for some weeks due to injury, while the continuing form of Baker kept Jim Blair in the reserves.

It was Scottish Cup time again and Edinburgh was in a frenzy because the draw had paired the Greens with their oldest rivals, the match to be played at Tynecastle. The two League meetings had been dull 0-0 affairs, but this was the Cup and so only a positive result would take either team into the next round. Hibs took the lead thanks to a superb diving header from John Hazel, only for Hearts to come storming back and equalise through Kevin Heggarty. With the game looking as though a replay was on the cards, Arthur Duncan sent those fans wearing green into a state of delirium when he fired a quite wonderful winner to dump Hearts out of the Cup.

Surely that Cup result would give the team the lift it needed to start moving up the League table? Sadly, it didn't. Once again, Hibs failed to impress while on the road and a very poor performance at Somerset Park saw Ayr United defeat them 2-0 with goals from McGovern and Reynolds. It certainly was a case of coming back down to earth with a bump after the heady success at Tynecastle.

The players didn't have time to feel sorry for themselves as their second successive away game took them to Ibrox, where Rangers would be sure to want to avenge the defeat they suffered earlier in the season at Easter Road. It was not to be for the light blues as Hibs won a point after Joe Baker equalised John Greig's opener. Indeed, Hibs might have managed a rare League double over the Glasgow outfit had Stanton's rocket shot gone in rather than coming back off the woodwork when the game was poised at 1-1. The encouraging thing for this up-and-down Hibs side was that they hadn't now lost to Rangers in the last four League meetings between the clubs.

Home advantage can mean so much in a Cup run and that's what Hibs had when they met Dundee in the quarter-final. The Dens Park men seemed content from the outset to keep things tight and try to get Hibs back to Tayside for a replay, but in defending deep they conceded a penalty and with Stanton and Blackley both reluctant to step forward after recent misses from the spot, the ever-confident Jimmy O'Rourke took the kick and duly sent the keeper the wrong way to secure a semi-final spot with a 1-0 win.

As the UK geared itself up for decimalisation, Hibs continued their poor run of League form by crashing 4-2 to Morton at Easter Road. While those fans buying a programme tried to decide whether they'd been done because the price had changed from 6d to 2.5 new pence, the Hibs defence was having problems of its own, and Gerry Sweeney, Per Bartram, Ernie Hannigan and Billy Osborne all helped themselves to a goal while only Johnny Graham and Joe Baker managed the same for Hibs. That win took Morton above Hibs in the League and pushed them towards a Texaco Cup qualifying place.

Dundee were given a quick chance to avenge their Cup defeat when the fixture calendar took Hibs to Dens Park the following Saturday, and take it they did by reversing the scoreline and winning 1-0, thanks to a solo effort by full-back Bobby Wilson. Hibs had lost Stanton at half-time as it became apparent that he had damaged his knee. In reality, the Greens should have won the match, but Baker and Davidson both missed really good chances while Cropley beat the keeper only to see his shot crash back off the crossbar. One positive note was the return of Eric Stevenson and the fact that he had a very good game in an unfamiliar midfield role.

There remained only two more League games before the Cup semi-final in which, it was now known, Hibs would face Rangers. The first of those was at home to St Johnstone. The Saints were sitting third in the table and arrived on the back of a good run, but it was still disappointing to see them overcome Hibs with goals from John Connolly and 17-year-old Jim Pearson giving them a 2-1 win. Jimmy O'Rourke struck a penalty as consolation for Hibs. Still, at least the club had made a move to help fans out by dispensing with the 2.5p price for the programme and increasing it to the much easier to deal with 3p!

If Hibs had a hoodoo team in those days it must surely have been Kilmarnock. The Ayrshire side seemed capable of beating the Greens at will, and it was no surprise when Hibs crashed 4-1 at Rugby Park in their last match before the Cup semi-final meeting with Rangers. Although it didn't help that Eric Stevenson was sent off, Hibs were never at the races and could have lost by more than the goals scored by Tommy McLean, Jim Cook, John Gilmour and Jim McCulloch. Blackley's goal put a better complexion on things, but nobody was fooled that this had been anything other than a shoddy performance by Hibs.

What chance could Hibs possibly have against Rangers at Hampden with a defence shipping goals like a sieve and a forward line that had lost its way? The bookies certainly didn't rate a Hibs win as likely, even though they'd taken three out of four points from Rangers in the League. The game was a bruising affair, the Rangers team proving to be physically stronger and more experienced in the national stadium. But with Stanton at centre-half and Alex Pringle drafted in from the reserves alongside him, the defence stood firm and Hibs were so very unlucky not to win the game at the death when Baker shot past keeper Peter McCloy only to turn away in agony as John Greig popped up on the goal-line to clear. No goals, then, and a replay required, but first the teams had some League business to take care of.

Falkirk were another side looking to qualify for the Texaco Cup courtesy of their League position and the Bairns did their cause the world of good by leaving Leith with both points in a 3-1 win. Minus Arthur Duncan – two cracked bones in his foot keeping him out – the home side lacked both pace and width. The home supporters were clearly running out of patience, not with the players but with manager Dave Ewing. Two goals from Alex Ferguson (yes, *that* Alex Ferguson) and one from Wilson Hoggan easily cancelled out Baker's effort for a Hibs team who had to go into their Cup replay on the back of this defeat.

Jekyll and Hyde Hibs gave Rangers one heck of a game in that replay, but once again missed chances cost dear and the Glasgow outfit scraped home 2-1 on the night. Jimmy O'Rourke, who had a magnificent game, scored for Hibs from a Cropley cross while Willie Henderson and Alfie Conn ended the Scottish Cup dream for yet another year.

Going into the last three League games for the season, Hibs were sitting in 13th place. While they were clear of any relegation worries, it was obvious that European football would not be a feature in the season to follow, and that was a huge disappointment to both club and fans. Airdrie arrived at Easter Road on 10 April 1971 sitting three points above Hibs, but left again with the gap reduced to one as a double from Baker and a single strike from Graham took the points in a 3-1 win, Drew Busby scoring for the Diamonds. Outstanding at centre-half that day was Pat

Stanton, whose form had gained him a place in the Scotland squad for an upcoming Nations Cup tie in Portugal.

Hibs travelled to Dunfermline for the penultimate League fixture and in a surprisingly entertaining game the sides drew 3-3, O'Rourke grabbing two and Cropley the other. Hibs fans who made the journey were astonished to see Erich Schaedler line up at centre-forward. Dave Ewing later explained that it was a tactic designed to keep Dunfermline's uncompromising centre-half John Cushley busy. It certainly worked: within a few minutes Schaedler and Cushley clashed in a crunching tackle and the Pars hard man was extremely quiet after that.

Dunfermline, who led 3-1 at one stage, scored through a Joe McBride penalty, Hugh Robertson and Barrie Mitchell. That draw had put paid to any chance Hibs had of qualifying for the following season's Texaco Cup, but in truth that chance had really slipped away much earlier after some dismal home defeats to the likes of Morton, St Johnstone and Falkirk.

The final League match of the season brought Clyde to Easter Road, the Bully Wee having fought for most of the season to stave off relegation. They succeeded in that quest, with Cowdenbeath and St Mirren making the drop, but they did not succeed at Easter Road as Hibs easily crushed them 5-1 with a hat-trick from O'Rourke, including two penalties and single strikes each from Baker and Hazel. Clyde scored through youngster Dom Sullivan, who went on to star for both Celtic and Aberdeen in the years ahead.

And so the League campaign was over, but the season was not yet finished for Hibs as they had agreed to play a series of friendlies following the late cancellation of their hoped-for tour to North America and Bermuda. Instead of the sunshine of Bermuda Hibs headed for rainy Manchester, which they used as a base for two scheduled games, the first against Wigan Athletic, at that time a non-League club. It was a decent game, with Baker getting the goal in a 1-1 draw. The following day, Hibs met Oldham Athletic at Boundary Park and lost 1-0 in a pretty dreary affair.

After the journey home, Hibs had a break of just two days before travelling up to Elgin, where they defeated the home side 3-0 with goals from O'Rourke (2) and Brownlie. Twenty-four hours later, Hibs went to Nairn and drew 1-1, Johnny Graham the scorer.

Back at Easter Road four days later, the Dutch side Maastricht visited in a return clash following the pre-season friendly won by Hibs the previous August. Again, the Greens were too strong for their opponents and ran out comfortable 3-0 winners, with goals from Graham, Cropley and Davidson.

After such a long season it seemed odd that Hibs would take on so many friendlies. They weren't finished yet: the team flew out to Spain for a working holiday during which they played Real Mallorca and lost 2-1, Baker scoring the Hibs goal.

All in all, it had been a poor League season, and the fans were mightily disgruntled that the departure of Willie MacFarlane and his replacement by Dave Ewing had offered no encouragement that things would improve.

Chapter Five

1971/72

TURNBULL TAKES THE REINS

It was a short but extremely eventful close season after the club's last competitive match the previous May. Just seven months into the job, Dave Ewing resigned to return south of the border, and in truth not many Hibs fans were disappointed with that turn of affairs. Ewing had failed to impress the Hibernian faithful with his coaching abilities and many felt the team had been underachieving with the Englishman at the helm.

Speculation was rife over the vacant post of manager, and full credit must go to managing director Tom Hart and his colleagues on the board for persuading Eddie Turnbull to leave a flourishing Aberdeen side and return to the club the former Famous Five member knew and loved so well. The Dons had come close to winning the championship the previous season, and Turnbull freely admitted that he would not have left for any other club than Hibs.

He inherited a decent squad of players, to which Bertie Auld had been added, and he would soon set about bringing in others. In the meantime he had four friendly matches set up in which to assess the players at his disposal for the start of the season.

Another change worth mentioning was that the programme had been increased to a 12-page affair and had been bumped up in price from 3p to 5p.

The first of the friendly matches brought Middlesbrough and World Cup 1966 winner Nobby Stiles to Easter Road. The Ayresome Park side defended stoutly throughout and then took the game with two late goals from John Hickton and Joe Laidlaw. New man Bertie Auld made his debut, but left the field injured at half-time. Another making his debut, thanks to an ankle injury which kept first-choice keeper Roy Baines on the sidelines, was Eddie Pryce, signed by Hibs in the close season from Kirkintilloch Rob Roy. The Hibs line-up that day was: Pryce, Brownlie, Shevlane, Blackley, Stanton, O'Rourke, Stevenson, Hamilton, Baker, Auld (Cropley) and Duncan (Davidson), which meant that eight of the team who would become known as Turnbull's Tornadoes were already in place – Erich Schaedler and Jim Black, who did not play, being the other two.

The following Monday evening Hibs faced the German side Schalke 04 at Easter Road and fought out an entertaining but goalless draw. Highlight of the evening was the appearance of the Famous Five, introduced to rapturous applause from around 9,000 fans at the game, and there to present 78-year-old Jimmy McColl with an inscribed gold watch to mark his having been at the club as player, trainer and general assistant since signing for Hibs in 1921.

Five days later, Hibs travelled to Middlesbrough to face the home side in the second of their agreed pre-season fixtures. They again failed to get the better of the English outfit in a 4-2 reverse. The home side actually raced into a 4-0 first-half lead, but Hibs redeemed themselves a little after the break with Joe Baker and John Hazel netting. In that crazy first half, Hickton (3) and Laidlaw again beat young Eddie Pryce in the Hibs goal.

On next to York and another defeat as the home side scored twice through McMahon, while Hibs could only counter through Eric Stevenson. Still, these were only pre-season games, designed to improve the match fitness of the players, and results were not held to be that important – unless you were a fan, when losing is never easy!

Back home at Easter Road, Hibs were preparing for the League Cup section games to begin, in the knowledge that their tough group contained Motherwell, Dundee United and Kilmarnock. It was to be in this week that Eddie Turnbull added the first of his Tornadoes signings when he captured the signature of 31-year-old goalkeeper Jim Herriot. Herriot had seen action with numerous clubs, including Dunfermline and Birmingham City and had been guesting for Durban in South Africa when he got the call from Easter Road.

He made his debut on Saturday, 14 August 1971 at Motherwell and kept a clean sheet as Hibs stormed to a 3-0 victory. The first half had seen John Brownlie hit the bar and the home side kept it goalless until half-time, but in the second period Hibs dominated and Alex Cropley opened the scoring early. A double from Johnny Hamilton secured the tie and on both occasions the woodwork was kinder than it had been to Brownlie, the Hibs number eight scoring via the post with his first and the bar with his second.

The first of two home games brought Dundee United to Easter Road and Jerry Kerr's men would offer stiff opposition, with the likes of Hamish McAlpine, Andy Rolland, Doug Smith, Kenny Cameron and Alan Gordon in their side. But the Greens proved too strong for the Taysiders and goals from Cropley and a Jimmy O'Rourke penalty won the points. A great start to the group stage saw Hibs at the top with Cropley among the early pacesetters for top scorer in the tournament. He was at it again in the next game when Kilmarnock visited Easter Road.

Killie arrived hoping to close the gap on Hibs, having managed to overcome Motherwell the previous midweek and haul themselves into second place behind the Greens, but Turnbull's men were not about to let that happen and secured a good 3-1 win, thanks to Cropley, Hazel and Baker. The visitors had lost their promising winger, Tommy McLean, to Rangers and manager Walter McCrae was unable to dip into the transfer market to seek a replacement as the fee paid by Rangers was used to help offset the club debt. Still, Killie were a decent outfit and Frank Beattie managed their goal in a game where they were never completely out of things.

The group fixtures now reversed and Hibs travelled to Tannadice to face United. This was Turnbull's Hibs and he had insisted that a team should look like a team, persuading the board that the players should be kitted out in smart green blazers bearing the club badge on the pocket and black trousers and shoes. Coming off the team bus in Dundee, they certainly looked both smart and imposing. The game itself saw Hibs win 4-1, but Turnbull was still not satisfied, insisting that the team could play much better! Wise words, no doubt intended to prevent his players from resting on their laurels.

Things had not started too well at Tannadice, with Alan Gordon opening the scoring for the Tangerines, but a brilliant headed goal from Baker levelled things up before the interval. Only in the last ten minutes did Hibs take control after the United full-back, Jim Cameron, had been sent off for a crunching tackle on John Brownlie. Superior numbers saw the visitors score three more times through Stevenson, Duncan and Cropley, who got his fourth in four games. This result ensured a quarter-final spot, even though there were two more group matches to play.

The first of those games brought Motherwell to Easter Road, the Steelmen looking to avenge their opening game defeat, but it was not to be as goals from Hamilton and Baker secured a 2-1 win, with McInally countering for a 'Well side which included Tom Forsyth and Dixie Deans.

The final group game at Rugby Park saw Hibs with the chance to secure 12 points from six games, a feat they had never before achieved in the competition, but a stuffy performance from the home side saw the game ending 0-0. At least Hibs were through, and their opponents in the quarter-final would be Falkirk.

Ahead of that there was the little matter of the opening League fixture, which just happened to be against Hearts at Tynecastle. Going into that derby, Hibs had injury troubles: Baker and Auld failed fitness tests, while Schaedler played despite a shoulder problem and Cropley struggled for a large part of the game with a groin strain. Nevertheless, Hibs won 2-0 with late goals from Cropley and Hamilton and a marvellous display in goals from Jim Herriot, whose clean sheet ensured that Hibs had not lost a goal to their oldest rivals in the last six League meetings.

A derby win seemed a good way to set up for the League Cup quarter-final first leg at Brockville. Falkirk had other ideas and ran out 2-0 winners, thanks to a soft penalty and a late long-range effort from Tom Young, which delighted the Bairns fans in the remarkable 18,500 crowd. It was a disappointing result for the Greens, but, make no mistake, this was a good Falkirk outfit that included players such as Stewart Rennie, ex-Hibee Mervyn Jones, Jim Shirra, Alex Ferguson and Alex Setterington.

Newly promoted East Fife were next up in the League and the Methil side arrived at Easter Road under the managership of former Hibs favourite Pat Quinn. Another well-known face in the ranks was right-back Bobby Duncan, who had left Hibs in the close season, but he was unable to help his new team to avoid defeat as Hibs won 2-1. The home goals came from a Stanton header and an O'Rourke penalty, ex-Ranger Billy McPhee netting for the visitors.

Another visit to Tannadice beckoned and another 4-1 win was the outcome as Hibs swept the Tangerines aside with a great display of passing football and goals from Stanton (2), O'Rourke (on his 25th birthday) and Hamilton. United's goal was scored by Kenny Cameron, but it was merely a consolation in a game dominated by the visitors from start to finish.

The League Cup quarter-final second-leg match against Falkirk at Easter Road saw the Edinburgh-born world lightweight champion boxer Ken Buchanan introduced to the crowd before the game. His presence failed to inspire Hibs into overhauling the visitors' 2-0 first-leg lead, and it was the Greens who suffered the knockout punch despite a Jimmy O'Rourke goal giving them a 1-0 win on the night. The vast majority in an amazing crowd of more than 27,000 fans roared the Hibs on, but it was not to be, despite two strong penalty claims.

League business beckoned again and undefeated Ayr United arrived at Easter Road with the future Scotland manager and former Hibs player Ally MacLeod at the helm. After a disastrous League Cup group in which they scored only two goals for the loss of 18, Ayr had got their act together and had been bolstered by the signing of Johnny Graham from Hibs and the return from injury of key players Joe Filippi and keeper Davie Stewart. In a very tight game a single strike by Auld secured the points for Hibs, keeping them joint top with Celtic.

Having beaten Motherwell home and away in the League Cup and having won the first four League games of the season, Hibs travelled to Fir Park confident of victory, but had to settle instead for a hard-earned 1-1 draw. The Steelmen had tightened up their leaky defence and took the game to Hibs. Jim Herriot turned out to be man of the match thanks to a series of wonderful saves, including a full-length dive to deny Dixie Deans late in the game. It had been Deans who scored the Motherwell goal and his was a name that would haunt Hibs defenders and fans in the years ahead. Thankfully, Hamilton continued his scoring efforts against 'Well, adding the Hibs goal in this game to the three he'd bagged against them in the League Cup matches.

In the week leading up to the next match, at home to Celtic, Pat Stanton and Alex Cropley were named in the Scotland squad for the forthcoming Nations Cup match against Portugal at Hampden. It was a fantastic honour for young Cropley. Nicknamed 'Sodjer', having been born in the army town of Aldershot, he shared with Bob Wilson, the Arsenal goalkeeper, the distinction of becoming one of the first two English-born players to be selected for Scotland.

In the match programme for the Celtic game, fans were informed that any father bringing their son to the game should be sure to use the special turnstile beside the car park as it was exclusive to a father-and-son combination and offered admission for a total cost of 45p! The item went on to say that this was a bright idea which would no doubt be copied by others, and the reader is left to speculate as to whether Hibs could add this innovation to the rest of their firsts in football.

Celtic actually arrived at Easter Road on the back of a shock 1-0 Parkhead defeat to St Johnstone, which had meant that they had slipped into third place behind Hibs in second and Aberdeen at the top on goal difference from the Easter Road men. It was a strong Celtic side, but Hibs were no slouches either and a single Lou Macari goal was all that separated the teams as the visitors took the points back to Glasgow.

Midweek saw Stanton and Cropley both turn in first-class performances as Scotland defeated Portugal, with Cropley in particular attracting praise for his tremendous distribution from midfield. Meanwhile, back at Easter Road, manager Turnbull was dipping into the transfer market in luring Alex Edwards away from East End Park – although the little Fifer arrived in the middle of a suspension, which meant that his Hibs debut would be delayed. As Edwards arrived, the Hibees' longest-serving player, Eric Stevenson, departed to join Ayr United. His departure was a wrench for the many Hibs fans who held him in the highest regard having watched him turn in so many wonderful performances for the club.

A visit to Pittodrie saw Hibs clashing with joint leaders Aberdeen. Although Hibs took the lead when Hamilton's cross was headed home by Duncan, goals from Joe Harper and Willie Young preserved the Dons' unbeaten record. It was a blow to lose to the two teams with whom Hibs were competing at the top of the table and Eddie Turnbull was fully aware that the capture of Alex Edwards could only be a part of his rebuilding exercise.

Losing to Falkirk in the League Cup quarter-final had hurt Hibs and they exacted their revenge big style when the Bairns visited Easter Road towards the end of October. Arthur Duncan took the headlines with four goals, while Auld and Hamilton added singles and Herriot denied the visitors whenever they threatened. It was great display of football and 6-0 was in no way flattering to Hibs.

October finished badly for Hibs as they made the trip to Shawfield to tackle a Clyde team who had been hammered 3-0 at home the previous week by Dundee United. As Jimmy Greaves would say, however, it's a funny old game, and Hibs came a cropper, losing 2-1. The hosts dominated possession and scored through former Hibee Joe McBride and Jim Burns, while a last-minute strike by Hamilton ensured that he remained top scorer so far. As if confirmation of that Greaves saying were needed, Falkirk went to Tannadice that day and thumped Dundee United.

At Easter Road the following Saturday, Hibs took on a Dunfermline team who had been displaying similar erratic form and managed to overcome them 2-0 with goals from Stanton and Duncan. This result kept Hibs in the pack of those clubs chasing Aberdeen and Celtic at the top, a pack which included St Johnstone, Hearts, Dundee and Rangers. The home win against the Pars was Hibs' tenth game of the season and their sixth win, taking them on to 13 points. Incidentally, Stanton's goal was extremely well received in the Stanton household as his wife, Margaret, astonishingly held the winning ticket in the club's Golden Goal competition and picked up £60 because of her husband's strike.

In a pleasant diversion from League business, Hibs welcomed Berwick Rangers to Easter Road to play in an East of Scotland Shield quarter-final tie. The Greens were just too strong for Berwick and easily won the game 4-1, Baker and O'Rourke claiming a double each. For this game, Eddie Turnbull gave a debut to teenager Derek Spalding, who had been turning in star displays for the reserves and looked totally at home in a first-team jersey. Berwick scored through a penalty by Hall.

Saturday, 13 November 1971, saw the long-awaited debut of Alex Edwards, and the little right-sided midfield man was instrumental in helping Hibs to achieve a deserved 2-2 draw against Airdrie. Ex-Hibs man Derek Whiteford got both Airdrie goals, while Duncan and a rare goal from Blackley, who was playing right-back in that game, earned the point for Hibs. Missing from the team that day was Alex Cropley, who had a foot in plaster following an injury picked up while playing for Scotland against Belgium at Pittodrie. Thankfully, the injury was not as bad as first feared and Cropley was soon on the mend.

The scheduled match against Partick Thistle at Firhill the following Saturday was a very late casualty of the early winter snow. Those Hibs fans who had already travelled through only to find the stadium locked up were left to face a disappointing journey home in driving snow and sleet. The postponement of that game meant Hibs lost a bit of ground on the leading pack and made it all the more important that they won their next home game against Kilmarnock.

The Rugby Park men had not had the best of starts to the season, finding themselves at the foot of the table after eight games, but a recent run of good form had lifted them to mid-table. Arriving on the back of three straight wins, against Clyde, Dunfermline and Airdrie, and scoring eight goals in the process, manager Walter McCrae's men fancied their chances of keeping that form going, but in a super game they fell 3-2, thanks to O'Rourke (pen), Baker and a home debut goal from Edwards. Sam Maxwell and Ross Mathie, just two of the five players in the Killie team whose surnames started with the letter M, earning them the somewhat unimaginative nickname in the press of the M Men, scored the goals for the visitors, who left feeling they had been worth at least a point.

The earlier postponed game against Partick Thistle at Firhill took place in the midweek following the Kilmarnock match and saw Hibs win again with a single goal scored by O'Rourke from an Edwards pass. It was a tough game and Thistle defended well, but Hibs broke them down eventually with the clever brand of passing football upon which manager Turnbull insisted. It's worth pointing out that when the teams met, both were in the top six and chasing the pacesetters Aberdeen and Celtic, so it was a good two points to win away from home.

Hibs were away again on the Saturday as they travelled to Muirton Park to face a St Johnstone side who had been riding high in the League but had lost their way a little in recent games. Hibs took full advantage of the biggest playing surface in Scottish senior football by securing a fine 2-0 victory, with goals from Hazel and Edwards. The latter revelled in the width of the park, which allowed him to display his fantastic passing abilities. Edwards was a great signing by Turnbull and already he was being talked about as the bargain buy of the season by those in the game.

Dundee were next to visit Easter Road and they did so on the back of a stunning 2-0 UEFA Cup victory over AC Milan at Dens Park. In fact, the Dark Blues had lost the first leg 3-0 in the San Siro and crashed out of the competition on aggregate, but they would surely prove a tough nut for Hibs to crack. In a very tight but even game Hibs triumphed 1-0, thanks to a penalty goal from O'Rourke after Cropley had been scythed down in the box by Dave Johnston. As ever, the players were entitled to relax on a Saturday evening after a game, but it's unlikely they would have accepted the invitation contained within a programme advert to dance the night away at the Americana Discotheque on Fountainbridge!

Next on the agenda was a tricky away tie at Greenock, where Morton had secured a number of decent results and were now sitting comfortably in mid-table. Hibs actually had to come from behind after Schaedler put through his own goal, O'Rourke snatching the equaliser with a well-placed header. This point kept Hibs in third spot, six behind leaders Celtic and five behind Aberdeen.

Christmas Day 1971 saw Rangers visiting Easter Road and going home with a nice gift of two points after grabbing a last-minute winner despite being second best throughout the 90 minutes. It was unfortunate for Hibs to relinquish their third place to Rangers, who had the 'Girvan Lighthouse', Peter McCloy, to thank after he pulled off a series of fantastic saves, notably from O'Rourke and Edwards.

The traditional New Year's Day derby match, this time at Easter Road, finished with what was becoming an equally traditional 0-0 draw. Bobby Seith's men defended exceptionally well, despite missing the injured Alan Anderson in the centre of defence, while Jim Herriot dealt well with any shots directed at the Hibs goal. The home team enjoyed the bulk of the possession, but neither set of supporters had much to cheer them on a miserably cold day.

East Fife had given Hibs a tough game earlier in the season, when the Greens scraped through at Easter Road by a 2-1 scoreline. When they visited Bayview just two days after the derby match, the Fifers managed to reverse that scoreline. Eddie Turnbull was disappointed that his side's cause was not helped by the dismissal of Edwards early in the second half. McPhee and Hughes had put the Fifers two goals up and although Stanton reduced the leeway from the spot, the visitors, despite dominating and making numerous chances, could not secure that elusive equaliser. This was the fifth loss in the League, each one by just the odd goal, and had even a couple of those turned out to be draws Hibs would have been in a stronger position to try to secure a UEFA Cup place by virtue of their League position.

Dundee United were next to visit Easter Road and arrived with their new manager Jim McLean at the helm, McLean having moved just a few weeks earlier from city rivals Dundee. United were skirting the relegation zone and desperate to put some points on the board, but they left Leith with nothing after Stanton, Brownlie and Duncan gave the Greens a somewhat easy 3-0 win. Playing at number ten that day for United was Alan Gordon, and the Hibs fans in the crowd would not be aware that within a fortnight they would be seeing him again when he joined Hibs, becoming the final piece of the Tornadoes jigsaw.

Hibs travelled to Somerset Park next to take on Ayr United and left with both points following a hard-fought 2-1 win, Brownlie and Duncan getting the goals. Jim Herriot was outstanding in goal, and his efforts were all the more remarkable because he had risen from his sick bed to take part. The Ayr goal was scored by Johnny Doyle from a cross by Eric Stevenson, who got a warm and friendly reception from the travelling Hibs fans. That day the draw was made for the third round of the Scottish Cup and Hibs were paired with Partick Thistle at Firhill.

After a poor start to the season, Motherwell were sitting comfortably in mid-table when they arrived at Easter Road to face a Hibs team buoyed by their last two results and with the fans looking forward to witnessing the debut of new centre-forward Alan Gordon. The bubble was burst that day by John Muir and Jackie McInally, who secured the 'Well goals in a 2-1 win, Billy McEwan scoring for the Greens. Under-23 cap McEwan's efforts at Easter Road were often overshadowed by the attention shown to others, but he was a decent player who worked hard in midfield and could slot in at full-back if required.

January was proving to be a hectic month as Hibs lined up to play their sixth fixture on Saturday, 29th. This game took the Leith side to Parkhead, where they would face a Celtic team locked in battle with Aberdeen for the top spot. As ever, Hibs gave everything they had but lost yet again by an odd goal as Celtic triumphed 2-1 with goals from Harry Hood and Dixie Deans, recently signed from Motherwell, while Stanton scored for the Easter Road side.

The Scottish Cup had long eluded Hibs, even the great League championship side of the 1950s failing to lift the trophy, and so it was with hope more than conviction that a large Hibs support travelled to Firhill on Saturday, 3 February, to watch their heroes take on Partick Thistle. They were duly rewarded by a fine 2-0 win for the visitors and a first Hibs goal for Alan Gordon, not to mention the absolute rarity of a goal from fullback Erich Schaedler. Thistle were never really in the hunt and Hibs deserved to progress to round four, where they would meet Airdrie at Easter Road.

Firstly though, title-chasers Aberdeen, with Turnbull's replacement, Jimmy Bonthrone, doing a fine job at the helm, came to Easter Road knowing that they could ill afford to drop any points if they were to stay in touch with Celtic. The Greens would be without Edwards, banned for a massive eight weeks because of his sending off at Bayview, and although his presence was missed, Hibs played their part in a great game, which finished 2-2. It's worth pointing out here that Aberdeen arrived with a record showing that in their previous 57 League matches they had conceded only 35 goals and had managed to keep a clean sheet in an astonishing 30 games. O'Rourke and Duncan pierced that tight defence while Joe Harper nabbed a double for the visitors.

A trip to Falkirk followed and with it the chance to do a League double over the Bairns. That was achieved – but at a cost, as Alex Cropley was stretchered off with a broken ankle. 'Sodjer' was a wiry but strong guy and he would suffer his fair share of injuries throughout his career because he knew no fear when going into the tackle. The game itself exploded into action from the off when Hamilton fired Hibs ahead after just ten seconds while Gordon and substitute Baker scored the others. Falkirk countered through Doug Somner and Alex Ferguson, but Hibs took the important two points on the day.

The Scottish Cup fourth round brought Airdrie to Easter Road and presented Hibs with the chance to progress to the quarter-finals, a chance they took with a 2-0 win after goals from Gordon and Baker. Airdrie put up a fighting display and held out for 75 minutes, but despite missing Edwards and Cropley Hibs were eventually too good for them and deservedly progressed to a home tie with Aberdeen, the Dons having secured their quarter-final place by narrowly defeating Morton 1-0.

March 1972 started for Hibs with a visit from lowly Clyde, a side struggling to avoid the relegation dogfight, and they returned to Glasgow no better off after a solo strike from Alan Gordon kept the points in Edinburgh. A familiar look was beginning to emerge in terms of the back six at Easter Road as the line-up that day once again read: Herriot, Brownlie, Schaedler, Stanton, Black and Blackley. It would be a while, though, before the front five of the Tornadoes team joined that six, due entirely to the suspension being served by Edwards and the broken ankle suffered by Cropley. Their absence was more often than not covered by the inclusion of Hamilton and Baker, with the odd appearance by Kenny Davidson.

Ahead of the Cup encounter with Aberdeen, Hibs suffered a 2-1 defeat at East End Park, where they never really got their passing game going. A Jimmy O'Rourke penalty was all Hibs had to show for their efforts, while Dunfermline secured the points with goals from youngsters Mackie and Paterson. It was not perhaps the best of preparations for the Scottish Cup tie with Aberdeen, but the Dons had a couple of blows of their own to endure when star defender Martin Buchan was transferred to Manchester United and midfielder Davie Robb was suspended from playing.

A huge crowd packed into Easter Road for the visit of the Dons and just 17 seconds after referee Bill Mullen from Dalkeith whistled for the game to start Jimmy O'Rourke took a pinpoint pass from Gordon and fired Hibs into the lead with a fierce left-foot volley from just inside the box. It was a stunning opening to what went on to be a classic cup tie, with the visitors forced to push forward after conceding the early goal. The Hibs defence, however, rose to the challenge magnificently, and when Baker slotted home the second goal for the Greens all thoughts turned to the semi-finals. The Hampden opponents would be either Motherwell or Rangers, who had drawn their quarter-final and would replay in the following midweek.

League form against the teams higher in the table had been good, but Hibs kept shooting themselves in the foot by dropping points to those clubs in the lower reaches. That trend continued when Airdrie visited the following midweek and went home with the points in a 3-1 win. Blackley was missing due to injury and his place was taken by Alex Pringle, while young striker Denis Nelson made his debut wearing the No.9 shirt. O'Rourke missed his first penalty in ten attempts, but Brownlie got his second goal of the season, from a free kick. The Airdrie keeper, Roddy

McKenzie, had a series of fine saves, and Drew Busby, Drew Jarvie and Willie Wilson scored the goals to win Airdrie much-needed points and gain sweet revenge for the recent Cup defeat at the hands of their hosts.

There was some good news for Pat Stanton during the week when his wife, Margaret, presented him with a baby boy. Just to make sure that the celebratory cigars would all be smoked, he was also named in the Scotland pool which would travel to Brazil in the coming close season.

The League table showed Partick Thistle to be just two places and two points behind Hibs in seventh when they visited Easter Road on 25 March, but there seemed a bigger gap based on the performances on the day when Hibs fired on all cylinders and recorded a very comfortable 3-0 win, with goals from O'Rourke (pen), Baker and an own-goal from full-back Reid. Thistle had lost striker Jimmy Bone to Norwich, but had Scotland pool member Alan Rough and future Celtic stalwart Ronnie Glavin in their team. Hibs, however, were just too strong for them, ex-Jag Arthur Duncan causing them particular problems throughout the 90 minutes.

The following Saturday, Hibs were meant to play Kilmarnock at Rugby Park and though they turned up to fulfil the fixture a late and torrential downpour of April rain saw the game postponed and rescheduled for the following Monday evening. Unfortunately, the two-day delay cost Hibs the services of Pat Stanton, who had to withdraw from the travelling party because of illness. Jim Black, who had a hip injury, was also absent. It was an odd-looking half-back line, then, with Billy McEwan, John Blackley and Alan Gordon wearing the four, five and six jerseys, but Hibs secured a point in a 1-1 draw and on the balance of play should probably have won the game. Gordon was outstanding alongside Blackley in the centre of the Hibs defence and was hugely unlucky in deflecting the ball past Herriot for the Killie goal. McEwan scored for Hibs, while Edwards never looked as though he had been away after ending his eight-week suspension.

It was now known that Hibs would face Rangers in the Scottish Cup semi-final at Hampden, but before that they had to meet St Johnstone at Easter Road in the League. The Saints, managed by Willie Ormond, were mid-table and had enjoyed their first-ever run in Europe when beating Hamburg and Vasas in the UEFA Cup before falling to Zeljeznicar of Yugoslavia. They met a Hibs side who were unstoppable on the day and they were crushed 7-1, their solitary strike coming from wing-half Alex Rennie. Hibs, prompted by the quite wonderful passing play of Alex Edwards in midfield and the speed of Duncan on the wing, scored through Gordon (2), Baker, Stanton, Edwards, Duncan and O'Rourke.

Not since 1967 had Hibs managed a League double over Dundee, but their earlier 1-0 win at Easter Road was added to with a fine 2-1 win at Dens Park, Hazel getting the first and Stanton the second after a great move ended with Gordon setting the skipper up with the chance. Jimmy Wilson had scored for Dundee, but Hibs were the better team on the day and fully deserved the points.

A Hampden semi-final against Rangers is always a daunting prospect and when the teams met on Saturday, 15 April, Hibs seemed somewhat overawed in the first half and trailed 1-0 at the break, having conceded a goal to Alex MacDonald. Whether it was the half-time cup of tea or the words of wisdom offered by Eddie Turnbull is unclear, but the Greens were a different team in that second period and it was no surprise when O'Rourke scored his 14th goal of the season to pull Hibs level. Arthur Duncan was causing mayhem down the Hibs left, but Rangers held on for a replay.

In between those two Cup games, Hibs had a visit from Greenock Morton, who had held them to a point at Cappielow earlier in the season. Morton had had a decent run of eight games in which they had suffered defeat only once. They defended stoutly throughout, but a rare goal from Blackley broke the deadlock and won the points for Hibs.

The Greens now had to face Rangers twice in Glasgow over a period of five days, firstly at Hampden in the Cup semi-final replay. In another exciting game, Hibs overcame any feelings of awe straight from the kick-off and goals from Stanton and Edwards sealed a Cup final place against Celtic on 6 May. This was a superb display from the Greens and the legions of Rangers fans present were making for the exits long before the game finished, so in control were Turnbull's men.

Ibrox was the venue for the second meeting, this time in the final League game of the season, and once again the Greens triumphed, gaining revenge for that last-minute 1-0 defeat on Christmas Day by winning 2-1, thanks to goals from a Jimmy O'Rourke penalty and Bertie Auld. The Rangers goal was scored by Colin Stein, but once again their fans were seen to be leaving early.

Only the Cup final now remained on the agenda and Hibs were well geared up for it following their good run of results, including those two great wins over Rangers. Once again, however, it was not to be as the Greens suffered a crushing 6-1 defeat at the hands of Celtic. Alan Gordon netted for Hibs, but the Glasgow side were dominant throughout. In front of more than 106,000 fans, Dixie Deans got a hat-trick, while Billy McNeill and Lou Macari (2) were the other scorers. At the end, the massive Hibs support still cheered their heroes, who had been totally overwhelmed, but the journey home was a long and sad one as the realisation sunk in that, once again, the open-top bus would not be required.

Chapter Six

1972/73

SEVENTH HEAVEN

There's no doubt that the disappointment of failing to win the Scottish Cup the previous May was uppermost in the minds of the Hibs support as this season approached, but little did they know that there were a few things about to happen which would go a long way to compensate for that Scottish Cup failure.

The previous season had seen the introduction of a new cup competition sponsored by the brewing giants Drybrough's. It involved the top-scoring teams from the First and Second Divisions and that meant Celtic, Rangers, Aberdeen (the holders) and Hibs from the First, along with Montrose, St Mirren, Dumbarton and Stirling Albion from the Second.

In preparation for that competition, the League Cup and the coming season, Hibs went on a short tour of Ireland, where they trained as well as taking part in three friendly games. The first was against Home Farm at Tolka Park in Dublin, and a 2-0 win was achieved, thanks to a double strike from Billy McEwan. Two days later, Hibs took on the Irish champions, Waterford, and again won 2-0, the goals this time coming from youngster Willie Murray and full-back John Brownlie. The tour wound up three days later with a 0-0 draw against Cork Hibs before the Greens returned home ready to face Montrose at Easter Road in the Drybrough Cup.

The Links Park outfit struggled to match the pace and fitness of a refreshed Hibs team, and it was no surprise when the home side ran out 4-0 winners on the day. In fairness to Montrose, it took Hibs 30 minutes to break them down, but once Hamilton had lobbed home the opener the fans began to wonder just how many goals the home side would get. Three more duly arrived, thanks to Duncan, Gordon and Stanton. Hibs actually had the best result of the opening ties, the others finishing: Celtic 2 Dumbarton 1, Aberdeen 1 St Mirren 0 and Rangers 3 Stirling Albion 1. The semi-final draw paired Hibs with Rangers at Easter Road and the game was played on the Wednesday next.

In a fantastic display of attacking football, with Edwards and Cropley in top form, Hibs thrashed Rangers 3-0 in front of a large and noisy home support. Stanton opened the scoring close to half-time and then in the second half Gordon got a double, the second a glorious header to send Hibs back to Hampden for their second Cup final inside four months. Once again they would face Celtic, the Glasgow side having edged out Aberdeen 3-2 after extra time at Parkhead.

A crowd in excess of 85,000 turned up on Saturday, 5 August, and the stadium was a sea of green as the teams ran out to an enormous roar. This was the old Hampden, and so Hibs fans were mainly in the Rangers end, meaning that the covered terracing made their singing and celebrating all the louder. And celebrate they did as Hibs raced into a deserved 3-0 lead, playing Celtic off the park with a double from Gordon. It would have been a hat-trick but for his shot at goal ricocheting off the leg of Billy McNeill, who went down as the scorer of an own-goal.

The Hibs supporters thought they were in heaven as the Cup looked destined for Easter Road when suddenly there was a pitch invasion by Celtic fans after some trouble appeared to break out on the terracing. Referee Bill Mullan had little option but to take the players off briefly while the mayhem was brought under control by the police and stewards. When play resumed Hibs had lost their impetus and Celtic came roaring back to 3-3, Jimmy Johnstone hitting a double and Billy McNeill scoring at the right end this time.

The large contingent of Hibs fans were stunned, while the Celtic supporters found their voice again. When Mr Mullan blew for the end of the 90 minutes, most in the stadium would have put their money on Celtic to go on and win the trophy in extra time, but Eddie Turnbull and his players had other ideas. Turnbull replaced the exhausted Hamilton with O'Rourke and it was to be an inspired move as Jimmy fired Hibs into a 4-3 lead. Players from both sides were feeling the effects of the draining Hampden playing surface and many had their socks around their ankles on that warm sunny day as the Glasgow outfit pushed hard for an equaliser. But it was Hibs who scored. Duncan went on a mazy run deep in the Celtic defence before crashing an incredible shot past keeper Evan Williams from a tight angle to put Hibs 5-3 up with time running out fast.

There were no more goals, and Hibs had gone some way towards avenging that Scottish Cup defeat by winning over Celtic at Hampden Park. The sight of skipper Pat Stanton climbing the stairs to the directors' box and then holding the cup aloft was a joy to behold as the Hibs fans celebrated wildly and noisily in recognition of their heroes.

There was to be no lap of honour at Hampden, presumably because of the troubles earlier in the game. The Hibs support would have to wait until the following Tuesday to salute the players when the cup was paraded ahead of the friendly match at Easter Road against West Bromwich Albion.

In the meantime, every newspaper report was read and savoured by the Easter Road faithful and one or two of the comments written are very worthy of repetition here. The *Sunday Express* enthused: 'What a super show. This was dream soccer, gloriously entertaining, a feast to savour through the years ahead.' The *Glasgow Herald* offered: 'Hibs' greater all-round consistency was instrumental in giving them a long overdue trophy success. Who would have thought there was a team anywhere in the world capable of scoring five goals against the Scottish champions?' while the *Daily Record* satisfied itself with: 'Hibs did Scottish football a considerable service.'

The evening of Tuesday, 8 August, was one of celebration, regardless of the fact that West Brom tried to spoil it by winning the match 2-0. Mind you, they had a pretty good team back then with the likes of Bobby Gould, Tony Brown, Asa Hartford and Ally Brown. It was Gould and Brown who got the goals. As ever, the match programme contained a few interesting items which caught they eye. One advert suggested that the best place to shop for sports items was Ronnie Simpson's in Rose Street, the former Hibs and Celtic goalkeeper having started his business there. Another wee gem which caught my eye was the paragraph stating: 'Some Stand patrons have indicated that they are dissatisfied with the stewarding whenever seats are bookable. Now stewards are wearing a numbered armband so that they can be identified if any spectator has a complaint to forward to the club secretary.' Problems with stewarding? – surely not!

With the Drybrough Cup safely tucked away in the trophy cabinet, Hibs set about trying to add to it by qualifying from their League Cup section, which included Queen's Park, Aberdeen and Queen of the South, with a rule change allowing the top two in the group to qualify. Queen's Park provided the first test for Hibs and played pretty well in only losing 4-2 at Easter Road, where Hibs had 19-year-old Bobby Robertson in goals replacing the injured Jim Herriot. The Greens scored through Hamilton (2, one pen), Stanton and Gordon while Queen's replied through Eddie Hunter and Ally Scott.

Next up was Pittodrie, where Hibs had a disappointing day, controlling great periods of the play and yet still managing to lose 4-1. The general consensus was that the Greens did not deserve to lose so heavily, but it's goals that count and Hibs only got one, from Edwards, while the Dons rattled their four in, thanks to Drew Jarvie (2), Stevie Murray and Joe Harper. It was a long journey home for both the players and the fans with much shaking of heads in disbelief at the outcome of the game.

Two home games would give Hibs a chance to get back on track and the first of those was against Queen of the South. A double from O'Rourke and a goal from Duncan gave the home side a comfortable 3-0 win. It could have been a bigger margin but for the form of the Queens keeper, Allan Ball, who defied the Hibs strike-force time and again with a string of wonderful saves, most notably from Gordon and Stanton. Around this time Hibs learned that they would meet the crack Portuguese outfit Sporting Lisbon in the first round of the Cup Winners' Cup and advertised places for fans who wished to travel with the team for that game. The all-inclusive cost was £59 each in a twin-bedded room and £62 for a single.

A quick chance to avenge that defeat by Aberdeen was given and taken when they came to Easter Road and lost 2-1, Duncan and O'Rourke grabbing the goals. Once again it was the balding Drew Jarvie who netted for the Dons, but the points remained at Easter Road. The most significant thing about this game was that it marked the first competitive match played by the team who would become known as Turnbull's Tornadoes. The starting line-up that day was: Herriot, Brownlie, Schaedler, Stanton, Black, Blackley, Edwards, O'Rourke, Gordon, Cropley and Duncan – names that to this day remain on the lips of those fans who were fortunate enough to see them.

The League Cup section had two more games to go, the first of those requiring Hibs to travel back to Hampden, the scene of their stunning Drybrough Cup victory a few short weeks earlier. This time the crowd was not 85,000 and there were not eight goals in the game, but Hibs beat Queen's Park 1-0, thanks to a goal from Alan Gordon, who clearly enjoyed that venue.

Palmerston Park, Dumfries, was the final destination in the section matches and Hibs enjoyed another good win over the Doonhamers when they ran out 3-1 victors with goals from Stanton, Duncan and Blackley. Queens, managed by former Hibs favourite Jim Easton, scored through Tommy Bryce.

The section finished with both Hibs and Aberdeen on ten points, but the Dons had a better goal difference and so in the next round Hibs would have to face Dundee United in a two-leg affair. That game was three weeks away, however, and the League campaign was about to start for Hibs, with a tough trip to Pittodrie.

Once again Hibs dominated most of the play and once again they got nothing for their efforts as a single first-half strike from Joe Harper won the game and gave the Dons two points when most observers felt it was a result which flattered them. Bobby Clark in the Aberdeen goal was by far the busier keeper and he brought off a number of good saves to deny Hibs any reward for their lead-up play.

The first derby match of the season brought a Hearts side to Easter Road who had failed to qualify from their League Cup section, where their opponents were Dumbarton, Airdrie and Berwick Rangers. Manager Bobby Seith must have been looking for better play from his men, but Hibs ran out easy 2-0 winners with goals from Cropley and Stanton. A major statistic from the game, and one which summed up the nature of the play, was that Jim Herriot had only one direct shot to deal with in the entire 90 minutes. Another interesting point was that Hibs played that game in an all-green top, the white sleeves being conspicuous by their absence.

That derby victory set Hibs up nicely for their trip to Portugal and when the players and fans flew out from Abbotsinch on the Monday they were joined by former Hibs heroes Gordon Smith, Willie Clark and Tommy Preston. Although the result was a defeat, Hibs played some of the best football ever seen in the Jose Alvalade Stadium and in later years Pat Stanton would say that this was the best performance he'd been involved in with a Hibs side in Europe. Hibs went at Sporting from the start and Cropley was unlucky when his shot crashed back off a post in their first attack. While the first half belonged to Hibs, it was goalless and the home side punished slack play after the interval with two quick goals from Fraguito and Manaca. Hibs stuck to the task and Arthur Duncan grabbed what might prove to be a vital away goal. Those fans who made the trip were somewhat bemused when Hibs took to the field wearing a purple and white outfit, but the colour change did not affect the play and the visitors finished the stronger team.

From Lisbon to Methil – these Hibs players were well travelled as they faced East Fife the following Saturday, and they came back with both points in the bag after Alan Gordon scored the only goal of the game. The Fifers tried packing the midfield area to stop Hibs playing their passing game and it was successful to a degree until Gordon broke the deadlock, but by then the home side could find no way back.

The League Cup first-leg tie against Dundee United would be the first of back-to-back meetings between the clubs, the League fixture being scheduled for the following Saturday. The match at Tannadice looked to be heading for disaster when United took a two-goal lead in at the interval with Ian Mitchell and Pat Gardner on target, but another of those famous Turnbull 'pep talks' seems to have done the trick because the Greens came out in the second half and blasted five goals past Hamish McAlpine without reply, four of them coming in a devastating 18-minute spell. The marksmen were O'Rourke (3, one pen), and Cropley (2) and as the players left the park at the end of the game there was a shell-shocked look on the faces of both the United players and supporters!

No doubt the Arabs were still feeling the effects of that midweek mauling when they came to Easter Road on League business that Saturday. Once again Hibs outplayed them and won comfortably by a 3-1 scoreline, thanks to a double from Gordon and a Jackie Copland own-goal. United's goal came from midfielder Jim Henry, who had been attracting the attention of Fulham and must have wished he'd gone there.

European nights at Easter Road have no comparison in the domestic game. They invariably draw bumper crowds, with the prospect of floodlit excitement on the cards. And so, when Sporting Lisbon arrived in Leith on Wednesday, 27 September 1972, more than 26,000 spectators packed the stadium.

Only a 2-1 win for Hibs would bring extra time, any other result ensuring that one team or the other would progress. The Easter Road men, once again wearing that all-green top, struggled a bit at the start of the game to gain control in midfield, but they did take the lead on 28 minutes when Gordon rose gracefully to power home an Edwards cross. That goal set the crowd alight, but they were stunned into silence just minutes later when a clearance from the Hibs defence struck referee Herr Maennig and fell kindly for Marinho to set up Yazaldi for an equaliser.

Half-time and another pep talk had Hibs buzzing in the second 45 as they swarmed down the famous Easter Road slope. In 65 minutes Hibs took the lead when Gordon fed O'Rourke and the number eight lobbed Damas in the Sporting goal. The volume from the terracings increased and so did Hibs' tempo as just a few minutes later Gordon rose again to head home a Schaedler cross to put Hibs 3-1 up on the night. The home side were rampant now and O'Rourke lashed home the fourth from a Brownlie pass. The visitors made substitutions to try to stem the flow, but they had no effect as O'Rourke completed his hat-trick and then an Arthur Duncan cross was turned into his own net by Damas. It was carnival time on the terracings as Hibs ended the game 6-1 winners on the night and 7-3 winners on aggregate against a very good Portuguese side.

September 1972 ended with a visit from Willie Ormond's St Johnstone. They were without a League win in four attempts while Hibs had won three and lost one, sharing top spot with Celtic. The Saints put up a good show on the day and it was end-to-end stuff at times. Henry Hall and Jim Pearson netted for the visitors, but that blossoming deadly partnership of Jimmy O'Rourke (2) and Alan Gordon ensured a 3-2 home win. Those strikes took Gordon on to 14 for the season and O'Rourke to 12 – astonishingly, they had shared 14 of the last 18 goals scored by the team!

October would prove to be a busy month with mixed results, starting with the second leg of that League Cup tie against Dundee United. The Tangerines, trailing by a three-goal deficit from the first leg, arrived at Easter Road knowing that the tie was dead as far as they were concerned, and appeared to use the game as an exercise in tightening their somewhat leaky defence. It seemed to work as Hibs failed to break them down and the match finished 0-0, with Hibs going through to meet Airdrie in the quarter-finals.

On the European front there was some doubt as to which side Hibs would meet next. The Danish club Fremad had appealed to UEFA, hoping to have the Albanian side FC Besa eliminated, even though the

Scandinavians had lost over two legs in the first round. UEFA rejected the appeal, however, and Hibs would face the Albanians, about whom very little was known.

Ahead of that lay a combination of League and League Cup games, the first requiring a visit to Dens Park, where a shot-shy Hibs side had much of the game but ended up losing 1-0 after some sloppy defending let Bobby Ford win both points for Dundee. That was a real disappointment and meant that Hibs had not scored in two consecutive matches. The loss at half-time of Alex Edwards, who was struggling with a head cold, didn't help, but the fact that Hibs had so few shots at goal was the real reason for the loss. Ironically, fellow pacesetters Celtic dropped a point and Aberdeen lost, but Hibs had failed to capitalise.

If five second-half goals at Tannadice had secured a place in the next round of the League Cup then surely the six Hibs scored in the second period at Broomfield would take them to the semi-finals, even though the return leg had not yet been played. In a quite stunning 45-minute spell, Hibs contrived to fall behind twice to Drew Busby goals, one of those being from the spot, and yet still won the game at a canter, Alex Edwards destroying the home defence with his pinpoint passing. The six goals came from Duncan (3), Brownlie (2) and a Jimmy O'Rourke penalty – referee Mr Gordon from Glasgow having a busy night.

As often seems to happen in Scottish football, even back then when the top division had 18 clubs, the fixture list threw the clubs together again just three days later at Easter Road in the League. Once again, Drew Busby netted for the Diamonds and his team-mate Columb McKinley got a second for the visitors. But it was Roddy McKenzie in the Airdrie goal who was the busiest on the night as Hibs thumped another five past him, thanks to a Jimmy O'Rourke hat-trick (one a penalty) and single strikes from Gordon and Duncan. Poor McKenzie must have had nightmares, having lost 11 goals in two games against the Greens. Knowing that he had to face them again in the second leg of the League Cup tie would have worried him further still.

Remarkably, the 5-2 win over Airdrie constituted Hibs' 25th game of the season and this was only mid-October. Still, it had been a good start, what with winning the Drybrough Cup, looking good for a semi-final place in the League Cup and sitting third in the League behind Dundee United and Celtic, with Hearts fourth and Rangers struggling in a poor 12th place. In all matches played to date, Alan Gordon had 14 goals, Jimmy O'Rourke 13 and Arthur Duncan nine – not a bad haul for this part of the season.

One more League game remained before the European tie and that was against Partick Thistle at Firhill. In a decent game, Edwards again pulled the strings in the Hibs midfield and the visitors ran out comfortable 3-1 winners, Gordon netting twice and Duncan getting the other. Joe Craig countered for the home side. That win kept Hibs in third place, two points behind Celtic and one behind Dundee United, while Rangers had improved to fourth and poor old Airdrie propped up the rest.

The Albanian Cup holders, FC Besa, were truly an unknown quantity when they came to Easter Road for the first leg of this Cup Winners' Cup second-round tie and Hibs' new signing, goalkeeper Jim McArthur, who was 20 and had joined the club that week from Cowdenbeath, must surely have been impressed by his new team-mates as they systematically destroyed the visitors with a 7-1 thrashing in front of a noisy and excited crowd of more than 22,000. Kariqi did manage to put the ball past Jim Herriot, but the Besa goalkeeper Arkaxihiu must have wished he had stayed in Albania as the shots rained in on him and those from O'Rourke (3), Duncan (2), Cropley and Brownlie reached the net. The second leg would be a formality and the fans left the stadium that night aware that the third round could bring the likes of AC Milan, Sparta Prague, Atletico Madrid or Leeds United to Easter Road.

Just five days after signing from Cowdenbeath, Jim McArthur made an unexpected debut against Dumbarton at Boghead after Jim Herriot failed to recover from a knock taken in the Besa game. The young keeper did well, although a number of his team-mates looked a little jaded after their recent busy schedule and Hibs were lucky to escape with a 2-2 draw. Duncan had put the Greens ahead, but former Hearts and Celtic striker Willie Wallace got them level and then Tom McAdam put them ahead. The Sons were then pushing for a clinching goal, but Hibs picked themselves up a bit and Gordon got a welcome equaliser.

November 1972 began with a League Cup visit from Airdrie. Trailing 6-2 from the first leg, they were soundly beaten yet again as Hibs punished their defensive frailties. Manager Turnbull, still without Jim Herriot, played young Bobby Robertson in goal and the keeper had a fine game, even though he lost a goal to McRoberts. At the other end, Roddy McKenzie shipped another four with O'Rourke getting two and Edwards and Stanton the others.

Another home game followed before Hibs were due to fly out to Albania, and Kilmarnock provided the opposition. Perhaps conscious of the fact that leaders Celtic were playing Dundee United that day and that something had to give points-wise at Parkhead, Hibs seemed determined to take any advantage that transpired, and take advantage they did with a fine 4-1 win over the Ayrshire outfit. Jim McArthur resumed in goals due to the continuing absence of Jim Herriot, but this was to be Pat Stanton's day as the skipper celebrated his call-up to Scotland's World Cup squad with a brilliant double in a 4-1 win. The other Hibs scorers were Duncan and O'Rourke, while Eddie Morrison scored for the visitors.

Although FC Besa were based in a town some 40 miles from the

Albanian capital of Tirana, they had decided that the game with Hibs deserved a better setting than their modest stadium offered and so the game was played in the capital's Qemal Stafa Stadium, which was in fact the National Stadium. There being little by way of entertainment in Tirana, Hibs decided to keep the players occupied by taking along some equipment which would allow the squad to play roulette and bingo. The club also brought the chef from Edinburgh's prestigious North British Hotel to ensure that there would be no problems with diets, and so the players were well prepared for the match itself. On an exceedingly bumpy and dry pitch it was difficult to settle into the passing game that Hibs preferred and although the local supporters realised their side had no chance of progressing they cheered long and loud when Pagria slotted the ball past young Bobby Robertson to put the home side ahead on the day. A second-half equaliser from Alan Gordon also met with huge cheers as the locals enjoyed themselves and the match ended 1-1, Hibs going through 8-2 on aggregate.

The Cup Winners' Cup now went into hibernation until February 1973 and Hibs and their supporters would have to wait for some time before learning the name of the next opponents. It was, however, known at that stage that clubs such as Spartak Moscow, Rapid Bucharest, Hajduk Split, Sparta Prague, Leeds United, AC Milan and Schalke would be in the hat.

Back in Scotland just four hours after taking off from Tirana, Hibs enjoyed the benefits of chartering a flight rather than spending endless hours waiting around in airport departure lounges, and the players were happy to be sleeping in their own beds that night.

Cappielow was the next venue for a Hibs side who were full of confidence following a string of good results and they kept that going with an emphatic 3-0 win, Jimmy O'Rourke getting his fifth hat-trick of the season, taking him to 25 goals in all matches. Jimmy really was a quality player and very popular with the fans, who had created their very own song for him using the tune from the Rupert Bear cartoons on TV. 'Jimmy, Jimmy O'Rourke, everyone knows his name' rang out from terraces around the country as the Hibs number eight banged goals in from all angles.

Hibs were still pushing Celtic hard at the top of the League when the other half of the Old Firm arrived at Easter Road on Saturday, 18 November 1972. It was a new-look Rangers side. Ex-Hibs man Colin Stein had departed in a deal which took him to Coventry City and brought the former Ayr Utd winger Quinton Young to Ibrox. Gers boss Jock Wallace had also recruited Joe Mason from Morton and Tom Forsyth from Motherwell. This new side had been taking time to gel, and Rangers were sitting only fifth in the League that day while Hibs were second. The visitors, though, were a better side on the day and while Stanton was on the mark for Hibs, Alfie Conn and Graeme Fyfe netted for Rangers in their 2-1 victory.

There was to be a quick opportunity to gain revenge for Turnbull's men as the teams would meet the following midweek in the League Cup semi-final at Hampden. A crowd of more than 46,000 turned up to watch a real cat-and-mouse display with both teams not at their best. But those who did attend will surely never forget the one goal that settled the tie, that being a quite magnificent solo effort from John Brownlie, who finished off a mazy run by crashing a shot past Peter McCloy in the Rangers goal. Hibs had reached their second Hampden final of the season, and once again the opposition would be Celtic, the Parkhead club having twice come from a goal behind to beat Aberdeen 3-2.

Newly promoted Arbroath entertained Hibs next in a League game at Gayfield Park and the visitors found their hosts in good form but managed to win 3-2 on a cold and very blustery evening. Two players notched doubles on the night, Billy Pirie for the home side and Alan Gordon for Hibs, who also scored through Arthur Duncan, the winger being set up beautifully by a defence-splitting pass from Cropley. Jimmy O'Rourke had to be substituted during that game due to a calf knock and his replacement was Bobby Smith, making his first-team debut.

A look at the reserve team Hibs were putting out around that time reveals a few interesting names, with players such as Derek Spalding, Willie Murray, Tony Higgins and Bobby Smith more or less regulars and new signing Des Bremner, from Deveronvale, making an instant impact by scoring one of the goals in the side's 3-0 win over Arbroath.

Only one more game remained before the League Cup final and it brought in-form Falkirk to Easter Road. Although they had not won an away game to date they had only actually lost one, and that was at Parkhead, so a tough afternoon was predicted. But Hibs had their tails up and cruised home 3-0 with goals from Gordon, Stanton and Duncan.

Cup finals do not come along nearly often enough for most Hibs fans' liking, so when they do there is always a huge support travelling through to roar on the team. That was very much the case on Saturday, 9 December 1972, a day noted with pride in the long history of the club. Some 71,696 fans piled into the stadium and those wearing the emerald green and white colours of Hibernian were desperate for their heroes to avenge the 6-1 thumping meted out by Celtic in the previous season's Scottish Cup final. Many pundits and neutrals had written off Hibs' chances because Jock Stein's side were packed with talent and led the League, having won 12 and drawn one of their 14 starts. Eddie Turnbull's team, however, had different ideas, and in a never to be forgotten 90 minutes they defeated the Glasgow side 2-1 to lift the trophy.

Praise for the victors was warm and plentiful, with telegrams of congratulations arriving at Easter Road from the Lord Provost of Edinburgh and Hearts FC among others. For the players and fans, there were two special occasions to savour: first, when Pat Stanton climbed the Hampden stairway and held the trophy aloft, and then, when the team got home that evening, the open-top bus ride through the city. Tens of thousands of fans lined the streets and the celebrations went on long into the night.

The goalscoring heroes that day were, aptly in my opinion and in the opinion of most Hibs fans, Pat Stanton and Jimmy O'Rourke, both great servants to the club, both Edinburgh lads and both dyed-in-the-wool Hibs fans themselves. Although every player played superbly that day the one man who stood head and shoulders above the others was Pat Stanton, whose display was best summed up by the *News of the World* sports reporter: 'The 1972 League Cup final will be remembered for years for one thing – it was the Pat Stanton final. If ever one player dominated a game it was the Hibs captain, whose part in this clash of the giants was immense.' Not even the consolation goal scored by Kenny Dalglish could take the glory away from Hibernian that day.

Easter Road was the place to be the following Saturday as the cup would be paraded in front of the supporters for all to see, but anyone arriving just a minute after kick-off would have missed the opening goal against luckless Ayr United, the Somerset Park men finding Hibs in stunning form. Cropley opened the Hibs account in just 40 seconds and the Greens went on to demolish the visitors 8-1, Cropley's goal being added to by Gordon (3), O'Rourke (3) and Stanton, with Alex McAnespie scoring for Ayr. The game marked a sixth hat-trick of the season for O'Rourke, while Gordon's third in that game – which put Hibs 4-0 up – was the Greens' 100th of the season to date.

L'Équipe soccer magazine, published that month, showed Hibs to be ranked joint fifth in Europe with Celtic lying ninth. Bayern Munich and Ajax shared top spot with Brian Clough's Derby third, Benfica fourth and Nice sharing the fifth spot with Hibs. The French publication awarded points to three teams giving the best performance in each country every week, and Hibs were right up there. Individually, Alan Gordon found himself sitting third in the race for the 'Golden Boot' award which went to the player scoring the most championship goals for his team. Eusébio of Benfica was top with 20; Gerd Müller of Bayern Munich was second with 19, and Gordon had 15 from 15 starts.

League leaders Celtic provided the next test and this time the game was at Parkhead. Jock Stein's men were smarting from that League Cup defeat and they would have been smarting even more when Alan Gordon gave Hibs a deserved first-half lead. The Edinburgh side created a number of chances but could not add to that lead and paid the penalty when Kenny Dalglish scored an equaliser with just 12 minutes left, the game finishing at 1-1.

Jimmy Bonthrone brought Aberdeen to Easter Road for the last game of the year, but had to do so without his star striker, Joe Harper, who had left to join Everton for a fee of £180,000, a record for a Scottish club. In his line-up, however, was the Hungarian midfielder Zoltan Varga, who had reached Aberdeen via Hertha Berlin, having first made his name with Ferencvaros in his home country. Varga was a superbly talented player whose control and passing ability would cause trouble for many defences in the months ahead. But on this particular occasion it was Alex Edwards who shone in prompting his team to win 3-2 in a game where the gap could and should have been much wider. Stanton, O'Rourke and Gordon, with a superb flying header, scored for Hibs while Drew Jarvie and Bertie Miller countered for the Dons.

Without doubt, 1972 was a grand year to be a Hibs fan, given that the Greens had won two trophies, were pushing Celtic hard for the title and had progressed into the third round of the European Cup Winners' Cup. It was difficult to imagine that 1973 could offer as much excitement, but it certainly started that way when Hibs visited Tynecastle just two days after the win over Aberdeen.

Derby matches in recent years had often been dull and goalless, and when the fans of both clubs turned up in Gorgie on 1 January 1973 they had little reason to think that the trend might change. True, Hibs were in good form, having scored a load of goals in a number of the matches leading up to the Ne'er Day encounter, but Hearts were going pretty well too. For their part, the fans were well equipped on that cold day to ward off the chill with half bottles of whisky in great evidence and frequent sips being taken as those bottles were handed around as friends in both colours wished each other a happy New Year.

In those days, Tynecastle, like almost every other stadium, had seating only in the main stand and segregation was a thing of the future, so other than the respective 'choirs' who stood under the sheltered terrace, the fans were intermingled throughout the terracing. The game started briskly with both teams looking to attack at every opportunity and within the first ten minutes Hearts had missed a couple of good chances to take the lead as first Donald Ford and then Donald Park shot wide from good positions.

Then the floodgates opened as the Gordon–O'Rourke partnership gave Hibs the lead in just nine minutes. A long throw from Schaedler, a flick on from Gordon and there was Jimmy O'Rourke to crash the ball past Kenny Garland to set the green parts of Tynecastle alight. Hearts were stung by this and tried to fight back, but Hibs stood firm with a solid defence and completely dominated the midfield, where Stanton and Edwards ran the show. Six minutes after O'Rourke's opener, an Edwards pinpoint pass picked out Alan Gordon at the edge of the box and in one movement he controlled the ball, stepped past Alan Anderson, the big Hearts centre-half, and stroked the ball beyond Garland to put Hibs 2-0 up.

Hearts were struggling to keep the Greens at bay and after another close thing when Arthur Duncan brought out a good save from Garland, Hibs scored again as Alex Cropley intercepted an attempted clearance by Thomson and headed the ball into the path of Duncan. Nijinsky took off, and no home defender could catch him as he slotted in number three after just 25 minutes.

Just as we find the case to be these days, a number of Hibs fans were late in making it to the ground and as they entered at 3.25pm they were greeted with both the news that Hibs were 3-0 up and the sight of many Hearts supporters heading home for an early steak-pie dinner with the family.

The latecomers were soon rewarded when Alex Cropley volleyed a superb fourth in the 35th minute and those same fans were still trying to get the tops off their bottles for a celebratory drink when Arthur Duncan headed a fifth, just two minutes later. The maroons were in total disarray and the look on their young left-back's face summed it up as he struggled to find a way to curb the Hibernian menace. That full-back would never forget or indeed be allowed to forget the outcome – Jim Jefferies was his name. In truth, Hibs could have had seven by half-time as first Edwards inexplicably lost his way when inside the six-yard box and then the same player cheekily lifted a free kick over the Hearts wall and, as the ball fell, Jimmy O'Rourke blasted it just wide.

Occasionally at such matches the home side would provide some sort of half-time entertainment to keep the waiting fans amused, but it wasn't needed that day as the Hibs fans in the ground made their own fun by singing and waving to the Hearts fans making for the exits.

When the second half started the more inebriated among the remaining Hearts supporters started singing, no doubt hoping their heroes would at least try to compete in the second period, but they were to be disappointed as Hibs retained total control and stroked the ball about almost at leisure. Stanton and his men knew that they would overtake Celtic for top spot if they could beat Hearts by six goals, although they cannot have seen that as a realistic target in the run-up to the game. But real it became as the Hibs skipper tore from midfield towards the Hearts penalty area and sent a shot beyond Garland which was heading for the net when Jimmy O'Rourke rushed in to make sure from about two yards.

It has to be said that were it not for the form of Kenny Garland in the Hearts goal that day there is every possibility Hibs would have reached double figures. As it was, Alan Gordon completed the rout with a seventh goal in the 75th minute. Hibs and their fans were truly in seventh heaven, beating their oldest rivals so comprehensively on their own patch and going top of the League as a result. The half bottles were empty as the Hibs supporters flocked out of Tynecastle and sang their way along Gorgie Road, but there would surely be a huge amount of alcohol consumed all over the city by supporters of both sides that New Year's night, whether in celebration of a fabulous victory or in commiseration after having been blown away by Turnbull's Tornadoes.

Could life get any better for Hibs fans after that magnificent seven? Sadly, no. Five days later, a series of events began which would ultimately cost the Easter Road side dearly.

East Fife were the visitors to Easter Road and the derby victory over Hearts encouraged more than 17,000 to turn up to watch what proved to be a bad-tempered affair. The Fifers, probably feeling that Hibs had to be stopped from doing to them what they'd done to Hearts, packed their defence and meted out some quite dreadful punishment to Alex Edwards as he tried to prompt attacking play for the home side. Methil man John Love was a particularly regular offender, crashing into Edwards on a number of occasions and mouthing off to the wee Fifer in an attempt to prompt a reaction. 'Mickey', as he was known to one and all, was a hugely talented player, but would be the first to admit that his temperament was fiery, and with no obvious protection being offered by referee Syme of Glasgow, the little Hibs number seven earned himself what would prove to be a very costly caution.

In the end, the game is best remembered for a shocking incident when East Fife full-back Ian Printy was involved in a tackle with John Brownlie which resulted in the Hibs man suffering a broken leg. Although it was a rough game, there was no malice on Printy's part as both players went into a hard tackle with equal commitment, but the sound of the sickening crack as the bone broke will live long in the memories of all present. In fact, Brownlie found out later that two bones had broken and the injury would keep him out of the side for some months.

Later in that same game, Alex Edwards, who had been kicked up and down the park by East Fife's John Love, took umbrage at a decision not going for him, threw the ball away and earned that caution which took him over the points limit, resulting in a 56-day ban. It meant that Edwards would eventually miss ten games, which proved extremely costly to Hibs in their challenge for the title. Hibs eventually won 1-0, with Gordon the last-minute scorer, but that fact seems almost incidental in hindsight.

Des Bremner was drafted in to replace Brownlie for the next fixture, which took Hibs to Tannadice. Although the Highlander had a good game a number of his colleagues did not, and Hibs disappointingly lost 1-0, Andy Rolland getting the only goal of the game. After the goal feasts of eight against Ayr United and seven against Hearts, it was disappointing that the Greens were strangely shot-shy at Tannadice. The defeat lost them two precious points in the title race, which had now also been joined by Rangers.

The Scottish weather claimed the next scheduled fixture, against St

Johnstone at Muirton Park, but there was more disappointment for Hibs when Pat Stanton appeared before the SFA Disciplinary Committee and was handed a 14-day ban due to an accumulation of bookings. In those days, the ban imposed was for a period of time instead of a number of games, and occasionally players could strike lucky and serve their ban without missing a game if the weather was 'kind' to them. No doubt that's why the rule was changed at some future date.

Another matter had entered the minds of Hibs fans as they learned that their favourites had been drawn against Hajduk Split in the third round of the Cup Winners' Cup. Nobody really knew much about the Yugoslav side other than the fact that they had disposed of Wrexham in the previous round on away goals. The draw had given Hibs home advantage in the first leg, but League business required attention ahead of that, with Dundee offering the next challenge at Easter Road.

In the week leading up to that game, Hibs found themselves in the recording studio, joining the ever-growing number of football teams releasing records. The 45rpm single had *Hibernian – Give us a Goal!*, written by chairman Tom Hart's wife, Sheila, as its 'A' side with, on the other, a little ditty called *Turnbull's Tornadoes*, written by lifelong Hibs fan James Macpherson, of Saughton Mains. I wonder if James realised that Hibs fans would still be singing that song some 30-odd years later.

With Pat Stanton missing through suspension and Brownlie through injury, Hibs struggled to find their usual cohesion and Dundee made it difficult for them by turning in a good performance. A finishing score of 1-1 was probably a true reflection on the play, although Hibs had finished the stronger team despite having lost goalscorer Alan Gordon at half-time because of a pulled muscle. That had been Gordon's 31st goal of the season in all competitions, while the Dundee counter came from John Duncan. The replacements for Stanton and Brownlie, 18-year-old Tony Higgins and Des Bremner, both turned in good, solid performances on the day and that was encouraging for the Hibs fans to see.

Scottish Cup time was here once again and Hibs had drawn Morton at Easter Road, the Cappielow outfit sitting low in the First Division some 12 places and 15 points behind Hibs. Although not in the best form on the day, Hibs won 2-0 with goals from Higgins and Cropley carrying them safely into the next round, where they would face Rangers at Ibrox – a daunting task, regardless of the form being shown by the Greens.

In the three meetings with Airdrie to date, Hibs had scored 15 goals for the loss of five and when the Diamonds hosted Hibs on League duty in February they were once again swept aside as Alan Gordon hammered all four goals in a 4-0 win on a very bumpy pitch. The whole team played well, and Gordon was in deadly shooting form as he gratefully accepted the chances set up for him by Edwards, Cropley and Duncan. That foursome took Gordon to 24 League strikes for the season and boosted his standing in the Golden Boot race.

With the suspension of Alex Edwards now started, Hibs travelled to Muirton Park, Perth, where they faced a plucky St Johnstone with Johnny Hamilton wearing Edwards' No.7 shirt. Hamilton put in a good shift as Hibs took the game 3-1 and even had the luxury of a missed penalty from O'Rourke. Scorers for Hibs that day were Duncan, in the first minute, Gordon and Schaedler. Fred Aitken struck for Saints. The press attention all went to Gordon, whose goal took him to the top of the tree in the Golden Boot race, one ahead of both Gerd Müller and Eusébio.

Ibrox was packed on the Saturday when Hibs faced Rangers in the fourth round of the Scottish Cup. The crowd of 63,889 (among them, the Hajduk Split coach, Branko Zebec) witnessed a pulsating game in which the Greens were very unlucky not to win through. Instead, they had to settle for a draw and a replay after goals from Willie Johnstone and Alan Gordon, his 37th of the season in all competitions, tied the game at 1-1.

The following midweek, Rangers arrived at Easter Road for the replay, which attracted a massive crowd in excess of 49,000, taking the attendance for both matches well over the 100,000 mark. In a rough game, Hibs scored through Duncan while Rangers countered through Tommy McLean. With the tie looking as if it was going to extra time, the visitors were awarded a highly controversial penalty, which McLean converted to take Rangers through 2-1 on the night. It was the first time Hibs had lost in the Cup to Rangers at Easter Road for 69 years and the first time they'd lost to anyone at Easter Road in that competition since Partick Thistle in 1962.

Being out of the Cup was an all too familiar feeling for Hibs fans, but there was a genuine belief that League glory might be achieved if the team could keep its championship form going – and, of course, there was still the UEFA Cup as well. Dumbarton provided the next League test and they were soon sent packing as Hibs hammered five past them without reply. A double from Cropley and goals from Gordon, Hamilton and Duncan kept Hibs hot on the heels of Celtic and Rangers while worsening the plight of the Sons, who were struggling near the foot of the table.

The easy win over Dumbarton seemed to set Hibs up nicely for the visit of Hajduk Split, a match in which Alex Edwards could appear because his ban did not extend to UEFA Cup ties. This was a quarter-final tie, but the Yugoslavs were a bit of an unknown quantity and so the Hibs fans turning up that night were not sure what to expect. Wearing their all-green tops, Hibs scored four times, Gordon hitting a hat-trick and Duncan getting the other, but in their rush to score as many as possible they lapsed twice defensively and allowed Ivica Hlevnjak to strike two very precious away goals. Despite those lapses, Eddie Turnbull was confident his men could progress to the semi-finals when the second leg was played two weeks later.

League duty next took Hibs to Rugby Park, where their record was pretty abysmal. Despite dominating the game and scoring twice through Higgins and a cracking 25-yarder from Stanton, they somehow contrived to drop a point by conceding soft goals to Eddie Morrison and Andy Dickson. This result meant that Hibs had not won a League match at Rugby Park for 15 years, and it was an important point dropped in the League race. Hibs were now five points adrift of joint leaders Celtic and Rangers, but they had two games in hand and so were still very much in the race.

A midweek game against Partick Thistle represented one of the games in hand, the need to win being self-evident. Win they did at Easter Road as Cropley converted a penalty and O'Rourke added a second, while the visitors failed to find the net. In fact, Hibs might have won by a landslide but for a stunning performance by the Thistle goalkeeper, Alan Rough, who stopped at least four more goals when lesser keepers would probably have been beaten.

Another home game followed, this time against an improving Morton side, who had lost only two of their previous seven League matches. With the Glasgow sides involved in Cup duty, it was a golden chance for Hibs to narrow the gap and they took it with a hard-fought 2-1 win. With former Hibs men Roy Baines and John Murphy in their line-up, the visitors made it hard for Hibs to play their passing game, but in the end Gordon and Higgins hit the net for the home side while Charlie Brown struck for Morton. Those two goals made Hibs the top scorers in the division with 72, while Celtic had 70, but time would show that goals would dry up for Hibs – and for Gordon.

On the Monday following that game, Hibs flew out to Yugoslavia holding a 4-2 first-leg lead and confident that they could get the result needed to take them into the UEFA Cup semi-finals. It all went horribly wrong, however, when goalkeeper Jim Herriot made two very uncharacteristic blunders in letting Ivo Surjak and Ivica Hlevnjak score, while John Blackley conceded an own-goal to give the Yugoslavs a 3-0 win on the day and a 5-4 win on aggregate. To compound the misery, Schaedler had to be replaced five minutes from time after suffering a dislocated collarbone and Gordon limped off with an injured knee at the end. These injuries were to cost Hibs dear in the weeks ahead as the League race drew to a close.

With morale dented if not low, Hibs returned to Scotland and had to face Rangers at Ibrox in the League. In a bad-tempered game, Hibs lost to a hotly disputed goal from Tommy McLean, most neutral observers among the press corps reporting he was clearly offside when he scored. John Blackley was so incensed at the decision to allow the goal to stand that he persisted in arguing with the linesman and gave referee Bobby Davidson little option but to send him off. It was a hammer blow to Hibs' League title aspirations, but Turnbull was no quitter and remained optimistic that his side were still in the hunt.

In goal that day at Ibrox was third-choice goalkeeper Jim McArthur and he had a fine game in front of more than 52,000, the vast majority of whom heaved a collective sigh of relief when a late effort from Higgins beat Peter McCloy only to crash back off the crossbar and be booted to safety.

A win against lowly Arbroath was a must if Hibs were serious in their contention that they were not out of the race, but a team badly weakened by injuries and suspensions could find no way past the visitors' defence and a dull 0-0 draw was the outcome. Arbroath manager Albert Henderson said later that holding Turnbull's men to a 0-0 draw was as good as doing the same to Celtic or Rangers, a nice compliment – but it was said with the knowledge that the point won probably guaranteed his side survival in the top League. Worryingly, Hibs had now gone three games without scoring a goal, and teams that don't score don't win.

There were five more games to go until the season ended, all in April and with three of them away from home, the first against Falkirk at Brockville. Three games without a goal soon became four as Hibs drew a blank, while Falkirk took the points with a single strike from John Markie. That defeat finally put paid to any lingering hopes Hibs had of winning the title, but a UEFA spot was still there for the taking and so a resumption of winning games was essential.

As the game at Fir Park had been postponed earlier in the season, Hibs now found themselves set to face Motherwell twice in five days, the first of those clashes coming on a Tuesday night in Lanarkshire. With Edwards having completed his suspension, the travelling fans had high hopes of a victory, but although the goal drought ended when Tony Higgins scored a real screamer, John Goldthorp struck for Motherwell and the game finished at 1-1. Goalkeeper McArthur had an outstanding game between the sticks and was as responsible as Higgins for ensuring that Hibs took something from a poor game.

End of season games often lack atmosphere and excitement, but with Hibs looking to clinch a place in Europe there was still much to play for. It was all the more disappointing, therefore, when they turned in a totally lacklustre performance in front of the home fans the following Saturday and went down meekly to Motherwell, a Peter Millar penalty winning both points for the Steelmen.

The penultimate game of the season took Hibs to Somerset Park, where they would face an Ayr United side only seven points behind them in the League. Eddie Turnbull took the chance to blood another youngster in 18-year-old Derek Spalding, who made a fine League debut in a 1-1 draw, O'Rourke scoring for Hibs and George McLean for the hosts. The introduction of Spalding reinforced Turnbull's view that Hibs had a number of promising youngsters on their books, and indeed the team at Ayr also included young Bobby Smith in the midfield.

Had things gone according to plan for Turnbull, the visit of Celtic on the last day of the season would have involved the two sides fighting it out for championship glory, but only Celtic could now attain that prize. Jock Stein's men needed to win, while Rangers had to annihilate East Fife at Ibrox and hope the Celts would slip up. On the day, Rangers managed only a 2-0 win, but it was academic anyway as Celtic clinched their eighth title in a row with a comfortable 3-0 win at Easter Road.

It had been an exciting season, of that there is no doubt, even though it had somewhat fizzled out in the end. But two cups, League and Drybrough, were not to be sneezed at, while thrashing Hearts 7-0 at Tynecastle would provide Hibs fans with a huge point-scorer over their maroon friends for decades to come. There had been a good run also in the UEFA Cup, where they reached the quarter-finals, and of course the third-place finish in the League guaranteed European football at Easter Road in the coming season.

There were some quite exceptional scoring performances, too, with Alan Gordon amassing an astonishing 42 goals in all competitions while Jimmy O'Rourke weighed in with 34 and Arthur Duncan 23 – making 99 goals between the three of them in League, Cup, League Cup, Cup Winners' Cup and Drybrough Cup.

Chapter Seven

1973/74

RING OUT THE OLD

With two trophies captured the season before, the Drybrough Cup and the League Cup, Eddie Turnbull was determined that Hibs would do even better this time, and when pre-season training began the club knew it had four targets: to retain the cups already held and to go for League and European glory.

After a very short summer break, especially for Pat Stanton and Erich Schaedler, who both saw action in the Scottish national side, Hibs re-assembled at Easter Road in preparation for a short trip to Scandinavia, where they would play three friendly matches ahead of the competitive games commencing on 28 July. A familiar face had left the club in the close season, goalkeeper Jim Herriot departing for St Mirren, but there were two new faces in the pack as Iain Munro joined from the Paisley outfit while Alex McGregor was signed after being released by Ayr United.

The tour of Scandinavia was not a success in terms of results but met its purpose in allowing the players to gain match fitness and to try out some new ideas in their play. First Division Hvidovre of Denmark provided the opening challenge of the tour. Hibs had most of the play, but they lost 1-0, Alan Gordon netting what looked a good equaliser only to see it ruled out for offside. Sweden beckoned and a match against Ostersund, where Hibs cruised into a two-goal lead thanks to a double from Gordon, only to take their foot off the pedal and allow their hosts to draw level. Once again, Gordon scored a 'goal' that was disallowed in mysterious circumstances, denying him a hat-trick and Hibs a victory.

The next and last stop was Trondheim, also in Sweden, where Hibs faced their toughest opposition yet, Rosenborg, and lost 1-0 to a first-half goal. Alan Gordon loomed large again in the proceedings and the big striker was incensed when, after being hauled down inside the penalty area, he was awarded only an indirect free kick by the local referee. Back home, then, to Edinburgh, via four flights which took the party from Trondheim to Oslo to Copenhagen to Turnhouse – where were easyJet when needed most?

The season proper opened when Hibs and St Mirren met in the first

Drybrough Cup game at Easter Road. Despite a heroic display by Herriot for his new team, the Buddies, Turnbull's men won 2-1 with goals from Munro, his first and on his home debut, and Duncan. Brian Third, brought in to replace Ally McLeod, who had departed for Southampton, got the consolation for the Buddies. That win took Hibs through to a tie with Rangers at Easter Road, a repeat of the draw from the previous season. Rangers had won 3-0 over Montrose at Ibrox to set up this 'semi-final', while in the other match Celtic, who beat Dunfermline 6-1 in the first round, met Dundee, who had struggled to dispose of Raith Rovers by a single goal after extra time.

Rangers arrived not having lost a competitive match in 1973, a run of 27 games without defeat, and hungry to win their first silverware of the new season. Newcomers to their squad included Johnny Hamilton, released in the close season by Turnbull and snapped up by Jock Wallace, and Doug Houston from Dundee. In a game played at blistering pace throughout, Des Bremner struck his first senior goal for Hibs, only to see Derek Parlane equalise for the visitors and take the game into extra time. With Jim McArthur and his stout defence holding Rangers at bay, it was left to young Tony Higgins to crash home the winner for Hibs and take them through 2-1 on the night.

With Celtic easily disposing of Dundee, they provided the Hampden opposition again in a repeat of the final of the previous season. Last time out, the game went into extra time, with Hibs winning a thrilling encounter 5-3. But on this occasion the game was much tighter, although it also went to extra time. Just when penalties looked inevitable, Bremner picked out Higgins, who shuttled the ball on quickly to Cropley. He looked up, passed to Gordon, newly named as the Hibs Supporters' Association Player of the Year, and the big striker hit a sweet left-foot shot under Ally Hunter in the Celtic goal in the dying seconds of the game. There was no way back for Celtic, and Hibs retained the trophy. They had beaten Jock Stein's men in three consecutive final meetings. The Hibs dressing room was a joyous place to be that Saturday afternoon in Glasgow, and the team arrived back in Edinburgh later to a heroes' welcome.

Now the task of trying to retain the League Cup would begin and Morton at Cappielow presented the first hurdle. After a poor first half, Hibs took control in the second with young Bobby Smith, on as a substitute for the injured Gordon, having a hand in the double scored by Higgins and the goal from Duncan. Cropley got the fourth, and teenager Neil McNab scored for Morton.

It was a good start to the section games and Hibs now had two home ties to further strengthen their position. First to come calling were Ayr United, who had also won their opening game by defeating Dumbarton 2-0. They provided very stuffy opposition and closed their men down well, but Des

Bremner broke the deadlock and won the points for the Greens with the only goal of the game. Bremner's goal was a beauty as he exchanged one-twos on the edge of the box with both Edwards and Higgins before crashing an unstoppable left-foot shot past Ayr keeper Davie Stewart.

Hibs now had four points on the board from two games, but the next opponents, Dumbarton, had managed just one when they shared the spoils with Morton. Having just missed being relegated from the League last season, the Sons were determined to make a better go of things this time and had periods in the game when they were very composed, especially at the back. Thankfully, the deadly Alan Gordon came to Hibs' rescue with a superb diving header, and a 1-0 win kept the Easter Road side clear at the top of the section.

Somerset Park provided the next venue and Hibs hit top form in beating Ayr 2-0, but victory came at a cost with in-form goalkeeper Jim McArthur breaking a bone in his hand, an injury that would keep him out of action for several weeks. Goals from Higgins and Cropley secured the victory, but McArthur somehow managed to play his part, too, as he battled on with his hand bandaged up and had a number of fine saves towards the end of the game as Ayr pressed.

Eddie Turnbull moved swiftly to secure a replacement and signed the 27-year-old Irish internationalist Roddy McKenzie from Airdrie. The big keeper went straight into the side to face Dumbarton at Boghead, but it was a nightmare debut for the new man as Hibs crashed 4-1, Gordon getting the consolation goal. Nevertheless, the defeat did not affect the group standings, and Hibs were still top when Morton came to Easter Road four days later.

In a stuffy match, the visitors set out to frustrate Hibs and largely succeeded in doing so, although the home side eventually triumphed by 2-1. Cropley grabbed a brace and 33-year-old Hugh McIlmoyle, a new signing who had spent his entire career in English football despite being born in Port Glasgow, struck for Morton.

The League Cup section was now complete, and Hibs would face Raith Rovers home and away in the quarter-final, but first they had to turn their attention to League business with an opening game against Partick Thistle at Easter Road on 1 September. Alex Cropley had finished top scorer for Hibs with four out of the 11 secured in the six games played.

When Partick came to Easter Road to begin their League campaign they did so on the back of a pretty poor League Cup section performance, having gained only one point from their six games, but they proved a handful for Hibs. The home side did eventually come out on top with a 2-1 win, thanks to a first top-team goal from youngster Bobby Smith and a second from Gordon, Tommy Rae hitting the target for the Jags.

Prior to entertaining Raith Rovers in the first leg of their League Cup quarter-final, Hibs had to face Hearts in the first derby of the season. A hungry home side went at Hibs from the start and the visitors were simply blown away as the Tynecastle men thumped them 4-1. Cropley was on target for Hibs, but an own-goal from Erich Schaedler, together with single strikes from Kenny Aird, Donald Ford and Drew Busby, kept the points in Gorgie.

Bruised and battered, at least mentally if not physically, Hibs next met Second Division Raith Rovers in the League Cup and had to fight every inch of the way to overcome the plucky Fifers with a 3-2 scoreline. Manager of Raith that day was the former Hibs goalkeeper George Farm, while in the dark blue No.8 jersey was yet another former Hibs man, the legendary Joe Baker, who grabbed one of their goals, the other being an own-goal by Des Bremner. Hibs struck through Smith, Stanton and Higgins, all with headers, and left the field knowing that the tie was far from over.

Three League games and two UEFA Cup ties would occur before the second leg, however, and the first of those brought East Fife to Leith. Missing from the Hibs starting line-up was Alan Gordon, due to a recurring muscle injury, and his No.9 jersey went to Higgins, who opened the scoring before Stanton got the second in a 2-1 win. On the bench for East Fife that day was ex-Hibee and now manager of the Methil men, Pat Quinn, while full-back Bobby Duncan also returned to his old stamping ground. Dailly scored the consolation goal for the visitors.

After the derby disappointment, Hibs had secured two victories as they made ready to face Keflavik of Iceland in the UEFA Cup first-round first leg at Easter Road. Little was really known about the visitors, but they gave a decent account of themselves despite losing the game 2-0. The goals from Jim Black and Tony Higgins gave Hibs a reasonable cushion for the second leg a fortnight later. Around the time of this UEFA tie, the Scotland pool to face Czechoslovakia in a World Cup qualifier was announced and included Hibs men Erich Schaedler and John Blackley. Their selection meant that the scheduled League fixture with Dundee United would be postponed, and so Hibs had ten days' rest following their European tie before meeting Ayr United at home in the League.

Yet another former Hibee arrived as manager of the opposition, and this time it was Ally MacLeod with Ayr United, who had recently signed Alex Ferguson from Falkirk. In a cracking game, Hibs won a lot more convincingly than the 4-2 scoreline might suggest, thanks to strikes from Duncan, Stanton, Cropley and an own-goal. Stanton also scored at the wrong end, Joe Filippi getting the other Ayr goal.

The second-leg UEFA Cup tie followed in the midweek after the Ayr game and Pat Stanton was once again on target as Hibs comfortably fought out a 1-1 draw to progress into the second round. The home side had scored through Zakariasson, but never looked likely to overturn the 2-0 deficit from the first leg, and their keeper, Olafsson, was the hero on a very wet and windy night on a dreadful playing surface.

Back in Scotland, Hibs met Aberdeen at Pittodrie and although they dominated large parts of the game they had to settle for a point in a 1-1 draw, with Gordon on target for Hibs and Jarvie successful for the Dons.

A third consecutive away tie took Hibs to Stark's Park, Kirkcaldy, for the second leg of their League Cup quarter-final. Leading 3-2 from the first game, Hibs kept a clean sheet and extended their aggregate win to 5-2 with goals from Duncan and Gordon. Another away tie awaited Hibs that month – they had drawn a plum tie against Leeds United in the UEFA Cup – but ahead of that Hibs had some League business to take care of as Falkirk came to Easter Road.

After the succession of former Hibs men arriving as managers of visiting sides, it was the turn of a former Hearts stalwart this time as John Prentice took up his place on the visitors' bench. Goals from Higgins and Gordon, their eighth and tenth of the season respectively, gave Hibs a comfortable home win and two valuable points, keeping them fifth equal in the table with Dundee United. Topping the League at that stage were Celtic and Hearts, with Aberdeen and surprise package Ayr United close behind.

Having played so many midweek games in the previous weeks, Hibs were glad to get a seven-day break before having to travel to Parkhead to face Celtic. Those players nursing bumps and lumps had the chance to rest, and behind the scenes there was the good news that John Brownlie, a long-term injury victim, was close to making a return to reserve team football.

Parkhead was never the happiest of hunting grounds for Hibs, but they managed a 1-1 draw, most media pundits feeling that they should have won. Gordon struck for the visitors in a game played for the most part in a torrential downpour. That Celtic encounter was the first of four consecutive away matches, which would bring a mixed bag of results.

Leeds United welcomed Hibs and a substantial travelling support to Elland Road on Wednesday, 24 October. Although the game finished goalless, Hibs were magnificent on the night and extremely unlucky not to score. Chances fell to both Higgins and Stanton, but a wayward shot and a great save denied the Hibs men their just rewards for excellent build-up play.

Footballers will tell you they love to play in the big games, and the Hibs footballers were getting every chance to do so. Having visited Parkhead and Elland Road, they now faced two trips to Ibrox in the space of four days. The first was on League business, and uncharacteristically the Greens folded easily in losing 4-0 to the Ibrox side. Two penalties from Sandy Jardine and single strikes from Alfie Conn and John Greig sent Hibs back along the M8 with their tails very firmly between their legs. Four days later they had the chance to make amends in the first leg of the League Cup semi-final, but despite a good showing by the visitors, Rangers triumphed 2-0 with a goal from Greig and an own-goal by Erich Schaedler.

Back in Edinburgh for the League visit of Clyde, Hibs found their shooting boots again and thrashed the Shawfield men 5-0, with a hat-trick from Stanton, one from the penalty spot, plus goals from Blackley and Cropley. With the return leg against Leeds coming up on the Wednesday, it was good to see the Easter Road men so deadly in front of goal and the fans left the Clyde game in happy and confident mood.

It was a crisp November evening in Edinburgh when Hibs and Leeds took to the field, knowing that whatever else happened the game would be played to a finish. A number of possible glamour opponents awaited the victors, including Feyenoord, Spurs, Nice, Fenerbahce, FC Twente, Marseilles and Lazio, but it would be the visitors who would get the chance to meet one of those teams. Despite having much of the possession, Hibs could not break down a resolute Leeds defence, in which Billy Bremner played an outstanding part as sweeper. Ninety minutes came and went, followed by 30 minutes of extra time, with neither team finding the net. And so it went to a penalty shoot-out. Given his success from the spot against Clyde, Pat Stanton stepped forward to take the first kick for Hibs and as he walked away to begin his run-up, referee Schiller of Austria adjusted the position of the ball on the spot. Stanton shot and missed, the only player to do so out of the ten elected to take the kicks, and Hibs were out. Stanton was devastated, and it was impossible not to feel for the man who lived and breathed Hibernian Football Club.

Unknown to the vast majority of people in the stadium that night, chairman Tom Hart was lodging a protest with the UEFA representative at the game, based on the fact that the Leeds manager, Don Revie, and his assistant had stayed inside the centre circle during the penalty shoot-out. Hart, who thought that this was against UEFA rules, actually lodged the protest prior to Stanton taking that first kick, so there was no question of sour grapes being involved: it was simply an attempt to ensure that both clubs abided by the rules of the competition. Hart and fellow director Tommy Younger flew to Zurich the following day and met the UEFA president, Hans Bangerter, as the draw for the next round was being made. Because of the formal protest by Hibs, the draw came out as Leeds United or Hibs v Vitoria Setubal of Portugal, but when the deciding committee met the following day the protest was dismissed and Leeds were through.

In the newspapers over the days that followed there was high praise from Billy Bremner, who told a *Sunday Mail* reporter: 'Hibs are a brilliant team and I cannot praise them enough. They did everything but score and if luck had been with them they would have won by three or four goals and we could not have complained had they done so.'

After the disappointment of crashing out of Europe in such cruel fashion Hibs had to turn their attention back to the League campaign and a visit to Fir Park on the following Saturday. A McClymont goal looked to have won the points for the home side until big Alan Gordon popped up in the last minute, latching on to a great pass from Munro to crash home the equaliser.

Hibs had one more game to play before meeting Rangers in the second leg of the League Cup semi-final and that was at home to an improving Dundee. In the Dundee team that day were former Hibee Thomson Allan and a future caretaker manager of Hibs, Jocky Scott. Games between these two sides were rarely short of excitement and this one was no exception, Hibs having to work very hard to secure their 2-1 win. O'Rourke netted a double while the prolific Gordon Wallace struck for Dundee. This win left Hibs in fourth place behind Celtic, Aberdeen and Hearts, though they had a game in hand over their city neighbours.

A significant presence in the winning Hibs team against Dundee was that of John Brownlie, making his first appearance since breaking his leg against East Fife the previous January. 'Onion' had missed no fewer than 50 first-team games during his lay-off and was accorded a warm welcome as he took to the field that Saturday.

The long-awaited second-leg League Cup tie against Rangers finally took place on Wednesday, 21 November, with the most unusual kick-off time of 1.30pm because of the power strikes and the possibility of extra time. In a rough-and-tumble affair, during which the referee seemed to be the busiest man on the park, Rangers shut up shop and Hibs could not find a way through, the game finishing goalless. In the space of two weeks, Hibs had been knocked out of both the UEFA and League cups. On the plus side, however, their League form was good, so that by the time they next played at Easter Road they would have risen to second place in the table, behind Celtic and above Hearts, Rangers and Aberdeen.

The weather that winter was not kind to football and many postponements were suffered, but Hibs managed to fulfil their next fixture when they visited Perth to play St Johnstone. The Greens started the game strongly and scored early through Gordon, but they laboured as they tried to extend their advantage, allowing the Saints to come back into the game more and more. Thankfully, the defence stood firm and O'Rourke sealed the points with a late second.

Three weeks would pass before Hibs played again and once more it was away from home, this time to Dunfermline. On a pitch cleared of snow but hard and quite slippy, the home side took the lead through Graham Shaw, but Hibs came storming back and forged ahead with goals from Stanton and Duncan. A resolute Dunfermline equalised through Jim Leishman before Gordon popped up six minutes from time to secure both points for the visitors.

Hibs were in good spirits when they took the field seven days later against Morton at Easter Road. This game pitched second-placed Hibs against a side just four places and five points off the bottom spot. The Greenock side had suffered a spate of single-goal defeats, but that run came to an end as Hibs hit five past the luckless Roy Baines, O'Rourke bagging a hat-trick and Gordon a brace. The match programme for that game contained a couple of interesting articles, the first of which came in the form of a 'Message from the boardroom', where the directors, condemning the stoning of Rangers supporters' buses, made it very clear that hooliganism from the home support would not be tolerated. Sadly, that was the way of things in the Seventies, when broken bus windows were part and parcel of visiting away grounds. Thankfully, this barbaric practice has long since ceased. The other article was of a brighter type as it informed the reader of a Hibs Cup win, the trophy in question being the *Edinburgh Evening News* 'Fives' Trophy, a competition hotly contested and won over four rounds without the loss of a goal in front of 1,600 spectators at Meadowbank.

The fixtures for 1973 ended with a visit to Firhill, where a single goal from Lawrie won the points for Partick Thistle. Alan Gordon was a flu victim and missed the game. It was both a disappointing result for Hibs and a dent to their hopes of catching League leaders Celtic.

Hibs were first-footed by Hearts on 1 January 1974 – the first day of the year in which the Gorgie outfit would celebrate their centenary. But Hibs were not in a giving mood and easily took the points in a fine 3-1 win, Cropley grabbing a double and Duncan the other. Donald Ford counted for a Hearts side who were riding high in the League.

Four days later, Hibs were at Methil to face an East Fife side anxious to move away from the relegation area. In a very physical encounter, Cropley gave Hibs a half-time lead before O'Rourke weighed in with a couple after the break, while Jim McArthur and his defenders kept a clean sheet at the other end. The win kept Hibs in second place, seven points behind Celtic with a game in hand, while Rangers and Hearts were third and fourth, both two points adrift of the men from Easter Road, Hearts having played one game more.

Mid-table Dundee United were next up and the Easter Road fans were treated to another 3-1 home win, with Hibs actually scoring all four goals thanks to a bizarre own-goal by Alex Edwards, of all people. To be fair to 'Mickey', he was doing what all good midfield players should do, attempting to help out the defence, when the ball struck Des Bremner as Edwards went to make a clearance. It came off the little number seven at an awkward angle and shot into the net. His team-mates, however, were also in scoring form and a double from O'Rourke plus a single from Stanton secured the points.

After the game the big talking point was the revelation contained in the programme that day. It announced that the Hibs chairman, Tom Hart, had chaired a number of 'secret' meetings, involving Hibs, Hearts, Celtic, Rangers, Aberdeen and Dundee, on the subject of proposed changes to the League set-up in Scotland. It's worth taking time out here to examine the proposals brought forward by the six.

First and foremost, there was the idea that there should be a Premier League, consisting of ten teams to play each other four times in the championship, which might be split into two competitions of 18 games or one tournament of 36 games. In the event of having two competitions, the top teams could play-off for the title – unless, of course, the same side won both sections. The other proposals were:

- A First Division to consist of the bottom eight teams in the present League plus the top two clubs from the Second Division.
- A Second Division to be made up of the remaining 17 teams and one new club. The 18-club division would cut out the need for one team to be idle each week.
- One club to be relegated from the Premier League and one to be promoted from the First Division, and one or two to move up and down between the First and Second Divisions.
- The League Cup to revert to the original format, with one qualifier from each group, and to be played as the first competition.
- The Drybrough Cup to be played at a different part of the season.
- A new Challenge Cup to be introduced for teams knocked out in the third and fourth rounds of the Scottish Cup.
- A Premier League guarantee of £1,000, or half the gate, depending which is the greater, but no change in the guarantee for the First and Second Divisions.

The theory, we were told, was 'to improve competition and provide more attractive matches to give the public the type of entertainment they want to see'.

From the resumption of League football in 1946/47, after the Second World War, the League title had been won by either Celtic or Rangers no fewer than 21 times out of a possible 29. Surely this bright new dawn would level the playing field a bit? Since its inception, the Premier League title has been played for 32 times, and the Old Firm have won it on no fewer than 27 occasions. Little has changed in terms of those teams dominating the League, but as the years have rolled by the quality of football has scarcely altered for the better. It is not insignificant that since the inception of the Premier League in 1998 the Scottish national side has failed to qualify for the finals of a major tournament. The Bosman ruling has certainly had an effect, but so, too, has the creation of a League system where fear of relegation overrides the will to develop home-grown talent and the creation of a side willing to try to go out and play open, attractive football week in week out. The late Seventies and early Eighties witnessed both Aberdeen and Dundee United enjoying success with home-grown talent, but it is only in recent years that clubs such as Hibs, Kilmarnock and Aberdeen have once again attempted to bring players through their youth systems rather than signing journeymen capable only of ensuring that relegation was not an issue.

Enough of the gloom and back to 1974, when football fans were regularly entertained by a very good Hibs side. Nevertheless, the home win over Dundee United was followed up by a somewhat disappointing 1-1 draw when Hibs visited Somerset Park to take on Ayr United. The conditions weren't good, but they were no excuse for a lacklustre performance which saw another point dropped and a bigger gap opening up in the chase to catch Celtic, who had secured a win. A solitary O'Rourke strike was countered by Johnny Graham's penalty goal for the home side.

The third round of the Scottish Cup saw Second Division Kilmarnock visiting Easter Road on Saturday, 26 January 1974. Former Celt Willie Fernie brought his men to Edinburgh with some hope of causing a Cup shock as his side were playing very well and were on the road to promotion into the top League. Early indications were that he might get his wish as Killie raced into a two-goal lead, but it would end in disappointment for the Ayrshire outfit as Hibs won through by a score of 5-2. Prolific Jimmy O'Rourke grabbed another double, taking him on to 13 for the season, while Edwards, Blackley and Stanton hit the others and Eddie Morrison struck twice for Killie.

The programme that day contained a nice piece on the reserves, for whom Willie Murray had found goalscoring form and John Brownlie had continued his comeback after his horrific leg break some 12 months earlier. It also contained, unusually, a representation of a restricted League table – ten teams to be precise – a sign of things to come perhaps? That table showed Celtic on 34 points, Hibs on 28, Rangers on 26, Ayr United on 25 and Hearts on 24, with Aberdeen, Dundee United, Motherwell and Arbroath hot on the heels of the men from Tynecastle.

Having safely negotiated passage into the fourth round of the Cup, Hibs were at home again the following Saturday when Aberdeen called on League duty. In the week leading up to that match, Hibs entered the transfer market, splashing out a record £120,000 to bring former Dons striker Joe Harper back north of the border from Everton. Little did the supporters know at the time, but the arrival of Harper would coincide with the beginnings of a break-up of Turnbull's Tornadoes. As for the game itself, Harper watched from the stands as his new side defeated his old one by 3-1, that man O'Rourke getting yet another double while Gordon contributed the other. Aberdeen's goal came from Davie Robb, but there was only ever going to be one winner in a game which Hibs dominated throughout. Des Bremner missed this one, a broken collarbone bringing to an end 53 consecutive first-team appearances, but there was a welcome return to the No.2 shirt for John Brownlie.

The Scottish Cup draw had paired Hibs with St Johnstone in Perth, but ahead of that tie the Easter Road men faced a tricky visit to Brockville on League business. In a dull 0-0 the only point of any real interest was that the game marked the competitive debut of Joe Harper, who took the No.9 shirt, Alan Gordon dropping to the bench. While the arrival of Harper was generally welcomed by the Hibs support the decision to drop Gordon was not a popular one. The big centre-forward had already bagged 16 goals for Hibs during the season. On a mudbath of a pitch, Hibs insisted on passing short and failed to create a single opening for their new striker, or anyone else for that matter.

Muirton Park boasted the biggest playing surface in Scottish football and when Hibs went there on fourth-round Cup duty they made use of every available inch in beating their hosts 3-1, thanks to a quite brilliant hat-trick from Jimmy O'Rourke, who took his tally for the season to 18, including two hat-tricks and five doubles. With Harper ineligible, Gordon returned and along with Duncan was responsible for setting up the goals for O'Rourke, while a Jim Pearson penalty offered some consolation to the Saints fans. Interestingly, 19-year-old Derek Spalding was drafted in at right-back and looked solid throughout the game, even though he was normally more at home in the centre of defence. A victory for Dundee over much-fancied Rangers meant that Hibs would face the Dens Park outfit in the quarter-finals.

With February in its third week, League leaders Celtic arrived at Easter Road knowing that a win would end the Hibernian challenge, and a win is exactly what they achieved with goals from Dixie Deans (2), Kenny Dalglish and Paul Wilson. The Celtic victory brought to an end Hibs' 20-game run without defeat at Easter Road. Despite Duncan and O'Rourke hitting the target for the home side, the 4-2 reversal gave Celtic a five-point lead at the top, and that was the state of affairs when the other half of the Old Firm arrived in Leith on 2 March 1974.

Rangers were sitting in third place, ready to take over second should Hibs slip up again, but wily old fox Eddie Turnbull shuffled his team about and the changes helped the home side to a deserved 3-1 win. Spalding was introduced to the defence and Harper, making his home debut, wore the No.7 jersey, with Stanton at eight, Gordon at nine and top scorer Jimmy O'Rourke not in the starting line-up. All of this served to confuse the men in blue as Hibs triumphed with Gordon getting two and Bremner the other.

With second place secured for the moment, it was time to turn attention to the Scottish Cup as Dundee arrived at Easter Road still buoyant after having knocked Rangers out in the previous round. In a humdinger of a game, the sides shared six goals, Gordon hitting a perfect hat-trick only to see victory denied by strikes from Jocky Scott, Jimmy Wilson and John Duncan. Scott would, of course, come back to Easter Road in the future, while big John Duncan made a real name for himself in later years when he joined Tottenham Hotspur. The official programme for that game included a couple of quite interesting adverts, one encouraging fans to buy a 'Golden Goal' ticket and another suggesting that if you booked a holiday at Butlin's you would be rewarded with the issue of Green Shield stamps.

The following week, Hibs were scheduled to meet Dundee on Tayside in a League encounter, but the weather forced a cancellation. Two days later, the pitch was declared playable and Hibs travelled to Dens Park for the Cup replay, taking with them a very large and noisy support. The game did not go the way these loyal fans hoped for as the home side recorded a 3-0 win in a match which was a lot closer than the scoreline would suggest.

With the Scottish Cup merely a dream again, Hibs turned their full concentration on to League business, the visit of St Johnstone to Easter Road giving them the opportunity to keep the momentum going at the top. Once again, supporters were treated to a six-goal thriller and, once again, it would end level at 3-3. An Alex Cropley penalty and strikes for Duncan and a first goal for the club from Harper, were cancelled out by counters from Henry Hall (2) and John Muir. It was another important point dropped in the race for the title – and all the more galling when it became known that lowly Dumbarton had played out of their skins and secured a point at Celtic Park.

Games were coming thick and fast now as clubs tried to recover those lost to bad weather, etc, but when Hibs met Motherwell at Easter Road on Wednesday, 3 April 1974, the situation regarding the backlog was not helped by the fact that the game was abandoned after just 18 minutes, a thick fog having descended over the stadium. Hibs were ahead, thanks to an Alex Cropley penalty, but that counted for nothing. Three days later, Hibs travelled to Boghead to face a Dumbarton side who were making a good job of crawling out of the relegation zone, their draw at Celtic Park serving as notice to Hibs that this would be a difficult game. Cropley once again scored from the spot and added another along with a strike from Duncan to give a total of three, but the Sons of the Rock would not be denied and scored three of their own through brothers Tom and Colin McAdam and John Bourke. Interestingly, the McAdam brothers would go on to play for the Old Firm, Tom ending up at Celtic and Colin at Rangers. John Bourke was a big, bustling centre-forward with whom Hibs were linked on more than one occasion, but a move to Easter Road never transpired.

The following midweek, Hibs were back at Dens Park trying both to avenge the Cup defeat and to secure two vital points. With crucial points having been dropped in recent games, Eddie Turnbull rung the changes and out went McArthur, Bremner, Black and O'Rourke. In came Roddy McKenzie, John Brownlie, Gerry Adair and John Hazel. The reshuffle worked, and Hibs ran out comfortable 3-1 winners, two goals from Harper and a single strike from Cropley cancelling out Jocky Scott's effort for the home side.

Tayside beckoned again on the Saturday as Hibs travelled to Gayfield Park to face Arbroath. But they came a cropper in losing 3-2, the goals of Stanton and Harper counting for nothing as Penman, Sellars and Fletcher secured two vital points for a side in a comfortable mid-table position. Despite this setback, Hibs were still clinging on to second place, although Celtic looked unassailable at the top, while Rangers and Aberdeen were snapping at their heels in third and fourth places respectively.

With just two days of rest following the setback at Gayfield, Hibs welcomed Motherwell to Easter Road to replay the game lost to fog a couple of weeks earlier. Realising that fans were being hit hard in the pocket with all of these games arriving over such a short space of time – Hibs would have four home games over nine days starting with this one – managing director Tom Hart sought to reduce admission prices but was overruled by the League Management Committee, which, in its infinite wisdom, decreed that normal admission charges should be levied. While appreciative of the attempts by Tom Hart, the fans were justifiably angry that a group of individuals who probably hadn't paid their way into a game in years could sit on high and make such a silly judgement. Some consolation was gained, however, with the winning of two points in a tight match settled only by a solitary strike from young Bobby Smith.

A mere two days later, Dumbarton arrived at Easter Road. As they had done at Boghead, Hibs struck three goals, but this time kept a clean sheet, so Gordon's fine hat-trick resulted in two more vital points for the Greens. That hat-trick took Hibs over the 100-goals mark for the season, and it was the fifth time the big striker had scored three or more goals in a game since joining the club. Another bright spot was the wonderful performance of young Derek Spalding at the centre of the Hibs defence and the excellent prompting from midfield of Alex Edwards, who had a hand in all three goals.

Hibs had five more games to play to see the season out and the first brought Dunfermline to Easter Road, where the points were shared in a 1-1 draw, Gordon once again the Hibs marksman as he took his tally for the season to 25.

Prior to going 'on the road', Hibs had one more fixture to play in front of their own fans and that was against an Arbroath side still enjoying the memory of a 3-2 win at Gayfield just ten days earlier. Once again, the sides were separated by just one goal, but this time it was the Greens who triumphed, thanks to strikes by Harper and Bremner. Almost immediately after the game had finished, the playing surface was ploughed up so that when the next season commenced it would have been completely resown.

In what would be the first of three away games in the space of just 12 days, Hibs travelled to Greenock and defeated Morton 3-0. Former Cappielow favourite Joe Harper bagged a double and Pat Stanton clinched the points with a third. It was a fine performance from a Hibs team who had endured a long and hard season but who seemed determined to finish with a flourish.

The wide, open spaces of Shawfield offered the next challenge, and Harper was once again on target as the sides fought out an entertaining 1-1 draw. The dog track at Shawfield ensured that you were 'miles' from the action as you stood on the terracing, and little did the fans present that day know that in years to come Clyde, a club with a long and proud history, would no longer play in Glasgow.

The curtain finally came down on season 1973/74 when Hibs travelled to Tannadice on 8 May and trounced Dundee United 4-1 with a cracking display. Munro grabbed a brace while Cropley and Harper were also on target to ensure Hibs would finish second behind Celtic.

Chapter Eight

1974/75

SO NEAR AND YET SO FAR

Scottish football was gearing itself for League reconstruction, and this would be the last season that 18 clubs would contend the top prize. From a Hibs perspective there were high hopes that the second place achieved last season would provide a platform to winning the title this time around, but everyone at the club knew that would prove a difficult task with strong challenges also being put in by the Old Firm and Aberdeen. In addition, Hearts were back in the top flight and they would also want to be involved at the right end of the table for a change.

As ever, Hibs warmed up for the new season by going on tour, returning to Scandinavia for the second season in succession for a short tour in Sweden in the hope that the players would get a feel for European football ahead of their entry in this season's UEFA Cup. From their base in Trondheim they had to make a four-hour bus journey in order to play the opening match against O.P.E. Ostersund. Hibs went behind to a soft penalty before drawing level in the second half, thanks to a goal by Pat Stanton. Further chances were made but not taken as Hibs struck the woodwork no fewer than five times before the match ended.

At this point, director Tommy Younger departed from the team hotel and headed for Zurich to witness the draw for the UEFA Cup and make arrangements for the games once the opposition was known. Meanwhile, Hibs played their second tour match against Rosenborg Trondheim, who had defeated them 1-0 some 12 months earlier. This time around it would be the visitors who triumphed as they took control of the game in its early stages and ran out 3-1 winners. Stanton was again on target as he nabbed a brace and Joe Harper got the other. Imagine the surprise the next day when Tommy Younger contacted Eddie Turnbull to advise him that Hibs had been drawn against Trondheim in the UEFA Cup. Younger was also able to inform the manager that Hibs were in a group of eight, and if they got past Trondheim their list of possible next opponents would include clubs of the stature of Atletico Madrid, Eintracht Frankfurt, Derby County and Hamburg.

The third and final tour match was played in the little town of Levanger, where the local residents had created a 3ft-high banner which they draped across the main street and which said 'Welcome Hibernian' in recognition of the fact that Hibs would be the first professional club to play there. Everyone was out in force for the match. Unfortunately, the heavens opened and there was a torrential downpour for most of the game, but it didn't deter the locals from staying until the end, and they very sportingly gave the Hibs players a standing ovation as they left the pitch, even though their team, Nesse Gutten, had been beaten 4-0. Harper opened the scoring inside the first 60 seconds before Iain Munro and Pat Stanton added two more. Hibs eased off somewhat at this point and contented themselves with scoring just once more through Alan Gordon.

Back home in Scotland, Hibs would begin the competitive season by taking part in the Drybrough Cup, a trophy they had won twice before and had every desire to win again. The tournament was played on a straight knock-out basis, and the draw brought Hibs together with Kilmarnock at Easter Road, the other ties being Stirling Albion v Rangers, Queen of the South v Dundee and Airdrie v Celtic. Their hold on the trophy remained intact as Kilmarnock were defeated 2-1, with goals from Duncan and Harper, while Killie's consolation came from Ian Fallis. Unsurprisingly, the other three First Division sides also came through unscathed, which meant a semi-final draw of Celtic v Dundee and Rangers v Hibs. This would be the third season in a row that Hibs had faced the Ibrox club at the same stage of the tournament. The four ties had produced a total of 16 goals, all of which added to the appeal as far as spectating was concerned. Holders Dundee needed extra time to dispose of Queen of the South, and did so thanks to a John Duncan hat-trick; Graham Fyfe scored twice for Rangers to see them safely through, and Celtic cracked four past hapless Airdrie.

As always, the first match programme of the season is worth a mention. At a cost of just 5p it was a good read and contained items of genuine interest as well as the usual quota of advertisements. The Killie programme brought confirmation that Hibs had a difficult League Cup section to negotiate, having been drawn with Rangers, Dundee and St Johnstone. A full record of all results from the previous season for both first and second teams was every stats fan's dream. Mention was made of the fact that John Blackley and Erich Schaedler had enjoyed a somewhat shorter close season than their team-mates because they had been in the Scotland pool for the World Cup in Germany. There was a short report on Hibs' participation in a five-a-side competition held in Musselburgh, where they lost to Falkirk with a predominantly young team consisting of Pat Carroll, Lawrie Dunn, Bobby Smith, Arthur Duncan and Willie Murray. The programme also included news of the club chairman, Sir John Bruce, who had been seriously injured in a car crash but who seemed to be slowly on the mend; stats on appearances and goalscorers for the first team, with Pat Stanton missing only two games of the 58 played and Alan Gordon finishing top scorer, and finally adverts for Leith Provident, Bandparts, Pennywell Service Station, The Brunswick Bar and Ronnie Simpson's Sports Shop in Rose Street.

In the midweek after disposing of Kilmarnock, Hibs welcomed Rangers to Easter Road for the semi-final of the Drybrough Cup. For the first 20 minutes, Hibs pinned the Gers back in their own half but could not find a way past goalkeeper Stewart Kennedy. That failure proved costly as the visitors started to fight their way back into the game and scored twice before half-time through Alex McDonald and Derek Parlane. Things went from bad to worse when Graham Fyfe extended Rangers' lead, but Hibs hit back with a double from Harper to set up a nail-biting finish. Unfortunately, Hibs could not get the goal that would force extra time, and so Rangers progressed to the final. One pleasing aspect from that game was the return to form of big Tony Higgins, who replaced Iain Munro during the second half. For such a heavy-set man, Tony was masterful at controlling the ball and remarkably adept at dribbling and weaving his way past defenders.

On that same night, the reserves took on Cowdenbeath at Central Park and ran out 3-1 winners, the goals coming from Lawrie Dunn, who played at centre-forward and scored twice, and Alex McGregor. Both Jimmy O'Rourke and Alan Gordon featured in the Hibs midfield and Jim Black steadied the defence at centre-half.

Off the field, Hibs were delighted to announce that managing director Tom Hart had been elected to the League Management Committee, and Tommy Younger had been re-elected to his position in the SFA. Hart's inclusion in the League Management Committee came at an appropriate time because he was able to lend his weight to the argument about not extending the use of the offside rule employed for the Drybrough Cup into League football. Hart, like Eddie Turnbull, did not like that rule and his vote was among those that decided not to effect any change to the current rules.

Failure to reach the Drybrough Cup final meant that Hibs had a blank Saturday ahead prior to the start of the League Cup matches. They did, however, play on the following Monday night at Easter Road when the Dutch side NEC Nijmegen arrived for a friendly. It was shirt-sleeve weather at Easter Road and the fans basked in the sunshine as the game unfolded into the Joe Harper show. The little striker, at his sharpshooting best, scored all the goals in a 5-0 win to double his tally for a season not yet properly started. The visitors never knew what hit them, and Harper could have had six had a late shot not rebounded off a post to safety. On the terracing there might have been a fan or two wondering when a Hibs player had last scored so many goals in one game and they might have been tempted to plump for Joe Baker's triple hat-trick against Peebles Rovers in the Scottish Cup, but they would have been wrong because that honour fell to the mercurial talent that was Willie Hamilton when he rattled home seven goals in a 15-0 win against Ottawa All Stars during Hibs' tour of Canada in 1965.

Pat Stanton was not risked in the Dutch game as he was troubled by a niggling injury. His No.4 jersey went to Bobby Smith and John Blackley deputised as captain on the night. Meanwhile, Hibs were spending some £25,000 to upgrade their floodlights so as to comply with the new standards set by UEFA for clubs playing in European competition.

At last the League Cup matches could now get under way, and Hibs had a tough opening game against Rangers at Easter Road. The Ibrox club had already started their campaign with a game against St Johnstone, where they took a two-goal lead, and were then pegged back to 2-2 before Derek Parlane popped up to secure a late winner. The good news for Hibs was that former Queen's Park amateur Parlane was actually suspended for this game, which meant one fewer goal threat in the opposing forward line. With Alan Gordon starting his first game of the season in an unfamiliar midfield role, Hibs had Rangers on the back foot from the off. It was Gordon who opened the scoring and the home side added two more through Duncan and Harper to take the tie 3-1, Rangers scoring through Parlane's replacement, Ally Scott. That was the best possible start for Hibs in a section that would be tight throughout.

Hibs then travelled to Dens Park for a game in which all of the action came in a pulsating first half. Harper found the target for the Greens after a great run and cross by Brownlie allowed Duncan to fire in a low cross, which Harper diverted past keeper Thomson Allan. Minutes later, Brownlie was stretchered off with an ankle injury that would lead to him missing games, but once again his most able deputy, Des Bremner, stepped into the right-back position. Concentration waned at this point and Hibs lost two scrappy goals to Jocky Scott and Bobby Hutchinson that won the points for the hosts, despite Gordon coming close on two occasions, only to be thwarted by Allan.

Preparations were being made for Hibs' trip back to Trondheim to face Rosenborg in the UEFA Cup and supporters were advised that a limited number of places were available on the club's charter flight. The cost of the flight was £35 return, but hotel charges would be extra. Given that Hibs were planning on staying two nights, the fans would have to take that expense into account. By contrast, British Rail announced it would be running a football special to Perth for the return League Cup match and return tickets would cost £1.15.

Ahead of any journey to Perth, the Hibs support had the match against St

Johnstone at Easter Road to look forward to. The visitors were bottom of the group, but caution was still required as they arrived having scored three goals at Ibrox. Sadly for them, they'd conceded six, but they clearly knew the way to goal and Hibs did not want to slip up after that defeat to League Cup holders Dundee. With Hibs playing superb passing football and the ball spending more time on the ground than it did in the air, the home side easily won the game 4-0. But for Derek Robertson in the Saints' goal it might have been a lot worse. Although he had a string of excellent saves, he couldn't stop Bobby Smith scoring twice while Harper and Duncan each notched singles.

A popular player departed from Easter Road that week when Jim Black rejoined Airdrie. Jim left with everyone's best wishes, but would be back in Edinburgh in the weeks ahead to receive his Player of the Year Award from the Hibs Supporters' Association.

A second home game in succession for Hibs gave them the opportunity to draw level at the top of the group with Rangers as the Ibrox club had, at that stage, played a game more. In fact, any kind of victory would put Hibs ahead as they enjoyed a better goal average. In the event, they recorded a 4-2 win as Smith, Gordon, Duncan and Harper all found a way past Thomson Allan in the Dundee goal. It wasn't all one-way traffic, Jocky Scott and John Duncan scoring for the visitors in the last five minutes, but in truth Hibs never looked likely to lose the game.

Hibs were in the driving seat in the group now, although they faced two tough away matches where results had to be good if they were going to qualify. In fact the home support had seen the last of their favourites for three games: once the League Cup section was finished, Hibs would open their Premier League campaign with a visit to Pittodrie.

The first of those away games took Hibs to Muirton Park on Saturday, 24 August, to face St Johnstone, who were giving a debut to their latest signing, Jimmy O'Rourke. After 12 years at Easter Road, where he had signed on as a schoolboy, Jimmy had moved on to pastures new with the very best of wishes from everyone associated with Hibs. Indeed, a few days after his arrival, numerous telegrams and letters began to arrive from Hibs fans eager to wish him well and to thank him for the many fine games he had played in green and white. If Jimmy felt emotional that day, he put it to one side and gave a thoroughly professional performance, even though his side went down 3-1 after Stanton, Gordon and Edwards had countered a goal from Bobby Thomson. Many years after that game, I was told in conversation with Pat Stanton that Jimmy, his lifelong friend, had kicked him in the ankle at one stage and when Pat gave him a puzzled look, Jimmy merely winked and ran off. Despite that, they remained good friends in the years ahead.

The final League Cup section match would be a showdown with Rangers at Ibrox, and the winners would progress into the quarter-final against Kilmarnock. In a pulsating 90 minutes, the match was won in the last minute by a single goal from the boot of Alex Cropley, who had come on as a substitute for Alex Edwards late in the game. It was a stunning victory and the travelling fans loved every minute of a first-rate performance from their favourites.

Two good away wins on the trot soon turned into three when Hibs won a five-goal thriller in their opening League match at Pittodrie. Watching from the terracing, it looked in the first half at least as though Hibs might be on to a bit of a hiding, but Jim McArthur was in brilliant form and made several excellent saves. Eventually, Ian Purdie gave the Dons the lead. Hibs looked as though they would struggle to contain the Aberdeen attack for much longer when up popped Cropley to tap the ball home for an equaliser after superb work by Harper had made the opening. In the second half the Dons once again took the lead when Billy Pirie angled a shot just inside McArthur's left-hand post, but Hibs would not give up and four minutes from time Harper levelled with a cracking free kick. As time ticked down towards the final whistle, Harper again found Cropley in the box and he slotted home the goal that took the points back to Edinburgh. During the game, Hibs lost John Blackley to a knee injury and also Alan Gordon, who was knocked unconscious and had to be carried off, so it was to the credit of the players that such a fine win was recorded.

The first home League match of the season brought newly promoted Hearts to Easter Road. The Tynecastle men had been beaten 2-1 by St Johnstone on the opening day, but they had won their League Cup section and were by no means an easy touch, with one or two new faces in their line-up. George Donaldson had been released by Rangers and Bobby Seith quickly signed him up, while John Gallagher, signed from Queen's Park, replaced the injured Alan Anderson at centre-half. Referee Bobby Davidson would have a busy afternoon, but not until Hibs had taken an early lead when a Smith shot was deflected past Kenny Garland by defender Jimmy Cant. The home side dominated thereafter and should have doubled their lead close to half-time when Garland saved Harper's penalty kick. Just past the hour mark, a Harper cross into the Hearts box was volleyed home by Duncan. A Des Bremner trip on Rab Prentice then won Hearts a penalty, which Donald Ford converted to give Hearts a glimmer of hope. That glimmer should have been snuffed out when referee Davidson awarded the third spot kick of the match, but Cropley's effort was well saved by Garland and the game finished at 2-1 to Hibs. Watching from the stand that day was chairman Sir John Bruce, now fully recovered from his car-crash injuries.

Two good League wins set Hibs up nicely for the first leg of the League Cup quarter-final tie against Kilmarnock at Rugby Park. Twice behind on the night, Hibs fought back each time and eventually drew the game 3-3.

Harper, Gordon and Cropley were on target for the Greens, while Eddie Morrison and two from Ian Fleming made it honours even, although Hibs might have won the tie had Harper not missed a penalty for the second game in succession.

Hibs headed west again on the following Saturday to meet Partick Thistle at Firhill and they were in devastating form as they ran riot over a bedraggled Jags side that seemed to have no answer to the smooth passing play of the opposition. Harper recovered from the disappointment of that penalty miss at Rugby Park by nabbing two goals, and there were singles for Gordon, Brownlie and Munro. Harper was now on 18 goals for the season in all competitions. Thistle got their consolation strike from Joe Craig, but the former Jags winger, Arthur Duncan, had a painful end to the game when a head knock ended up confining him to hospital for three days.

Sitting proudly at the top of the League as the only team with maximum points from their opening games, the Greens next set out for Trondheim to face Rosenborg in the first-round, first-leg tie in the UEFA Cup. Although Hibs had played in Norway before, this would be their first competitive game there, and it brought an excellent result: a 3-2 win. With the rain coming down in torrents, Stanton, who got the opening goal, Blackley and Derek Spalding were particularly impressive, as was Gordon, who got the second goal. With only one European goal, against FC Besa of Albania, to his name going into this match, Alex Cropley got his second – not only Hibs' third on the night but also the club's 100th goal in European competition. Both Rosenborg goals were scored by Odd Iversen, a tricky forward who impressed manager Eddie Turnbull and made him aware that the player would have to be marked more closely in the home leg. Arthur Duncan missed the trip following his concussion and was replaced by Iain Munro.

When Jim McLean brought Dundee United to Easter Road they, too, had had a great result in European competition. The Tannadice club were in the Cup Winners' Cup and had scored a useful 3-0 home victory over Romanian side Petrosani, making them favourites to progress to the next round. In terms of the League, the Arabs were lying fourth, having won two and lost one of their opening three games. Leading the line for them that day was a very promising young centre-forward by the name of Andy Gray, who was attracting interest from England and had been the subject of a failed bid of £75,000 by Nottingham Forest. Gray played well that day, but he would not score as Hibs won 3-0 to maintain their unbeaten start and top spot in the League, in front of a crowd of just under 15,000. Cropley opened the scoring early from the spot, Hibs' 50th goal in the 18 games played so far, and Gordon added a second before turning provider for the third which was again scored by Cropley. The busiest man in the stadium that night was Hibs' trainer Tam McNiven, who had to treat Edwards,

Harper, Schaedler, Blackley and Cropley at various stages throughout the game.

Wednesday, 25 September 1974, brought Kilmarnock to Easter Road for the second leg of the League Cup quarter-final tie. The first game had finished at 3-3 and so there was all to play for as the author watched from the terracing on his 22nd birthday. This match would be the first to be played under the new floodlights – four times brighter than the old ones and twice as bright as the standard set by UEFA for European competition. On the night, the lights were outdone by a Hibs side that shone brightly with a cracking 4-1 win to take the tie 7-4 on aggregate and advance the club into the semi-finals. Duncan got the ball rolling with an early strike, although he only played in the first half, retiring with a groin injury. Killie were proving stubborn in defence, though, and Hibs had to wait until 18 minutes from the end before Stanton doubled their lead. Eddie Morrison then reduced the deficit, but Cropley scored the goal of the game with a stunning left-foot volley. Munro, on for the injured Duncan, wrapped it all up with a fourth goal in the closing minutes. There was the exciting possibility of an Edinburgh derby if Hearts could overcome Falkirk in their quarter-final tie, but the Bairns won that one, and so it would be the men from Brockville who would stand in the way of Hibs reaching the final of the League Cup.

Things were going extremely well for Hibs at this point. They topped the League and were in the semi-final of the League Cup, as well as looking favourites to advance into the second round of the UEFA Cup. But history had shown that when Hibs were on a high something would happen to bring them back down to earth with a bump, and this time it was St Johnstone who did it. In the same League Cup section as Hibs, they had conceded no fewer than 23 goals in the six matches played, but their League form was somewhat better and they had enjoyed good wins over both Hearts and Dundee United when they arrived at Easter Road at the end of September. Their line-up included Jimmy O'Rourke, making his first appearance at Easter Road since leaving to join the Saints, and as fate would have it he notched the only goal of the game. It was quite bizarre to see him score against Hibs, and his celebrations were somewhat muted – even he looked stunned when the ball hit the net. The 100 per cent record had gone, and Hibs knew that to win the title they really had to beat teams such as St Johnstone at home.

The St Johnstone defeat was hardly the ideal preparation for Hibs' next match, against Rosenborg Trondheim in the second leg of their UEFA Cup tie. The Greens enjoyed a 3-2 first-leg win, but manager Turnbull was taking no chances as he fielded the strongest XI available to him. In a fast start to the game, Odd Iversen eluded his marker and shot the visitors ahead, causing some concern that Hibs might just let this tie slip through their fingers. From that moment on, however, Hibs dominated, and by the end of the 90 minutes Arve Thunshelle, the teenage Rosenborg keeper, must have had a very sore back because he had to pick the ball out of the net on no fewer than nine occasions. Quite simply, Hibs were a class apart and the goals were raining in from all directions as Harper, Munro, Cropley and Stanton each scored twice, the other coming from Alan Gordon. Cropley's goals both came from the penalty spot and it was good to see that Hibs finally seemed to have put their penalty hoodoo to rest.

All that occupied the minds of the Hibs supporters now was who the opposition might be in the second round. A host of big names were still in the hat, including Cologne, Hamburg, Derby County, Lyon, Porto, Juventus, Spartak Moscow and Napoli. When the draw was made that Friday, Hibs landed a plum tie against Italian giants Juventus – a mouth-watering prospect.

Goals in Europe seemed easy to come by, but Hibs had somewhat dried up on the domestic front and they failed to score for a second League game in a row in the 0-0 draw with Dundee at Dens Park. Both sides had opportunities to score, but it was a day of missed chances and good goalkeeping.

In the following midweek, Hibs met Falkirk at Tynecastle in the semi-final of the League Cup. It was a dour affair, with the Bairns seemingly more intent on stopping Hibs from scoring than trying to win the game themselves. It was a poor show and did nothing to encourage people to watch football, but there was one ray of sunshine and that came 20 minutes from the end when Gordon carved open the Falkirk defence with a pinpoint pass that Harper fired home from 18 yards. That goal sent Hibs through to the final, where they would meet Celtic. Arthur Duncan limped out of the game with a recurrence of his groin strain, but the club were confident that he would be fit for the busy schedule ahead.

Only one more game remained before Hibs would face three crucial fixtures in the space of a week – Celtic away in the League, Juventus at home in the UEFA Cup and then Celtic at Hampden in the League Cup final. That one game brought a struggling Motherwell, fourth from bottom, to Easter Road to face Hibs, riding high in third place. It was sore-back time for the goalkeeper again as Hibs rediscovered their scoring touch in League games with a superb 6-2 win. Star of the show on the day was Iain Munro, who scored twice and had a hand in two others, while Gordon, Spalding, Stanton and Cropley all added to 'Well keeper Stewart Rennie's woe. The Steelmen did manage a couple of goals of their own, from Bobby Graham and John Goldthorpe. After the game, the Hibs squad set off for Turnberry to enjoy a change of routine before the big week that lay ahead.

Parkhead was the venue for game one of the big three and it was League points on offer. After such a promising start, Hibs had faltered somewhat in losing to St Johnstone and then only drawing with Dundee, but spirits and optimism got a lift from the demolition of Motherwell. On the day, however, Hibs never really got going at all and once early goals were conceded the heads went down a bit and Celtic scored five times without reply. The scourge of Hibernian defenders, Dixie Deans, got a hat-trick while Stevie Murray and Jimmy Johnstone completed the rout. The only good thing to come out of the game was the fact that Arthur Duncan came off the bench for the second half and got in some match practice before the midweek duel with Juventus.

Having lost the first leg of their first-round UEFA Cup tie to Voerwarts of Germany, the Italian giants Juventus turned the tie around by winning 3-0 at home to take them forward to a second-round tie against Hibs. The Turin-based team were packed with quality players, including the then most expensive player in Europe, Pietro Anastasi, who joined the club from Varese for a staggering £440,000. The centre-forward was bound to be a handful, but this was no one-man team as among the starting XI would be Roberto Bettega, Antonello Cuccureddu, Gaetano Scirea, who cost Juve £400,000 from Atalanta, and Claudio Gentile. On top of all that, their goalkeeper, Dino Zoff, was the international number one and would be desperate to make amends for losing five goals on his last visit to Easter Road when he played for Napoli. On the bench they had 36-year-old Jose Altafini. It was some line-up, but one player who would not take part in the first leg was Fabio Capello, who had been booked in both legs of the first round and so had to sit out a one-match suspension.

The excitement in the stadium was palpable as the teams ran out, Hibs in their traditional green and white and the visitors in their famous black and white striped shirts with white shorts and socks. The game was played at a blistering pace, and anyone who thought the visitors would adopt the Italian 'catenaccio' style was proved mightily wrong by the free-flowing Juve. Catenaccio is a style of play that is like a boxer holding his opponent in a clinch – quite simply, it denies you the opportunity to play by fair means or foul and packs the defence to restrict goalscoring opportunities. Hibs scored two great goals that night through Stanton and Cropley and actually led 2-1 at that stage, but the visitors got four, thanks to Claudio Gentile, Antonello Cuccureddu and a double from substitute Jose Altafini.

Having watched many world-class footballers over the years, I can honestly say that Altafini was up among the best. He may have been 36, but his pace was frightening and his ball control mesmerising. It's worth mentioning a bit about Altafini, as he had enjoyed a wonderful career in football. Although born in Brazil, he spent almost his whole professional career in Italy, playing first for AC Milan, where he scored 120 goals in seven seasons before leaving to join Napoli for six seasons and then on to Juve. He played well over 400 League games in Italy and scored around 230 goals – a phenomenal achievement in a country where defensive play was the norm. He also had the distinction of representing Brazil in the 1958 World Cup and Italy in the 1962 competition. While in the Brazilian side, he was known as Mazzola and played alongside an up-and-coming young star named Pelé. At Easter Road that night, the Hibs supporters, while obviously wishing their heroes had won, were sufficiently impressed by the play of Juventus to clap the visitors off the park when the final whistle blew.

Trying to overturn a 4-2 deficit in the second leg would be a mammoth task, but Hibs had enjoyed good results in away ties before and so all hope was not yet lost. Fans wishing to follow the team in Italy were given the chance to buy a seat on the club's charter flight, although they were warned that the admission fee in Turin would be a hefty £6.00.

A 4-2 home defeat was hardly the ideal preparation for the next match, when Hibs faced Celtic in the League Cup final at Hampden. Eddie Turnbull and the huge travelling support all hoped that the players would be sufficiently motivated to seek revenge for the drubbing at Parkhead. In the event, Hibs certainly played a whole lot better than in that League encounter. The one thing that Turnbull had drummed into his players was that they should avoid losing an early goal, but that's exactly what they did, and the task of winning became all the harder. Although Hibs got within a goal on two occasions they never led at any time and ended up losing the match 6-3. Once again, Dixie Deans punished a defence that seemed incapable of marking him and he got his second hat-trick in a week, while Jimmy Johnstone, who teased and tantalised the Hibs defence all afternoon, weighed in with one, as did Paul Wilson and Stevie Murray. Rarely does a side score three goals in a Cup final and lose, but spare a thought for poor Joe Harper, who scored two and saw his hat-trick shot deflected into the net by Billy McNeill. Whether Joe got two or three was a point debated for a long time afterwards – his shot was netbound when it struck McNeill at the last second. Hibs had lost, but had played their part in providing a thrilling 90 minutes for the 53,848 spectators.

October had proved a disappointing month for Hibs, so everyone was looking for better luck in November, which certainly started well when Hibs thrashed Morton 5-0 at Easter Road in a League match. There was a real 'Edinburgh' feel to the visitors' starting XI, with ex-Hibs men Roy Baines and Alex McGhee being joined by the former Hearts trio of Jim Townsend, Kevin Hegarty and Neil Murray, but manager Erik Sorensen could only look on in dismay as his side were ripped apart and even contributed to their downfall in conceding an own-goal. The other Hibs scorers were Duncan, Munro from the penalty spot, Stanton and Harper, his 25th of the season in all competitions.

The following Wednesday, Hibs were in Turin for the second leg of their UEFA Cup tie with Juventus and in the first half had a number of good chances to work their way back into things as Duncan struck a post and Dino Zoff had a quite wonderful save to deny Stanton. A stomach bug kept Harper indoors at the interval and he was replaced by Edwards, but the Italians must have decided they had taken things too easy in the first half as they rattled four goals past Jim McArthur to win the tie 8-2 on aggregate. Roberto Bettega, Jose Altafini and two from Pietro Anastasi put a reflection on the scoreline that didn't do Hibs any favours.

From the Stadio Delle Alpi to East End Park, Hibs could now put thoughts of Europe behind them and concentrate on the next League match with Dunfermline. Leading by an Alan Gordon goal and looking comfortably in charge of the game, it looked as if the two points were in the bag for Hibs until Erich Schaedler got sent off. Booked for a foul challenge in the first half, he got a second yellow for making some kind of remark to referee Kenny Hope. It was the first time in his career he had been sent off, and he was extremely upset by the decision. The Pars grasped the opportunity to make their extra man count and equalised through Alex Kinninmonth, who secured his side a share of the points. Harper lasted only 70 minutes after his stomach bug returned to cause him problems, and he was replaced by Bobby Smith. Schaedler would now face a suspension and would join Edwards on the sidelines, the latter having picked up a four-match penalty after getting a number of yellow cards in recent games.

On the Wednesday following that draw in Fife, Hibs travelled to Rugby Park to face Kilmarnock in the knowledge that two points had not been won there since 1958, when manager Eddie Turnbull was in the winning side. Certainly the clubs had not played every season since then, because Killie had had spells in the Second Division, but it was still a monkey the club would like to get off its back. Although controlling the play for long spells, Hibs could not find a way past Jim Stewart in the Killie goal. He had three top-drawer saves and was helped by the woodwork on another occasion, while both Harper and Munro missed the goal when it looked easier to score. Inevitably, the hosts took the lead in a rare attack when Derrick McDicken beat an unprotected Jim McArthur. That seemed to spur Hibs on, and they set up wave after wave of attacks, only to continue to be thwarted by Stewart. Finally, John Blackley found the net to secure his side a 1-1 draw. With injuries and suspensions taking their toll, Hibs had given the first starts of the season to Willie Murray and Iain Munro, both of whom had reasonably good games.

Mid-November brought struggling Clyde to Easter Road hoping to gain some points to help them climb away from the joint bottom spot in the

League. The Bully Wee had conceded fewer goals than a number of teams above them, but it was their inability to score enough that had them in trouble. Manager Stan Anderson had a decent pool of players at his disposal, including ex-Celtic goalkeeper Evan Williams, Willie McVie, Brian Ahern, Dom Sullivan and goalscorer Joe Ward, who would go on to join Hibs later in his career. As expected, the visitors proved very difficult to break down and it took a classic piece of opportunism by Harper midway through the second half to score the only goal of the game and get Hibs back to winning ways.

The programme for the Clyde match carried a fine photograph of managing director Tom Hart presenting long-time club employee Jimmy McColl with a copy of a newly released book, *100 Years of Hibs*, by Gerry Docherty and Phil Thomson. The book contained some 71 pictures and carried a foreword written by Matt Busby. Costing just £1.75, it had been published by John Donald (Edinburgh) and was available in the club shop. McColl would be able to enjoy many happy memories from the contents of that book – he had joined Hibs in 1921 and been a player, trainer and a host of other things during his long association with Hibernian.

Mindful of the fact that his side were not gelling quite as they should, Eddie Turnbull shuffled the pack a bit for the next match, against joint leaders Rangers at Ibrox. With the suspended Erich Schaedler out, Des Bremner filled in at left-back and had an outstanding game there. Bobby Smith was drafted into the midfield and looked quite at home alongside Stanton, Munro and Cropley. The hosts went into the game as the only undefeated side in the UK, but Hibs had turned them over twice in the League Cup. That became a wonderful hat-trick of victories after Harper headed home an inch-perfect Duncan cross for the only goal of the game. Hibs had 11 heroes on the park that day, as no substitutes were used, but the shining star was goalkeeper Jim McArthur who saved everything that came his way and became the first keeper to get a clean sheet against Rangers in a League match. As the final whistle sounded, word filtered through from Tynecastle that Hearts had drawn with joint leaders Celtic, so it was a good weekend for Hibs in catching up two points on Rangers and one on Celtic.

Ayr United provided the opposition at Easter Road on the last day of November, a month in which Hibs had taken six points from a possible eight, had gone without a loss and had ended Rangers' long unbeaten run into the bargain. Going into this game, the visitors had strung together a fairly decent run of results that had lifted them from second bottom to mid-table, and manager Ally MacLeod had dabbled in the transfer market, bringing in Johnny Gibson from Partick Thistle, with Doug Somner and Doug Mitchell moving in the opposite direction. The visitors certainly made life difficult for Hibs, whose lead, thanks to Arthur Duncan, proved short-lived when Davie McCulloch equalised. The clock was ticking down rapidly when a superb run and cross by Duncan set up a second and winning goal from the head of Pat Stanton.

During the following week, Hibs sold Alex Cropley to Arsenal, allowing the popular midfielder to realise an ambition to play in English football and swelling the club coffers in the process. The Gunners had been tracking him for a year and were delighted to get their man. His debut came in an away game at Carlisle, where his new team lost out to the home side. On the very same day that Cropley departed, manager Eddie Turnbull secured the signature of a player he had long admired – Ally McLeod, who joined Hibs from Southampton. The 22-year-old was born in East Kilbride and had joined up at The Dell from St Mirren some 18 months earlier. His first-team appearances had been few and far between as he found himself competing for a starting place with Mike Channon and Peter Osgood. Indeed, he had been loaned out to Huddersfield when Hibs made their bid to sign him. His claim to fame when with St Mirren was that he once scored four goals in a game against Rangers, and he would go on to find the net regularly for Hibernian.

After such a rewarding November, Hibs hoped to carry on their good form into the next month and started that quest with a visit to Broomfield to face mid-table Airdrie. In quite appalling conditions, the visitors dominated the first half but could find no way past McWilliams in the home goal. Both Derek Spalding and Willie Murray were injured and unable to continue in the second half, which meant that substitutes Erich Schaedler and debutant Ally McLeod played the last 45 minutes after the defence had been reshuffled to put 'Shades' at left-back and Des Bremner into the middle alongside John Blackley. The match finished at 0-0, taking Hibs' unbeaten run in the League to seven games.

With the busy festive period fixture schedule fast approaching, Hibs were handily placed in third spot behind Rangers and Celtic, the Old Firm clubs jointly sharing the lead four points ahead of the Greens. With his side's fixture the previous weekend falling victim to the weather, Dumbarton boss Alex Wright watched Hibs drawing 0-0 at Airdrie and would have set his tactics for an Easter Road clash accordingly. The Sons of the Rock were flirting with relegation and were keen to start earning the points that would move them clear, so Wright was delighted to be able to field his strongest XI in a side that included John Cushley, a tough, no-nonsense central defender, veteran striker Willie Wallace and centre-forward John Bourke. Hibs were able to welcome Alex Edwards back into the side after he had served out his suspension, and he was in fine form, setting up both Harper and Duncan to give the Greens a 2-0 win. Edwards was busy all over the park and made a particularly important contribution when, with Hibs just the one goal up, he anticipated a McAdam header that had beaten

Jim McArthur and hooked the ball over his head to safety from virtually on the goal-line.

Postponements were starting to affect a number of clubs, but Hibs were continuing to benefit not only from their undersoil heating system but also the arrival of the Carrick Knowe golf course greenkeeper, Alex Kerr, to take on the job of groundsman. His efforts had the playing surface in immaculate condition.

The Saturday before Christmas had Hibs at Gayfield to meet lowly Arbroath on a freezing cold afternoon, with the wind howling in off the sea. With Spalding still out injured, Bremner retained his place at the heart of the defence and proved to one and all that he could excel no matter what position he was in. A twin strike-force of Harper and MacLeod was capable of causing any defence problems, but it was the ever-reliable Arthur Duncan who did the damage to a pressurised home defence. 'Nijinsky' struck twice to win the points for Hibs. With Jim McArthur keeping a clean sheet, it meant that only one goal had been conceded in the last five games. The two points enabled Hibs to make up ground on Rangers, surprisingly beaten at Airdrie, and widen the gap on fourth-placed Dundee United as they also lost.

During the following week, Des Bremner turned out for the Scotland Under-23 side against their English counterparts at Pittodrie and although the Scots lost, Bremner had a fine game and would be sure to appear again in future.

The holiday fixture squeezed in between Christmas and New Year brought together two sides enjoying lengthy unbeaten runs when Aberdeen visited Easter Road. Despite a slow start in the League race the Dons were now handily placed in fifth spot, but Hibs were soon pinning them back and Arthur Duncan's rich scoring vein saw him come close to extending it when he hit the post. The home side had the chance to go ahead when referee Marshall awarded a penalty after Willie Young upended Edwards in the box, but Munro failed to convert it, meaning that Hibs had now missed an incredible six penalties in the season to date. In the second half, Duncan again hit the woodwork and Bobby Clark pulled off wonder saves from Stanton and Harper before Billy Pirie caught the Hibs defence at sixes and sevens to sneak home the only goal of the game late in the second half.

And so 1974 came to an end and Hibernian entered their Centenary Year with a visit to Tynecastle on New Year's Day. The Gorgie side had consolidated their position in the Premier League after gaining promotion, and all thoughts of being involved in a relegation battle had been swept aside as they occupied seventh place, some six points ahead of the bottom club, Arbroath. In what could only be described as a dour affair, neither side could find the net to lift the Ne'er Day hangovers from their fans.

The chance to get back to winning ways came just three days later when

Bertie Auld's Partick Thistle visited Easter Road. The Jags had taken a thumping at Firhill the last time the sides met early in the season, but their form had improved greatly following that 5-1 reversal and they now sat in mid-table despite losing Ronnie Glavin to Celtic in an £80,000 deal. John Arrol had displaced Alan Rough in goal, while centre-back Alan Hansen was drawing the attention of clubs down south with his polished style of play. This would turn out to be a game that Hibs had to display their never-say-die qualities in coming from behind twice to secure a draw. Thistle centre-forward Joe Craig grabbed a double, Hibs countering through Stanton and Hansen's own-goal.

On the following Monday, the draw was made for the third round of the Scottish Cup and a number of top ties came out of the hat, including Hearts v Kilmarnock, Aberdeen v Rangers and, perhaps the biggest tie of all, Hibs v Celtic. Those encounters were a fortnight away, however, and Hibs had two difficult League matches to negotiate first, both away from home and both requiring a trip across the Forth Road Bridge. Around the same time, free-scoring Alan Gordon was transferred to Dundee, a move less than popular with the fans, who had now witnessed both O'Rourke and Gordon being shipped out when they were still finding the net on a fairly regular basis.

Tannadice was next on the fixture list, and Hibs arrived there just one place above their hosts in the League table. This would be a match to remember for two young debutants. Goalkeeper Hugh Whyte and winger Pat Carroll stepped up from the reserves and both had fine games in an excellent 3-1 win. Indeed, it was from a corner by Carroll that Hibs took the lead, Hamish McAlpine punching the ball into his own net when trying to clear his lines. Bremner added a second before David Narey pulled one back, but the match was won when big Tony Higgins headed home from close range.

Seven days later, Hibs were at Muirton Park to meet St Johnstone, and both Hugh Whyte and Pat Carroll retained their starting places. Unfortunately, Schaedler failed a late fitness test and so his No.3 jersey went to Munro. The Saints had both a former and future Hibee in their team. The former was, of course, Jimmy O'Rourke, who repeated his goalscoring feat of earlier in the season, and the future Hibee, Duncan Lambie, scored a second from the penalty spot. Hibs also scored twice, the first coming early in the game from Bobby Smith and the second from the spot as Tony Higgins, who saw his initial strike parried by Derek Robertson but followed up to knock the rebound home. That goal from Higgins was the 99th of the season in all competitions and meant that Hibs had lost only once – against Aberdeen – in their last 14 League fixtures.

January 1975 would end with a visit from Celtic in the Scottish Cup. Amazingly, it would be the first time the clubs had clashed in the Cup at

Easter Road since a 1961 replay, which the visitors won thanks to a John Clark goal. In the Hibs team that day were Joe Baker and Johnny MacLeod, but they could not find a way past Frank Haffey in the Celtic goal. In actual fact it had been 80 years since a Hibs v Celtic tie had come up in the Cup, and though Hibs won that day Celtic lodged a protest and the match had to be replayed, with the Glasgow side coming out on top.

All of that was in the past, of course, and Hibs would have to be at their best to get past Jock Stein's free-scoring Celtic side. With £80,000 Ronnie Glavin on the bench, it seemed as though the Celts were not really missing Lou Macari and David Hay, who had been transferred for fees in excess of £200,000 to Manchester United and Chelsea respectively. For Hibs, Hugh Whyte started in goal again, but Murray dropped to the bench when Eddie Turnbull switched his forwards around to try to test the visiting defence. Celtic scored early, however, through that man Dixie Deans again, and although Bremner hit the post, the only other goal came from Stevie Murray to put Celtic into the draw for round four.

Hibs were back at Easter Road on the first day of February to face Dundee in a League match. Like Hibs, they really only had one trophy to play for – although in their case it was the Scottish Cup – as they were well off the pace in the League race. They'd negotiated a difficult third-round tie at Shawfield and got through thanks to a goal from ex-Hibs striker Alan Gordon that earned them another away tie against St Johnstone. Hugh Whyte was once again in goal and in recognition of his early promotion to the first team there was an interesting article about the youngster in the match programme that day. Born in Kilmarnock, he was the youngest player in his primary school team – which was why, he reckoned, he became a goalkeeper. His secondary school did not have a football team and so Hugh played for Ayr Boswell Boys' Club and helped them to win the Scottish Boys' Club Cup before joining Hurlford United. Celtic seemed keen on him and he trained with them for a couple of weeks, but Hibs offered him a contract and he jumped at the chance. Studying medicine at university, he trained with Hibs on a part-time basis and was still not 100 per cent certain whether his future lay in football or medicine. His immediate future lay in the game against Dundee, of course, and he played his part in a fighting 2-1 win after Hibs had trailed 1-0 to an early Anderson goal. Pat Stanton equalised, thereby securing Hibs' 100th goal of the season, before Higgins bagged the winner in a spirited finish by the home side.

One player not in action at this time was reserve centre-half Davie Steedman, who was in plaster from his neck to the base of his spine after contracting a spinal virus around Christmas time. It was really unfortunate for the youngster as he had been showing good form in the second XI and had been hoping to follow team-mates Hugh Whyte and Pat Carroll into the first-team pool, but the club were determined that he should get the best of treatment in his quest for recovery before he pulled his boots on again.

During the week following the Dundee match, the reserves took on St Johnstone at Easter Road and thrashed them 6-1 in what was a marvellous triumph for Ally McLeod, the striker scoring five times. With Alex Edwards providing the ammunition, Ally always seemed to be in the right place at the right time, although one of his goals came from the penalty spot. Pat Carroll got the other Hibs goal, while Lindsay Muir and Les Thomson also put in fine performances.

Back in October, Hibs had thrashed Motherwell 6-2 at Easter Road, but the Steelmen got their revenge when Hibs took them on at Fir Park on 8 February. Prior to the game, Hibs had signed 32-year-old man of many clubs, Roy Barry, and he must have wondered whether he had made a wise move after Hibs crashed 4-1 on his debut appearance. Everything had looked fine for the visitors, who led at half-time through a Higgins goal, but a series of second-half defensive blunders were punished heavily by the home side, and poor Hugh Whyte was beaten on four occasions. The 'Well goals, from Willie Pettigrew (2), Willie Watson (pen) and Bobby Graham, made it a miserable 45 minutes for the Hibs players and their travelling supporters. Derek Spalding had been the man to make way for Barry, who didn't get off to the best of starts in terms of impressing the fans of his latest club.

Barry, who joined Hibs from Crystal Palace, started out in football with Musselburgh Athletic, and his first senior club was Hearts. Next stop was Dunfermline, where he played in the same side as Alex Edwards before heading down to Coventry and then on to Crystal Palace. His ambition was to move into coaching and he had actually lined up a post in the USA when Hibs persuaded him to join up at Easter Road, an offer he was only too happy to accept as he had supported the club as a boy.

Having been knocked out of the Scottish Cup, Hibs faced a blank Saturday in mid-February and had contemplated seeking out a friendly fixture down south, but plumped instead for playing their East of Scotland Shield semi-final match against Berwick Rangers at Easter Road. The other semi would pit Hearts against Meadowbank, and the two finalists were likely to meet in April. Eddie Turnbull brought Jim McArthur back into the starting line-up and there were also places for Edwards and MacLeod. With the game just 15 minutes old, Edwards was carried off with what proved to be a chipped bone in his ankle, which would keep him out for several weeks. Pat Carroll came off the bench as his replacement and proved a most able deputy as Hibs cruised to a 3-0 win, despite Tony Higgins missing an early penalty. Harper opened the scoring with his first goal for nine games while his second-half replacement, Duncan, got the second and Higgins the third.

The reigning League champions, Celtic, would provide the next Easter Road challenge for Hibs and they arrived with a new loan signing, Peter Latchford, who had moved from West Bromwich Albion. Up against a potent strike-force of Kenny Dalglish, Dixie Deans and Paul Wilson, Hibs had to be at their very best in securing a wonderful 2-1 win, thanks to a brace from the effervescent Arthur Duncan. The pace of 'Nijinsky' was just too much for the Celtic defence and he was unlucky not to score a hat-trick after robbing Roddy McDonald late in the game, waltzing past Latchford and then slipping at the crucial moment in steering his shot wide of the post. Defensively, Hibs were solid and Dixie Deans, so often the hammer of Hibs, was kept very quiet by Roy Barry, who used all of his experience to deny the Celtic man even a sniff at goal. The visitors pulled one back late in the game through Paul Wilson, but there is no doubt the better team won on the day, with Stanton and Bremner dominating the midfield area throughout. The result took Hibs to within three points of Celtic, who were second going into the game, but Rangers won that day and maintained their seven-point advantage over the Easter Road men.

For the fifth time this season, Hibs would face Kilmarnock when the Ayrshire club arrived at Easter Road on the first Saturday in March. Two League Cup games, a Drybrough Cup match and a League clash at Rugby Park had resulted in two wins for the Greens and two draws, so Hibs went into the game in confident mood, especially as their visitors were in the bottom half of the League table. Killie had two quality goalkeepers on their books, Jim Stewart and Alan McCulloch, together with a central defensive partnership of Brian Rodman and Derrick McDicken, but it was at the other end of the park that manager Willie Fernie had been having problems. The recently signed Davie Provan, however, was now proving adept at providing the right kind of ammunition for their forwards, Eddie Morrison and Gordon Smith. From a Hibs perspective, Higgins and Edwards were injured and Pat Carroll was given an outing at No.7. An even first half produced opportunities for both sides, but the second belonged to Killie as they scored twice through Eddie Morrison and Ian Fallis to record a somewhat unexpected win.

Pat Carroll was just 17 and had impressed greatly in the reserves to earn a place in the starting XI. Capped at schoolboy level, he was signed by Hibs on an 'S' form, having caught the eye playing with Sauchie Thistle. While on that 'S' form, he played for Scotland against England at Wembley, where he had an outstanding game, and Hibs wasted no time in bringing him on to the professional staff on his 17th birthday.

As the points won against Celtic had been somewhat cancelled out after that unexpected loss to Kilmarnock, Hibs were anxious to get back to winning ways when they travelled to Cappielow to face a Morton side fighting for First Division survival. The single-goal victory secured by the visitors was far from a reflection of the way the game had gone. Hibs dominated throughout, but missed chance after chance until eventually Ally McLeod scored his first competitive goal since joining from Southampton. Billy Osborne squandered the opportunity to equalise when he fired a penalty kick high over the bar. Tony Higgins had recovered from injury, but manager Turnbull didn't want to risk the big fellow on a mudbath of a pitch and so restricted him to the substitutes' bench, where he was joined by young Lawrie Dunn, although neither player was called into action. Alex Edwards was still on the treatment table, but even if he had been fit he could not have played because the SFA Referees' Committee suspended him for 28 days and fined him £150 following his ordering-off against Aberdeen in December.

There was quite a scrap going on at the foot of the last-ever First Division, and Dunfermline FC were among those involved when they arrived at Easter Road in mid-March. Going into the game, Hibs could still technically be champions, but to do so they had to win their remaining matches and hope that the Old Firm would slip up at some point. They stayed in the hunt with an impressive 5-1 win against the Pars, whose keeper, Geir Karlsen, had a difficult afternoon in conceding goals to Munro, who bagged an impressive hat-trick, Harper and MacLeod. After the match, Munro put his first senior hat-trick down to the tremendous service from the Hibs midfield, saying that he'd been set up six times during the game and was delighted to have taken half of them. The Pars' goal was scored by Graham Shaw.

A couple of interesting articles appeared in the match programme for the game where fans were advised that the club was somewhat dismayed to find that newly installed seats in the centre stand had been damaged because supporters had stood on them. As the installation had cost Hibs £7,500, it is perhaps no surprise that the management was set on encouraging fans to remain seated during games.

The other item concerned plans for the celebration of the club's Centenary Year. A plea had been made for former players to get in touch and the response had been really encouraging, with Willie Harper, John 'Cubby' Cuthbertson, Davie Shaw, Willie Finnigan, John Grant, Joe Davis, Peter Flucker, Peter Carruthers, Willie Hamilton, Bobby Kinloch, Joe McClelland, Hugh Higgins, Jimmy Thomson, Doug Moran, Alex Duchart, Gordon Black, Angus Plumb, Bobby Nutley and Peter Aird all intimating that they would come along, some facing the prospect of travelling a fair distance to meet up with old friends.

Hibs had not won a League match at Shawfield since October 1965, when John McNamee and John Baxter scored the goals to beat Clyde, but that long wait for another success ended when the Greens scored three without reply in this latest encounter. Boosted by the confidence gained from his hat-trick against Dunfermline, Iain Munro opened the scoring early for Hibs and the visitors never looked in danger of losing as Duncan added two more goals to secure the points.

March 1975 ended for Hibs with a visit from champions-elect Rangers, needing just a point to secure their first title for 11 years. The best Hibs could hope for was to win and delay the inevitable, but there was no doubt, regardless of the result in this game, that Jock Wallace's side would finish top of the pile. With a huge travelling support roaring them on, the visitors took the lead through ex-Hibs centre-forward Colin Stein, but the home support was noisy too and raised the roof when Ally McLeod equalised. Later in the game it looked as though the hosts would spoil the party after MacLeod notched what looked a perfectly good goal, only for referee Paterson from Bothwell to mystify everyone by chalking it off. The match ended 1-1, and Rangers lifted the title, but Hibs were still in with a shout to finish second and, if nothing else, looked favourites to qualify for Europe in the coming season.

The race for the runners-up spot in the First Division had Celtic and Hibs neck and neck, which would make for an exciting last few weeks in the League campaign. A tricky tie at Somerset Park against a much improved Ayr United would certainly test the nerve of the Easter Road men and, as it turned out, John Brownlie in particular. Duncan had given Hibs the lead, but two defensive blunders allowed Davie McCulloch and Alan Phillips to put the home side ahead with time ticking down fast. As the game was drawing to its conclusion, Hibs were awarded a penalty and Brownlie was nominated to take it. He demonstrated how such kicks should be taken when he rattled the ball past Hugh Sproat to secure a valuable point. That was Hibs' 15th penalty award of the season, but they'd managed to miss no fewer than six, the 'offenders' being Harper, Higgins, Munro and Cropley, so it was satisfying for manager Eddie Turnbull that he seemed now to have a player who would hit the mark when needed.

Only three games remained for Hibs to secure that second place in the League and going into them they needed just three points to make sure. The first of the three brought Airdrie to Easter Road. Although they were in the lower half of the League they had reached the final of the Scottish Cup after a semi-final replay win over Motherwell, and so would be facing Hibs with a degree of confidence. Unfortunately for the Diamonds, they met a Hibs side in full flow and were hammered 6-1, Harper bagging a hat-trick and Bremner, Smith and Duncan adding to Airdrie boss Ian McMillan's woes. Jim McArthur had a very quiet day, although he was beaten once by Billy Wilson, but most of the action was at the other end of the park.

On the Monday of the following week, Des Bremner joined the Scotland Under-23 squad as they flew out to Gothenburg to face Sweden. He could be forgiven if he had mixed feelings, given that Hibs were up north to play

Des's old club, Deveronvale, in a testimonial match the following night. It turned out to be a canter for Hibs. Harper and Brownlie got doubles, one of Brownlie's coming from the penalty spot, while Smith and Carroll were also on target in a 6-0 win in front of the home side's biggest crowd for ten years. Over in Sweden, Des was doing well, too, as Scotland defeated the home nation and Bremner was singled out for praise by boss Jock Stein.

The penultimate League game of the season saw Hibs visit Boghead knowing that a point would be enough to secure second place and guaranteed participation in the coming season's UEFA Cup. Dumbarton, however, had an agenda of their own and set about the visitors with a purpose, scoring twice through Colin McAdam and Jim Muir before Hibs decided enough was enough and started off on the comeback trail. Having switched from the left wing to the right for the second half, Arthur Duncan began to get behind the home defenders and cause them serious problems. It was Duncan who pulled Hibs level with a great run and finish after Smith had scored the first, and it was Duncan's pass to Erich Schaedler that allowed the full-back to deliver a swerving cross that the Sons defender Dennis Ruddy sliced past his own goalkeeper for what proved to be the winning goal.

Saturday, 26 April 1975, marked the end of Hibs' League campaign when bottom club Arbroath visited Easter Road and went down 2-1, the Hibs goals coming from Brownlie and Edwards while the visitors countered through Derek Rylance. The match programme contained an announcement that referee Jim Callaghan, who had been on the Grade 1 list for 13 years and had been officiating at senior games for 28, including ties abroad in the various European competitions, would be retiring after this game. With all due respect to the whistler, an article on possible European rivals for Hibs certainly drew a deal more attention. A whole host of big names had qualified, including Feyenoord, Barcelona, Hertha Berlin, Torino, Sporting Lisbon, Anderlecht, Olympiakos, Hajduk Split, Ferencvaros and Magdeburg, and so there was much to look forward to in the coming season.

Having refused an invitation to play two friendlies during a short trip to Poland, Hibs had just one game left to play before the squad started its close season and that took the Greens to Tynecastle for the final of the East of Scotland Shield. Winning 1-0, courtesy of a third-minute goal by Arthur Duncan, Hibs missed a number of glorious chances to extend their lead and paid the price 11 minutes from time when Donald Park equalised. Extra time followed, and in the last of those 30 minutes Park shot home to win the game for Hearts.

Chapter Nine

1975/76

DERBY DOMINANCE

It was the dawning of a new age for Scottish football as league reconstruction created a Premier Division containing only ten clubs, with two groups of clubs below, the First and Second Divisions. Everyone seemed to go into this with high hopes of moving the game in Scotland forward, but that optimism would eventually be proved somewhat misplaced as clubs such as Ayr United, Airdrie, Partick Thistle and Dundee found their time among the elite to be somewhat restricted. Given that the top league by its very nature tended to accommodate the best-supported clubs, those outwith would feel the damaging effects of lower attendances for decades to come.

Down at Easter Road, few were worried about matters such as those. After all, Hibs had finished second the previous season and there was no reason to even consider the thought that the lower leagues would ever be part of their world. Hibs had a first-class manager, a board willing to invest and a pool of players among the best in the country.

During the summer of 1975, Eddie Turnbull underwent two fairly major operations and did not travel with the club when Hibs set off for a pre-season tour of Ireland. The first-team coach, Wilson Humphries, was made caretaker manager for the trip and a successful trip it was. The first match took place at Flower Lodge Park against Cork Hibs on a pitch where the grass was lush and probably just a little too long, but that didn't stop the touring side winning 2-0, with goals from Joe Harper and a John Brownlie penalty. Roy Barry suffered an early injury to his foot and soldiered on until half-time, but it was felt best not to risk further damage and so Pat Stanton moved to centre-back, Tony Higgins coming off the bench to fill Stanton's midfield role.

From Cork it was on to Waterford, where, apart from putting in some hard training sessions, the players also enjoyed a round of golf or a bit of sunbathing on the nearby beach. That combination seemed to work well for Hibs as they easily defeated their hosts 6-0 at Gorey Park, even though they had introduced a few youngsters into the set-up. Lindsay Muir and Pat Carroll started the game and Willie Murray joined in from the bench when he replaced Iain Munro. Prior to leaving the park, Munro had got his name on the scoresheet, as did Joe Harper with two, Pat Carroll, Ally McLeod and Bobby Smith. Harper's double could have been a triple but he had a goal disallowed in what Wilson Humphries described as 'an Irish hat-trick', much to the amusement of all who heard him say it.

The third game in what was a mere five-day spell of action came when Hibs travelled to Dublin to face the Irish champions, Bohemian, at Dalymount Park. A tougher game was anticipated and so it proved to be as Hibs won by a solitary goal scored by MacLeod. The Irish side defended well without ever troubling Hibs at the other end of the park, but they had no answer to a clever move between Arthur Duncan and MacLeod, who fired home from ten yards. Alex Edwards suffered a slight groin strain and was replaced by MacLeod, while Muir caught the eye with a very impressive performance alongside Stanton at the back.

Back home in Scotland, the draw for the League Cup had been made and Hibs found themselves in a section with Dundee, Ayr United and Dunfermline. The Greens had won the Cup three years earlier after having toured Ireland pre-season, and everyone was hoping for a repeat performance this time around. The first two games in that section would have to be played without John Brownlie, whose booking in the previous season's East of Scotland Shield final at Tynecastle meant suspension. There had been little or no transfer activity at the club, possibly because Eddie Turnbull had taken the summer months to recover from his operations, but there was one addition to the ground staff when 18-year-old centre-half Bobby Aitken joined from Airdrie Boys' Club. Aitken had been serving his apprenticeship as a painter, but decided to give that up to sign full-time with Hibs. One nice touch worth mentioning is the fact that while in hospital Eddie Turnbull had many visitors from the world of football, including the Hearts boss, John Hagart, who popped in a couple of times to keep Eddie up to speed with all the local football chat.

Nineteen-seventy-five was, of course, the Centenary Year of Hibernian Football Club, and as part of the celebrations Hibs invited the English League champions, Derby County, north for a friendly match on 4 August. The Rams had shot to prominence in English football when Brian Clough was their manager, but he along with assistant Peter Taylor had now moved on and the club was left in the capable hands of Dave Mackay and Des Anderson. Mackay was a legend in both the Scottish and English game, having starred for both Hearts and Tottenham Hotspur as well as representing Scotland in his day. As you might expect from a championship-winning side, there were a host of household names in Derby's starting XI, which included Bruce Rioch, Roy McFarland, Colin Todd, Kevin Hector, Kevin Hinton and Francis Lee, but there was no place for Charlie George, recently acquired from Arsenal for £100,000. For their part, Hibs lined up with the old familiar faces that had served them so well in the previous season, although there was a place on the bench for Muir, who had impressed so greatly in pre-season, while Edwards missed out because of that groin strain suffered in Dublin.

It was an even contest for the most part, with Hibs matching their opponents in most areas of the park, and so it was probably inevitable that only one goal would separate the sides. Unfortunately for Hibs, that goal came from the boot of Bruce Rioch. Muir had replaced Blackley at half-time and gave an excellent account of himself alongside Roy Barry at the heart of the home defence.

The new season brought with it a revamped programme, which now cost the princely sum of 10p. As always the advertising revenues were important to Hibs and among those paying to have their services advertised that season were Selecta Travel, based at 42 Dalry Road, the Americana Discotheque, Fairbairn's off-licence at 11 Albert Street, Butlin's and the Sound Centre at 17 Easter Road, where you could buy cut-price LPs, including the latest from the Carpenters and Cat Stevens.

The UEFA Cup draw had been made by this time and Hibs could scarcely have asked for more difficult opponents when their name came out of the hat to face Liverpool. The sides had met competitively just four years earlier, when the Anfield club won 1-0 in Edinburgh and 2-0 in Liverpool, with crowds in excess of 30,000 at Easter Road and 40,000 on Merseyside. That encounter was some weeks away yet, and having completed their pre-season schedule, Hibs were now set to begin their domestic season with participation in the League Cup.

The quest for Cup glory began with a visit to Easter Road by Dundee, who had had a successful Scandinavian pre-season tour and an impressive home win in a friendly against Arsenal, for whom Alex Cropley had scored in a 2-1 defeat. Manager Davie White had a number of good players at his disposal, including ex-Hibs men Thomson Allan and Alan Gordon, while he was extremely excited about the form of a youngster promoted from the reserves who went by the name of Gordon Strachan. For Hibs, a winning start to the section was crucial, and they did that in some style with a 2-0 victory. MacLeod opened the scoring from the penalty spot, taking on that task in the absence of the suspended Brownlie, while Harper delighted the home fans by selling a wonderful dummy to Thomson Allan before rolling the ball into an empty net. Hibs were well served by Bobby Smith and Arthur Duncan, who provided width on either side of the park, and were happy to finish the game so much in command. Watching from the stand was Eddie Turnbull, back at Easter Road but not yet back in action as manager until his recuperation was complete. Also in the stand were representatives from Liverpool, having their second look at Hibs: they had also attended the Derby County match.

With two points on the board, Hibs headed for Somerset Park to face Ayr United, but it would not be a happy outcome as the home side triumphed 2-1, thanks to goals from Gerry Phillips and Rikki Fleming. MacLeod hit the target for Hibs and all the goals came in the first half, with Hibs trying manfully to equalise in the second period but being unable to find a way through the stuffy home defence.

With both Brownlie and Edwards available again, caretaker boss Wilson Humphries made changes for the next game, against Dunfermline at Easter Road, and those changes had a positive effect as the home side won 3-0 despite being reduced to ten men. The Pars had proved difficult to break down, and Humphries had replaced MacLeod with Bremner, when Pat Stanton was controversially sent off by referee Brian McGinlay. The ten men buckled down, however: inspired by Edwards, Joe Harper scored twice and Duncan got the other. After the match, it became known that Stanton planned to appeal against his dismissal, arguing that although he had tangled with Alan Evans he had not, as suggested by the referee, 'spoken out of turn' during the incident.

Off the field, there was news regarding young centre-half Derek Spalding, who was busy planning his end-of-season wedding in the knowledge that none of his team-mates would be likely to attend as the ceremony was taking place in Chicago, home of his fiancée, Heather. There was information, too, about tickets going on sale for the upcoming Liverpool match, although they would only be needed in the main stand and the seated enclosure, those for the latter being priced at £1.50. Finally, word had reached Easter Road that the referee for the Liverpool tie would be from Holland, the official for the second leg at Anfield coming from West Germany.

The home win against Dunfermline meant that the Easter Road side now topped their section. Ayr United, without a loss so far, had won their home fixture 2-1 and Hibs had to redress the balance by beating them at Easter Road to ensure continued leadership of the group. That's exactly what they did. It was a close game, to be fair, but Hibs probably held the edge overall and deserved to take both points thanks to a goal from Munro and an own-goal from Rikki Fleming. Ayr's goal came when their promising young winger, Johnny Doyle, set up ex-Hibs man Johnny Graham, who beat Jim McArthur with a low angled drive from ten yards.

The match programme for the game against Ayr at home had an interesting article about Des Bremner, who was pictured with an array of trophies on display in front of him. A number of Supporters' Club branches had voted Des Player of the Year, but there were also trophies reflecting his success on the badminton court, indicating that he excelled not just at one sport but two. Also in that programme came news that because only 21 of the 38 senior clubs in Scotland planned to run a reserve team, the Scottish Football League had decided to split the 21 teams into two leagues, in one of which Hibs joined the other nine Premier League clubs.

The penultimate section match in the League Cup took Hibs to East End Park to face a Dunfermline team who had not won any of their games so far. Before the kick-off, the home side presented Hibs with a lovely silver salver to mark the club's 100th year. It was duly returned to the Easter Road boardroom, where it sat nicely alongside the three crystal decanters presented by Rangers and the silver salver gifted by Cork City during the pre-season tour. A huge travelling support swelled the attendance, and the journey was made more than worthwhile when the Greens swamped their hosts 4-0. With Duncan out injured, Bobby Smith took the No.11 jersey and celebrated his call-up by scoring the final goal after Harper had bagged two and Stanton the other.

During the following week, Hibs sent a sizeable deputation down to Elland Road to watch Liverpool take on Leeds United in the League. Wilson Humphries and John Fraser were accompanied by Tom Hart and Tommy Younger, all four being mightily impressed as the Merseysiders won 3-0 in a game in which Peter Cormack was one of their star performers. Also during that week, Hibs called up two teenagers to the playing staff. Seventeen-year-old full-back Colin Campbell gave up a job with the Civil Service to turn professional with Hibs, while the other signing, Joe Forte, joined from Haddington. Interestingly, Campbell would feature in the first team in times to come – but not at full-back!

A win at Dens Park would put Hibs in the quarter-finals of the League Cup, and that win duly arrived as the visitors took the game 2-1. It was another of those encounters where the final scoreline didn't tell the full story. Hibs had dominated for almost the entire 90 minutes, but had come up against goalkeeper Thomson Allan at his sparkling best. Eventually, Harper headed home a fine cross from Schaedler and Brownlie scored from the penalty spot after Allan had fouled Harper. Dundee owed their goal to Iain Munro, who steered the ball past Jim McArthur after being put under pressure by Alan Gordon in the Hibs penalty area. Having won the section, Hibs then found out that their quarter-final opponents would be Montrose.

Attention now turned to the start of the Premier League campaign, and what better way to begin that long journey than with a home game against your oldest rivals? Having narrowly failed to qualify from their League Cup section, John Hagart's men were hoping for better success in the League and the Hearts boss had assembled a useful-looking side. The newest face in the line-up belonged to defender Don Murray, who had joined the club from Cardiff City and had already been made captain of the side. He was joined in the starting XI that day by the likes of goalkeeper Jim Cruickshank, left-back Jim Clunie, midfielder Drew Busby and outside-left

Rab Prentice, while wearing the No.4 jersey was Jim Jefferies. It was a typical derby in relation to the number of goals scored, but the standard of play set by both teams was exceptionally good in front of some 23,600 fans. In the end, a single strike by Harper kept the points in Leith and set up bragging rights for the Hibs support in the weeks ahead. The match made history in one respect in that the referee was Edinburgh man Eddie Thomson, who became the first capital-born whistler to officiate at an Edinburgh derby in a championship match.

In the match programme from the derby game came the interesting news that Arthur Duncan, Joe Harper and Des Bremner would be flying out to Denmark on the Monday following as they had been named in the Scotland squad playing Denmark in the European Championships. Actually, Bremner was scheduled to play in the Under-23 fixture and the other two in the full international, but it was good to have such representation at national level and even better to hear that Des had struck the winning goal in his game, while Joe Harper did the same in the full international.

Having lost their opening game, Dundee United were determined to make amends when Hibs visited Tannadice on the first Saturday in September. An early penalty gave Graeme Payne the chance to put the home side ahead and he was fortunate when Jim McArthur got a hand to the ball but could not keep it out. Hibs then went in search of an equalising goal and had the home side pinned back in defence for long periods, but could not find a way past Hamish McAlpine. There were loud shouts for a penalty late in the game when Duncan tumbled in the box, but referee Bill Anderson waved them aside. Two points dropped, then, but encouragement from the fact that Hibs went down fighting and tried to play attacking football throughout.

In the following midweek, Hibs faced Montrose at Easter Road in the first leg of the League Cup quarter-final. The game marked the return to duty of Eddie Turnbull, following his illness and recuperation. Although not a Premier League side, Alex Stuart's Montrose had enjoyed a good start to their season and so would be sure to present a difficult encounter for the home team. They might not have had any household names in their side, but they did have some useful players, such as Dave McNicoll, who had signed from Dunfermline following Kenny Watson's transfer from Montrose to Rangers. Ex-Dundee United men Kenny Cameron and Stuart Markland had played at Easter Road before, and so this tie would hold no fears for them. The visitors set out to frustrate Hibs and they largely succeeded in that task in restricting the Greens to a narrow 1-0 win, Harper scoring from a free kick six minutes from time. After the match, a disappointed Eddie Turnbull said that only Jim McArthur, John Blackley and Iain Munro had played to form, the remainder of the side being well below par.

The back page of the match programme that night informed us that Des

Bremner had a very optimistic view of Hibs' chances of progression in the UEFA Cup. Apparently, Des had fixed a date for his wedding, but had promptly changed it when he discovered that it clashed with the date for the third-round UEFA Cup ties. There was also news that 24 hours after the second-leg tie with Montrose, Pat Stanton had an important meeting in Glasgow, where he would appear before the SFA Referees' Committee to appeal against his ordering-off against Dunfermline some weeks before.

Having beaten Ayr United in the home game of their League Cup section, Hibs were looking for a repeat performance when the Ayrshire club visited Easter Road in mid-September. Ayr arrived having played a total of ten competitive games with only one defeat, so they would be a hard nut to crack. With Alex Edwards in sparkling form, Hibs had most of the possession, but a combination of poor finishing and good goalkeeping by Hugh Sproat kept them out until well into the second half, when referee Gordon pointed to the spot after Harper was bundled over in the box and Brownlie stroked home the only goal of the game. It would have been nice to win by more goals, but the two points were very welcome, and the game threw up another clean sheet for Jim McArthur and his fellow defenders. In fact, McArthur had conceded only three goals to date and all of those were from the penalty spot.

Off the park but still very much a football matter, was the news that having attended the appropriate courses during the previous summer in Largs, Pat Stanton had acquired the necessary qualifications to become a football coach. Pat was only one of three players to satisfy the examiners, the other two being Cameron Murray and a certain Walter Smith. At this point, of course, Pat had no plans to give up playing, but he was certainly now equipped to stay in football once he decided to hang up his boots at some future time.

In the following midweek, Hibs welcomed Liverpool to Easter Road for the first leg of their first-round clash in the UEFA Cup. Manager Bob Paisley had, like Eddie Turnbull, only ever played professionally for the one club, and when his playing days were over he initially took charge of the Liverpool second string before becoming assistant to Bill Shankly. He assumed control of the first team just a year before this tie took place. Packed with quality, the Liverpool first XI included household names such as Ray Clemence in goal, Phil Neal and Emlyn Hughes in defence, Peter Cormack, Ray Kennedy and Steve Heighway in midfield and, of course, Kevin Keegan and John Toshack up front. On a miserable night weather-wise, with rain pouring down almost throughout the whole match, Hibs took the game to their illustrious opponents and scored a quite wonderful goal when Munro and Duncan combined brilliantly down the left to create a chance for Joe Harper to open the scoring. Despite pressure from Hughes, Harper finished well and the Hibernian tails were up. At the other end, Jim McArthur saved well from both Heighway and Keegan before Hibs had the chance to double their lead after the Dutch referee awarded them a penalty. It was a nervy moment for players and fans alike, and there was a huge groan of disappointment when Brownlie watched in despair as Ray Clemence saved the kick. The game ended at 1-0, and there is little doubt that a 2-0 lead to take to Anfield would have been very handy indeed, but Hibs still had cause for optimism as they had played very well throughout this home tie.

One tough game seemed to be following another at that time and so it was almost inevitable that having faced Liverpool on the Wednesday, Hibs would meet Rangers at Ibrox on the following Saturday. Showing no signs of their midweek exertions, Hibs took the game to their hosts and enjoyed long periods of dominance without managing to break the deadlock. In a relatively rare raid upfield, the Glasgow side opened the scoring in the luckiest of ways when a wayward shot by Derek Parlane looked to be going wide only for Blackley to stick out a boot and send the ball past a stranded McArthur. That incident seemed to spark Hibs up even more and they were soon level, thanks to a rocket shot from Brownlie. After that equaliser, both sides had half-chances to win the game but neither could capitalise and the spoils were shared at 1-1.

Next up for Hibs was a trip to Links Park, Montrose, for the second leg of the League Cup quarter-final tie. Leading 1-0 from the first game, the Easter Road men got off to the perfect start when Duncan scored in the first minute, but clearly the hosts were working to a different script and set about pinning the Hibs defence back. With no Stanton in the starting XI, his appeal against that red card having failed, Hibs struggled to control the midfield and it wasn't long before full-back Les Barr struck an equaliser. With Hibs truly under the cosh, Bobby Livingstone put the home side 2-1 up and level at 2-2 on aggregate, his goal taking the game into extra time. During the half hour, Smith rattled a shot off the post and both Blackley and Harper were denied by brilliant Dave Gorman saves. As time ran down and a penalty shoot-out looked a distinct possibility, disaster struck for McArthur when a 40-yard punt forward by Les Barr was totally misjudged by the Hibs keeper and it sailed over his head, into an empty net. Once again, chances galore were made but not taken and that was the sixth game in a row that Hibs had managed only one goal. It was a gloomy drive home that night as fans came to terms with the fact that Hibs had been knocked out of the League Cup when everyone had anticipated another trip to Hampden for the semi-final, and it was an even gloomier picture the following morning when the news broke that Pat Stanton had handed in a transfer request.

The last Saturday in September saw Hibs welcoming St Johnstone to Easter Road on League business, the game giving the home side the chance to prove that their additional shooting practice at training would be put to good effect. The tie heralded another Easter Road appearance for Jimmy O'Rourke and as ever the player received a warm welcome from the home fans, clearly not holding a grudge against O'Rourke for the fact that on the last occasion he'd played against Hibs at Easter Road in the League he'd scored the only goal of the game and ended the unbeaten run of Eddie Turnbull's men. In a whirlwind start, Hibs opened the scoring in just 24 seconds through Munro and they went on to score three more in comfortably winning the game 4-2. The other Hibs scorers were Duncan, MacLeod and Harper, while Duncan Lambie and, yes, you've guessed it, Jimmy O'Rourke found the target for Saints. Man of the match that day, by a country mile, was Des Bremner with a typical display of non-stop action, although it should be borne in mind that Des combined his athleticism with a great footballing brain.

In the days leading up to the UEFA Cup first-round second-leg tie against Liverpool at Anfield, Eddie Turnbull suggested that if Hibs could score just one goal they would qualify for round two. It was a bold statement, but made in the knowledge that Hibs had more than matched their opponents in the first leg and so had absolutely nothing to fear. A sizeable support followed the Greens south and they were soon celebrating as Hibs equalised an opener from John Toshack when Edwards shot home from just inside the box. At that stage, Hibs were looking good and led the tie 2-1 on aggregate, but with the Kop roaring its heroes on Toshack scored two more to get his hat-trick and take Liverpool through 3-2 on aggregate. Although available again for selection, Pat Stanton did not start the match and much of the talk on the supporters' buses as they made the long trek home was that with Stanton in the team Hibs might just have qualified. In reality, however, Hibs had been beaten on the night by a better team.

When the season had started Hibs had high hopes of doing well on four fronts, but now they were reduced to seeking success on just two – the League and the Scottish Cup. The latter was some weeks away from commencing when Hibs welcomed Dundee to Easter Road at the start of October. Hibs were sitting in third place in the table and the visitors second bottom. Since the clubs last met, Dundee had done business in the transfer market, Jocky Scott leaving to join Aberdeen and Ian Purdie and £30,000 coming the other way. The new man made his mark for Dundee by providing a perfect cross for Gordon Wallace to head past McArthur, but Hibs also scored, and for the second game in a row the marksman was Edwards as the game ended in a 1-1 draw. That evening it was announced that Arthur Duncan had been named by the Hibs Supporters' Association as their 1974/75 Player of the Year, and a well deserved award it was, too.

The League table had a familiar look to it by this time, with the Old Firm in the top two places, but leading the chase behind them were Hibs and

Motherwell, and those sides clashed at Fir Park on 11 October with both knowing that a win would keep the pressure on the leading two. The first half belonged to Hibs and they went into the half-time break holding the lead after Harper had scored a cracking goal. For the first 25 minutes of the second half Hibs kept control and should have doubled their lead, but a furious onslaught by the home side in the last 20 minutes of the game saw them draw level through Willie Pettigrew and then take both points when a header from Gregor Stevens beat McArthur as virtually the last action of the match. It was a sore one for Hibs: not for the first time, their inability to kill opponents off when in control of a game had cost them dear.

Saturday, 18 October 1975, is a day the author will always remember due to the very unusual circumstances surrounding Hibs' visit to Parkhead on League business. With the ground packed and a fairly big travelling support trying its best and often succeeding in out-singing the home 'choir', Hibs turned on a devastating display of pacy, fluent and outstanding football, with pick of the bunch Des Bremner in quite wonderful form at the centre of the Hibs midfield. The visitors swarmed around the Celtic goal at every opportunity and took the lead when a deep cross by Duncan was magnificently headed home at the back post by Bremner.

With just 15 minutes left, Harper scored what looked like the crucial winning goal, but the Celtic supporters were disgruntled with their team's efforts and a minor pitch invasion stopped play for a while after fans standing in the infamous 'Jungle' took matters into their own hands. Referee Bobby Davidson restarted the game once the fans had been cleared off the pitch, but by this time a bank of fog was enshrouding the stadium and visibility became very poor as a result. Around five minutes of playing time remained, but Mr Davidson decided the game would have to be abandoned and took the players off the park. Within ten minutes, visibility was back to normal as the fog rolled on to a new destination.

There is no doubt Hibs had that game won and if the fans had not invaded the pitch the match would have been over before the fog rolled in. Unsurprisingly, Hibs appealed to the Scottish League on that basis, asking for the tie to be awarded to them. Equally unsurprisingly, the Scottish League rejected the Hibs appeal and ordered that the match should be replayed on 10 December.

A week later, managerless Aberdeen, sitting in second-bottom spot in the League, arrived at Easter Road. Results had been poor during the opening weeks of the campaign and a heavy defeat by Celtic had prompted Jimmy Bonthrone to tender his resignation. The Pittodrie board was extremely reluctant to accept it, but finally agreed with Bonthrone's view that a change of manager might improve the fortunes of the club. Coach George Murray held the reins until an appointment could be made, and he had a good squad of players at his disposal, including goalkeeper Bobby Clark,

Willie Miller, Jocky Scott, Davie Robb, Drew Jarvie and Arthur Graham. Indeed, it was a major surprise that such a talented side were struggling so badly, but there was no room for sentiment in the Hibs camp as the home side ran out worthy 3-1 winners. Bremner, Smith and an own-goal by Drew Jarvie counted for Hibs while Davie Robb struck the Aberdeen goal.

On the following Monday evening, Hibs held a Centenary Dinner, with almost 200 guests in attendance. Officials from both the Scottish League and the SFA joined former players from different eras, including four of the Famous Five and the oldest former player, John Lamb, who was 84 and had signed for Hibs in 1910.

November would be a busy month for Hibs with five games scheduled, and the first of those came when Hibs visited Tynecastle on League business buoyed by the news that Pat Stanton had withdrawn his transfer request. Hearts were tucked in nicely behind Hibs in the League race and they were the better team in the first half of this tense encounter, although the interval arrived with no goals on the board. Some 15 minutes into the second half, Hearts broke the deadlock when Ralph Callachan beat McArthur from close range and for a while after that the Gorgie side, cheered on by their fans in the near 25,000 crowd, looked as if they might increase their lead, but Hibs stuck in and slowly started to take the initiative. With the game in its closing phase, Smith and Harper both tested Jim Cruickshank in the home goal, but with both points seemingly destined for Tynecastle, Pat Stanton popped up deep into injury time to head home a cross from Brownlie and gain the draw. Those were the days before 'time added on' became a public feature in the game, and although such time was played, nobody knew how much would be added as it was solely at the discretion of the referee – in this particular case, Ian Foote. For years afterwards, Hearts fans would insist it was a 95th-minute goal, but the truth is that Pat scored in the third minute of added time. To be fair, Pat himself would some years later admit that he had been offside when he put the ball in the net!

Earlier in the season Hibs had lost narrowly at Tannadice and now had the opportunity to gain revenge for that defeat as Dundee United arrived at Easter Road having lost at home to Porto in their UEFA Cup tie the previous midweek. One bright note for Jim McLean's men was that the £40,000 handed over to Dumbarton for centre-forward Tom McAdam had paid early dividends, the big striker hitting two goals against St Johnstone in his first match for his new club. McAdam had been brought in to replace Andy Gray, who had been sold to Aston Villa for a six-figure sum, and he was on target again in beating McArthur to get United's goal in this 1-1 draw. The Hibs goal came from a Brownlie penalty early in the game and there was disappointment on the home terracings that chances had again been missed to finish the opposition off.

During the following week, Hibs were given a civic reception by Edinburgh District Council, and Lord Provost John Millar was host for a buffet dance attended by players and officials from the club. A presentation was made to the club and added to the long list of Centenary gifts received from varying sources. Hearts had given a beautiful inscribed rose bowl, while a number of clubs had given inscribed silver salvers and crystal. Perhaps the most unusual gift came from Morton in the shape of a coffee table inlaid with Morton's club badge. One player missing from the celebrations that day was Des Bremner, who had the perfect excuse as it was his wedding day. The civic reception also missed out on the company of Jim McArthur and Bobby Smith, who both attended Bremner's big day instead.

Hibs had a casualty with a difference that week as trainer Tam McNiven injured his back lifting a kit hamper and was in considerable pain as a result. It was a case of 'physician, heal thyself', though, and Tam was soon mobile again.

It was back to football business at the weekend as Hibs travelled to Ayr looking for the win that would keep them very much in contention at the top of the League. Delaying his honeymoon until the close season allowed Des Bremner to occupy his usual midfield berth, while young Mike Wilson found a seat on the bench alongside Bobby Smith. The home side opened brightly and the impressive Johnny Doyle put them ahead with an early goal, but Duncan soon equalised and then MacLeod gave Hibs the lead. Showing much better form than had been on display against Dundee United the previous week, Hibs went on to control the remainder of the match and score a third goal, Duncan again being the man on target. It was Hibs' first away win in the League since the 2-0 'victory' at Parkhead had been annulled and it created a situation in the Premier League where just five points separated Rangers at the top from St Johnstone at the bottom.

The top five teams in the Premier League were covered by just one point when leaders Rangers came to Easter Road in the second half of November. The Ibrox men had stuttered slightly a few weeks back in losing two games in a row, but recent form had seen them scoring nine goals in their last two games. They arrived as League Cup holders, although St Etienne had ended their European dream by winning both legs of their second-round tie. In a pacy encounter with lots of good football on display, Hibs ran out 2-1 winners after Stanton had headed two beauties. Quinton Young scored for the 'Gers.

Hibs were on the road again a week later when they headed north to face St Johnstone at Muirton Park on a day that was to be a personal triumph for the popular Arthur Duncan. The flying winger was in top form, scoring a hat-trick and being brought down in the box for a penalty that Brownlie duly converted. The Saints were outplayed on the day and yet still managed to score three goals of their own, Charlie Smith nabbing two and his namesake Gordon another as the Hibs defence was guilty of sloppy marking.

The first Saturday in December took Hibs to Dens Park, where things went wrong virtually from the off. An early strike by Alex Caldwell had the visitors on the back foot for a long spell and when they did eventually start getting forward in search of an equaliser Caldwell popped up to add a second. In truth, Hibs rarely troubled the home defence and the day of misery was compounded by the late dismissal of John Blackley, who had incurred the wrath of referee Brian McGinlay and paid the ultimate penalty for one rash challenge too many.

In the following midweek, Hibs were at Parkhead to replay the game that had been abandoned due to fog earlier in the season with Hibs leading 2-0. It was a different story this time around as they had to settle for a 1-1 draw. Dixie Deans found the target for Celtic, while the visitors got their goal from the unlikeliest of sources, Erich Schaedler curling a long shot home when keeper Latchford was caught off his line. That was Erich's first goal since February 1973 and it was fully deserved on a night when Hibs played particularly well. John Brownlie had an outstanding game and was promptly called up to the Scotland squad, while Roy Barry also put in a good shift against a high-scoring and very mobile Celtic forward line.

Hibs were sitting joint top of the Premier League when Motherwell visited Easter Road in mid-December, but the visitors were only one place and one point behind them. Testimony to Motherwell's form was the fact that they had drawn five and lost one of their first six matches in the League race and yet they had fought back with a number of winning displays in recent weeks and had in their forward line Willie Pettigrew, once on the Hibs books as a youngster and a player who now ranked as one of the top scorers in Europe in the race to win the 'Golden Boot'. Already he'd scored 18 goals in domestic competition and was proving a hot handful for opposing defenders. He had been ably backed up by close-season signings Willie McVie, Colin McAdam and Vic Davidson, who had arrived from Clyde, Dumbarton and Celtic respectively. In a thrilling first 45 minutes, Hibs went ahead thanks to a Stanton header and might have doubled their lead had MacLeod's strike not come back off the post. The visitors were much livelier in the second half and struck the woodwork late on, but Jim McArthur was in great form and kept a clean sheet to give Hibs a 1-0 win. Just fewer than 16,000 fans turned up that day and they were well entertained by two sides looking to get forward at every opportunity.

With the holiday fixtures looming large as well as the halfway point in the League race, Hibs entertained joint leaders Celtic at Easter Road on the Saturday before Christmas. They say that Christmas is all about giving and not receiving, and the Hibs players certainly lived up to that description by inexplicably giving the visitors three soft goals. The defence that had played so admirably against Motherwell just seven days earlier could only stand and watch as Dixie Deans, Johannes Edvaldsson and Jackie McNamara all found the net, with only Arthur Duncan scoring at the other end. It was bitterly disappointing to lose 3-1 and more so because Celtic really didn't have to work very hard for the points.

The last game of 1975 took Hibs to Pittodrie to face a rejuvenated Aberdeen side that had found some form since Ally MacLeod had left Ayr United to fill the manager's chair vacated by Jimmy Bonthrone. Ally had his new side playing with a confidence not evident before his arrival and they were well worth the point they earned in an entertaining 2-2 draw. John McMaster and Billy Williamson struck for the home side, while Bremner and Duncan countered for Hibs and Jim McArthur saved a penalty. An interested spectator in the stand that day was former centre-half Sam Waldie, who had made the long trip from Inverness with his son, who was sporting a Hibs scarf to display where his allegiances lay! Waldie senior had signed for Hibs just after the Second World War and stayed at Easter Road for five years.

The festive period was tinged with great sadness around Easter Road when word came through that Sir John Bruce, chairman of the club until he retired during the last close season, had died in the Western General Hospital on 30 December, in his 70th year. Sir John, always a staunch Hibs supporter, had been a director for eight years. A surgeon by profession, he had used his expertise over the years to operate on a number of injured Hibs players and was respected throughout the world as an expert in his field.

The New Year began with the traditional derby match between Hibs and Hearts, with the Greens having home advantage on this occasion. The Gorgie side were doing well in the League and could boast the longest unbeaten run in the first half of the season, going eight games without defeat either side of losing to Celtic at Parkhead and then Tynecastle. Add to that good away wins at Dundee, Rangers, St Johnstone and Dundee United, and it was evident they were a match for anyone on their day. The Hibs side required a reshuffle at the back as Schaedler missed his first game of the season and that opened the door for Derek Spalding, who had come on as a substitute at Pittodrie the previous week. In goal for Hearts was Jim Cruickshank, whose recent displays had resulted in him being called into the Scotland squad. In a whirlwind first 23 minutes, Hibs found themselves 3-0 up, a scoreline they would protect for the remainder of the game as Hearts simply could not recover. Smith got the ball rolling in the 15th minute and Arthur Duncan added two more in the 19th and 23rd.

The match programme for that derby meeting carried a pen picture of former player Jock Weir, who had left the club around 30 years earlier to join Blackburn Rovers. He had attended the club's Centenary Dinner, and the programme carried a splendid picture of Jock in full Highland dress for the occasion. A teenager when he joined Hibs in season 1940/41, he scored a hat-trick in his first senior match, against Partick Thistle. When he left to join Blackburn it was said the fee was the highest paid for a player moving south up until that time, but he lasted only 12 months at Ewood Park before being transferred back north, to Celtic, before moving on to Falkirk and lastly Dumbarton. A speed merchant, Jock once clocked 9.8 seconds over 100 yards in a trial for the Powderhall Sprint.

A midweek thaw in Dundee looked as though it had arrived in time to make Tannadice playable for the visit of Hibs, but on the Friday night the temperature dropped to well below freezing and the pitch failed a Saturday-morning inspection, so the players got an unexpected weekend off. That day the draw for the third round of the Scottish Cup was made and Hibs came out of the hat to face Dunfermline at Easter Road later in January.

There were two new faces in the Ayr United party that arrived at Easter Road for the next League match. Alex Stuart had replaced Ally MacLeod as manager and there was a new signing, Malcolm Robertson from Raith Rovers. Robertson was an Edinburgh lad but worked in Greenock, so the move to the west coast suited him well. With Schaedler still ruled out, Spalding retained his place in the starting XI and played his part in an impressive 3-0 home win. Harper got two and was only denied a hat-trick by Hugh Sproat's fine goalkeeping, while Brownlie got the other from the penalty spot. Those were Harper's first goals for ten games and the little striker was glad to see that drought end. Brownlie had to take his penalty twice after referee Kyle spotted a Hibs player inside the box at the first attempt, but 'Onion' kept his nerve and took his tally to six penalties scored out of the last seven awarded.

The Premier League was still exceptionally tight at the top when Hibs travelled west to face Rangers at Ibrox in mid-January. The Glasgow side, sitting joint top with Celtic, maintained their position by winning this game 2-0. Hibs had their chances and should have scored either side of half-time but failed to do so and paid the price as Derek Parlane and Tommy McLean found a way past McArthur. Schaedler was back after injury, but Blackley dropped out due to suspension and the defence didn't have its usual solid look at times. The defeat meant that Hibs dropped to fourth place, albeit still only four points off the lead.

The latest quest for Scottish Cup glory began when Dunfermline visited Easter Road towards the end of January. Although in the First Division, the Pars were in decent form and included the fastest footballer in Scotland in their ranks. Kenny Thomson had earned that distinction when competing against other players in a special race arranged around the Meadowbank Sprint. It was a close thing, with Thomson reaching the finishing line just ahead of Arthur Duncan. But Dunfermline went into this tie missing their two most influential players through injury: Alex Kinninmonth had suffered a burst blood vessel in his leg and top scorer Ian Hall was recovering from a cartilage operation. Their absence would prove costly as Hibs cruised into the next round with an emphatic if narrow 3-2 win. With a few players struggling to find their form, Hibs made it difficult for themselves by conceding two very sloppy goals to Allan Reid and Ian Hunter, but Stanton, Harper and Smith scored the goals to set up a fourth-round clash at Easter Road against Dundee United.

On the same afternoon, the reserves played a friendly match against Partick Thistle at Firhill and earned a very creditable 3-2 win. Down 2-0 at one point, Hibs replaced Pat Carroll and Joe Forte with Mike Wilson and Brian Ross and the changes certainly worked as the Greens stormed back into the game and scored through Alex McGhee, Lindsay Muir and Ally McLeod. The centre-half trialist from previous games had earned a contract and so it was that Ally Brazil wore the No.5 jersey for Hibs that day.

During the following week, Hibs went on the transfer trail and secured the services of goalkeeper Mike McDonald from Stoke City. The former Clydebank stopper had been taken south by Stoke after that club's bid for Aberdeen goalie Bobby Clark had been rejected. Giving up his job as a wages clerk to go full-time with his new club, McDonald found his chances of first-team football were restricted and he only managed nine starts in his time there before Stoke shelled out £300,000 for Peter Shilton. Still, Mike had the opportunity to work with Shilton and the great Gordon Banks and felt his game had improved greatly as a result. At 6ft 3in and weighing more than 14st, he was an imposing figure between the sticks and would be easily capable of dealing with 'robust' centre-forwards.

McDonald made his debut that weekend when basement club St Johnstone were the visitors to Easter Road. Even though the League card was barely into its second half, the Perth club already looked doomed, with just two wins from 22 starts and a mere six points on the board. It was worth bearing in mind, however, that nine of the League defeats had been by the odd goal and indeed that had been the case when Hibs won 4-3 at Muirton Park some weeks earlier. It would be a quiet debut for McDonald, who was hardly troubled by the Saints attack, but the same could not be said for his opposite number, Derek Robertson, who was beaten five times on a tricky surface as Hibs went nap through a double from McLeod and others from Smith, Duncan and Phil Roberts, who put through his own goal. A welcome boost to the goal difference was engineered in the main by the clever midfield play of Alex Edwards, although Willie Murray, who had come off the bench in the first half to replace the injured Pat Stanton, also had a hand in one of the goals. Watching from the stand were the injured

Joe Harper and Jim McArthur – the latter perhaps thinking McDonald might be difficult to dislodge!

During the coming week, there were a number of significant announcements. Firstly, the club reported, ahead of its pending annual general meeting, that a trading profit of £47,000 had been achieved, although it was acknowledged that the transfer of Alex Cropley had prevented a loss. News also emerged that two Hibs players, Alex Edwards and Bobby Aitken, were due to face the SFA Referees' Committee in the following week, both having amassed enough points to warrant suspension. Finally, and sadly, news reached the club of the death in his 80th year of Hugh Shaw. Shaw was truly a Hibernian legend, having served the club as player, trainer and manager between 1918 and 1961 – which meant, of course, that he was there when the three League titles had been won in the late Forties and early Fifties.

With a game still in hand, Hibs went into their next match, against Dundee at Easter Road just four points behind leaders Celtic. This would be the fifth meeting of the season between the two. Hibs had won both of the League Cup ties but had only managed a draw and defeat in the League games. Although Dundee were in the lower half of the League, they had scored as many goals as Hibs, with Gordon Wallace the chief marksman. Mike McDonald retained his place in goal and made a strong statement of his intention to keep that place by having another shut-out. Thomson Allan, on the other hand, was beaten four times, Smith, Duncan, MacLeod and Stanton all finding the target. Significantly, Duncan's goal, a real beauty when he superbly controlled an Alex Edwards cross before firing home, was his 98th senior goal in the green and white of Hibernian as well as being his 12th in the League this season.

Having disposed of Dunfermline in the third round of the Scottish Cup, Hibs now faced Dundee United in what would be the home side's fourth consecutive match at Easter Road. It was the first time for 18 years that the sides had clashed in the competition. This current United team were a tough nut to crack, and Hibs had to settle for a 1-1 draw and a replay at Tannadice as Bremner's goal was cancelled out by Henry Hall. The draw for the quarter-finals had been made that afternoon and the winners of the replay would meet Motherwell at Fir Park.

By pure chance, Hibs would be at that stadium in their next match for a League encounter. In what many were calling a Cup rehearsal – which, given the fact Hibs had yet to face Dundee United in a replay, was somewhat premature – a close game was settled by one flash of brilliance when a cross from Brownlie saw Smith peel off his marker to steer a header high past Stewart Rennie's outstretched right hand. Smith was certainly settling into his role as a more regular starter in the first team and his versatility served him well in that he could play full-back, midfield or striker, depending on the wishes of the manager.

With Motherwell awaiting the winners, Hibs next travelled to Tannadice for that Cup replay and on a crisp February evening the Greens took the game to their hosts from the off, going into the lead through an unlikely source when Dundee-born Derek Spalding, in for the injured Roy Barry, struck a magnificent shot into the roof of the net from all of 35 yards, the sheer pace on the ball leaving Hamish McAlpine stranded. The home side set about looking for an equaliser, but Hibs were solid at the back and anything that did get through was ably dealt with by McDonald. Hibs looked the most likely to score next and that's exactly what they did when Edwards forced the ball home from close range and took the Greens into the next round.

That 2-0 replay victory should have boosted confidence, but this was a Hibs side with unpredictable tendencies, and when they visited Parkhead that weekend the travelling fans could only stand in depressed silence as the Glasgow side ruled the game from start to finish. Up until that day, Mike McDonald's performances had been quite good, but a four-goal blast from Celtic put a different complexion on things. A Dixie Deans penalty, along with strikes by Bobby Lennox, Paul Wilson and Kenny Dalglish, simply compounded the misery as Hibs lost not only the match but also Ally McLeod, who left the field in agony having broken his collarbone.

Neck and neck in the Premier League with just one point separating them, Hibs and Motherwell clashed at Fir Park in the Scottish Cup fifth round (quarter-final) on the first Saturday in March. A huge travelling support made its presence felt with loud singing throughout the match and the players certainly responded to that encouragement. Recovered from injury, Roy Barry was recalled and slotted into the back four alongside Blackley. Derek Spalding was given a midfield role and Alex McGhee was called up from the reserves to replace the injured McLeod in attack. Motherwell were at full strength and a rip-roaring Cup tie ensued. Goals from Willie Pettigrew and ex-Hibs star Peter Marinello were cancelled out by a cracking 18-yard drive from Spalding and a cool finish by Duncan to take the tie into a replay. After the match, manager Turnbull joked about having unearthed a new goalscorer in Derek Spalding and singled out both Alex McGhee and Lindsay Muir, who had replaced a limping Roy Barry in the second half, for particular praise. In general, he was more than happy with all of his players as they had shown a massive improvement on the form displayed at Parkhead the week before. The other quarter-finals played that day allowed the semi-final draw to be made, and so the Hibs and Motherwell players knew before they went into their replay that the 'prize' for winning through would be a semi-final clash with Rangers at Hampden.

Scottish Cup rules dictated that in the event of a draw the replay should be played on the first available midweek date, and so, four days after drawing at Fir Park, the sides met again at Easter Road. Roy Barry was injured again and Hibs gave a starting place to young Lindsay Muir, who operated in a midfield role with Spalding dropping back into the centre of defence alongside Blackley. In another very good and very entertaining Cup tie, the game went to extra time but still the sides could not be separated and the match finished at 1-1. Stanton scored for Hibs and Bobby Graham for Motherwell. Both sides had chances to win but could not find that all important second goal. During the extra-time period, Erich Schaedler was carried off on a stretcher and spent the night in the Royal Infirmary undergoing tests; thankfully, there was no serious damage. After the game it was announced that the sides would meet at neutral Ibrox the following Monday evening in their second replay.

The match programme for that first replay had an interesting article concerning a previous Cup meeting between the sides. Twenty-five years earlier, and in front of a staggering crowd of 48,800 at Tynecastle, Motherwell had beaten Hibs 3-2 in a semi-final clash that saw the Steelmen score in the first minute when a cross from ex-Hibs man Johnny Aitkenhead was headed home by Archie Kelly. Hibs then settled into the game on a muddy pitch, but tragedy struck when left-back John Ogilvie suffered a double fracture in his leg. As there were no substitutes allowed in those days, Bobby Combe switched to left-back and Hibs played the remainder of the tie with just ten men. Missing the guile of Combe in the middle of the park, Hibs battled on bravely and equalised through Lawrie Reilly, but Kelly scored again for 'Well to give them a 2-1 half-time lead. An early third goal made it a long second half for Hibs, even if they did score again through Reilly to give them a fighting chance. But when they also lost Willie Ormond to injury it was beyond the nine remaining men to equalise, although Gordon Smith did have the ball in the net only for referee Gerrard to disallow it for offside. The Hibs team that day included the immortal forward line of Smith, Johnstone, Reilly, Turnbull and Ormond.

The third meeting with Motherwell was put on the back burner for the weekend because Hibs had another playing engagement to fulfil before the game would take place and that involved a visit to Tynecastle on a cold and miserable Saturday afternoon in mid-March. It was the fourth and final meeting of the season and Hibs went into the game holding the upper hand, having won two and drawn the other against John Hagart's men. A crowd of 18,528 watched a milestone match for Arthur Duncan, whose goal not only won the game for Hibs but was his 100th in competitive games for the club. Stanton came close to making it 2-0, but was denied by a fine save from Jim Cruickshank, while at the other end McDonald was well protected by a back four minus the injured Schaedler. Willie Murray and Lindsay Muir came off the bench during the game and they both played their part in winning the two points that took Hibs to within four points of leaders Celtic.

Ibrox Park was a bedlam of noise for the Cup replay with Motherwell and the Hibs support in particular was in fine voice, watching the Greens dominate a first half and score through Harper. Two further golden opportunities to score were missed, however, and Motherwell capitalised by equalising when Peter Marinello scored from the penalty spot. They went on to score a second through ex-Aberdeen winger Ian Taylor. Hibs came storming back to put the 'Well goal under siege, and Blackley was unlucky to see his strong header beat keeper Stewart Rennie but then crash back off the base of a post. Arthur Duncan, celebrating another milestone in his 300th game for the club, also came close, but time ran out for Hibs and the Scottish Cup dream was over for another year, to the bitter disappointment of everyone connected with the club. In fact, Hibs had played six ties in the competition, scoring ten goals and losing eight in front of more than 100,000 spectators.

Targets still existed for Hibs as it was still possible to take the title and, of course, grab a qualifying spot for European competition in the coming season. But points from the remaining games were vital, and so it was hugely disappointing that Hibs lost their next game against Dundee United at Easter Road. A lacklustre performance saw Hibs struggling to create any real opportunities while United, anxious to earn the points that would take them away from the relegation zone, were content to sit in and hit on the break. It was from one such break that Henry Hall scored the only goal of the game and in doing so he administered a major blow to Hibs' title hopes.

On the following Wednesday evening, Easter Road hosted a European Championships match between Scotland and Holland at Under-23 level. The Dutch led 2-0 from the first game and Scotland hoped to overcome that with home advantage in the second leg. In front of an impressive crowd of 32,593, the young Scots, with Hibs men John Brownlie and Des Bremner in their ranks, got level in normal time and with no further goals arriving in extra time, the match went to a penalty shoot-out. Brownlie scored from his kick, but Joe Jordan and Tommy Craig missed, and so Scotland were eliminated.

A visit to Somerset Park gave Hibs a chance to get back to winning ways against a side who had only the doomed St Johnstone below them in the League and had lost their three previous Premier League games to the Greens. But once again Hibs were below par and lost the game 2-0 after Rikki Fleming and Malcolm Robertson scored for the home side. Even the dismissal of Ayr United's Jim McSherry 15 minutes from time made no difference. That defeat effectively removed any lingering thoughts that Hibs might have had of seeking to win the League, but it was important to get back to winning ways in the remaining games to ensure a UEFA Cup spot.

During the following week, the Greens took on Aberdeen at Easter Road in a rearranged League match. Since landing the job as manager, Ally MacLeod had seen a major improvement in the fortunes of the club, who now occupied a respectable mid-table position. A new face appeared in the Dons side, MacLeod having secured the services of striker Ian Fleming from Kilmarnock, while young centre-half Willie Garner was putting in some good performances to justify the manager's faith in him after promotion from the reserves. Hibs gave a couple of youngsters a start, Willie Murray wearing the No.8 jersey and Mike Wilson the No.9. Five goals were scored on the night. Murray and Lindsay Muir got the strikes that cancelled out those by Jocky Scott and Ian Fleming before, in the dying moments, John Blackley popped up to score the winning goal. It was a night of 'firsts' for Hibs, with Murray and Muir, who had come off the bench to replace the injured Edwards, getting their first senior goals and Blackley finding the target for the first time since November 1974. Although not on the scoresheet, the man of the match on the night was Arthur Duncan, whose tireless running and ability to deliver dangerous crosses into the box kept the Dons defence on edge all night.

The win over Aberdeen had Hibs in third place in the League, with Celtic and Rangers ahead of them fighting it out for the flag, but the Greens had their own interests to consider as Motherwell were challenging for that third spot, and the next League match, against Rangers at Easter Road, was sure to present a tough challenge. The Glasgow outfit were hungrier for the points on the day and a disappointing Hibs performance led to a 3-0 win for the visitors. John MacDonald, Martin Henderson and Derek Johnstone all beat Mike McDonald, while at the other end Peter McCloy had a relatively easy afternoon of it. After the match, word filtered through that Motherwell had won, making the race for third spot all the tighter.

At Ibrox on the same day, Ally McLeod made his comeback after recovering from his injury and linked up well with Joe Harper in attack to help the Greens win 3-2, Harper netting twice and Pat Carroll getting the other. Playing at outside-left that day was 19-year-old Gerry McCabe, who had played a couple of successful trials for the reserves while still with Polkemmet and had won a contract as a result. Harper, who had somewhat fallen out of favour at Easter Road, actually played his last game in the green and white of Hibernian that day before being transferred to Aberdeen.

There would be more transfer dealings that week, although the players on the move would have to content themselves with reserve team football initially because the transfer deadline date had passed. Leaving Easter Road was Iain Munro, who joined Rangers, while the Ibrox pair Ally Scott and Graham Fyfe joined Hibs in return. Of the two, Fyfe was the more experienced, having played in the Rangers midfield in European Cup matches, while Scott had joined the Ibrox club from Queen's Park in 1971. Another departure from Easter Road that week involved first-team coach Wilson Humphries, who severed his links with the club after three years. John Fraser, the reserve team coach, was immediately moved up to fill the gap.

An away visit to relegated St Johnstone gave Hibs the chance to get two more points on the board and they achieved that in a comfortable 2-0 win. Alex McGhee got his first senior goal of the season and Bremner weighed in with the other. At Easter Road on the same day, Messrs Fyfe and Scott featured for the first time in green and white as the second string won 3-0, Fyfe scoring the opening goal.

Up at Dens Park, Hibs fought out a 1-1 draw, but the point was won at a cost as Bremner had to leave the field with a shin wound that would require eight stitches and Edwards strained a groin, making both doubtful for the few remaining crucial League matches. Those injuries meant a reshuffle, with Lindsay Muir, Bobby Smith and Ally McLeod across the middle and young Alex McGhee up front. In fact, McGhee gave Hibs the lead, but before the end Bobby Ford equalised.

Saturday, 17 April 1976, was crunch day in terms of whether Motherwell or Hibs would secure third spot in the League and with it a guaranteed UEFA Cup place the following season. It could not have been closer as both sides had the same number of points and the same goal difference, although 'Well had scored more goals. Injuries made team selection very difficult for Eddie Turnbull, who put Willie Murray, Lindsay Muir and Alex McGhee in his starting XI, with Willie Paterson on the bench. Bobby Smith emphasised his versatility by filling in at right-back for the suspended Brownlie, and the way he marshalled the threat of Peter Marinello throughout the game was a delight to watch. When Duncan failed to appear for the second half following an early knock to his right knee, Willie Paterson came on to make his first-team debut and was involved in the move that ended with Alex McGhee firing Hibs into the lead. Motherwell then pressed forward looking for an equaliser, but it would be Hibs who scored the only other goal of the game when MacLeod took responsibility after a penalty was awarded and sent Stewart Rennie the wrong way.

Only three League games remained now and the first of those brought title-chasing Celtic to Easter Road. This was a game that the Parkhead side desperately needed to win in order to push leaders Rangers all the way in the title race, but Hibs had other ideas and won 2-0, with Smith and McLeod doing the honours, the latter from the penalty spot. Hibs' victory did little to help Celtic's cause but did a lot to ensure a third-place finish for the Easter Road side.

The penultimate game of the season meant a trip to Aberdeen, where the hosts were in a winning mood and duly disposed of Hibs by a 3-0 scoreline.

There was more woe on the last day of the season when another away trip, this time to Tannadice, brought another defeat, Mike McDonald twice having to pick the ball out of the net. Hibs had arrived in Dundee from the Highlands, where they had been playing in a testimonial match against Inverness Thistle. They won that one by 4-1, with goals from Ally Scott (2), Bobby Smith and John Brownlie.

Chapter Ten

1976/77

THE END OF AN ERA

Hibs kicked off the 1976/77 season with their third trip in five years to Ireland, where they were always assured of a friendly welcome. In their last two visits they had been undefeated and had not conceded a single goal, but manager Turnbull was wise enough to know that the games played were more about gaining match fitness than winning.

Dublin hosted the first game when Bohemian put up a strong fight and lost only to a John Brownlie penalty. Two days later it was the turn of the reigning Irish champions to host Hibernian. Dundalk were considered by all to be a decent outfit and so it was encouraging that Hibs dominated the game, especially in the midfield area, and ran out worthy 4-0 winners with Des Bremner (2), Lindsay Muir and Pat Stanton all getting their names on the scoresheet. Finally it was on to play Drogheda United, who finally scored a goal against Hibernian when Clarke gave the excited home fans reason to cheer. Sadly for the hosts, Hibs managed three goals of their own through Ally Scott (2) and an Ally McLeod penalty. So pleased were the Drogheda board with Hibs' decision to play them that they laid on a fine after-match dinner for the touring party.

A new face had appeared in the green and white of Hibernian on that tour. George Stewart, who had been playing centre-half in the Dundee team relegated at the end of the previous season, was snapped up by Eddie Turnbull with a view to bolstering the defence. An Edinburgh lad and a Hibs supporter to boot, George was over the moon when the Hibees came looking to offer him a contract because it ended what he thought of as a 13-year wait. As a young lad, he had played for Tynecastle Boys' Club and was being courted by both Dundee and Hibs. Feeling that chances of first-team football might be more likely on Tayside, he plumped for Dundee. Now, though, he was home in Edinburgh and absolutely delighted to be there. A second player to join the club in the close season was John Lambie, who joined the coaching staff in place of the now departed Wilson Humphries.

The League Cup group saw Hibs matched up with Montrose, St

Johnstone and Rangers, who had won the domestic treble the previous season, so it was accepted that it would be a tough task trying to qualify for the later stages. The first challenge came in the shape of an away trip to Montrose and the Angus club put up stiff resistance in losing only 1-0, with Scott on target for Hibs. Meanwhile, Rangers were thumping five past St Johnstone to confirm their intent to make every effort to hold on to the League Cup.

Rangers provided the next opposition when they visited Easter Road on Wednesday, 18 August 1976. The match drew a large crowd, including representatives of FC Sochaux of France, against whom Hibs had been drawn in the first round of the UEFA Cup. Chairman Tom Hart and manager Eddie Turnbull already had plans to view the French side in an upcoming match against St Etienne, and it was no surprise that the French club were also doing their homework.

The Rangers match was fast and furious with both sides looking to gain the two points on offer. Both keepers, McDonald for Hibs and McCloy for Rangers, were kept busy throughout the 90 minutes and on the balance of play the end result of 1-1 was probably fair. Ironically, both goals were scored by 'old boys', Ally Scott finding the net for Hibs and Iain Munro doing the same for Rangers. Man of the match was undoubtedly John Blackley, who looked to be continuing the form that had won him the Player of the Year Award from the Hibernian Supporters' Association. Up against the fearsome striking partnership of Derek Parlane and Derek Johnstone, 'Sloop' was in command throughout in stifling their forward play and denying them any real goalscoring opportunities. The Rangers defence played well, too, and after the game manager Jock Wallace singled out full-back Alex Miller for praise as he felt Alex Edwards had been much less influential thanks to Miller's marking of him. Miller, of course, would later go into management and had a ten-year spell with Hibs in that capacity.

A trip to Muirton Park, Perth, followed and many Hibs fans made the journey there not only aboard the usual buses laid on by the Supporters' Club branches but also by train, thanks to British Rail, which had put on a 'football special' at a cost of £2.10 return. The match itself finished 2-1 to Hibs, with Scott getting a double. Duncan Lambie, brother of the new Hibs coach, struck for the Saints, but there was a disappointing occurrence of crowd unrest and a number of Hibs fans were among those taken out of the ground by the police. The vast majority of fans present were on their best behaviour, but as ever it was the actions of the few that made the headlines the following day.

When Hibs visited Ibrox the following Wednesday night, both sides had a record of two wins and a draw in the group so far, and it was pretty well accepted that the victors of this meeting would be the team to progress to the last eight. On the night, the home side was just too strong for Hibs and coasted to a 3-0 win with an Alex Miller penalty and strikes from Sandy Jardine and Tommy McLean. Manager Turnbull was left to bemoan the fact that several players had not performed to their best and that the midfield had not ventured forward quickly enough to support Scott in the Rangers penalty area. Turnbull was trying to remodel the side, and some players were taking longer than expected to adapt to the new shape, but he declined to name names.

There was still an outside if unlikely chance that Hibs could qualify, but they needed to win their remaining two group games and hope that Rangers slipped up. The first of those games brought St Johnstone to Easter Road, and in the match programme chairman Tom Hart took the opportunity to lambast those Hibs fans who had been ejected from Muirton Park the previous week. With some dismay, he reported that of the ten spectators led out by the police, eight were from Edinburgh and three of that eight were still at school. Sadly, crowd disturbances were fairly common in those days, but Hart was determined that the good name of Hibernian would not be dragged through the mud and agreed with the Supporters' Association that if any of those ejected were members they should be immediately expelled.

Of course, the vast majority of fans went to the game to cheer on their team, and a decent crowd turned out at Easter Road in the hope that St Johnstone would be put to the sword. The visitors struck two sweet goals, but not sweet enough to prevent Hibs from running away with the game as poor Derek Robertson in the Saints goal was beaten nine times. Two Brownlie penalties, doubles from Muir and McLeod, plus singles from Bremner, Scott and Duncan, wrapped up the points and sent all in green home happy. Nine goals is a rarity in games and yet Hibs were doing it for the second time in as many years, Rosenborg being the victims last time out. That Ally Scott goal was his fifth in the competition and the ex-Ranger seemed to be enjoying himself in his new colours.

One more League Cup tie was required to be fulfilled and that brought Montrose to Easter Road. There wasn't a big crowd that night, and no-one was really expecting that anything of great note would occur. But how wrong they were. Arriving at the ground on that early September evening, fans were totally stunned to learn that Pat Stanton had been transferred to Celtic in a deal which brought Jackie McNamara to Easter Road. This seemed unbelievable, and there was an angry reaction from the terraces throughout 90 goalless minutes as fans vented their frustrations. To many, Pat Stanton *was* Hibs. A man who lived and breathed emerald green and white, a man who had captained the side and led them to three consecutive Cup final wins over Celtic, a man who had clocked up over 650 games since making his debut against Motherwell in 1963, a man whose loyalty to Hibernian was to be rewarded by the granting of a testimonial game.

In those days, fans relied heavily on local newspaper reports and stories/rumours from those who might just know what was going on. Today's instant information available via the internet was not even a dream at that time and certainly hadn't yet featured on the BBC's very popular science programme, *Tomorrow's World*. Over the days and weeks that followed Pat's departure, the common belief was that there had been a fall-out with manager Eddie Turnbull. Whatever the reason, Hibs fans could not have been more dismayed and many vowed, illogically but led by feelings of the heart rather than the head, to give McNamara a hard time. In its simplest form, Jackie would be held responsible for Pat's departure. It was, of course, a wholly ludicrous way of thinking, but passions were running high and the Hibs support needed someone to blame.

In the week following that tie with Montrose, Hibs were working hard preparing for their first League tie of the season, which brought Dundee United to Easter Road. The fans may have been reeling at the departure of Pat Stanton and no doubt a number of the players would also have been shocked, but football life goes on. Eddie Turnbull was determined to remould his side into an outfit that would win more games than it lost. The game heralded the debut of McNamara, who was given the midfield berth vacated by Stanton, and although he had a decent game he was on the losing side as United won 2-1. There were two penalties in the game, John Brownlie scoring for Hibs and goalkeeper Hamish McAlpine for United, who grabbed a very late winner thanks to a fine strike by new signing Gordon Wallace.

An inauspicious start for McNamara, then, as a subdued home support still mourned the loss of one of its greatest heroes. Fans were genuinely in the doldrums over Pat's departure and it would take a while before they recovered – although some never would, such was the reverence in which the player was held. The match programme that day, incidentally, confirmed that even although Pat had left the club he would still be getting his planned testimonial.

Having claimed third spot in the Premier League last season Hibs had started badly in losing at home to Dundee United, but there was improvement in the next game which saw the Easter Road men pick up a point in a 2-2 draw away to Motherwell. Hibs certainly came out of the blocks at 3pm and within 30 seconds they had the lead as Scott pounced on a loose ball in the box after Brownlie's snap shot had only been parried by Stewart Rennie in the home goal. Hibs dominated for long periods and were stunned when Bobby Graham equalised in a breakaway move that caught the defence flat-footed, but all looked to be good again when Willie Murray struck a second Hibs goal in the last five minutes of the game. Then the curse of the former player, a well-known footballing phenomenon, saw Peter Marinello equalise with almost the last kick of the ball.

Four days after securing that draw at Fir Park, Hibs welcomed Sochaux to Easter Road for the first leg of their first-round UEFA Cup tie. Eddie Turnbull and Tom Hart had watched the French side go down 2-0 to St Etienne the previous midweek, but the manager saw enough to ascertain that Sochaux would present a tough challenge, even though it was only their second foray in Europe. By comparison, Hibs were seasoned campaigners. Sochaux had finished third in their domestic league last season and were very close to winning the title outright, despite having few real 'stars' in the line-up. Keeper Joel Bats would go on to play for his country, while top scorer Robert Pintenat had already made international appearances and had notched 22 goals for Sochaux the previous season.

In a closely fought game, played in good spirit, Hibs secured a first-leg lead thanks to a goal from John Brownlie. Pintenat always looked lively for the French, but John Blackley, playing his 23rd game in Europe for Hibs, managed to subdue the striker throughout the 90 minutes. With McNamara ineligible, Lindsay Muir was drafted into midfield and gave a good account of himself, being involved in the build-up to Brownlie's goal.

Game three in the Premier League brought reigning League champions Rangers to Easter Road. Like Hibs, the Ibrox men had not had the best start to the season, drawing 2-2 with Celtic after being two goals up and then fighting out a dour 0-0 draw with newly promoted Kilmarnock, who provided stuffy opposition on the day the League flag was unfurled in Govan. Bobby Smith, who had started the season at left-back, had been pushed into the midfield against Sochaux and Eddie Turnbull decided to leave him there for this game, with Schaedler once again slotting in at left-back. It proved to be a bit of a master stroke by the gaffer: Hibs were a goal down to a Colin Smith strike when 'Smudger' Smith blasted the ball past Peter McCloy from 25 yards to earn them a valuable point. It was an absolute belter of a shot from the man who would go on to play many games for Hibs in many different positions and whom the *Mass Hibsteria Fanzine* had dubbed 'The Perminator' in honour of his bushy Seventies perm. On a more sombre note, George Stewart, who had started the season really well at his new club, suffered a groin injury in what was a pretty physical game.

Jackie McNamara had been recalled to the starting line-up after missing out against Sochaux, and it is fair to say that his performances were winning the disgruntled fans over after his arrival to replace Pat Stanton. Although he was aware of the resentment, he did not allow it to impair his performances. In the programme for the Rangers game, he commented: 'I was delighted to join Hibs and I feel confident that I have a lot to give them.' Time would prove those words to be very true.

A second home game in succession for Hibs brought Aberdeen to Easter Road on 25 September, and despite plenty of goalmouth action neither side could find the net. Bizarrely, going into that game, the fourth of the season, Hibs, Hearts, Celtic and Rangers had still to record their first win. It was Dundee United who were setting the pace, with Aberdeen tucked in behind them. If nothing else, this game gave the defence a boost in keeping a clean sheet as the next game was away to Sochaux in the UEFA Cup. Hibs were taking the narrowest of leads to France, and it was important that they tried not to concede a goal to give the French side hope.

In the event, the Sochaux encounter was a tense and sometimes bad-tempered affair as the home side's frustration grew due to their failure to break down a resolute Hibs defence. In fact, Hibs could have sealed it but for the fact that Smith's shot crashed back off the crossbar with Joel Bats well beaten. At the end of the 90 minutes neither side had scored, so Hibs progressed to the next round, where they would face the Swedish side Osters Vaxjo.

Having negotiated safe passage in Europe, Hibs returned to Scotland for an away game with Celtic, who had themselves been on European duty the previous midweek in Poland. Both sides looked determined from the off and when Tony Higgins put Hibs in front the home crowd was silenced. That silence persisted as Hibs continually took the game to the Parkhead men, and it was hard to see where an equaliser might come from until referee Gordon of Newport took a hand in proceedings. John Brownlie brilliantly tackled and dispossessed Johnny Doyle in the Hibs 18-yard box, and as the Celtic man went to ground the referee pointed to the spot. Even the Celtic players had the good grace to look stunned at this award, but they took advantage of the lifeline offered and Kenny Dalglish earned them a point they never looked worthy of getting.

Hibs had been due to meet Kilmarnock next, but that game was postponed and they took advantage of an otherwise blank weekend to visit Newcastle United for a friendly match. Ally Scott was on target for Hibs and it was generally accepted that a draw would have been a fairer result on the balance of play, but the hosts won 2-1. Over the years, Hibs and Newcastle United had met in friendlies on numerous occasions, first in September 1894, when Hibs travelled to Tyneside and won 3-1.

With five draws and one defeat to date, Hibs were suffering from drawing too many games and their League position needed a boost, with many thinking that their next opponents, newly promoted Partick Thistle, could provide them with points. In fact, the Jags frustrated Hibs throughout a dull 90 minutes when neither team could find the net. It is interesting to note that playing for Partick Thistle that day were goalkeeper Alan Rough, whose heroics would one day raise loud cheers at Easter Road, and Alan Hansen, who would go on to carve out a place in the history of Liverpool FC before hanging up his boots to take up TV punditry.

The following midweek brought Osters Vaxjo to Easter Road for the first leg of the second-round tie in the UEFA Cup. Manager Turnbull had been to Sweden to watch the opposition lose 4-3 to Djurgaardens, a side Hibs had met and beaten in the past. His view was that the Swedes were a decent outfit and looked likely to attack rather than follow the set pattern of defending away from home in Europe. Like Sochaux before them, Osters did not arrive with a team full of star players but one or two had good experience and international caps. Keeper Goran Hagberg and midfielder Anders Linderoth were the pick of the bunch, but fans attending that night were going to see many players they had not heard of before.

There was a feeling of great sadness around Easter Road that evening with news of the death of club stalwart Davie Shaw. As a player, Shaw had captained Hibs to their first post-war League championship in 1947/48, having been signed as a youngster in 1939 by Willie McCartney. Capped nine times by Scotland, he joined Aberdeen in 1950 and remained there for 17 years as player, trainer and ultimately manager. Just 60 years old, he would be fondly remembered and sadly missed by all who knew him.

As to the match itself, Osters proved Eddie Turnbull right by playing a brand of attacking football rarely seen from visiting teams in European ties. But they could not find a way through a resolute Hibs defence, which recorded its third clean sheet in that season's competition. At the other end, Blackley took a break from his defensive duties to put Hibs ahead and doubled the advantage from the penalty spot.

A visit to Somerset Park, Ayr, on Saturday, 23 October, saw Hibs finally secure that elusive first Premier League win of the season – largely due to the heroics of Mike McDonald in goal. The game ebbed and flowed, with Graham, from the spot, and Ingram scoring for Ayr, but Hibs securing a 3-2 victory through a Brownlie penalty and strikes from Smith and Duncan. In the latter part of the game, Ayr were throwing everything into attack and won a late penalty, but McDonald pulled off a magnificent save to ensure a win bonus for himself and his team-mates.

Four days later, Hibs were back in Ayrshire to face newly promoted Kilmarnock, a side languishing near the foot of the table. Fighting as if for their lives, even this early in the season, Killie were well worth the point earned in a 1-1 draw. Des Bremner was the marksman for Hibs, while a future SFA head honcho, Gordon Smith, found the net for the home side.

When Hearts visited Easter Road on Saturday, 30 October, their League record to date made dismal reading: eight games played, none won, six drawn, two lost. Twelve goals had been scored but 15 conceded, leaving the Gorgie men on just six points and third from bottom of the table. Add to that the fact that they arrived having lost a midweek match at Hampden which saw Celtic qualify for the final of the League Cup, and you can maybe understand why there were a few nervous fans wearing maroon scarves inside the stadium.

The programme for that game carried the grim news that a former Hibs and Hearts favourite, the mercurial Willie Hamilton, had died in Canada at the age of just 37. Willie was adored at Easter Road and played many fine games in green and white, his best performance arguably coming against the giants of Real Madrid. A footballing genius, he had his troubles off the park, but it would be his performances on it that left fans with some wonderful memories.

Given the 'draw' record of both Hibs and Hearts, it should have come as no surprise to those present that the spoils would be shared that day. A cracking goal by young Willie Paterson was cancelled out by Hearts' tricky winger, Bobby Prentice, and both sets of fans went home happy not to have lost but equally disappointed not to have won.

That match was the last for Hibs before they travelled to Sweden for the second leg of their UEFA Cup tie against Osters Vaxjo. To date, Hibs had not conceded a goal in the competition and were the only side with a clean sheet, although Dynamo Kiev and St Etienne had matched that feat in their European Cup games. The players had won comfortably at Easter Road and were confident of progressing, but they were in for a shock as Osters hammered them 4-1 to go through 4-3 on aggregate. Scott scored for Hibs, but it was a huge disappointment to crash out of the tournament at a stage where progression could have brought a quality side to Easter Road and would have boosted the club income.

Back in Scotland, a tricky trip to Tannadice was next on the agenda. Dundee United were setting the pace at the top of the League and were scoring freely. They added another two goals to their tally in a 2-1 victory over Hibs. Bobby Smith found the target with a typical long-range effort, but Gordon Wallace and Tom McAdam won the points for the home side, although the winning strike was hotly disputed as having been offside. Although the goals won the game for United, special mention must be made of the heroics of Hamish McAlpine in the home goal as he pulled off a serious of quite wonderful saves to deny the Hibs forwards.

Another blank Saturday followed as teams were out of action to help Scotland's World Cup qualifying campaign. In the following midweek, Stoke City arrived at Easter Road for a friendly. City had the distinction of being the second oldest League club in England, behind Notts County, and they had a number of very useful players on their books. In goal would be veteran Gordon Banks, who had won a World Cup winners' medal in 1966 but who had later suffered a serious injury to an eye in a car accident which was to cut short his career. He still played in benefit games and friendlies and it was a bonus that he turned out for Stoke that night, giving the home support a chance to see the great man in action. Also in the Stoke line-up was England cap Mike Pejic and a promising youngster by the name of Garth Crooks, who scored the only goal of the game as Banks and his defensive colleagues closed out the Hibs attack.

Three days later, Hibs were at Ibrox and yet again were involved in a draw, their ninth in 12 starts and their third of the season against Rangers. It could all have been so different. After being dominated for the opening half hour, during which Derek Parlane gave Rangers the lead, Hibs came storming back to run the show for the rest of the game. A Jim Steele own-goal got Hibs level just before the interval, but despite having the better of the game in the second half they could not get that elusive winner. Their cause had not been helped any by the fact that Alex Edwards had to leave the match in the first half after being on the receiving end of a number of robust tackles. The absence of the little playmaker's guile in midfield meant that chances to win the game were not created so fluently.

In the midweek following the draw at Ibrox, Motherwell came to Easter Road on League business just one point ahead of Hibs, and the hope was that Turnbull's men could leapfrog their Lanarkshire opponents, who had former Hibs favourite Jimmy O'Rourke wearing the No.9 jersey. Just as he had done for Hibs, Jimmy was scoring freely and came into the game having notched eight goals in eight games. He failed to find the target that night, but team-mates Willie Pettigrew and Bobby Graham did, to give 'Well a 2-0 win.

Things were starting to look a little bleak for Hibs by this time as they were perilously close to the wrong end of the table. Indeed, the two clubs below them had managed more wins than Hibs. A change of form to winning ways was somewhat overdue when they travelled to Pittodrie to face an Aberdeen side riding high near the top of the table. Hibs played well and probably deserved something from the game, but a solo strike by Joe Harper sent them home empty handed. Alex McGhee had been given his chance in this game, and although the youngster played well he could not find a way past a very well organised Aberdeen defence.

A cold snap at the start of December meant that Hibs were out of action until the 18th, when they played Partick Thistle at Firhill. Yet again, they could manage only one point. On a snow-covered pitch both sides struggled to put together any sort of passing game and although Graham Fyfe managed to score his first Premier League goal for the club, Doug Somner equalised within 60 seconds to cut the celebrations short. To be fair, Fyfe's goal was a bit special as he rifled the ball home from 30 yards with Alan Rough well beaten. The big goalie did redeem himself with two wonderful saves to deny young Alex McGhee, who had retained his starting place in the team.

Christmas Eve 1976 brought lowly Ayr United to Easter Road and it was not lost on the fans that the Somerset Park side were the only one Hibs had beaten that season in the League. Ayr manager Alex Stuart had been strengthening his team and had signed both 6ft 3in centre-forward Walker McCall and goalkeeper Andy Geoghegan from Aberdeen to bolster his squad. Both played in a stuffy game in which the sides were separated only by a goal from Ayr's Joe Filippi. Fortunately for Hibs, it was an own-goal, and it gave the Easter Road side only their second League win of the season. Going into that game, Hibs had scored fewer goals than any other team and so it was perhaps no surprise that they needed an Ayr player to win them the points.

The winter weather kicked in again with a vengeance, forcing postponements galore, and one of the casualties was the New Year's Day fixture at Tynecastle, for which the police had insisted not only that there should be a maximum attendance of 30,000 but also that the match should be all-ticket. As it turned out, Hibs did not play again until 5 January, against Dundee United at Easter Road. The game had been originally scheduled for the 3rd, when frost made the pitch unplayable. United had led the League for a spell, but had shaded a little going into this game. Given Hibs' ineffectiveness in front of goal and United's dip in form, it was perhaps unsurprising that the game ended at 0-0. Alex McGhee had the best of the chances for Hibs, but was generally well marshalled throughout by David Narey at the heart of the United defence.

In the match programme for that game there was an interesting article on former player Jock Brown, a goalkeeper who had joined Hibs in 1941. One of those players whose Hibs career was lessened by the need for service in the Second World War, Jock nevertheless enjoyed his time at Easter Road, playing in teams alongside the likes of Bobby Baxter, Davie Shaw, Matt Busby, Gordon Smith and Bobby Combe. After retiring from football, he turned his attention to rugby and became physiotherapist to the Scotland rugby team. In time, his sons Peter and Gordon would go on to win many Scotland rugby caps as they chose to play that sport in preference to football.

The following midweek, Hibs travelled west to take on Motherwell, who were in the same bottom half of the table as Eddie Turnbull's men. Once again, it was honours even in a 1-1 draw, Brownlie netting for Hibs, his eighth of the season, and old favourite Jimmy O'Rourke finding the target for the Steelmen. In his time at Easter Road Jimmy had scored goals aplenty, and his old club would have loved to have a goalscorer with his strike rate on their books again. Perhaps letting Jimmy go was not one of Turnbull's better judgement calls?

Another cold snap hit the fixture card and Hibs were idle until 22 January when a thaw enabled the home game against Aberdeen to go ahead. The Dons arrived as League leaders and had conceded just 19 goals in 18 games, indicating just where their main strengths lay. With a game fewer played, Hibs went into the match having conceded just 18 goals, but the main difference was in the number of goals scored, with the Dons on 34 and Hibs on just 15. Chances were at a premium on a tricky surface and neither side could find the net, even though Hibs dominated in large parts of the game. The result meant that Hibs had now drawn 12 of their 18 games.

The programme issued for the Aberdeen game contained an article giving the quite surprising news that Hibs had accepted an offer to tour Australia in the coming close season. In recent years the club had only toured relatively close to home and so a trip to the other side of the world was quite something. The plan was to play six matches in three weeks and ex-pat Hibs fans who had made a new life for themselves Down Under must have been drooling at the prospect of seeing their favourites in the flesh again.

When Hibs headed to Tynecastle to fulfil the fixture postponed on New Year's Day, Hearts were mid-table and had suffered like Hibs in drawing too many games, so a share of the spoils was clearly on the cards. On the night, Hibs dominated their hosts and won the game thanks to a magnificent strike by Ally McLeod, who showed no ill effects from playing his second game in two days following a reserve team outing. The defence stood firm throughout and it was a very happy Hibs support that made its way home that night. That victory made it nine straight League games without defeat against Hearts and, more importantly given the hullabaloo their fans would make in the years ahead, it was the 22nd year in a row that Hibs had remained unbeaten at Tynecastle in the New Year derby. Certainly, Tynecastle was a much happier hunting ground at that time than it would prove to be in future.

Next up was a trip to Glasgow to face title-chasing Celtic, and for once a normally solid defence had a bit of a nightmare in conceding four goals. Ronnie Glavin (2), Johannes Edvaldsson and Joe Craig scored for the Hoops while at the other end Smith and another from McLeod put a better complexion on the scoreline.

Astonishingly, just a day after losing at Parkhead, the Hibs first team were back in action when they met Partick Thistle at Easter Road in the Scottish Cup. This would be the first time Hibs had played on a Sunday and it was to be a winning first as they put Thistle to the sword by 3-0. The weather had cost Thistle competitive games and this was their first for three weeks, their rustiness very much in evidence. Smith, McLeod and Bremner scored the goals which took Hibs through to round four, where they would meet Arbroath at Gayfield. Hibs and Thistle had been bumping into each other in the Cup quite regularly and had met in 1965 when Thistle were beaten 5-1. Jackie Campbell, the Thistle defender, had played that day and was in the team again for this tie some 11 years later, a club stalwart if ever there was one.

After that double header, the players had six days to recover before heading to Rugby Park to face Kilmarnock in the League. Killie's season had been of nightmare proportions and they were stuck at the bottom of the League both before and after this game, which Hibs won with an Ally McLeod goal. Hibs didn't play to their best but were still strong enough to take both points, something they had not managed to do in a League game at Rugby Park for some 19 years. It was a relief for the club to finally end that hoodoo as well as continue their slow but steady climb up the League table. That was McLeod's fourth goal in four games and there was little doubt his return to fitness was making a noticeable change for the better in Hibs' results of late.

With all of the postponements caused by the bad weather it meant that there would have to be a good few midweek games to clear the backlog, and it was in the next midweek that Rangers came to Easter Road. Sitting third in the League, they were six points behind Celtic with a game more played, and they were still smarting at having lost their last match when Dundee United beat them at Ibrox. Hibs were a further six points behind Rangers, and there was no change at the end of the game, which finished in a 0-0 draw. It was a bruising battle, with Alex Edwards in particular coming in for some rough treatment – all the harder to take when the Hibs man was booked for protesting too loudly about that treatment to referee Tommy Muirhead.

The following Saturday brought Partick Thistle to Easter Road, this time in the League and having managed to get some games under their belts they were not nearly as rusty as they had been for the recent Cup tie. Indeed, they very much gave as good as they got and Bobby Smith's goal, his fifth in the League for the season to date, was cancelled out by a smart strike from Denis McQuade.

More news came out on the close-season tour front when Hibs announced that the original trip to Australia was now turning into a bit of a world tour. Hong Kong would provide a stopover on the way to Australia and while there Hibs would play Hong Kong Rangers. After that it would be two matches in Australia before the club would move on to New Zealand for games against Auckland FC and Caledonia. From there it was on to Tahiti against Papeete and a yet to be named second side before finishing up in either Acapulco or Los Angeles.

The Scottish Cup tie with Arbroath was next up on the fixture list, and on a very muddy pitch Hibs were extremely fortunate to force a replay with a late equalising goal by John Blackley, much to the relief of the travelling fans. The home side had given their visitors a torrid time and led for a long time through Tommy Yule's goal. The incentive to get through this tie was obvious in the shape of a very lucrative home tie against either Dundee or Aberdeen, but Hibs came within just minutes of losing out on that possibility.

It was Scottish Cup replay time when Arbroath visited Easter Road and that awful Cup hoodoo was to strike Hibernian once again. Despite an early lead, provided by MacLeod, Hibs contrived to miss chance after chance and the visitors made a much better job of theirs in scoring through Tommy Yule and John Fletcher. A disgruntled crowd poured out of Easter Road that night and it would be of little consolation for them to know that the players were equally upset at the defeat. This latest defeat meant that it had now been 75 years since Hibernian's name had appeared on the Scottish Cup, and little did the fans know that the 75 would extend into triple figures in the years ahead.

Three days later, Hibs set out for Somerset Park, Ayr, in the knowledge that the previous two meetings had won them four points. Both of those games had been close and this third meeting followed the same pattern, with Hibs winning 2-1. A headed goal by Walker McCall was cancelled out by Duncan's strike and Higgins, one of a number of new faces in the team after that shocking Cup exit, scored the winning goal.

In the following midweek, basement boys Kilmarnock arrived at Easter Road desperate for the points that might keep them in with a fighting chance of survival, but Hibs were in no mood to do them any favours and dominated throughout, winning the game 2-0 with goals from Smith and McLeod.

A blank Saturday for the first team meant that the fans could turn up in numbers for the Second XI Cup semi-final tie against Aberdeen at Easter Road. The Dons fielded a fairly strong XI, but Hibs won the game relatively comfortably by 2-0, Ally Scott getting both goals. It was a good game and Derek Spalding, Jackie McNamara and Ally Scott were the pick of the bunch for Hibs.

Having enjoyed a ten-day break, Hibs next travelled to Tannadice to face a United team still very much in the race for the League title. In the first half hour Hibs looked the better side, but fell behind to a Paul Hegarty header when the big defender found himself some space at a corner. Hibs fought back and were awarded a second-half penalty, but that wily old fox Hamish McAlpine saved Brownlie's kick and the points were lost. That had been the first penalty Hibs had been awarded for five months, and so Brownlie was somewhat out of practice, but it would be wrong to take anything away from the keeper's outstanding save. The game saw defender John Blackley go through the 400-appearance mark.

The third Edinburgh derby of the season brought Hearts to Easter Road on Wednesday, 23 March 1977. The previous two games had produced a draw at Easter Road and a win at Tynecastle. As the sides lined up for kick-off, Hibs were fifth in the table with 26 points while Hearts were third from bottom with just 20. Add to that the fact that in the last 19 League games between the two clubs Hearts had only one win, and you can imagine that the home supporters were in a relatively confident mood. As it turned out, they had every right to be as Hibs cruised to a 3-1 win, thanks to goals from that man McLeod again, Smith and Ally Scott. Willie Gibson scored for Hearts, but it was little more than a consolation for the Gorgie men, who had Malcolm Robertson, signed from Ayr United for £25,000, making his debut.

Earlier that week, two stalwarts of Hibs' oldest rivals had passed away. Willie Bauld and John Harvey had been great players for Hearts and were much respected in the game. In the derby match programme, the club passed on its deepest sympathy to the families.

Also in the match programme that evening was exciting news of yet another first for Hibernian Football Club. A three-year sponsorship deal had been struck with leading British sports goods manufacturer Bukta, and it would see the company's name displayed on the front of the Hibs jerseys from the start of next season. The SFA had given consent to clubs to explore this area of sponsorship and Hibs were the first to announce a deal, although the SFA would first be required to sanction the use of the sponsors' name on the front of the shirt. It was a groundbreaking deal that would bring welcome cash to the club.

With the season in its last quarter, Hibs had recovered quite well from a slow start. Without so many draws early in the campaign, the Easter Road men might have gone into their next match, at home to Motherwell, better placed than just fifth and a full five points behind fourth-placed Aberdeen. As it was, Hibs had another of those days when they dominated proceedings, took a first-half lead through McLeod and then threw it all away in the second half when slack marking allowed Willie Pettigrew to score twice. It was so frustrating to be on top and then lose out and Eddie Turnbull must have been tearing his hair out by the time the final whistle blew.

That goal from Ally McLeod was his 11th of the season, which may not sound a lot but was an impressive strike rate, given that he had been out for a long time with knee problems and had played only 20 games. At the other end of the park, Erich Schaedler put in another sterling performance, and it's a pity his defensive team-mates had those costly lapses.

Wednesday, 30 March, brought Celtic to Easter Road on League business in a game that had been postponed earlier in the season. It would be the first of two meetings between the sides in the space of a fortnight and Hibs would have home advantage on both occasions. Celtic arrived as League leaders, some five points ahead of Dundee United with a game in hand, but Hibs made it a difficult afternoon for them and the final result of 1-1 was fair on the balance of play. Once again, the Hibs marksman was McLeod, while Ronnie Glavin netted for the Celts. There was a certain irony in that game in that the best player on the park by a long way was Pat

Stanton, perhaps trying to demonstrate to his old gaffer that there was plenty of life left in him yet.

Hot on the heels of that joust with Celtic was a visit to Ibrox to face the other side of the Old Firm. It was a close game, but Rangers came out on top by 2-1, goals from Derek Parlane and Derek Johnstone coming after Smith had given the Hibees a half-time lead.

The second of what would be a run of three away games followed when Hibs visited Pittodrie and earned a very creditable 0-0 draw. Both sides had chances, but defences won the day and neither manager felt the result unjust, although McLeod's spot kick attempt might just have stolen the points for the visitors had goalkeeper Ally MacLean not made such a good save. That was the third goalless draw between the pair this season. Making his Hibs debut that day was Ally Brazil, a reward for his string of fine performances in the reserves.

In the following midweek, Hibs travelled across town for the fourth and final Premier League meeting of the season against Hearts. The Gorgie club were struggling in second-bottom place in the League and things looked bleak for them after two stinging shots from outside the box by Bremner flew past Jim Cruickshank in the home goal, but Willie Gibson pulled one back to give them hope and in the dying seconds of the game Jim Brown squeezed the ball beyond McDonald to salvage a point. The result, however, would not be enough to help Hearts avoid relegation. Astonishingly, it was the 17th League draw of the season for Hibs, equalling a record that had stood for more than 50 years, Falkirk having drawn 17 out of 42 games in the 1920s.

Saturday, 16 April 1977, saw the League title won at Easter Road – not by Hibs but by their visitors, Celtic, who won 1-0 thanks to a Joe Craig goal. Hibs gave the Celts a good run for their money and Brazil was outstanding in the home midfield, but for once McLeod could not find the net and it was the visiting fans who stayed on to celebrate after the final whistle. Notably, Des Bremner clocked up his 200th appearance for the club in that game and man of the match by a big margin was Erich Schaedler, who looked fresh and eager despite the season nearing its end.

The next midweek brought Ayr United to Easter Road, and although their good away form had been a major contribution in keeping them in the Premier League, it deserted them that night as Hibs recorded their fourth win of the season over the Somerset Park side, with goals from Scott and Bremner, the latter hitting the target with a superb diving header to meet a corner taken by Arthur Duncan. Missing from the side was Derek Spalding, who was serving a suspension. In fact, his absence was about to become permanent because, having married a Chicago lass, he planned on emigrating to the United States at the end of the season.

That midweek tie against Ayr was Hibs' 16th home League game of the season and a staggering eight of those had been played in midweek because of the severe winter weather. As midweek games generally attracted fewer spectators, a significant drop in gate money was the result, and so that Bukta sponsorship money would be all the more welcome when it arrived.

The last home game of the season brought relegated Kilmarnock to Easter Road and it was a typically dull affair with no goals and very little creative play by either side. It was a landmark game of sorts, though, as Hibs bagged that unenviable draw record for themselves. A week later, the season ended with a disappointing 1-0 away defeat to Partick Thistle. This meant that Hibs had finished with the best defensive record in the Premier League, but only bottom-placed Kilmarnock had scored fewer goals. The curse of the draw had scuppered Hibs from attaining a higher finish.

Unfortunately, the proposed 'world tour' was cancelled after negotiations broke down, leaving everyone at the club a tad disappointed, and who could blame them?

Chapter Eleven

1977/78
'SHADES' DEPARTS

With no 'world tour', the playing staff had the summer off and came back fully refreshed and ready for another tilt at the domestic prizes on offer. There were no new faces on the playing staff, but there was an addition in the boardroom as Alan Hart, son of chairman and managing director Tom, joined the club. At just 27, Alan still played a bit of football himself and had been a centre-forward with Edinburgh Albion and Portobello Volta in the Maybury League. A quantity surveyor by profession, his favourite Hibernian memory was of the defeat of Barcelona in the Fairs Cup.

By way of preparing for competition, Hibs travelled north for a short tour of the Highlands and based themselves in Elgin. Three games would be played and the first of those was against Deveronvale, the club from which Hibs had signed Des Bremner and for which his brother, Kevin, still played. In the pouring rain, Arthur Duncan was giving the home defence a torrid time and set up a number of the goals in a 6-0 win. Ally McLeod led the way with a hat-trick, while Des Bremner celebrated his return to the Princess Royal Park in Banff with a smart double and Ally Scott, on in the second half for Duncan, got the other.

Inverness Thistle proved a tougher nut to crack even after Bremner had opened the scoring in the first 60 seconds of the game. Thistle struck back to equalise before George Stewart headed his first goal in Hibernian colours. Thistle equalised again, but a second-half strike from McLeod secured victory for the visitors.

The tour ended against Elgin City at Borough Briggs Park, where the home side were blitzed 7-0 by a rampant Hibs outfit. Ally Scott got two, with Bremner, Duncan, Pat Carroll, Smith and Willie Paterson all finding the net. The tour had been very useful for honing up the match-practice levels of the players, and it was particularly pleasing to note that the midfield players had weighed in with a few goals, something that had been missing from team performances during the previous campaign.

This season would be the one which heralded changes to the Scottish League Cup format. It would no longer be played on a group basis but would be a straight home-and-away draw, with the aggregate winners in each tie moving through to the next round. This season, too, would see Hibs competing for the first time in the Anglo Scottish Cup, formerly known as the Texaco Cup, the company having ceased its sponsorship of the tournament. Hibs would first play against Ayr United and the winners of the two-leg tie would progress to face English opposition. The clubs from south of the border, drawn into four regional qualifying groups, included the likes of Bolton Wanderers, Blackburn Rovers, Fulham, Chelsea, Birmingham City and Sheffield United, while Hibs were joined in Scotland by clubs such as Motherwell and St Mirren.

The first Anglo Scottish Cup game brought Alex Stuart's Ayr United to Easter Road. The Somerset Park side had narrowly avoided relegation from the Premier League in the previous season, thanks largely to their good away form, so this tie would not be an easy one. Giant striker Walker McCall was on target for Ayr, but Smith and McLeod found the net to win the day for Hibs and give them a lead to take west in the second leg. Those goals were crafted by Des Bremner and Arthur Duncan, who continued to show the fine form displayed on the Highland tour.

Out of the team that night due to injury was Alex Edwards, newly voted Player of the Year by the Hibs Supporters' Association, a victory he achieved by a handsome margin. A wonderful footballer with a keen eye for the killer pass, he had certainly earned his reward with countless excellent performances the previous season. The only sour note about the game against Ayr was that big George Stewart took a sore one on the knee and finished the game limping.

The match programme, increased in price from 10p to 12p due to higher printing costs, included one or two interesting articles and adverts. John Blackley, whose summer had been spent touring South America with the Scotland squad, recounted a tale of the half-time break in the Boca Juniors stadium in Argentina. He had been out on the park with the other substitutes and undertook a bit of juggling with the ball. 'I have a habit of resting the ball on the back of my neck if I want a breather,' he said. 'At first I wondered what the fans were shouting about and when I realised it was my juggling act I kept it going until the interval was over. As I left the park I gave the fans a bow and they loved it!' This was typical Blackley behaviour, as throughout his time at Easter Road he would always have a laugh and a joke for the fans.

Further news included the fact that there was now a Premier Reserve League which would mirror the clubs in the top flight and replace the haphazard set-up of previous seasons. There were high hopes for the Hibs 'wee team' as they'd run the League close and reached both their Cup finals in the previous season. In terms of adverts, it's perhaps unsurprising that the new kit sponsors, Bukta, featured prominently, while the tailors Tom

Martin had a half-page spread suggesting that there was no other place to buy the latest men's fashions. Once you'd bought your threads, you might then take your car to ACE Accessory Centre, Edinburgh, where all your motoring needs would be met!

Saturday, 13 August, heralded the start of the Premier League campaign and brought Motherwell to Easter Road. The Lanarkshire side had hit goalscoring form in their Anglo Scottish Cup game, when Alloa conceded seven with ex-Celt Vic Davidson nabbing five of them. They arrived in confident mood, but without the services of ex-Hibee Jimmy O'Rourke, who was recovering from illness. In their side, though, were another ex-Hibs man, Peter Marinello, and the previous season's top scorer in the League, Willie Pettigrew. All in all, with Hibs also finding the net regularly, the fans might have expected a goal feast, but it was exactly the opposite as both sides cancelled each other out and neither keeper was beaten. On Hibs' substitutes' bench that day was 19-year-old centre-forward Gordon Rae, signed from Whitehill Welfare. Gordon didn't get on the pitch, but it wouldn't be too much longer before he made his mark.

The home leg of the League Cup tie with Queen of the South marked the full debut of Gordon Rae, but it was to be a disappointing night as the Dumfries side upset all the odds by winning 2-1. McLeod counted for Hibs, who missed a hatful of chances to put the tie out of sight and lost two very soft goals at the other end when Tommy O'Hara and Peter Dickson, from the penalty spot, beat Mike McDonald in the Hibs goal. In the Queens side that night were keeper Allan Ball and right-back Iain McChesney, who between them had clocked up more than 1,100 first-team appearances, by any standards a remarkable achievement.

With the disappointment of losing that Cup game still fresh in their minds, Hibs next travelled to Ibrox to face a Rangers side they had not beaten in three years. Manager Turnbull made one enforced change, due to an injury to Duncan, and he brought in Ally 'Benny' Brazil at the back, allowing him to push Bremner further up the park. This meant a second successive game and Premier League debut for young Gordon Rae, who was on hand to scramble the ball into the net after Peter McCloy had failed to hold a shot from Smith. That happened early in a game which Hibs dominated, a late Bremner strike from a superb McLeod through ball sealing the points in a 2-0 win. It was a great performance from Hibs and among those who particularly caught the eye was Erich Schaedler, who left Ibrox that night to make his way to Kelso where the Jedburgh Hibs Supporters' Club presented him with his Player of the Year award.

On the following Monday, Hibs travelled to Somerset Park for the second leg of their Anglo Scottish Cup tie. Leading 2-1 from the first game, Hibs found themselves pegged back to level terms on the stroke of half-time when Walker McCall headed powerfully home. But the Easter Road men came back into it in the second half and scored twice through Bremner and Smith after Ally Scott had twice opened up the Ayr defence with pinpoint passes. A late strike by Willie McCulloch levelled the match, but Hibs progressed 4-3 on aggregate and would face Blackburn Rovers in the next round.

With barely 48 hours to recover, Hibs were in action again on the Wednesday when they visited Palmerston Park for the second leg of the League Cup first-round tie. In a tense affair, veteran keeper Allan Ball was in sparkling form to deny Hibs, and the 0-0 result meant that Queen of the South would progress but that Hibs were out. It was a blow to bow out so early and miss the chance of more lucrative ties in the later rounds, the revenue from which might have allowed Eddie Turnbull to dip into the transfer market. As it was, the only likely way a new face or two might appear was if Hibs could arrange player swaps, something which Turnbull had been working on but so far without success.

Newly promoted Clydebank offered the next challenge when they visited Easter Road on League business. Having sold their star man, Davie Cooper, to Rangers in the summer for £100,000, the Bankies were finding football at this higher level quite tough and were already at the foot of the table. Mind you, they were only there on goal average, and sitting just one place above them were Celtic, so they were in exalted company. Manager Bill Munro had constructed a side with a blend of youth and experience, but they struggled as Hibs proved too strong for them and won the points with goals from Brazil and Scott, which took the Hibees to the top of the League.

With League Cup ties due to be played on 3 September, Hibs would have had a blank Saturday, but a reserve team friendly was quickly arranged with Hearts at Easter Road and the wee Hibs won 4-2, with goals from Paul McGlinchey, Pat Carroll, John Brownlie (pen) and Alex McGhee. The following Tuesday, the first team welcomed Newcastle to Easter Road for a friendly and triumphed 3-0 as McLeod (2) and Higgins found the target. Most notable from this game was the fact that Eddie Turnbull experimented by playing Jackie McNamara at sweeper, and although the Hibs man took a knock late in the game he looked very accomplished in a role that was soon to become permanent.

Tannadice was the next venue on League business and Hibs lost out 2-0 in a match in which they had more than held their own but which saw United double their lead on the stroke of half-time with a highly controversial penalty. Future Hibs man Billy Kirkwood had given the home side the lead, but Hibs were pressing forward at every opportunity for an equaliser until referee Kenny Hope of Glasgow pointed to the spot after Blackley and Derek Addison collided in the box. Blackley was booked for protesting. His complaints were certainly justified, and the sporting press, reporting on the game, came firmly out on his side. Significantly, Smith was replaced during the second half of that game by Jim McKay, a player who had been brought from Brora Rangers on trial for a month and had actually come off the bench in the game against Newcastle. The 21-year-old mill worker had shown in both games that he might prove a decent acquisition and certainly Eddie Turnbull was keen to secure his signature.

Victory over Ayr United had set up a tie against Blackburn Rovers in the Anglo Scottish Cup quarter-final, and the Lancashire club visited Easter Road on 14 September 1977. Founded in the same year as Hibs, Rovers were original members of the English League and had won their championship on two occasions as well as the FA Cup on six. Their form going into this game was not at its best and in their last two games they had tumbled out of the League Cup in a replay at Colchester and then lost their unbeaten League record at home to Blackpool. Nevertheless, they were treating this competition seriously and fielded their strongest side with England Under-21 keeper Paul Bradshaw in goal and Glen Keeley, Derek Fazackerley, Noel Brotherston and David Wagstaffe among the other starters. A 2-1 win on the night gave Hibs the narrowest of leads for the second leg, but the Easter Road men should have had more than McKay and McLeod's goals for their efforts. As it was, a late Noel Brotherston strike kept the tie in the balance.

Glasgow was the next port of call when Hibs took on Partick Thistle in the League and after a disappointing and frustrating 90 minutes it was the Jags who secured the two points with a well-taken goal by Bobby Houston. After a bright start to the season, during which Hibs had even topped the League at one point, two consecutive League defeats brought everyone back down to earth with a resounding bump.

Alex Ferguson brought newly promoted St Mirren to Leith on 24 September, when they were sitting fourth in the League just one point ahead of Hibs. The Buddies were a useful outfit with a number of very promising youngsters, including Tony Fitzpatrick, Billy Stark and Frank McGarvey in their line-up, but Hibs were too good for them on the day in securing a 2-0 win with goals from Higgins (a stunning drive from all of 25 yards) and McLeod. The respective League positions were thus reversed. The match programme that day contained an article advising that the forthcoming match against Celtic at Parkhead would see Hibs wearing their new change strip if agreement could be reached about the size of the lettering that would advertise the sponsors, Bukta, on the front of the jersey. The outfit was described as 'a purple shirt, with green and yellow banding on white sleeves and white shorts', but unfortunately the picture which accompanied the article and which was captioned 'Hotel hairdresser Ann Macbeth models the new TV strip' was in black and white! Hibs had suffered from the TV companies blacking out their games on the grounds that the sponsors' name on their shirts amounted to 'free advertising'.

The following midweek, Hibs travelled south to Ewood Park to meet Blackburn Rovers in the second leg of their quarter-final tie in the Anglo Scottish Cup. Higgins struck another 25-yard beauty which proved to be the only goal of the game and took Hibs through 3-1 on aggregate. Their semi-final opponents would be Bristol City, who had recovered from a two-goal deficit to eliminate Partick Thistle in their own quarter-final tie. The other semi-final would feature Notts County and St Mirren, County having knocked out Motherwell and St Mirren having defeated Fulham in the other quarter-finals.

The first opponents in October were reigning champions Celtic. After a very shaky start to the season, they were finding their feet and climbing the League steadily. Not for the first time this season Hibs found themselves the victims of a poor refereeing decision, and it was to cost them the opening goal right on the stroke of half-time. The Hibs players were adamant that referee Bill Anderson had blown for an infringement just before Johannes Edvaldsson stroked the ball past Mike McDonald, but their protests went unheeded and that goal inspired Celtic to score another two through Ronnie Glavin and Joe Craig. There is little doubt that the controversial goal upset Hibs, who until that point were in command of the play, and McKay's late solo effort was of little consolation to the Easter Road men.

This was a game that would be remembered for a number of reasons. Firstly, Hibs wore their TV-friendly purple away strip. At the same time, Jim McKay's trial spell ended and Hibs had to allow him to return to Brora, who had refused to accept the offer made for his signature. But more significantly, it turned out to be club captain John Blackley's last appearance for Hibs. In the days following the Parkhead defeat, Blackley was transferred to Newcastle United and once again the news was met with dismay by a disgruntled Hibs support. Certainly, it was too good an offer for the club to turn down and everyone wished Blackley the best of luck, but fans were left wondering if the transfer fee would be invested in a replacement.

On the following Tuesday night, a subdued Hibs support trooped into Easter Road to watch their favourites take on Meadowbank Thistle in the semi-final of the East of Scotland Shield. The winners would face Hearts in the final after the Gorgie side had defeated Berwick Rangers in the other tie. Hearts were not in the Premier League, so a win over Meadowbank would at least allow Hibs fans to witness one derby this season. With George Stewart installed as skipper following the sale of Blackley, Hibs were far too strong for Thistle and cruised home 4-1 with goals from McLeod (2), Duncan and Higgins against a penalty converted by Jim Hancock.

Ayr United provided the next opposition in a Premier League game at Easter Road. Hibs had already beaten Ayr at the same venue earlier in the season in the Anglo Scottish Cup when they won by 2-1, but on this occasion the match went the other way, with Ayr scoring three goals. Defender Bobby Tait put through his own goal for Hibs, while Gordon Cramond and John Christie were Ayr's other scorers. Needless to say, the atmosphere was somewhat subdued following Blackley's departure and the lack of any replacement, and Hibs fans were left wondering which player might be next to go if the club were happy to sell and seemingly unwilling to buy. Eddie Turnbull was still looking to do player swaps, a clear reflection of Hibs' financial position.

In the week leading up to the next fixture, which would take Hibs to Pittodrie to face League leaders Aberdeen, Hibs secured the services on loan of Rangers striker Martin Henderson. The big centre-forward had been allowed to join Hibs on a three-month loan deal with a view to the move becoming permanent if it suited both player and club. While any new signing was a welcome move, it was a little bit baffling that a centre-forward was seen to be the priority when the side had arguably been weakened in defence after the sale of John Blackley. In any event, Henderson made a winning debut at Pittodrie where, against all odds, Hibs won 2-1. Drew Jarvie netted first for the Dons, but Joe Smith put through his own goal and McLeod scored a spectacular winner. Hibs had gone into the game minus the injured Schaedler, which meant a move to left-back for Smith, with Higgins dropping into midfield to accommodate Henderson up front. The 12,000 crowd made plenty of noise, and those Hibs fans among them would, for once, be making the long journey home in happy mood. It was later revealed that the reason why a 'goal' slotted home by Henderson had been chalked off by the referee was because the player, unsure of his new team-mates' names, had shouted 'Leave it' and was penalised for doing so.

Hibs had been due to play their first-leg semi-final of the Anglo Scottish Cup at Ashton Gate, but the Bristol City stadium was having work done on its generators and so Eddie Turnbull agreed to the first leg being switched to Easter Road, where the game took place on 19 October 1977. Nicknamed 'the Robins', City had a decent squad of players including the likes of Kevin Mabbutt, Don Gillies, Norman Hunter, Gerry Sweeney, Gerry Gow and, of course, ex-Hibs favourite Peter Cormack. 'Corky', as the former Hibs man was known, had looked forward to his return to his old stamping ground and fans who remembered him as a favourite were equally excited at the prospect of seeing him again. Sadly, it was to be for all the wrong reasons that Corky would make his mark on the game as he was sent off for a quite shocking challenge on Des Bremner. Norman Hunter was also dismissed in a stormy encounter which ended 1-1. Duncan was on target for Hibs and Don Gillies for City, but Hibs could have won the match had keeper John Shaw not saved McLeod's late penalty kick.

In the aftermath of the game, Tom Hart suggested that Hibs might forfeit the tie rather than run the risk of another bad-tempered encounter in the return, but he changed his mind when he heard that the club would be fined £2,000 if they did not fulfil the fixture.

Hibs travelled to Motherwell next, and even a fantastic first-half penalty save by McDonald couldn't inspire his team-mates on to a win. Hibs had chances, McLeod shooting just past and Henderson hitting the post, but the only goal of the game came from Gregor Stevens.

There would be one more game before the return match with Bristol City and that brought League leaders Rangers to Easter Road. Bremner missed this one through injury, and during the game Brownlie was carried off with an ankle knock which required an X-ray. So it was no surprise when Rangers took revenge for that earlier Hibs win at Ibrox by winning the game thanks to a Sandy Jardine penalty. In the first half, Higgins was hauled down inside the Rangers 18-yard box by Tom Forsyth, but referee Paterson of Bothwell waved aside the claims of the Hibs players. This game had the TV cameras present, and because Hibs could not wear their purple TV strip, Bukta were asked to come up with an alternative and supplied canary yellow jerseys with green trim.

The first day of November had Hibs in Bristol where they met and lost to City in the second leg of their Anglo Scottish Cup tie. In torrential rain, City scored first through Kevin Mabbutt and although McLeod soon equalised it was to be a case of Hibs always having to come from behind during the game. It finished 5-3 to the hosts, who scored again through Mabbutt and added goals from Tom Ritchie, Gerry Sweeney (pen) and Trevor Tainton. McLeod struck a second for Hibs and Henderson got their third with his first goal in Hibs colours – although, strictly speaking, they were not fully Hibs colours. The rules stipulated that two teams could not wear shorts of the same colour in a game. As City wore white shorts, Hibs had to borrow a black set from their hosts.

Back home in Scotland, Hibs were uncomfortably close to the foot of the table when they travelled to play bottom club Clydebank at Kilbowie Park. With Alex Edwards recalled to the starting XI, there were hopes that Hibs could get back to winning ways, but a poor performance resulted in the third consecutive 1-0 defeat in the Premier League. Billy McColl got the only goal of the game and in the process dragged Hibs just a little bit closer to that bottom spot which they themselves still occupied.

An interested spectator in the stand for the next game was John Blackley, injury preventing him from playing for Newcastle against Wolves that day. Instead, he watched Hibs and Dundee United playing out a 0-0 draw. Although disappointed that his old side didn't win, he felt that the result was not only fair but also encouraging in that United were still pushing for the top spot. Certainly, goals were hard to come by and Hibs had only managed ten in the League to date. They had just played their fourth game in a row without finding the target.

A second consecutive home game brought Bertie Auld's Partick Thistle to Easter Road. The Jags occupied third place and were very difficult to break down as Auld had them so well drilled at the back, with Alan Rough between the sticks and Andy Anderson filling the jersey once worn by Alan Hansen, who had been transferred to Liverpool for a six-figure fee. Up front, the wily Doug Somner and new signing from Rangers Alex O'Hara were causing opposition defences some difficulties.

For once, Hibs would not draw a blank, but although they scored twice through McLeod and Stewart the visitors bagged three, with Bremner's unlucky own-goal being added to by Andy Anderson and a Doug Somner penalty. Interestingly, the match programme carried an article that day on the dearth of goals in the Scottish game. As Hibs were drawing 0-0 with Dundee United in the previous week the other four Premier League games produced just four goals and three draws. United's Jim McLean blamed the ten-club League, which, he argued, had clubs concentrating on not losing rather than winning. Few on the terraces around the country would disagree. Carefree attacking football was now a thing of the past, and it seemed like a lifetime ago, rather than just a few short years back to season 1959/60, that Joe Baker alone had scored 42 goals in the season.

Hibs drew yet another blank in their next encounter, against St Mirren at Love Street. The Buddies had lost 2-0 earlier in the season at Easter Road, but exacted revenge with goals from Frank McGarvey, Billy Stark and Bobby Reid. Bobby Smith played at left-back that afternoon because in the days leading up to the game Eddie Turnbull had finally managed to complete one of those player swaps he'd worked so hard on for most of the season. The swap involved Erich Schaedler moving to Dens Park to join Dundee, with centre-forward Bobby Hutchinson coming the other way. Hibs fans were really sorry to see Erich leave: he was a very popular player who always gave 100 per cent and was another of the Turnbull's Tornadoes to fly the nest. Equally, they would welcome Bobby Hutchinson in the hope that he would bring his goalscoring expertise to Leith and put it to good use.

The new player's route to Easter Road was an interesting one. Twenty-four years old, he hailed from Glasgow and started his footballing career with Queen's Park before moving on to Aberdeen, not to join the Dons but to find work. While playing minor-team football he was spotted by Montrose, who offered him a contract and two years later sold him to Dundee for £20,000. In his four seasons at Dens, he not only scored 40 goals but also provided many assists for his team-mates by making darting diagonal runs and taking defenders with him to leave space which was then exploited.

At Easter Road on the Saturday when the first team were losing at Love Street, the wee Hibs turned in a fine performance in winning 3-1, thanks to a hat-trick from Alex McGhee. Playing as a trialist centre-half for Hibs that afternoon was a young lad by the name of Craig Paterson, son of former stalwart John, who played in defence behind the legendary Famous Five. Craig, from Penicuik, topped the six-foot mark and John Lambie predicted he would have a good future in the game – never a truer word was spoken.

Somerset Park was the next place that Hibs would play and they were looking to avenge the 2-1 defeat inflicted on them by Ayr United at Easter Road in October. As Ayr were just below Hibs going into the game, it was vital that a good result be achieved in order to keep relegation worries at bay. Because of injury and illness, Eddie Turnbull had to shuffle the pack a little and Des Bremner was moved to the centre of the defence, where he had an excellent game. A solitary goal settled the issue and it came from the boot of Arthur Duncan, his first since March – when, coincidentally, Ayr had also been the opponents. Another who played well that day was new signing Bobby Hutchinson, whose non-stop display had the home defence working hard throughout.

Still struggling to get goals, Hibs badly needed a further injection of firepower even after the signing of Hutchinson and it was made known at this time that Eddie Turnbull had been trying to persuade Motherwell to allow Jimmy O'Rourke to come home to Hibs. The Steelmen, however, were also finding goals hard to come by and refused to part with him. One other piece of news that reached Easter Road that week about a former Hibee was that Alex Cropley had suffered a double leg break while playing for Aston Villa in their Midlands derby against West Brom. 'Sodjer' had been there before and had recovered fully, and every Hibs fan no doubt wished him a full and speedy return to action.

Still very much in pursuit of Rangers at the top of the League, Aberdeen arrived at Easter Road in mid-December. From the off, Hibs took the game to their visitors and it was no surprise when Willie Murray shot them ahead in the first half. The Dons tried to rally, but Hibs kept them pinned back and the points were sealed when Arthur Duncan headed a second. After the game, Duncan joked that his goals were like buses, you wait ages on one and then two arrive back to back! An absolute standout for Hibs that day was Jackie McNamara, who played at sweeper and never put a foot wrong. The fans had been slow to take to the man who replaced Stanton, but there was now no doubt in the minds of the supporters that this McNamara guy could play a bit.

A busy festive period began with the visit of Motherwell to Easter Road on Christmas Eve 1977. Both clubs were in the bottom four, and both set out their stall to win the game, which led to some fast, furious and exciting football for the entire 90 minutes. Hibs scored first when McLeod coolly slotted home a penalty, but the visitors hit back when a shot from Jimmy O'Rourke was only partially stopped by McDonald and Willie Pettigrew was on hand to knock the ball home. An injury to Hutchinson saw him replaced by substitute Willie Murray, and it was the new man who nabbed the winner with a smart drive to the left of the diving Stewart Rennie. It was a vital two points for Hibs, lifting them into a mid-table position alongside a strangely struggling Celtic.

New Year's Eve saw Hibs at Ibrox, where table-topping Rangers were considered to be too strong for most visiting sides. Eddie Turnbull had said after the earlier 1-0 defeat to the Gers at Easter Road that he thought there was very little between them. On this occasion, a fighting 0-0 draw seemed to reinforce the manager's view. Indeed, in some quarters Hibs were considered unlucky not to take both points, after not one, but two very strong penalty claims were waved aside by referee Anderson.

On the second day of the new year, Hibs would normally have faced Hearts, but their old rivals were now in the league below, so Clydebank provided the opposition. The basement boys from Kilbowie, who were trying desperately to cling on to their Premier League status, packed their defence and hoped for a goal on the break. Alex McGhee and Ally McLeod had different ideas, however, and their goals meant that Hibs had taken five of the six points available over the festive period.

In an attempt to give the Edinburgh footballing public some kind of derby match to look forward to, Hibs and Hearts had agreed to meet on the third of that month in the East of Scotland Shield final, but the pitch was unplayable and the match was postponed, so there was no immediate return to Easter Road for former Hibs man Willie Ormond, newly appointed as manager of Hearts. The weather was not being kind in general and all clubs, in the days when undersoil heating was but a pipe dream for the future, suffered with cancellations.

Tannadice was playable at the end of that first week in January and Hibs went there looking to improve upon a pretty dismal record against Dundee United in recent times. As always, the home side proved a hard nut to crack, but McLeod found his shooting boots and beat Hamish McAlpine in the home goal with a fierce drive. Unfortunately, John Bourke scored at the other end and so Hibs had to be content with a draw.

A series of postponements followed as the winter weather worsened and Hibs made inquiries down south about the possibility of a friendly to keep the players in trim. Brighton and Blackpool were possibilities, but at the end of the day the logistics made it impossible and so the players had time off from playing and did extra training sessions instead. One player who did have a game to look forward to was Benny Brazil, who had been selected for the Scotland Under-21 pool for the forthcoming international against Wales in Wrexham. This was a real boost to the young Hibs man, who had only recently broken into the first team at Easter Road. The adaptability already displayed for his club, where he had performed well both in defence and midfield, meant that he had caught the eye of the Scotland manager and would have an opportunity to add to the Scotland Youth caps already in his possession.

On the last Saturday in January 1978, Hibs finally took to the field of play again when they hosted East Fife in the Scottish Cup third round. The Fifers had a new player/manager, Dave Clarke, who had been handed the reins after former Hibs man Roy Barry had resigned the previous week. At just 27 years old, Clarke had played his entire career to date for the Bayview club and was a very popular appointment with the fans. It would not, however, be a winning start to his managerial career as Hibs brushed the Fifers aside with a convincing 4-0 win. McLeod got a double, with Duncan and McGhee on target for the other two. That win took Hibs through to a fourth-round tie at Easter Road against Partick Thistle, but that game would not take place for a further five weeks as the Scottish winter took a firm hold and caused cancellations galore.

In fact, Hibs would not play another competitive game for another four weeks and had to resort to picking up a couple of friendlies to keep the players match fit. The first of those took place in London, where the weather was being somewhat kinder, Hibs beating Crystal Palace with the only goal of the game, scored by skipper for the day Ally McLeod. Centre-forward Bobby Hutchinson thought he had broken his scoring duck when he lashed a shot home from 25 yards, but it was disallowed when the linesman flagged offside against a colleague.

A week later, Dens Park was deemed playable for a visit by Hibs and despite a good showing by the Dark Blues it was the visitors who took the honours with a fine 2-1 win, Brazil and Higgins getting the goals.

At the end of February the weather relented a bit and Hibs were back in competitive action when they made the trip to Pittodrie, but it would be a horror show in the mud as the hosts cruised to a 3-0 win. A George Stewart own-goal nudged the Dons ahead before Davidson and Miller added to the tally and sent the Greens home pointless.

A Wednesday night fixture in Ayr should have allowed both clubs to start making inroads into the backlog of fixtures, but Hibs were left fuming after arriving to play the game only to discover that Ayr had applied for, and been granted, a postponement because most of their players were suffering from a flu outbreak. The problem was that no-one thought to tell Hibs, and so they and a good number of travelling supporters had to turn around and make the long journey home. Hibs intimated that they would be protesting to the Scottish League – and who could blame them in the circumstances?

At Easter Road, the reserves drew 2-2 in an exciting game enjoyed by a fairly decent crowd. Gordon Rae and Lindsay Muir put Hibs two up after being fed defence-splitting passes by Alex Edwards, but the Dons fought back and after Brian Turner was harshly sent off for what looked like a simple push, they struck two late goals to share the spoils. This result was achieved without a coach, as John Lambie had left the club and new man Stan Vincent, a former Hibs player, had not yet taken up his duties.

That Ayr United postponement meant that Hibs' next game was in the Scottish Cup against Partick Thistle at Easter Road on 4 March 1978. As both clubs were in the Premier League and one must obviously be eliminated from the competition it meant that by the time the fourth round had been played out only five of the ten Premier clubs would have survived. Clydebank, Ayr United, St Mirren and Motherwell had already fallen, and Hibs fans were praying they would not be joining that list. Arriving for the game, fans were informed via the match programme that Hibs would be undertaking a summer tour of Canada, where they would play a total of seven matches. Previous trips to Canada, in 1965 and 1967, had proved to be most enjoyable for all concerned and this latest group of players had games in Toronto, Calgary, Vancouver, Edmonton, Winnipeg and Ottawa to look forward to. More immediately, though, was the task of trying to progress in the Cup, and Thistle proved, as usual, to be stubborn opponents. Wave after wave of attacks came to nothing and the match ended 0-0. The replay in Glasgow was scheduled for the Monday night because of the already heavy backlog of fixtures.

Monday came around and Hibs set off for Firhill, as did 12 coachloads of fans and innumerable cars, but on arrival in Glasgow they were told the match had been called off by the referee, Mr Gordon of Newport, due to a waterlogged pitch. Twenty-four hours later, those who could do so made the journey again, and although the pitch was like a mudbath the game went ahead. For the first half hour it was all Hibs, but they couldn't find a way past keeper Alan Rough. The old maxim, 'if you don't take your chances you may just be punished', was true to form when a defensive mix-up allowed Jim Melrose to head the opener for the Jags. Just on the hour mark, McLeod fired an equaliser, his 22nd goal of the season, but Thistle stole it when another defensive blunder allowed Melrose to grab his and Thistle's second. Another Cup exit for Hibs, who had the opportunities to put the game out of sight but came up against a goalkeeper at the top of his form.

With the Cup no longer a concern, Hibs could turn their attention to improving the League position. Two games a week was the likely situation as efforts were made to eat into that backlog, and the first of those matches brought St Mirren to Easter Road. The Buddies were two points ahead of Hibs, but had played three games more, so there was a chance for Eddie Turnbull's men to put some pressure on them. The St Mirren manager,

Alex Ferguson, had been adding to his squad and had signed Jimmy Bone from Arbroath along with Iain Munro from Rangers, the latter returning to Love Street having left there some years before when he signed for Hibs. Things looked as though they might just go a bit pear-shaped for Hibs when the visitors took the lead, but that goal provided the incentive needed to up their game and they then proceeded to take St Mirren apart, eventually running out 5-1 winners. Bobby Hutchinson finally got off the mark with two well-taken headed goals, while Brazil, Higgins and McLeod (pen) completed the rout.

The match programme for the St Mirren game contained the sad news of the death of Jimmy McColl. Born in Glasgow in 1892, Jimmy was a goalscoring centre-forward in the great Hibs team of the Twenties and then went on to be club trainer to the Hibs sides who won the Scottish League on three occasions after the Second World War. His playing career had also seen him at Celtic, Partick Thistle and Stoke City and he'd even given management a bash with Belfast Celtic, but Jimmy was a Hibs man and Easter Road was his 'home'. A winner of no fewer than 36 medals during his playing days, Jimmy gave more than 50 years of service to Hibernian and would be missed by all who knew him and all who were lucky enough to have seen him play.

On the Wednesday following that cracking win over St Mirren, Hibs went through to Fir Park to take on Motherwell, who had been showing good form, especially at home. To the neutral observer it must surely have looked a home banker, but the visitors had other ideas in securing a very impressive 4-2 win. Leading 2-0, Hibs allowed the visitors back into the game at 2-2 in the second half, but a strong finish brought two more goals for the Greens and two very welcome League points. Vic Davidson and Gregor Stevens scored for the Steelmen, with McLeod (2), Bremner and Willie Murray on target for Hibs.

Another away game followed on the Saturday when Hibs visited basement boys Clydebank at Kilbowie Park and boosted their goal tally to 11 in three games with a convincing 3-0 win. Another two from the prolific McLeod and a solo strike by Hutchinson had Hibs on easy street and, in truth, keeper Mike McDonald, himself a former Clydebank player, had a very easy 90 minutes as the home side struggled to cause the Hibs defence any problems. Man of the match was Des Bremner, who had a fantastic game, the highlight being his involvement in Hutchinson's goal. Des headed a cross clear of his own 18-yard box and then proceeded to run the length of the park to receive a pass which he whipped into the box for Bobby to smash home. The big Highlander not only had magnificent stamina but also great footballing ability, and it was little surprise that he was such a favourite with the Hibs support.

High scoring continued to be the theme in the following midweek, when

Ayr United were the victims as Hibs cruised into a 3-0 half-time lead. The Easter Road men lost their way a little in the second half, when Ayr got a boost from scoring two goals themselves, but wrapped up the points with a fourth, scored by McLeod from the spot. The other Hibs goals came from a Hutchinson double and one from Murray, Ayr countering through Danny Masterton and Dave McCulloch. Incidentally, that penalty from McLeod took his tally for the season to 27 in all competitions, 11 of those in the League.

When Dundee United arrived at Easter Road on 25 March 1978 they did so in the knowledge that in the previous 11 meetings Hibs had yet to beat them. There had been a number of draws and no fewer than five odd-goal defeats. It was all the more enjoyable, therefore, for the home crowd to watch their favourites record a 3-1 win. For once, the dependable Hamish McAlpine in the United goal made an error and Higgins was quick to take advantage by slotting the ball home. Murray's defence-splitting pass allowed McLeod to grab a second and Higgins added his second and Hibs' third before United struck through Graeme Payne, but it was too little too late for the Terrors. Amazingly, that was the first time in the season to date that United had conceded more than two goals in a League game. The icing on the cake for Hibs was that it catapulted them into joint third with Motherwell, who had played three more games.

Sitting third in the table at the end of March was a much healthier position than early season results had suggested, and even though Hibs were too far back from Rangers and Aberdeen to make a serious challenge for the title they could still have quite some say in where the League flag might end up, with both clubs still to play at Easter Road. First to meet that challenge were Rangers, who arrived in Leith with their strongest possible XI in the starting line-up. In a tough, sometimes brutal game, Derek Parlane put the visitors ahead and the Rangers players seemed to lose the plot when Higgins went down under a challenge from John Greig and referee Bob Valentine of Dundee pointed to the spot. The visitors argued that Higgins had been outside the box, although the big fella later said he had just crossed the 18-yard line when Greig fouled him. The 'debate' lasted for what seemed an age and all the while Ally McLeod stood calmly waiting to take the kick. Finally, peace was restored and the Hibs man proved he had nerves of steel by sending McCloy the wrong way and scoring the goal which earned the Greens a 1-1 draw in front of 21,245 fans.

One sad bit of news that day was a notice in the programme reporting the death of the chairman of the Hibs Supporters' Association. A retired army captain, Bill Collins was also chairman of the Hawkhill Branch, and the author had the pleasure of being both minute secretary and secretary during his time in that post. Bill was a true gentleman who always had encouraging words to offer, and I enjoyed my time working with him on that committee.

April started with a visit from Partick Thistle, who had ended Hibs' Scottish Cup dream earlier in the season as well as beating them home and away in the League. Bertie Auld's men, who had new signing Colin McAdam in the centre of their defence, had progressed in the Cup and were due to make a semi-final appearance, but arrived at Easter Road on the back of a heavy midweek defeat from Celtic in the League. On the day, Hibs, with former favourite John Blackley watching from the stands, ran out comfortable 3-1 winners. Hutchinson got the ball rolling and then Duncan bulleted an unstoppable shot past Alan Rough to double the lead before Alex O'Hara pulled one back. Any thoughts of getting a point were soon removed from Bertie Auld's mind when McLeod struck the third and final goal of the game.

Next up was a trip to Parkhead for the first of three meetings with Celtic in a ten-day spell. After a fairly even first half, Hibs were awarded a penalty early in the second when Willie Murray was tripped in the box. McLeod rifled a low shot past Peter Latchford to establish a lead. Seven minutes later, Bremner pounced on a loose ball in the box and fired home a second, only to have referee Tommy Muirhead disallow it. Hibs players protested vehemently and even the Celtic players looked confused, starting to walk to the centre circle for the kick-off when the ball hit the net. Mr Muirhead would not be persuaded, and the goal did not count. At 2-0 up, Hibs would have fancied their chances, but it was not to be, and when George McCluskey hit a late double the visitors were down and out.

Back in the west at the weekend, Hibs faced a St Mirren side they had comprehensively beaten just a few games earlier. That being so, it was all the more perplexing that they lost 3-0 to the Buddies. The opening goal was painful to take for Hibs: a poor shot by Leonard was heading into the safekeeping of Mike McDonald's hands, only to take a deflection off John Brownlie and trundle past the now wrong-footed keeper. A penalty claim was turned down and Hibs also hit the post twice, but further goals from Bobby Reid and Frank McGarvey ended any hopes of a fightback. A late effort by Tony Higgins, celebrating his 100th appearance for the club, came off the underside of the bar and bounced out, summing up the kind of afternoon Hibs had endured.

The second of three rapid-fire meetings with Celtic took place at Easter Road on 12 April 1978. Hibs were still sitting in third place despite the two most recent setbacks, while Celtic were down in sixth, some three points behind Hibs with a game less played. This had been a really poor season for the Parkhead men, one which would bring them no silverware at all – changed days since their nine-in-a-row League dominance in the very recent past. Kenny Dalglish had departed for Liverpool, and Celtic seemed to be struggling without him. In this particular clash, Hibs came out of the blocks with all guns blazing, taking an early lead through Higgins after great play by Brownlie and McLeod had set up the chance and being unlucky not to add to it before half-time. Celtic, to their credit, also played an attacking game and created a number of chances before George McCluskey grabbed their equaliser. Eddie Turnbull felt that on the balance of play Hibs should really have taken the points, but he praised Celtic for playing attacking football, something many visiting Premier League sides just refused to do for fear of losing away from home. The draw left both clubs still in the hunt for a UEFA Cup spot, as the teams finishing third and fourth would qualify. Setting the pace in that race were Dundee United, level with Hibs but with two games in hand.

A mere four days later Celtic were back at Easter Road, but this time they would not deny Hibs their first win of the season against the Glasgow side. Arthur Duncan opened the scoring with a smartly taken back-post header, while Higgins continued his recent good form with a well-taken double and Alex McGhee nabbed the other. Celtic struck via Mike Conroy, but they were second best throughout as Hibs played the kind of free-flowing, attacking football for which they had once been famous. The win secured two very useful points in the fight for that UEFA Cup place and dented Celtic's hopes at the same time.

Two away games followed in rapid succession, the first at Firhill against Partick Thistle. Alex McGhee gave the visitors the lead on a dry and fiery pitch, but the home side fought back to win the points with goals from Ian Gibson and Alex O'Hara in a stadium devoid of any real atmosphere, so few in number were the spectators. On the same day in Edinburgh, the reserves drew 1-1 with Motherwell, a trialist getting the Hibs goal. This would herald the start of another run of consecutive games, being the first of five that the reserves would play in the space of ten days. A number of the regulars in that team were keen to show what they could do in the hope that they might be part of the group who would be jetting off to Canada at the end of the season. There was at least one place certainly up for grabs, as first-team regular Ally Brazil was remaining in Scotland for a cartilage operation.

The second away game for the first team took them to Somerset Park to face an already relegated Ayr United. Once again the turnout was poor and once again Hibs failed to secure any points in going down 2-0 after missing more chances to score than you could count on both hands. That UEFA Cup spot was under threat. Hibs had just one more game to play and were joint fourth with Celtic, Dundee United having already secured third place.

The League season would draw to a close with a visit to Easter Road from Aberdeen, who had pushed Rangers all the way in the title race, and Hibs went into it knowing that defeat was not an option if they wanted

UEFA Cup football. Ian Scanlon scored for Aberdeen and Hibs looked as if they might be about to have one of those days when chances galore went begging, but Duncan latched on to a great cross from Brownlie to level things up. It was just a draw, but it was enough to secure fourth place, and after a gap of one season Hibs would once again enjoy a UEFA Cup adventure in 1978/79.

With the important business of competitive football out of the way, Hibs still had another couple of engagements to fulfil before setting off on that trip to Canada. The first of those was the long-awaited testimonial game for Pat Stanton. The game would be between Hibs and his present club, Celtic, with a fair sprinkling of guest players on both sides. A crowd in excess of 25,000 turned out to honour the player who had been a mainstay at Easter Road for the largest part of his career, and the great man was cheered throughout, playing for Celtic in the first half and Hibs in the second. Hibs won 2-1, and the winning goal came from the penalty spot, the kick being taken by none other than Patrick Gordon Stanton. After the match, an emotional Pat thanked everyone who had helped make it such a special day for him, including Rangers and Hearts, both of whom had donated money to his testimonial fund, proving his popularity in the game.

During the following week, Eddie Turnbull raided relegated Clydebank to bring Gerry O'Brien to Easter Road. The new man had once been a team-mate of Ally McLeod's when the pair played for Southampton and had been with Clydebank for his second stint there before joining Hibs. An early priority for the player was the need to ensure that his passport was up to date, as he would be joining his new club on their summer tour, but ahead of that he would make his debut when Hibs entertained Hearts in the East of Scotland Shield final on Saturday, 7 May 1978.

This game, initially scheduled during the New Year period but postponed due to bad weather, brought Hearts across the city as First Division runners-up. Under the guidance of former Hibs man Willie Ormond, the Gorgie side would return to the Premier League at the first time of asking and it was a real bonus for capital football fans as they'd certainly missed the excitement of a derby match. In fact, Hearts only clinched promotion on the very last day of the season, when Eamonn Bannon headed the winning goal at Gayfield, securing promotion and condemning Dundee to another season in the lower league by the narrowest of margins.

This derby would see Edinburgh referee Dougie Ramsay in charge and it would be the first time he had refereed either club, because in those days referees did not officiate in games involving teams from their home town or city. The game was played in good spirit and Ramsay had very little to do other than to note the fact that Hibs won the Shield, thanks to a goal by debutant Gerry O'Brien – a goal which earned him the instant appreciation of the Hibernian faithful!

'SHADES' DEPARTS

And so the domestic season drew to a close with Hibs securing fourth place, Ally McLeod and Mike McDonald achieving perfect attendance records in the League, and McLeod finishing top scorer by a huge margin with 32 goals in all competitions, including 16 in the League.

The summer tour of Canada had finally come about and it was good news for young Craig Paterson, Gordon Rae and Willie Temperley, who were included in the travelling party. During the tour, Ally McLeod lived up to his reputation as principal marksman, scoring 16 of the 36 goals Hibs notched up in their seven matches across the country. Undefeated, they managed five wins and two draws. Although it was McLeod who hogged the scoring headlines, it was Tony Higgins and Willie Murray who won the many man-of-the-match awards on offer. Higgins in particular was outstanding throughout the whole trip and never more so than in Edmonton, where he gave a quite superb performance against the local All Stars.

All of the games were played on artificial surfaces and it took the players a couple of games to properly adjust, but once they had done so they were able to demonstrate the kind of passing football that Eddie Turnbull always wanted his men to achieve. The opening game brought a 1-1 draw against Ontario All Stars, with McLeod the scorer, but they fared better in the second match in beating Calgary Kickers 4-1. McLeod got two this time, the others coming from Duncan and Higgins.

The most testing match came next as Hibs took on Vancouver Whitecaps, who boasted players of the quality of Kevin Hector, Alan Hinton, Phil Parkes and Steve Kindon, all of whom had played at the highest level in the English League. The game finished at 2-2, but not without a deal of controversy. Willie Murray and Arthur Duncan had shot Hibs into a two-goal lead, but the Whitecaps fought back and got two of their own, the second from a hotly disputed penalty. Hibs then scored again through McLeod, but the goal was disallowed, much to the disgust of the players, Eddie Turnbull and the many ex-pat Scots in the crowd. Such was the uproar that the incident was debated in the newspapers and on the TV sports channels for several days after the event and the general consensus was that the referee had robbed Hibs of a deserved victory.

Vancouver Island Vistas were next to face the tourists and quite simply Hibs overwhelmed them with a stunning 9-0 win. McLeod got four, Higgins and Duncan two each and Bremner the other. Edmonton All Stars fared little better in the next game, Hibs scoring seven without reply. McLeod got a hat-trick and Duncan a couple, while Higgins and Willie Paterson rounded it off. While accepting that the calibre of opposition was not great, it was gratifying to see Hibs, and especially McLeod, scoring so freely.

Two more games remained and the first, against Manitoba All Stars, brought the visitors a 6-0 win, McLeod getting another four and big

George Stewart venturing forward from defence to get the other two. The final game of a most enjoyable trip took place in Ottawa against the Tigers and Hibs rattled in another seven. McLeod and Brownlie each got two, the other goals coming from Higgins, Duncan and Bremner.

As the touring party set off for home there were broad smiles all around and none more so than on the faces of Paterson, Rae and Temperley, all three of whom had taken part, from the bench, in no fewer than six of the seven games, gaining good experience and learning just what it was like to play at first-team level.

Above: Napoli arrive at Turnhouse in 1968 in confident mood. *www.scran.ac.uk*

Below: Joe McBride scoring one of a hat-trick against Lokomotiv Leipzig on his home debut. *www.scran.ac.uk*

Right: Arthur Duncan shortly after signing for Hibs. *www.scran.ac.uk*

Below: Pat Stanton, Alex Cropley and Eric Stevenson enjoying a cup of tea! *www.scran.ac.uk*

Left: Joe Baker returns to a hero's welcome. *www.scran.ac.uk*

Below: Eddie Turnbull addressing the players at training. *www.scran.ac.uk*

Above: Hibs fans out in force at Hampden. *www.scran.ac.uk*

Below: Pat Stanton about to be presented with the League Cup. *www.scran.ac.uk*

Above: Hibs players in early S43 mode as they record Turnbull's Tornadoes. *www.scran.ac.uk*

Below: Evidence of Leeds boss Don Revie being on the park during the penalty shoot-out. *www.scran.ac.uk*

Above: Action from the Hibs v Norrkoping game in December 1978 at Easter Road.
www.scran.ac.uk

Below: Norwegians Svein Mathisen and Isak Refvik looking proud in their Hibs kit.
www.scran.ac.uk

Left: The one and only George Best in action against St Mirren. *www.scran.ac.uk*

Below: Tam McNiven with the players he looked after so well. *www.scran.ac.uk*

Above: Action from a friendly against Moscow Dynamo which Hibs won 2–0. www.scran.ac.uk

Below: Action from a friendly against Dutch champions Feyenoord which Hibs won 4–2. www.scran.ac.uk

Chapter Twelve

1978/79

HAMPDEN HEARTBREAK

Between arriving back from Canada and preparing the team for a pre-season tour of the Highlands, Eddie Turnbull had been busy in the transfer market, with players both joining and leaving ahead of the new campaign. Lindsay Muir departed to St Johnstone and Alex McGhee to Dundee, while centre-half Rikki Fleming was signed from relegated Ayr United. Turnbull thought he had a second signing, only for the deal to fall through at the last minute. The target was ex-Hearts man Ralph Callachan of Newcastle United. The manager had been tracking him for some time and was disappointed that the deal fell through.

An influx of young players meant that other new players who would be seen around Easter Road included Jim Farmer (Stonehouse Violet), Rab Kilgour (Whitehill Welfare), Colin Campbell (Edinburgh University), Gordon Leitch (Hutchison Vale), Alan Quilietti (Gairdoch), Brian Fairlie (Whitburn), Steven Brown and Dave Huggins (both Tynecastle Boys' Club) and Andy Johnstone, who had been released by Liverpool. As is the way with football, in the course of time some of those youngsters would make it, but most would not.

Other items of news in the run-up to the season were that club director Tommy Younger was in line to become president of the SFA, the last Hibs man to hold that post being Harry Swan, and that Ally Brazil, who missed the trip to Canada, was still recovering from his cartilage operation (it took months back then, but modern-day methods mean minimal time before a player is back training again). Finally, of interest to all the 'bad boys' at clubs, a new disciplinary code was introduced. Effectively, this meant that a player could now be cautioned five times before having to sit out a game. Each caution would earn the offender up to two points. Deliberate trips, pushing, kicking, etc, would draw the maximum two, while such offences as handling, gesticulating and talking back would attract a one-point penalty. A red following any type of yellow would attract five penalty points, and a straight red six.

As had been the case at the start of the previous season, Hibs took themselves north to play a number of pre-season friendlies and started off with a 2-0 win against Inverness Thistle. Pat Carroll and Ally McLeod scored the goals and young Colin Campbell was handed his first-team debut in a team that also included Craig Paterson in central defence alongside George Stewart. The next game took place at Dens Park, where First Division Dundee were swept aside in a 4-1 scoreline. Bobby Hutchinson scored against his old club before going off with what turned out to be badly bruised ribs. Ally McLeod got two, one of them from the spot, and Arthur Duncan got the other. Then it was off to Elgin to defeat City 2-0, McLeod and Pat Carroll finding the net.

Having received a bye in the first round of the League Cup, Hibs' first competitive action was a League match against Dundee United at Tannadice. Like Hibs, United were in that season's UEFA Cup and had been unlucky in the draw, which pitched them against top Belgian outfit Standard Liege, while Hibs had been paired with IFK Norrkoping of Sweden. Those games would arrive in due course and were probably not in the minds of the players as they fought out a 0-0 draw. Both sides had periods of dominance but neither could find a goal, which was probably a fair reflection of the match.

On the same day, Stan Vincent's reserve team won 1-0 against United at Easter Road. With the defence well marshalled by the ever improving Craig Paterson, it was new boy Alan Quilietti who got the only goal when his persistence forced a defender into making a mistake, allowing him to steal the ball away and fire it home. Further changes to the reserve League set-up meant that the wee Hibs would only play 18 League matches, the second half of their season being filled with cup ties and/or friendlies. This was undertaken to help avoid the clutch of games played late in the season, a situation which had affected all teams in the last two seasons.

During the following week, Eddie Turnbull finally got his man when Ralph Callachan joined the club from Newcastle in a deal which took rightback John Brownlie in the opposite direction. At just 23, Callachan had a lot of playing years ahead of him and would soon fit into the Hibs midfield, but there was a tinge of sadness among the Hibs support at the departure of Brownlie – yet another of Turnbull's Tornadoes to leave Easter Road. Accepting that football teams evolve and by the nature of the game players move around, it was still a blow to those who remembered the flowing football of just a few seasons ago. The only Tornadoes still at the club were now Arthur Duncan and Alex Edwards.

Hibs' next challenge came in the shape of reigning League champions Rangers, who arrived at Easter Road under the guidance of their new manager, John Greig. Having lost at home in their opening game to a late St Mirren goal, the Gers were in a determined mood and were looking to take the two points back to Ibrox, but despite having the likes of Derek

Johnstone, John MacDonald and Derek Parlane in their line-up they could not find a way past Mike McDonald. Unfortunately, Hibs suffered the same fate at the other end of the park and so recorded their second consecutive 0-0 draw. One feature of that game was the surprise inclusion of Rab Kilgour at right-back. The youngster had impressed against Dundee United reserves and had shown up well in training, and so Eddie Turnbull pitched him in, which allowed Des Bremner to move into the midfield. Kilgour had a solid game and proved the manager was right to take the chance in playing him against very strong opposition.

Brechin City would provide the opposition for Hibs in the second round of the League Cup, but before that two-leg match took place Hibs had the matter of a derby match at Tynecastle to negotiate. Hearts were back in the top flight after spending the previous season in the First Division and were determined not to return to that lower level. The Gorgie men started the better and Donald Park put them ahead. Not having beaten Hibs in a Premier League game up until then, Hearts hung on grimly and looked like ending that hoodoo, only for McLeod to head home an inch-perfect O'Brien cross in injury time. Unfortunately, the game made headlines in the newspapers the next day not because it had been a decent match but because there had been severe crowd trouble. At the earliest opportunity, Eddie Turnbull wrote in his programme notes: 'Officials of this club wish to attract the spectator who can enjoy his or her football in peace. That is why Hibs appeal to the fans to refrain from chanting obscenities at the opposition players or manager and to set an example by pinpointing the troublemakers for the police. Local rivalry can be good for the game, but the bitterness which was evident at Tynecastle last week cannot be allowed to continue. Hibs and Hearts used to meet in the friendliest circumstances; players and officials on both sides are extremely close, so why shouldn't it be the same on the terracings and in the stand?' Strong words indeed, but when you read some of the stuff on modern-day internet site messageboards it seems that little has really changed in terms of Hibs–Hearts rivalry.

Four days after the derby draw, Hibs travelled to Glebe Park to meet Brechin City in the second-round first leg of the League Cup and proved to be too strong for the Angus outfit, despite having McNamara sent off for two bookable offences. The goals came from Rae, who was about to turn full-time with the club, Smith and Callachan, his first for Hibs. New boy Rikki Fleming had to leave the field with a badly cut leg that required nine stitches and it looked as if the big defender might be out for a few games.

The second leg was played on the Saturday after the first and once again Hibs scored three, McLeod getting a brace and Callachan doubling his total in green and white. Brechin's only response was a goal from Dick Campbell, a player who would in time find his way into football management. As expected, Fleming sat the game out, but Hibs found an able deputy in Gordon Rae, who looked as though he had played in central defence all of his life. That win took them into round three, where they would meet Clydebank, who had been relegated from last season's Premier League.

The programme for the Brechin game announced the very good news that Jimmy O'Rourke was back at Easter Road, although his role would be in assisting with the coaching of the young players as opposed to terrorising opposition defences while playing in the first team. Needless to say, Jimmy was delighted to be back at Hibs as his love for the club had never been a secret. Indeed, Eddie Turnbull once said of Jimmy: 'He has "Hibernian" stitched across his chest,' which sums O'Rourke up perfectly.

With their UEFA Cup tie looming up fast, Hibs had a home game against St Mirren, who had won two of their first three League games under new manager Jim Clunie. Clunie had played for St Mirren in the past and left Southampton to take the reins from Alex Ferguson, who had moved on to Aberdeen. The Buddies had a good crop of players and had recently added goalkeeper Billy Thomson, signed from Partick Thistle, to help stiffen their defence, but they could not keep Tony Higgins out and his goal ended up winning the points for Hibs by the narrowest of margins. Hibs hadn't played particularly well, but did enough to get the home win and Higgins's goal was a peach. For such a big man he could show a deft touch when it mattered and his goal came when he drifted past two defenders before thumping a right-foot drive beyond Thomson. There was disappointment, though, when both McLeod and Bremner limped off during the game, the former with a groin strain and the latter a pulled hamstring. Not good news in advance of the UEFA Cup tie, a game for which Ralph Callachan was not eligible having signed past the deadline date.

The St Mirren match programme intimated that the Hibernian Supporters' Association had awarded its Player of the Year trophy to Jackie McNamara, who had beaten off opposition from Ally McLeod and Des Bremner in winning it. Few would argue that the award was not fully deserved, as since finding his niche as sweeper, Jackie Mac had been outstanding in Hibs' colours. There was news, too, that Eddie Turnbull and John Fraser had twice been to Sweden to study Norrkoping. The manager was confident that an in-form Hibs could see them off, but he sounded a word of caution to the effect that the Swedes would probably pack their defence to frustrate Hibs, so it was important that the fans should not only be patient but also offer their vocal support for the whole 90 minutes.

Wednesday, 13 September 1978, brought IFK Norrkoping of Sweden to Easter Road for the eagerly anticipated UEFA Cup first-round, first-leg tie. Hibs would be without the injured Des Bremner, but there was better news when Ally McLeod passed a late fitness test. The Swedish club officials had been entertained to lunch that day by Tom Hart, who presented each of their party with a watch as a memento of the game, their first competitive one in Scotland. The visitors had a number of Swedish internationalists in their side, including goalkeeper Jan-Ake Jonsson, midfielders Gert Hellberg and Leif Anderson and top-scoring centre-forward Par-Olof Ohlsson. Hibs, however, would miss not only Bremner but also Ralph Callachan. This would not be the first time the sides had met: back in 1947, a touring Hibs side lost a friendly to Norrkoping 3-1.

The game itself, Hibs' 63rd in Europe, was much more open than Eddie Turnbull had anticipated and the Swedes attacked with every chance they got. Thankfully, Tony Higgins was still in the goalscoring frame of mind that saw him strike the winner against St Mirren and he managed to put two past the Swedish keeper, while Willie Temperley got a third. Unfortunately, Hibs had suffered a lapse in the first half which saw their visitors score twice in two minutes through Ohlsson and Svensson. That left Hibs with a narrow 3-2 win. Star of the show that night was Arthur Duncan, who slotted in as an emergency right-back and was outstanding in doing so. His tenacity in the tackle, his ability to read the game and perhaps, most of all, his still blistering pace, caused the Swedes no end of problems. It was the most slender of leads and Hibs would have to be at their best in the return tie, where a 1-0 Norrkoping victory would be enough to eliminate them, the away goals counting as double in the event of a draw over the two legs.

Hot on the heels of that UEFA tie was a Saturday afternoon visit to Parkhead to face Celtic. Having already taken a point off the other half of the Old Firm, Hibs went one better in snatching the game with a coolly taken goal by Temperley. The youngster collected a neat Tony Higgins pass and shot right-footed beyond the diving Peter Latchford for the only goal of the game. There was some criticism afterwards that Hibs had been overly negative, but Eddie Turnbull pointed out that it would have been folly to have played any other way with so many inexperienced players in his side. As it was, the most experienced player in a Hibs jersey was makeshift right-back Arthur Duncan, who had another fine 90 minutes.

The next game saw Hibs, third in the League, face second-spot Aberdeen at Easter Road. The Dons' new managerial partnership of Alex Ferguson and Pat Stanton were enjoying an unbeaten start to the season, with only four goals conceded in five starts. They were exceptionally solid at the back, with Jim Leighton in goals and a central defensive partnership of Alex McLeish and Willie Miller, flanked by full-backs Stewart Kennedy and Chic McClelland, while other notable names were Dom Sullivan, Joe Harper, Steve Archibald and Drew Jarvie. For Hibs, Duncan was retained at right-back and Hutchinson returned to lead the attack. A little over 12,000 spectators watched on as Gordon Rae, outstanding in a midfield role, headed Hibs ahead. On the stroke of half-time, McLeod scored from the spot after Smith had been upended in the penalty box. Drew Jarvie got one for the Dons, but Hibs won the game 2-1 and leapfrogged Aberdeen into second place behind Celtic.

On the Monday following that fine home win over Aberdeen, Hibs flew out to Sweden for their midweek UEFA Cup return game against Norrkoping. On the day of the match it rained incessantly and the pitch was like a bog, making good football a near impossibility for either side. At the end of 90 energy-sapping minutes, neither side had found the net and so Hibs progressed to round two, where the likes of Valencia, Everton, Benfica, Torino, Arsenal, AC Milan, Napoli and Olympiakos lay in wait. It was not the most inspiring performance by a Hibs team in Europe, but they had played better in times gone by and been knocked out, so it was smiles all round when the official party returned to Edinburgh on the Thursday. There was no bigger smile than the one on the face of Colin Campbell, who had only joined Hibs on a temporary contract and could not have dreamt that he would soon be involved in a UEFA Cup tie. Hibs' next opponents would be the current leaders from the French League, Racing Club Strasbourg, and that would surely be a huge test for the Easter Road side.

The League campaign continued and next up was a visit to Easter Road by newly promoted Morton, who had started the season reasonably well with one win and three draws from their seven games. Benny Rooney brought his side to Edinburgh hoping that the Hibs players might be a bit leg-weary after their midweek exertions in Sweden, and his wishes seemed to come true as ex-Hibs man Ally Scott opened the scoring early in the match. Hibs dug in, though, and got an equaliser very late in the game, thanks to the alertness of Ally McLeod, whose quick thinking saw him reach a short back pass, allowing him to slot home and save a point for Hibs. That took them on to 11 points from eight games, but more importantly extended their unbeaten run in the League – a feat which no other club could match at that stage.

The League Cup third-round, first-leg tie with Clydebank was played on a balmy October evening at Easter Road, and the visitors put up stuffy resistance in restricting Hibs to just a 1-0 win, the goal coming from a penalty strike by McLeod. Eddie Turnbull would have preferred a wider winning margin to take into the second leg, but the Bankies defended resolutely and Hibs just couldn't make their superiority tell. It was already known that the winners of the tie would qualify to meet Morton in the quarter-finals, but at this point it was still really anybody's game, with Hibs fans hoping their team would be more creative in the second leg, when Clydebank would surely have to play a more attacking game.

Two consecutive away League games followed, interspersed with the second leg of that League Cup tie with Clydebank, and so a busy period lay ahead. The first of those League games took Hibs to Motherwell and they got off to a wonderful start when Hutchinson headed the ball home in the second minute, but the Steelmen came back with a vengeance and scored twice through Ian Clinging and Mike Larnach before McLeod equalised from the penalty spot. With time running out, Motherwell were then awarded a penalty kick, but Mike McDonald brilliantly saved Peter Marinello's effort low to his left-hand side. That save inspired Hibs to push forward again and Gordon Rae secured a 3-2 win and both points with a stinging low drive just a couple of minutes from the end. Results elsewhere meant that Hibs now shared top spot with Celtic, Dundee United and Aberdeen in what was shaping up to be a very tight League.

Part two of the Clydebank Cup tie saw Hibs get off to a good start when George Stewart scored his first competitive goal for 11 months to put his side one up on the night and two up on aggregate. To their credit, Clydebank kept plugging away and got their reward with a goal by John McCormack, but Hibs never looked like losing another, while the Bankies' keeper, Hunter, pulled off a string of fine saves to deny Hibs increasing their lead.

Back in the west the following Saturday, Hibs finally surrendered their unbeaten League record in going down 2-1 to Partick Thistle at Firhill. The visitors looked a tad jaded in going behind to an Alex O'Hara strike, but perked up a bit when Higgins equalised before half-time. The second half belonged mainly to the Jags and they capitalised on some slack marking, which allowed O'Hara to get his and Thistle's second and winning goal.

On the Monday, a charter flight took the Hibs party to Strasbourg for their UEFA Cup second-round, first-leg tie, but missing from the group was Jackie McNamara, who had not recovered from an ankle knock suffered in the Partick game. This meant a swift return by the now recovered Des Bremner, and there would be a place in the starting XI for Gordon Rae. The French club were in good form, not only leading their league race but also undefeated at home for two years. And they had a number of very experienced French caps in the starting line-up. Goalkeeper Dominique Dropsy had starred for France in that year's World Cup and he was joined by fellow internationalists Francis Piasecki, Albert Gemmrich and a left-back by the name of Raymond Domenech, who would later manage his national team. On the night, the hosts were just a bit too strong for Hibs and ran out 2-0 winners, Piasecki and Gemmrich the scorers. The Piasecki goal was somewhat controversial as it came from the penalty spot after Mr Kuti, the Hungarian referee, awarded the kick when it seemed that the alleged offender, Rikki Fleming, had clearly won the ball when he tackled Piasecki in the box. The small band of Hibs fans who had made the journey must have been shocked to be charged £20 to sit in the stand and another 40p for their programme. At Easter Road, those fans would have had to pay only a fraction of those sums.

After their earlier visit to Sweden on UEFA business, Hibs had struggled in their next game in only managing to draw at home with Morton. When the team returned from France, a tougher match awaited them with a visit to Easter Road by joint League leaders Dundee United. Signs of tiredness were not in evidence in the first half, and Rae volleyed home a peach of a goal to give Hibs the lead, but this United team did not get into joint top position by giving up when they went behind, and in the second half they got a deserved equaliser through a Graeme Payne drive which McDonald got a hand to but could not keep out.

On the Wednesday of the following week, a Scotland Under-21 team, managed by Eddie Turnbull, took on their Norwegian counterparts at Easter Road and won 5-1. Skipper and outstanding player on the night was Hibs' very own Ally McLeod, appearing as one of the over-age players allowed under the rules. Ally scored a great goal and urged his young team-mates on to a five-star performance in front of a very decent crowd. Playing for Norway that night was a young centre-forward by the name of Isak Refvik, and it would not be too much longer before his name was mentioned at Easter Road again.

The luxury of a week without a midweek fixture was not something Hibs had enjoyed for a while, but after the draw with United, Eddie Turnbull had a full six days to prepare his players for their next challenge, an away League game at Ibrox. This break also gave injured players more recovery time, and one such player was Jackie McNamara, who was back in the side at Ibrox. The loss of two goals in five minutes through an Alex Forsyth penalty and a Gordon Smith header gave Hibs a mountain to climb, but they did not just sit back and accept defeat; instead, they went at Rangers and were rewarded when McLeod headed home from close range. The same player then beat Peter McCloy all ends up with a raking shot, only to see the ball thudding back off the crossbar. In the dying minutes, Hibs could and should have had a penalty when Hutchinson was sent crashing to the ground, but referee Alexander waved away the protests and the game ended at 2-1 to Rangers.

Wednesday, 1 November 1978, brought Strasbourg to Easter Road for the second leg of the UEFA Cup tie. The visitors set out their stall to defend their 2-0 lead from the first leg, and Hibs threw everything at them to break the deadlock. If Hibs could get the tie back to a 2-2 scoreline after 90 minutes there would be extra time and penalties, if needed, but keeper Dropsy failed to live up to his name and produced a string of fine saves throughout. Only an Ally McLeod penalty, after the Hibs man had been punched to the ground with 25 minutes left, got beyond him, and so Hibs went down 2-1 on aggregate and out of the competition.

After that disappointment, Hibs had an Edinburgh derby to face when Hearts came to Easter Road on the Saturday. Hibs were now lying third in the League, while Hearts, struggling since their return to the top flight, were second bottom. A Gordon Rae goal gave the home fans reason to cheer, but two shocking defensive blunders gifted Hearts a brace as Denis McQuade and Derek O'Connor cashed in to take the points to Tynecastle. It's always a blow to lose a derby match, and the Hibs fans just weren't used to it – Hearts' win was only their second in the last 23 meetings between the teams.

An interesting development was reported in the derby-day match programme, which revealed that Hibs were on the trail of two amateur footballers from Norway. Midfielder Svein Mathisen, who played for the Norwegian champions, Start Kristiansand, was a schoolteacher by profession, while Isak Refvik played for Viking Stavanger and was a motor mechanic. Refvik had been noticed by Eddie Turnbull when he starred for the Norwegian Under-21 side beaten by Scotland just a few weeks earlier, and the Hibs manager very much liked what he saw. The intention was for both players to join the club for three months to establish whether they might be offered professional contracts and indeed whether the players themselves could settle in the capital. Unlike in modern times, these were days when the introduction of foreign players was both unusual and fraught with problems over being allowed residence in the country. Morton and Dundee United in Scotland had already travelled this route with some success, and so Hibs were hopeful that everything would work out.

In the next midweek, Hibs visited Cappielow for the first leg of their League Cup quarter-final tie with Morton. In a very physical game, McNamara was sent off and ten-man Hibs struggled thereafter, going down 1-0 to a goal by Bobby Thomson. That was Jackie's second red in the competition. Together with his bookings in other games, it took him over the ten-point mark, meaning an automatic one-game suspension.

It was the west coast again on the Saturday as Hibs took on St Mirren at Love Street, and once again they would fall to a single-goal defeat after Billy Stark struck for the Buddies. The loss of Stewart to injury early in the second half didn't help much, but on the day the best team won.

Since the arrival of the two Norwegians in Edinburgh, club secretary Cecil Graham had been wrestling with the mountain of paperwork issued by the Home Office in relation to the granting of work permits. He had even travelled to London to see if his personal attendance at the Home Office might speed the process up. Meanwhile, the negotiations between Hibs and the Norwegian clubs and the players themselves had been a smooth affair, and both Refvik and Mathisen signed amateur forms with Hibs to tide them over until the work-permit situation was resolved.

The quarter-final, second-leg League Cup tie with Morton was next on the agenda for a Hibs side who had suffered three odd-goal defeats in their last three outings. Morton had a number of very good players, including

Dennis Connachan in goals, defender Neil Orr and midfielders Bobby Russell and Andy Ritchie. Ritchie was a real enigma in the Morton ranks. His seemingly lazy style made him look as though he would rather be somewhere else than playing football, but this was totally deceptive as he was a truly gifted player and arrived at Easter Road having scored a hat-trick against League leaders Dundee United the previous Saturday. The night did not belong to Ritchie or Morton, however, as the home support got its first look at the Norwegians and immediately took both players to heart. Mathisen's prompting from right midfield was a joy to behold, while Refvik stole the show with both goals in the 2-0 win that took Hibs into the semi-final. Isak's goals were both set up for him by Ralph Callachan, the first from a well-placed free kick and the second from a superb left-wing run and cross. There was a scare when Morton were awarded a penalty, with Hibs just the one goal ahead, but Andy Ritchie blasted the spot kick high over the bar. The win meant Hibs joined Rangers, Celtic and Aberdeen in the semi-final draw.

One bizarre fact which came to light at this time was that although Hibs had left open-ended air tickets for the two Norwegians to travel to Scotland, they chose instead to make the trip by boat, taking the ferry which docked at Leith. This was November, don't forget, and the North Sea could be rough and punishing, but it clearly didn't affect the players, who had not met previously and used the time to get better acquainted.

Mathisen, fluent in English, gave up his teaching job to join Hibs and was hoping that a move to full-time professional football would help him add to the seven caps he already had in playing for Norway, while Refvik had his eye on progression from the Under-21 set-up. Both players had rejected offers to move to the United States or Holland, and Hibs were hoping this might be the start of a time when the club could confidently look overseas for players who would improve the team. Certainly, if any future foreign signings made the same impact as these two Norwegians had done, the Hibs support would welcome them with open arms.

Prior to arriving at Easter Road to join Hibs, the Norwegians had not actually played for three weeks. Even after reaching Scotland, their training sessions had been few because they were in such demand for interviews and the like. That didn't stop Eddie Turnbull naming both in his starting XI on the Saturday, when Celtic arrived in Leith. The Parkhead club had a couple of new faces of their own on show: Davie Provan, newly arrived from Kilmarnock, and Murdo MacLeod, signed from Dumbarton for £100,000. Having already won at Parkhead, Hibs were looking for a double against the Glasgow side, but had to be content with a point in a 2-2 draw. Hutchinson and Callachan were on target for Hibs, while the visitors countered through new boys Provan and MacLeod in what was a thoroughly entertaining game. Prior to kick-off, Celtic had been in third place in the League with 17 points, while Hibs were third bottom, above Hearts and Motherwell, with 14 points. It really was a tight League, with just four points separating top and second bottom.

That midweek, Hibs met Berwick Rangers in the semi-final of the East of Scotland Shield at Easter Road and ran out comfortable 4-0 winners. Eddie Turnbull put out a mixed side containing a few reserve players, with Jim Farmer and Stevie Brown being handed their debuts. In a one-sided affair, the goals came from Hutchinson, Farmer, Smith (pen) and an own-goal.

Aberdeen was the next port of call for Hibs, who came an absolute cropper in going down 4-1 in a game perhaps best forgotten. The visitors never really got going and lost goals to Harper (2), Fleming and Sullivan, Hutchinson getting the consolation goal.

Torrential rain caused the postponement of Hibs' next scheduled game, against Morton at Cappielow. The Pools Panel sat on such occasions, and they declared that in their view Morton would have won if the game had gone ahead. Time would tell as to just how accurate that prediction might be. Edinburgh weather was somewhat kinder, and on the Friday evening prior to that postponement the reserves met at Easter Road, Hibs running out 2-0 winners with goals from Willie Murray and Willie Temperley.

The saga of work permits for the two Norwegians was still dragging on, and Cecil Graham seemed to be employed almost full-time on working his way through the government red tape. The matter seemed to be hung up on the number of times each player had represented his country at full international level. Refvik was only 22 and had yet to make an appearance in the full side, although he had played a number of games at Under-21 level. Hibs' first request for work permits had been declined, but the club appealed and pointed out that the rules seemed to be different in Scotland and England. The Home Office agreed to review the matter, and meantime the players just carried on with training and getting to know their new team-mates.

While the rest of the first-team squad enjoyed a break from playing, Ally McLeod was in Portugal along with Eddie Turnbull. The Hibs manager was in charge of the Scotland Under-21 team and Ally was their skipper. The Easter Road goalscorer converted a penalty and scored a second from open play in a fine 3-0 win for the young Scots.

The enforced break from playing ended on 9 December, when Motherwell arrived at Easter Road for a League match. After a bright start, Hibs had slumped in terms of their League form and indeed their last win had been against Motherwell at Fir Park. Since then they'd managed just two draws and four defeats. That run without a win continued as the sides, with Jackie McNamara making his 100th appearance for the club, drew this latest clash 2-2. A Willie Pettigrew double for the visitors cancelled out goals from Hutchinson and Higgins in what was Hibs' last game before facing Aberdeen in the League Cup semi-final.

That day's match programme delivered the interesting news that stringent checks were now being made at home matches to ensure that the season ticket used to gain admission was actually current. Apparently, a number of fans had gained admission to games using last season's ticket. The club was unhappy at this practice and urged fans to leave the removal of the voucher for each game to the turnstile operators. Also, fans were informed that the New Year derby would be an all-ticket match at Tynecastle, and terracing tickets were on sale at the club shop for the princely sum of £1.00 each – changed days indeed. Finally, Hibs had, it seemed, beaten off competition from a number of English clubs to sign two players from Tynecastle Boys' Club. Both played for the Under-16 team and they were Peter Docherty, a centre-half and pupil of St David's in Dalkeith, and Martin Munro, a sweeper who attended Liberton Senior Secondary.

The following midweek saw Hibs and Aberdeen meet at neutral Dens Park in that Cup semi-final. British Rail had laid on football specials from Waverley at a cost of £3.50 return and hundreds of fans made use of the service while many more flocked north in buses and private cars. Dens Park was packed to the rafters, with both sets of fans in the 21,000 crowd roaring their lungs out to urge their team to victory, but after 90 minutes the game was still locked at 0-0, although Aberdeen had finished normal time looking by far the stronger side. Extra time got under way and Hibs missed two gilt-edged chances to take the lead. First, Callachan chipped Bobby Clark in the Aberdeen goal, but got too much on the ball and it sailed over the bar. Just 60 seconds later, Hutchinson was clean through with only the keeper to beat but shot straight at Clark, who saved easily. Two minutes into the second half of extra time, tragedy struck for Hibs when a harmless-looking cross by right-back Stewart Kennedy sailed over the head of Mike McDonald and nestled in the back of the net for the only goal of the game. It was galling for McDonald, who had made a number of excellent stops when Hibs were under pressure. The goal put Aberdeen on the road to Hampden to meet Rangers in the final and left Hibs and their fans facing a depressing journey home. What neither side knew at this point was that they would clash again in a Cup semi-final later in the season, only this time it would be at Hampden.

Partick Thistle travelled to Edinburgh to take Hibs on in a League match on Saturday, 16 December 1978, and home fans arriving for that game were given a first-hand opportunity to gauge Eddie Turnbull's mood in relation to the seemingly never-ending saga of the work permits being sought for Isak Refvik and Svein Mathisen. The local newspaper had carried a story saying that Hibs were having problems, and it wasn't an exaggeration by any means. There follows an account of the manager's take on this matter, reproduced in full. Under the heading of 'If only England hadn't opened their doors' Turnbull wrote:

'It's a great pity that foreign footballers were allowed into England this season, for the arrival of Messrs Ardiles, Villa, Golac, etc, resulted in Government legislation to tighten up on the allocation of work permits. Scotland, never previously troubled by any restrictions, has had to fall into line with England and that adds up to a farcical situation.

'English clubs can pay huge fees for players; Scottish clubs cannot compete financially and yet are prevented from recruiting amateur talent from other countries.

'So Isak Refvik cannot obtain a work permit because he has yet to play in a full international for Norway. Hibs, in effect, are being penalised for appreciating the potential of a young player with eight U21 caps. It would seem that Hibs are in a better position to judge the ability of the player than any Government official.

'There seems to be some fear in Whitehall that foreign players could be brought over by Scottish clubs and transferred to England. Surely it would be the simplest matter to lay down that any continental player would be ineligible to move south.

'This week's talks in London did not resolve the Refvik case. Despite the blessing of the SFA and the Players' Union, Isak cannot become a professional at the moment. Thankfully the Government do not have any voice in the running of football in normal circumstances.'

Clearly, Turnbull was incensed with this ridiculous situation and was not afraid to speak his mind on the matter, a trait which followed him throughout his football career and beyond. The man called a spade a spade, and his forthrightness was often a breath of fresh air in a sport where officialdom is quick to jump on those who speak their mind.

As to the game against Partick Thistle, it finished 0-0, was a drab affair and deserves no further mention from me.

When Hibs travelled to Tannadice two days before Christmas 1978, little did they know that it would be their last competitive game for more than a month, as the severest of winters was about to grip Scotland. United were sitting proudly at the top of the League, and the smart money was on a home win. Anyone who followed the smart money was duly rewarded when United edged home 2-1. Hibs performed well, and many present felt that a draw would have been a fairer result, but it was not to be. Jackie McNamara opened the scoring for United when he inadvertently deflected the ball beyond the reach of McDonald, and then Graeme Payne added a second before Bremner pulled one back for Hibs. Despite a concerted effort in the closing stages of the game, the visitors could not get that elusive second goal and the points stayed on Tayside.

At Easter Road on the same afternoon, the reserves fared much better in defeating United 2-1 with goals from Willie Temperley and Gerry O'Brien. A perfect Gordon Leitch cross set up the first goal and man of the match

O'Brien got the winner late on. This game would be the last for the club for Bobby Smith, who was on the point of being transferred to Leicester City. 'Smudger' had caught the attention of Leicester boss Jock Wallace and was enthusiastic about this fresh challenge in English football. Manager Turnbull drove south with the player to conclude the deal, and while at Filbert Street he was delighted to bump into former colleague John Ogilvie, the pair having starred for Hibs during the days of the Famous Five.

Smith's departure prompted Eddie Turnbull to move into the transfer market for a replacement and as a result Duncan Lambie, brother of former Hibs coach John, signed up from the German second division team Furth, having previously played in Scotland with both Dundee and St Johnstone. The fact that Lambie had been playing in Germany and had not won any full caps for his country would seem to suggest that the German government saw no need to interfere in football – if only the British government were the same! Another player leaving Easter Road was reserve centre-forward Brian Fairlie. A part-timer at the club, his departure was due to his employers sending him to Wolverhampton for a two-month training course. Hibs quickly tried to fix him up with some games while down there and Roy Barry took him under his wing at Nuneaton, where he was manager.

With the domestic card wiped out by heavy snow and severe frosts during the latter part of December and for most of January, Hibs looked further afield than the UK to fix up a game that would offer much-needed match practice. A four-day trip to Israel was organised and the players jetted out for a spell in the sun and a game against a Tel Aviv XI. Left at home was Des Bremner, whose wife Pat was heavily pregnant and due at any time, but Lambie made the trip and was handed his debut in the Israeli capital. Indeed, the only goal of the game arrived when a Lambie shot came back off the post and Isak Refvik popped up to net from close range. Back in Scotland, Des Bremner was counting his blessings as wife Pat gave birth to twin boys – a big surprise for the couple, who had been expecting just the one baby.

At long last the weather broke towards the end of January and Hibs, having 'lost' five fixtures to Mother Nature, recommenced their League campaign with a visit from Aberdeen. The Dons had not sat idle during the break and had spent some time in Portugal, where they defeated the Lisbon club Belenenses 5-0, old adversaries of Hibs. It has to be said that both sides in the Easter Road game were a little ring rusty, but there were some decent passages of play on a heavy surface in the 1-1 draw. Arthur Duncan, now more or less permanently entrenched in the left-back position, scored for Hibs and Aberdeen countered through Joe Harper.

The Scottish Cup draw had taken place during the enforced shutdown and it paired Hibs with Dunfermline at East End Park. The game against the Second Division pacesetters took place on Sunday, 28 January, drawing in a crowd in excess of 11,000. Drawing was the operative word really as the teams banged in a goal each during a tense 90 minutes. On a frosty surface, both sides struggled to play controlled football and it was a relief to the travelling fans when Higgins popped up with an equaliser after Mike Leonard had put the Pars in front. A replay would be required, but again the weather turned nasty and Scottish football ground to a halt for a fortnight.

Twenty-four hours before the first team played that Cup tie, Hibs hosted Hearts in the reserve derby and swept them aside in style. The pitch was not ideal, but both sets of players gamely tried to adapt, Hibs being the more successful in that regard. On a day when Hearts goalkeeper John Brough was the busiest man on the park, Hibs dominated from the off and led 4-1 at half-time with goals from Willie Murray (2), Pat Carroll and Willie Paterson. The second half saw Brough make a string of saves to keep the score respectable but he was helpless in stopping Svein Mathisen and Willie Temperley taking the Hibs total to six. Temperley's goal was something special. He gathered a high ball on his knee, flicked it over the head of his opponent, caught it with his knee again and then smashed the ball into the roof of the net. A special goal, a sixth goal against Hearts in a 6-2 victory, something that would occur again in the years ahead!

With the Scottish Cup replay postponed because of the weather, Hibs were next in action at Fir Park, where they faced bottom club Motherwell. Despite their lowly position the home side were only a couple of points adrift of Hibs and so both sides knew just how crucial a victory was to them. On the day, the Steelmen gave it their best shot, but they met a Hibs side that had McLeod back on the goal trail after a fairly lengthy famine. Ally actually got the third that day as Hibs had already scored through Bremner and Callachan in a game that finished at 3-0 to the visitors.

That good win on the road set Hibs up nicely for Dunfermline's visit on the Monday following. The game was played on a pitch cleared of snow in a massive effort by ground staff and volunteers earlier in the day, and all the hard work was worthwhile as Hibs cruised to an easy 2-0 win, with goals from McLeod and Callachan. The Pars, with ex-Hibees Hugh Whyte and John Salton in their side, tried hard to match their hosts but to no avail. Hibs' reward for progressing to round four was an away game against Meadowbank Thistle.

A couple of items in the match programme for that game brought the fans up to speed on developments involving Hibs. Firstly, the Department of Employment had put forward the recommendation suggested by the SFA that Under-21 and 'B' cap internationals be allowed to play in Scotland up to a maximum of ten. The government paper also pressed for a 'one foreigner per club' rule, but the SFA was actively canvassing for that to be increased to two. Regrettably, this farcical situation would not resolve itself in time for Hibs to retain the services of Mathisen and Refvik who returned home after their three-month spell with Hibs. Their departure prompted Eddie Turnbull to comment: 'It was sometimes outrageous the way Refvik was treated in his quest for a work permit and Whitehall can be proud of how it handled matters.' Bitter, but entirely understandable, words from the manager. The other item of interest was an announcement that the brewing giant Skol had agreed to sponsor a four-club pre-season cup tournament involving Hibs, Hearts, Manchester City and Coventry City with the hope that if it were successful it would be repeated in years to come.

The weather yet again kicked in to decimate the football fixtures north of the border, and Hibs found themselves out of action until 21 February, when they played Meadowbank Thistle in the fourth round of the Scottish Cup. This tie had given Meadowbank home advantage, but after discussions between the clubs and Edinburgh Council it was decided to move the game to Easter Road, where the expected number of spectators could be more easily and safely accommodated. Struggling near the foot of the Second Division, it was always going to be a big ask for Meadowbank to pull off a shock result, and in the end Hibs ran out winners by 6-0. The goals were shared among five different players, with only McLeod getting a double while Callachan, Brazil, Duncan and Higgins all found the target. Brazil and Duncan were playing at right- and left-back respectively, and that fact alone perhaps illustrated that traffic was virtually one-way for the biggest part of the game. That victory was made all the sweeter as it set up a home quarter-final tie against Hearts after the Gorgie side eliminated Morton at Tynecastle.

Three days later, Hibs were back at Easter Road on League business against Morton. The League table continued to be extremely tight and the visitors arrived two points ahead of Hibs in sixth place and yet only three behind leaders St Mirren. The teams below Hibs were Celtic, Hearts and Motherwell, but with the weather playing havoc with fixtures, a number of teams had games in hand. Bremner gave Hibs a deserved lead, but the home side, without suspended skipper George Stewart, could not build on that goal and lost an equaliser when Jim McArthur took a sore one to the face and was left stranded as Bobby Thomson slotted home from close range. Incredibly, that was the seventh draw in Hibs' last eight games, and while a draw is always better than a defeat, it was also frustrating as better finishing and defending would have had Hibs challenging near the top.

March 1979 began with Hibs again at home and this time their opponents were high-flying Dundee United, who had got the better of the Easter Road men in recent times. In a tight match, Bremner's fourth goal in five League games won the points for Hibs and brought to an end a barren home spell – it had been eight games since they had won in Leith. Bremner's goal came when second-half substitute Gordon Rae supplied a pass that the popular Highlander slotted home from 12 yards.

A fourth consecutive home game for Hibs brought old rivals Hearts to Easter Road for the Scottish Cup quarter-final tie on 10 March 1979. One player who would not feature in this or any future game for Hibs was Willie Paterson, who had been transferred to Falkirk in the days leading up to the game. Another player might have featured, though, as chairman Tom Hart and director Tommy Younger had travelled south to Liverpool in the previous week to watch Trevor Birch turn out for their reserves. Hibs had considered that they might take him on loan, but the player was stated to have 'not come up to expectations'. This was the first time Eddie Turnbull would manage a Hibs side facing Hearts in the Cup, although the teams had met 18 times in the competition before this match, Hearts holding the upper hand with ten wins. Hibs needed to set about closing that gap, and that's exactly what they did in winning 2-1 and progressing to a semi-final game against Aberdeen. Goals from skipper George Stewart and Gordon Rae either side of half-time did the trick, with Derek O'Connor putting a better complexion on the final score from a Hearts perspective. Hibs had been in total control at 2-0, but a disturbance behind the goal seemed to upset their rhythm and after O'Connor pulled that goal back it was a tense and bruising final 20 minutes. In goals for the maroons that day was John Brough, recalled because ex-Hibs goalkeeper Thomson Allan had turned out for Meadowbank in their six-goal mauling in the last round. A certain Jim Jefferies played at centre-half and future Hibee Malcolm Robertson wore the No.11 jersey.

Ironically, Hibs were lined up to host Hearts in the League at Easter Road just seven days later, but ahead of that they had a tricky midweek visit to Ibrox to negotiate. Hibs arrived in Glasgow undefeated in 1979, but records like that are just meant to be broken and a Gordon Smith goal won the points for Rangers to end that impressive run. Hibs had their chances when Colin Campbell broke clear but shot straight at McCloy and then an off-balance Tony Higgins contacted the ball on the six-yard line, but his effort screwed over the bar.

Hearts visited Easter Road again hoping to fare better than they had seven days earlier as they were sitting at the wrong end of the League table and didn't fancy dropping to Division One for the second time in three seasons. In a typical blood-and-thunder derby there was action galore, but when the dust settled at the end of the game both sides had to be content with a point. Colin Campbell, in for the injured Hutchinson, scored for Hibs, but the visitors equalised from the spot when Willie Gibson's low shot beat Jim McArthur in the home goal. That was two derbies in a week, and there was another coming up fast as the SFA had scheduled a Tynecastle meeting for later that month.

After a break of seven days, Hibs travelled to Love Street to face a St Mirren team who had briefly topped the table. The Easter Road men put in a five-star performance in twice coming from behind to win 3-2, the first time they had taken two points in Paisley since December 1966. Frank McGarvey shot the Buddies into an early lead but ex-St Mirren player Ally McLeod equalised with a well-taken goal. The home side then scored again through Jimmy Bone, but again Hibs bounced back when Higgins smacked home an equaliser from 12 yards. With play raging from end to end, both defences were severely tested and it was the St Mirren rearguard that was found wanting when Campbell headed home the third and winning goal.

A busy March, during which Hibs would play six League games, saw the Easter Road side at Tynecastle for game five of the six. The win at Paisley had lifted the confidence levels and taken Hibs up to fourth spot in the League, just six points behind leaders Dundee United with a game in hand. Hearts, on the other hand, had not managed to get out of the bottom three places at all and were somewhat vulnerable in second-bottom spot, six points behind Partick Thistle with just one game in hand. In an often bruising encounter, Higgins limped off after just half an hour and was replaced by Stevie Brown, whose performances in the reserves had caught the eye. A later X-ray would reveal that big Tony had suffered a hairline fracture in his leg and would be out for two or three weeks. Brown played well having been given this opportunity, as did the versatile Gordon Rae, who played up front alongside Colin Campbell. Willie Gibson, whose penalty goal had earned Hearts a draw at Easter Road, was once again on target, from open play on this occasion. Hibs countered with goals by McLeod and Callachan to win the game 2-1, earn another two valuable points and increase the pressure on their neighbours at the bottom of the League.

Fixtures were coming thick and fast at this stage but so, unfortunately, was the snow, which had returned with a vengeance. A meeting between the football authorities and the Electricity Board was arranged to take place in Glasgow, and though Hibs were invited they couldn't attend – because heavy snow made travelling impossible! The talks had been called to examine ways and means of using electric power to beat the kind of weather that had wrecked the football schedule. Initial findings suggested the use of an electric blanket, which would be laid on top of the pitch and stop the ground from freezing, but the cost, at £50,000, was probably too prohibitive for most clubs to consider. A fleeting discussion took place regarding the possibility of undersoil heating, and further meetings were planned to explore that and other possibilities.

The last day of March brought Celtic to Edinburgh for the Easter Road club's sixth match of that month. The Parkhead club had suffered more than most from postponements and this would be only their fourth League match in 1979, leaving them 15 more games to fit in before the end of the season, just two months ahead. Those postponements, as much as anything else, probably accounted for the fact that Celtic were in seventh place in the League, one point behind Morton but with an incredible six games in hand. Buoyed by their derby victory, Hibs went at Celtic from the off and were two goals up inside the first 15 minutes. A Callachan cross was bulleted home by the head of George Stewart and when Rae added a second things looked bleak for the visitors, but they managed to steady the ship and not concede any more, while late in the game they got some consolation from Ronnie Glavin's well-hit penalty. Worthy of note is the fact that Stevie Brown, who had come on for the injured Tony Higgins at Tynecastle, retained his place and put in an impressive 90 minutes.

It had been a most productive month for the Easter Road men, whose only defeat was that narrow 1-0 loss at Ibrox. Of the six games played, Hibs had won four, drawn one and lost one, scoring nine goals and conceding just six in the process.

April began with the news that Eddie Turnbull had been having discussions with Derby County manager Tommy Docherty about the possibility of former Dundee centre-forward John Duncan joining the Easter Road side until the end of the season. The injuries to both Tony Higgins and Bobby Hutchinson meant Hibs were a bit light in that area of the park, but an injury to Duncan himself meant that the proposed move never materialised.

St Mirren and Hibs next clashed at Easter Road in Hibs' penultimate game before the Scottish Cup semi-final tie with Aberdeen at Hampden. Arriving intent on revenge for that recent 3-2 reversal at Love Street, the Buddies got their way with a 2-0 win over a shot-shy Hibs side who illustrated all of the misgivings Eddie Turnbull had regarding the lack of current firepower at the club. Frank McGarvey and Billy Stark did the damage and halted Hibs' recent impressive run of League performances into the bargain.

By a quirk of fate, the one League game Hibs still had to play ahead of their trip to Hampden was against Aberdeen at Pittodrie. As well as competing for a Cup final place, both sides still had hopes of qualifying for a UEFA Cup spot through their final League position. Those Hibs fans who made the journey north must surely have left Pittodrie asking how Hibs had not won the match. A host of chances came and went as the visitors dominated the first 80 minutes. In fact, they had put the ball in the net via Colin Campbell only to see the 'goal' chalked off for offside. The last ten minutes belonged to the Dons, but Jim McArthur earned his wages with three super saves and the contest ended 0-0.

The players then lined up to face each other once again at Hampden on Wednesday, 11 April. Hibs went with the same starting XI, but Aberdeen made a couple of changes, bringing in Steve Archibald for Mark McGhee and replacing Cooper with Hamilton in defence. A huge crowd piled on to the terraces at Hampden and the atmosphere was electric as both sides attacked from the start. It was Aberdeen who broke the deadlock when Archibald showed tremendous skill in controlling a Strachan pass before sending a curling shot beyond McArthur and high into the net. The Dons fans duly celebrated and the Hibs fans fell silent for the moment, but they were soon cheering wildly again when Gordon Rae hit a fantastic equaliser past the diving Gardiner in the Aberdeen goal. The game was level at half-time and a tense second half duly unfolded with the tie being decided from the penalty spot, when McLeod coolly slotted home the second and winning goal for Hibs. It was a wonderful and fully merited win by the men from Easter Road and set up a May final against the might of Glasgow Rangers.

On a high from that Cup success, Hibs travelled to Greenock at the end of that week to face a Morton side who had more than held their own after being promoted into the Premier League that season. This would be the first of two meetings between the clubs over a four-day period as the fixture backlog was still being cleared. The first half of the game most definitely belonged to the home side and it was no surprise when Bobby Thomson gave them the lead, which they held until half-time. Whatever Eddie Turnbull said to his players in the dressing room it certainly had the desired effect as within minutes of the restart Callachan fired home an equaliser. It was a very open game now, and Hibs looked to have taken the lead when Rae found the target with a header that referee Alexander originally gave and then chalked off after consulting his linesman. Morton then went up the park and won a penalty, which Andy Ritchie converted, leaving Hibs to chase the game. All credit to the Greens, though, as they stuck to the task and got a deserved late equaliser from Callachan, his first double for the club.

On the following Wednesday Hibs were back in Greenock for that second meeting but this time they would leave empty handed. Home goalkeeper Roy Baines was in fine form and stopped everything Hibs could throw at him, while at the other end some slack marking allowed Bobby Russell, Dave McNeill and Andy Ritchie to find the target. It was a poor showing from Hibs and the points lost over the two games with Morton saw them slipping back down the table again.

When Motherwell visited Easter Road on Saturday 28 April they were already relegated, but that hadn't stopped them beating Rangers in their last game and so Hibs would have to be at their best to secure the two points on offer. After a slow start, when both teams seemed to be sizing each other up, Hibs went into overdrive and hammered four past the luckless Stewart Rennie in the Motherwell goal. Rae got the ball rolling and Callachan soon added a second, taking him into double figures for the season. Motherwell then hit the bar, but they would rarely threaten the Hibs goal and when Bremner and Campbell made it 4-0 the points were safely tucked away for Hibernian.

In the following midweek, Hibs went to Firhill to face Partick Thistle and suffered their heaviest defeat in a very long while. Eddie Turnbull decided to rest several players, with the hectic finish to the League campaign and the small matter of a Cup final in mind. The defence, minus George Stewart, Jackie McNamara and Benny Brazil, was all at sea and the visitors were four goals down inside the first 21 minutes. Ralph Callachan then pulled one back, but the Jags scored another two, making the final score a very painful 6-1. The Jags scorers that day were Jim Melrose (3), Donald Park, Doug Somner and Alex O'Hara.

Three days later, the teams clashed again at Easter Road and those players rested in the previous game were back in their positions. Needless to say, the Hibs fans were hoping for revenge after that hiding in midweek and certainly the home side took the game to Thistle throughout, but at the end of the day only one goal separated the sides and it was Ralph Callachan who won the points for Hibs.

There were only two more League games for Hibs to play before the season ended and these involved matches with the Old Firm. Celtic came first, while the Rangers game would not be played until after the Scottish Cup final. The match at Parkhead, on a Tuesday night, afforded Hibs the chance to have a ten-day break before the Hampden match. Perhaps the Easter Road men had their eyes on that Cup tie or perhaps Celtic were the better team on the night, but the bottom line was that the hosts scored three times through Mike Conroy, Davie Provan and Danny McGrain before Callachan slotted home a late consolation. That goal made Callachan top League goalscorer after a rich run of form over the previous five or six weeks. Making his Premier League debut that night was Jim Farmer, who came off the bench to replace a tiring Stevie Brown. Farmer slotted in at right-back, with Brazil moving to the left and Arthur Duncan into the midfield spot vacated by Brown. The result meant that with one League game still to play Hibs had amassed 35 points from 35 games, more than enough to keep them well clear of the relegation slots, which were filled by Hearts and Motherwell, but too few to win them a place in Europe.

Although Hibs were preparing for that Cup final, they did have a match on the Saturday before it when they took on Meadowbank Thistle in the final of the East of Scotland Shield at Easter Road. Eddie Turnbull fielded a reasonably strong side and the Greens were far too powerful for their lower-league opposition and ran out easy 4-0 winners. Campbell did his selection prospects no harm at all by grabbing a hat-trick, while the fourth came from an own-goal. Significantly, Higgins, now recovered from that hairline fracture, came on as a substitute for Stevie Brown and gained some welcome match practice.

The build-up to the Scottish Cup final was both tense and exciting for a Hibs support dreaming of ending the abysmal run that had commenced so many years before. All around Leith, the banners and scarves were hung from windows and many shops decorated their window displays in green and white with good luck messages abounding. Everyone with a ticket was counting the minutes until the big day, but little did they suspect that the big 'day' would turn out to be three big days.

With the game being broadcast live on two television channels, the crowd on Saturday, 12 May, was recorded as 50,610, with the Rangers support under its traditional covered end while the Hibs fans were on the open terracing at the other. The stadium was a sea of colour and the singing fans of both sides were doing their clubs proud. It was a very tense 90 minutes, with both sides looking extremely nervous, and goal chances were few and far between. Many felt that Hibs were denied an obvious late penalty when Campbell was sent crashing in the box, but referee Brian McGinlay waved play on. On the day, neither side could score and so a replay was required, to take place four days later at the same venue. This time, a crowd of 32,952 turned out on a very wet and windy evening. The Hibs supporters were drenched throughout but never stopped singing as the players on the park sought the elusive opening goal. One or two near things at either end caused heart-in-the-mouth moments, but when the 90 minutes were up not a single player had managed to find the net.

A third and, as it turned out, final match, in front of 30,602 fans, took place on Monday, 28 May 1979, and had to go to extra time before a winner finally emerged. Hibs started the brighter, and a fantastic move down the left involving Rae, Campbell and Duncan ended with Higgins slipping the ball past Peter McCloy to put the Easter Road men a goal up. Shortly after that, Callachan held his head in his hands as his rocket shot beat McCloy but came back off a post and was booted to safety by Ally Dawson. A second goal at that stage would have seriously tested the mettle of the Rangers players, but it was not to be. Slowly, the Ibrox men fought their way back into the game and scored twice through Derek Johnstone. Hibs would not lie down, and with 12 minutes left substitute Hutchinson, on for goalscorer Higgins, was tripped in the box and referee Ian Foote pointed to the spot. As cool as you like, Ally McLeod stepped forward and sent McCloy the wrong way to make it 2-2.

The game therefore went to extra time, and the tension was palpable on the terraces as both sets of players, showing obvious signs of fatigue, went in search of the winning goal. It looked as though Rangers would get that when they were awarded a penalty, but Jim McArthur brilliantly saved substitute Alex Miller's spot kick. With just 11 minutes left, tragedy struck for Hibs when a dangerous cross into their box by Davie Cooper had Arthur Duncan leaping to try and reach the ball ahead of Derek Parlane, only to knock the ball past his own goalkeeper and give Rangers what turned out to be a 3-2 win and the Scottish Cup. It was devastating to lose that way and made all the worse because of Arthur Duncan's misfortune. Duncan was a magnificent servant to Hibs and was widely admired by the Hibs support and all the players who had played alongside him. No-one then, or to this day, would ever point a finger of blame at the Hibs man, and quite rightly so.

Dejected but loyal to the final whistle, the Hibs supporters made their way back from Glasgow that night knowing that their side may have lost but had given everything in trying to bring back that elusive trophy to Easter Road.

And so we came to the final League game of the season. Just three days after winning the Scottish Cup against Hibs, Rangers arrived in Edinburgh looking to repeat their winning scoreline but they would not succeed as the home side got a modicum of revenge in winning the game 2-1, thanks to goals by Brazil and Rae.

Chapter Thirteen

1979/80

RELEGATION – DESPITE BEST EFFORTS

After last season's late finish it was a pretty short summer for the Hibs squad, and there would be no pre-season tour of the Highlands this time around as the Easter Road side had entered the Anglo Scottish Cup and, of course, the Skol Festival Trophy was also on the cards.

Eddie Turnbull had been busy in the weeks leading up to the new season and there were a number of new faces around when the players reported back for training. Jim Brown, former captain of Hearts, joined on a free transfer, although his contract was as a part-timer because he had a job in the financial sector. Two players were picked up from Leeds United, Glasgow-born centre-forward David Reid and Fifer David Whyte being acquired for what was described as a reasonable fee. Last but not least was Derek Rodier, signed from Edinburgh University, where he would continue to study chemistry while fulfilling his footballing duties. Brought on to the ground staff was Peter Docherty, a 17-year-old centre-half from Tynecastle Boys' Club.

Having altered the rules in relation to disciplinary points and suspensions at the start of last season, the SFA were at it again before a ball was even kicked this time around. The ten-point ceiling equating to a one-match ban was reduced to eight, while the penalty incurred for an ordering-off, whether by the showing of two yellow cards or one red, was set at five points. The message was clear – stay out of trouble with the referee or suffer the consequences. Ironically, both Jackie McNamara and Ally Brazil would miss the start of the season in serving suspensions carried forward from the previous campaign. One other interesting move by the SFA was to introduce extra time in the Scottish Cup final to avoid the kind of marathon that Hibs and Rangers had found themselves in last season.

The competitive season kicked off for Hibs on 28 July with a visit to Love Street in the Anglo Scottish Cup first round, first leg. Buddies manager Jim Clunie had also been busy in the transfer market after selling Frank

McGarvey to Liverpool, Jimmy Bone to Toronto and Tony Fitzpatrick to Bristol City. In came bustling centre-forward Doug Somner from Partick Thistle, centre-forward Frank McDougall from Clydebank and winger John Dempster from Queen of the South. All three new signings took part in that opening game, as did Jim Brown for Hibs, and the match was a good advert for the game as it finished at 3-3 after Saints had held leads of 2-0 and 3-2. Bobby Torrance (2) and Jackie Copland scored for the home side with George Stewart, Jim Brown and Tony Higgins countering for Hibs on a very wet Saturday afternoon.

Three days later, the sides clashed again at Easter Road in a second leg tie that would determine which side progressed into round two, where English opposition awaited. During the game, George Stewart went down heavily under a challenge and it looked grim for the big centre-half as he was stretchered off. Whether that unsettled Hibs we will never know, but Billy Stark shot the winning goal for the visitors, taking them through on a 4-3 aggregate. Later precautionary X-rays revealed no serious injury to Stewart, which was at least one piece of good news for Hibs.

Attention now turned to the opening game of the Skol Festival Trophy, which brought newly promoted Hearts to Easter Road. Fans were encouraged to come along to watch the matches in this mini-tournament, in which the Edinburgh clubs were joined by Manchester City and Coventry City, and the admission price to the terracing was a mere £1.50. With Craig Paterson in central defence in place of the injured George Stewart, Hibs took the game to their oldest rivals and goals from Gordon Rae, with a smart header, and Colin Campbell, with a fierce shot from 12 yards just five minutes before the final whistle, won the match for Hibs. Willie Gibson had opened the scoring for Hearts. Ralph Callachan, continuing the good form shown at the end of last season, won the man of the match award, which came with a prize of £100. Immediately following that derby match, the two English clubs faced each other, making the £1.50 admission price an absolute bargain.

Two days later, Hibs were at Tynecastle to face Manchester City, who had lost their opening game but were soon ahead in this one when Henry slotted the ball past Jim McArthur to give his side the lead. Hibs were not to be denied, however, and should have been level, but Callachan struck a penalty past the post and then Bobby Hutchinson headed over the bar when it looked easier to score. Their persistence was rewarded, though, when Brown smashed home from close range to earn Hibs a draw and himself £100 for being man of the match. Coventry City beat Hearts that day, and so when they met Hibs at Easter Road on the Wednesday night they knew a draw would be enough to win them the trophy. With big Jim Blyth in goal and a central defensive partnership of Jim Holton and Terry Yorath, City ground out a 0-0 draw and topped the group to take the trophy back south. Man of the match in that final game was Jackie McNamara, and it meant that a Hibs man had lifted the £100 prize in all three games in which the Easter Road side were involved. One disappointing note for the sponsors of a highly entertaining tournament was the poor turnout at games. The brewing giants had underwritten the tournament to the tune of £50,000, but gate receipts came nowhere near to matching that.

Involvement in both the Anglo Scottish Cup and Skol Festival Trophy now complete, Hibs turned their attention to the Premier League and their opening game, which brought Rangers to Easter Road. The sides had clashed that often at the end of last season that the players must have been getting sick of the sight of each other – although there were one or two new faces around to freshen things up a bit. The Ibrox side had already secured one trophy for the season as they defeated Celtic 3-1 at Hampden in the final of the Drybrough Cup. For their part, Hibs were weakened defensively by the unavailability due to suspension of both McNamara and Brazil. Drafted in to replace them were youngsters Jim Farmer at right-back and Craig Paterson in central defence, but those lads, along with their nine team-mates, found Rangers too strong on the day and lost 3-1. With the visitors two up through Alex McDonald and Davie Cooper, Gordon Rae's strike brought fleeting hope of a revival, but a Bobby Russell goal soon put an end to that.

In the following midweek, Hibs welcomed Meadowbank Thistle to Easter Road for the semi-final of the East of Scotland Shield. Although virtually at full strength, Hibs huffed and puffed for long spells and Jobson's goal for the visitors had those watching biting their nails for a while. Eventually the players got going and goals from Stewart, Brazil and Hutchinson earned a respectable 3-1 win.

Aberdeen at Pittodrie provided the next Premier League challenge. Hibs dominated the first half but could not find a way past Bobby Clark in the Aberdeen goal. Right on the stroke of half-time, Steve Archibald scored against the run of play and in the second half the Dons took control of midfield, adding two more goals from John McMaster to record a comfortable 3-0 win and leave Hibs without a point from their first two matches.

Back at Easter Road, the reserves, with George Stewart making a comeback after injury, were ripped apart by Aberdeen, who had inflicted similar batterings on the wee Hibs last season. The Dons, with Dom Sullivan, Joe Harper and Ian Scanlon in their attack, won the game 6-1, with Harper on target five times. The home support was generous in its applause of that achievement and Harper was quick to acknowledge their applause. The Hibs goal was scored by David Whyte, but it truly was a consolation as the Dons were far and away the better side on the day.

Newly promoted Dundee were next to visit Easter Road, and they were met by a warning shot from Eddie Turnbull in his programme notes. He explained that, statistically, newly promoted teams were at the highest risk of going straight back down again since the formation of the Premier League. Of course, the fact that two clubs faced the drop from a League that contained only ten to begin with, increased that probability. Indeed, the League was not proving popular with fans, as the cut-throat business of avoiding relegation seemed to bring out an attitude of 'avoid defeat at all costs' in the play of visiting teams. Many games were proving to be dull affairs and front men were usually faced with a wall of defenders whenever they neared the opposition penalty area.

As if to defy that school of thought, this game was a belter with loads of open play and seven goals into the bargain. Hutchinson grabbed two and McLeod, Callachan and Rae added three more, while Dundee countered through a Craig Paterson own-goal and Ian Redford penalty. The goal of the game was undoubtedly scored by Callachan when he waltzed past several defenders, rounded Ally Donaldson in the Dundee goal and coolly stroked the ball home to a tumultuous roar from the crowd. Best goal belonged to Ralph, but best performance most certainly belonged to Ally McLeod, who was in majestic form throughout. He opened the scoring himself and then proceeded to open up the Dundee defence with a string of pinpoint passes that had the popular Hibs man looking to be back to his best form. Five goals and the first two points of the season certainly sent the Hibs support home happy that night.

The League Cup draw had now been made and for the third time in five seasons Hibs would face Montrose over two legs, the first at Easter Road in the midweek following the Dundee game. Former player/manager Kenny Cameron having left the club, new boss Bobby Livingstone brought his Montrose side to Edinburgh hoping that they could inflict a shock result on the Premier League side. In his line-up were future Hibees Stewart Beedie and Gary Murray, but Hibs were just too strong for the men from Angus and ran out 2-1 winners, with Rae and Higgins on target for Hibs and Harry Johnston for Montrose. It was quite a one-sided affair, but poor finishing and a number of good saves by Jim Moffat kept the tie alive for the second leg on the Saturday at Links Park.

In that game, a nervy start by Hibs saw Gary Murray open the scoring for Montrose to level the tie at two goals each, but Hibs soon got back into their stride and started to bombard the home goal. The whole of the second half seemed to be played in the Montrose half, but no goals were forthcoming and so the match went into extra time. Again, Hibs pummelled the home goal and eventually substitute Willie Murray, on for Colin Campbell, provided a pinpoint cross for Higgins to head the winner and take Hibs forward to a quarter-final clash with Kilmarnock.

After the game, the Hibs chairman, Tom Hart, had some harsh words to direct at an element of the Hibs support who had been chanting pro-IRA slogans and songs. A press statement was issued and it was emphasised that it was squarely aimed at a small group of supporters, as the vast majority of the travelling support had not been involved. The statement read: 'Hibs will not tolerate any behaviour of this kind from our supporters. This is a non-sectarian club with no religious or political links and I have asked the police to help us deal with the culprits. I have seen the Eire flag at some of our matches and anyone waving the tricolour will be put out of the ground or denied admission in the first place if the flag is spotted outside the stadium. Hibs want to put their own house in order and we mean to stop these young fans who chant irresponsibly. Support the team by all means, but cut out the nasty stuff even if provoked by rival supporters. I deplore bigotry in any shape or form and will not have Hibs involved in any way.'

Safe passage in the League Cup was followed by a visit to Kilmarnock in the hope that Hibs could improve on their record so far – one win in three starts. Once again, Hibs dominated a game they ended up losing, and it was small consolation to the manager and the travelling support that Killie boss Davie Sneddon agreed his side had been outclassed throughout. It was becoming quite a worry that possession was not being turned into goals: in a tight Premier League, it was hard to climb the table once you found yourself at the wrong end. It had looked as though Hibs might just have to settle for a point, but in the dying moments Ian Jardine struck for Killie and there was no time for Hibs to respond. Looking for plus points you could point to the amount of possession Hibs enjoyed or to the excellent first-team debut of Derek Rodier, but those matters were of small consolation when set against the loss of two points.

Only St Mirren separated Hibs from bottom spot in the Premier League, and that was not a healthy state of affairs for the club, particularly when the next League match brought reigning champions Celtic to Easter Road, boasting an unbeaten start to this season's campaign. Manager Billy McNeill had not dabbled in the transfer market to any great extent, relying instead on the players who had stormed from behind to capture the title last season. As to the match itself, it was once again full of hard-luck tales for Hibs. Higgins had already scored when, near the half-hour mark, he shot for goal once again only to see Mike Conroy apparently handle on the line to stop the ball going in. Referee Jim Renton awarded a penalty, but many in the ground thought the ball had already crossed the line and so it should have been a second goal for Hibs. Neither Mr Renton nor his assistant saw it that way and a spot kick was awarded, which McLeod saw well saved by Peter Latchford. Had the second goal counted, who knows what the final score might have been, but at the end of the day Celtic scored three goals of their own, through Bobby Lennox, Mike Conroy and a Murdo MacLeod penalty.

There was some anger among the disgruntled Hibs supporters as they left the stadium, but that was nothing compared to the anger that was to come a few days later when Hibs announced that they had sold Des Bremner to Aston Villa. With more than 300 appearances under his belt for Hibs, Bremner was a firm favourite with the fans on account of his non-stop style and undoubted skill, qualities which Hibs could ill afford to lose. The deal took Des south and Hibs were reported to have received £275,000, plus Joe Ward, who had joined Villa just nine months earlier for £80,000. Manager Eddie Turnbull acknowledged the anger of the support, but argued that there were two main reasons behind the transfer deal. Firstly, Des had apparently asked for a transfer in the previous season but had been persuaded to stay – on the proviso that if an English club came in for him he would be allowed to leave. Hibs apparently offered Des a six-year contract and a guaranteed testimonial game in order to get him to stay, but he wanted to test himself in English football, where, apart from anything else, the wages would be far higher than he could earn at Easter Road. The second reason was that Eddie Turnbull was anxious to convert the possession his team was enjoying in games into goals, and he felt a new centre-forward was needed to fill that role. He had made a six-figure bid for Sandy Clark from Airdrie, but the Lanarkshire club turned that down without even consulting the player. Hibs were now firmly stuck at the bottom of the League, and it would fall upon the shoulders of Ward to get them away from that spot, although the manager made it clear he was still looking to strengthen the side.

Joe Ward got his first chance to impress when St Mirren arrived at Easter Road on Saturday, 22 September, for a Premier League clash. This match would also mark Ally McLeod's 200th appearance for the club, and it was McLeod who set Joe Ward up with a chance to open the scoring, but unfortunately for the new man Billy Thomson brilliantly anticipated the shot and pushed the ball behind for a corner. Hibs were well on top again but not scoring, and there was a huge collective groan from the home support when, in a rare attack, a Jimmy Bone shot found its way through a crowd of legs and rolled past the unsighted Jim McArthur into the net. Things went from bad to worse in the second half when Frank McDougall found himself unmarked in the Hibs penalty area and, with all the time in the world, controlled the ball before firing it past McArthur to give his side a 2-0 lead, which their play scarcely deserved. In his defence, Joe Ward had a reasonable debut and must have been wondering what was going on when sections of the crowd started to boo at 2-0. The explanation, of course, could be found in the League table, which showed his new club had just two points from six games.

A League Cup tie against Kilmarnock, with the first game at Easter Road, gave Hibs some respite from their miserable start in the League. The tournament, sponsored by Bell's, the whisky company, offered financial reward for advancement in the competition, and the winners would earn a place in next season's UEFA Cup draw. In the event, Hibs did themselves no favours by falling into their now predictable pattern of dominating a game they would subsequently lose. Killie opened the scoring when Joe Cairney scored from a suspiciously offside-looking position before Higgins struck to level the match. Although both Ward and Callachan hit woodwork, John Bourke scored the second and winning goal for the visitors. To compound the misery for Hibs, goalkeeper McArthur injured a hand, and this would keep him out for several games.

Hibs' next match, against Partick Thistle at Firhill in the Premier League, saw Mike McDonald in for the injured McArthur while Jim Farmer came in at left-back, Arthur Duncan pushing forward to replace the injured Callachan. Without really setting the heather on fire, Hibs created enough chances to win a string of games but found Alan Rough at his sparkling best between the sticks for the Jags. A goal eventually did arrive when Jackie Campbell deflected the ball into his own net, but by that time McDonald had conceded two at the other end, with Colin McAdam and Jim Melrose the marksmen. In the dying moments, Ward had a chance to grab an equaliser, but the player, showing the strain of not having yet scored for his new club, steered his shot wide and Hibs – inexplicably without McLeod in the line-up – were left stranded at the bottom of the table.

Benny Rooney's Morton side had been a surprise package this season and when they arrived at Easter Road in early October they sat second in the League, behind Celtic but only two points adrift. Given that they had only been promoted to the Premier League two seasons ago, they were certainly the exception to the rule in Eddie Turnbull's contention that promoted clubs were most likely to go straight back down again. In their seven games so far they had scored 20 goals as compared to Hibs' meagre total of just eight, the latter figure being five goals fewer than Andy Ritchie alone had scored for the visitors. On the day, Hibs found Morton keeper Roy Baines in outstanding form and only McLeod could find a way past the genial Englishman. Roddy Hutchison equalised for Morton, and Hibs had to settle for just the one point. In an effort to alter the Easter Road routine, Eddie Turnbull had taken the players to Turnberry for a few days, but any number of rounds of golf, snooker matches and table-tennis competitions seemed to have made little difference as Hibs still enjoyed good possession in their games without being able to find the net often enough.

In the following midweek, Hibs travelled down to Rugby Park for the second leg of their League Cup tie, which Kilmarnock led 2-1 from the first meeting. Within three minutes the tie was level as Higgins slotted home from eight yards, but Killie worked their way back after that early dent to their confidence and scored two goals of their own to win the match 2-1 and the tie 4-2 on aggregate.

With the League situation growing more desperate by the game, Hibs now faced two tough away matches at Tannadice and Ibrox. Tannadice had not been a happy hunting ground for the Greens, and so it was on this occasion as Dundee United scored twice through Willie Pettigrew and Ralph Milne. For their part, Hibs rarely troubled the home defence and even when they did create openings they could not beat Hamish McAlpine in the home goal.

The day after that Tannadice reversal, Hibs held an 'open day' at Easter Road and it was very well attended. Fans were given the chance to watch a training session and then to meet and chat with the players. A reserve side took on an all-star team and led 2-0 before comedian and ardent Hibs fan Bill Barclay, who was playing in goals for the all stars, announced to referee Eddie Thomson that he should help out given the quality of the defenders in front of him! In the end, Bill's side won and he announced that his feat was 'not bad for a Hibs goalkeeper this season', which got a laugh but proved to be scarily prophetic.

Next it was on to Ibrox to face Rangers, who had not started their League campaign too convincingly. From the off, Hibs took the game to their hosts. Early chances for Hutchinson and McLeod to establish a lead were both scorned and the match then hinged on a highly controversial refereeing decision by David Syme. With ten minutes to go until half-time, Jackie McNamara tackled Alex McDonald, and although it was certainly a free kick the referee stunned all present by brandishing a straight red card at the Hibs man. It was the harshest of decisions and effectively killed off any chance Hibs had of getting something from the game. Inevitably, the home side scored twice through Gordon Smith and Alex Miller (pen). Match reports after the game certainly added weight to Hibs' feelings of injustice with the *Sunday Express* reporter writing: 'If Syme had treated everyone as harshly as McNamara, we would have ended up with seven a side.' The *People* added: 'McNamara hadn't even been warned before that tackle, which was no worse than others that had gone unpunished.' It was a sickening blow to a Hibs side that genuinely looked as though they had the makings of winning the game, but once again the Greens would be on the wrong end of a controversial decision in Glasgow.

The last game of the first quarter of the season brought Alex Ferguson's Aberdeen to Easter Road. In his programme notes, Eddie Turnbull assured the fans that his hunt for a goalscorer was very much ongoing and he reminded them that sometimes identifying a player was not enough as the player's club had to be persuaded to sell. Hibs had already had a significant bid for Sandy Clark knocked back, but it was getting desperate now as Joe

Ward was clearly not the answer, having failed to find the net since his arrival from Aston Villa. In the Aberdeen match, for once it looked as though Hibs were going to get a much-needed win as they had the better of the play and led through a brilliant first-half header from Hutchinson, but Andy Watson equalised in the last minute of play.

November started with a visit to Dens Park and yet another hard-luck story for Hibs. Leading by a first-minute McLeod penalty, the first half and start of the second belonged wholly to Hibs, but in a crazy five-minute spell when defenders failed to clear the ball despite having the chance to do so, Peter Millar and John Fletcher struck for Dundee and earned their side a 2-1 win. It was distressing to watch a Hibs defence play so poorly – all the more so when former Hibs favourite Erich Schaedler was putting in his usual solid performance for the Dark Blues.

Now adrift at the foot of the table by a worrying five points, Hibs next faced Kilmarnock at Easter Road. The newly promoted Ayrshire side had had a decent start to the season, with five wins and three draws out of 12 starts. Having recently beaten Hibs both home and away in the League Cup, they were confident of getting a result against a struggling side. As for Hibs, they had shown some encouraging form in their last two games, scoring first in each but subsequently paying the price for lapses in defence. In the game itself, Hibs once again enjoyed the bulk of the possession, but once again a defensive lapse allowed Killie to score through George Maxwell. McLeod netted for Hibs and the Greens had to be content with a draw. A guest of the club that day, watching from the stand with his wife and making the half-time lottery draw, was none other than George Best.

The programme from that home match with Kilmarnock had, as always, a few paragraphs informing the fans of goings on in and around the club. One such article drew attention to the fact that from then on the match programme would only be sold inside the stadium and cited a couple of reasons why that decision had been taken. Firstly, it seemed that a number of 'new' sellers had absconded with sums of money collected from their sales and the police were in the process of pursuing those individuals. The other reason given was that the sellers in the ground would get more protection, as there had been instances of assault when they had stood outside the ground. All of that was somewhat depressing to read, but a lift to the spirits came with the final paragraph on that same page: 'Hibs have been discussing the transfer of George Best with Fulham during the week and are keen to sign him. The Irish star will decide on his next move after playing in a testimonial match at Ipswich on Tuesday.'

It seemed to be a thing of fantasy that Hibs, struggling at the foot of the Scottish Premier League, could even think of making such a signing. This was a world-famous footballer, arguably the best the British Isles had ever produced. Of course, he was in the twilight of his career after his heady days with Manchester United, when he had won a European Cup winners' medal along with a string of other successes and awards, but the mere mention of his name was enough to send a spine-tingling shiver of excitement down the back of any Hibs fan. Could it possibly be true that Best might join Hibs? Certainly, the fact that he had been at Easter Road that day fired the optimism of those present, and spirits were lifted even higher when it was revealed that Eddie Turnbull and Tom Hart had travelled to Ipswich to watch George play in that testimonial game.

Five days after appearing as a guest at Easter Road, George Best signed on the dotted line for Hibernian. The deal, costing Hibs a £50,000 transfer fee, was done in London, the only bad news being that because of an ankle knock George's debut would be delayed.

With all of that mind-blowing news flying around Scottish football circles, Hibs travelled to Parkhead to face Celtic, a daunting task given the Parkhead side's lofty position at the top of the League. The visitors had failed to win any of their previous six away games, and that number increased to seven when the home side strolled to a 3-0 win with two goals from Johannes Edvaldsson and one from Bobby Lennox.

During the following week, George Best slipped quietly into Edinburgh and on his first night in the capital was a dinner guest of chairman Tom Hart. The next day at Easter Road, the press room was packed to capacity as the football journalists took the chance to interview a player who, in their wildest dreams, they could never have expected to see playing in Scottish football. Outside the stadium, a large number of fans had gathered hoping for a glimpse of this stunning new signing and perhaps even an autograph if they could get close enough. One matter confirmed to the press that day was that George would definitely be making his Hibs debut at Love Street, Paisley, on the coming Saturday. Another matter, which the press seemed hellbent on establishing, was how much Hibs were paying the player, but quite rightly the club refused to comment on a matter which was personal to the player and his arrangement with the chairman. Since then, the general consensus has been that George was paid £2,000 per appearance, and the money came directly from Hart. Those details have never been confirmed or denied, but it seems safe to assume that the Northern Irishman was getting a healthy whack to turn out for Hibs.

When the teams ran out at Love Street and the Hibs support got their first chance to see George Best wearing the No.11 jersey they were part of a crowd that exceeded 14,000 – more than treble the normal attendance. The place was buzzing as both sets of fans watched in awe as the great man picked out passes with ease and dribbled his way forward at every opportunity. Ideally, when George scored for Hibs in the dying minutes it would have signalled the end of a fairy-tale winning debut, but unfortunately two Doug Somner shots had already beaten Mike McDonald, in for the injured McArthur. Joe Ward, still to open his account for Hibs, limped off early in the second half with a jarred knee that would cause him future problems.

Watching Best that day, it was obvious that he was carrying a little too much weight, was slower than he had been in the past and was struggling at times with the pace of the game, but one undeniable fact stood out above all of those apparent flaws: the man was a footballing genius who understood that often the ball can do the work for you, and that if you can read the game, an art at which he excelled, endless running was just not required.

Edinburgh was buzzing during the following week as Hibs' next game was against Partick Thistle at Easter Road, and it would mark the home debut of George Best. On the day, the crowd exceeded 20,000, around four times the norm for such a fixture. Best, of course, was the attraction, and when you consider what the gate receipts would have been for the game it highlights what a good business decision the chairman had made in signing the player and paying wages out of his own pocket. Thistle must have been delighted, too, as their share of the gate was around £8,500.

The match itself was not exactly a purist's dream, but it saw a determined Hibs side, under the promptings of Best, record its first victory in 14 weeks in winning 2-1. Ralph Callachan was tripped in the box and McLeod duly converted the penalty before Hibs doubled their lead when a shot from McLeod was deflected beyond Alan Rough by Brian Whittaker. The Jags were then awarded a penalty, which Jim McArthur saved from Colin McAdam. Then Alex O'Hara netted to ensure a nervy finish to the game, but Jackie McNamara – the Hibs Supporters' Association Player of the Year for the second successive time – rallied the defence brilliantly to keep the visitors out.

Tom Hart must have been delighted to see his team win at last and he had double reason to celebrate as he was named Mackinlay's Scotch Whisky Personality of the Month for introducing George Best to Scottish football. At the same time, he must have felt a little sorry for Andy Roxburgh, who only got second prize for his sterling work with the Scotland Under-21 side.

Because Dundee United were appearing in the Scottish League Cup final the following Saturday, their scheduled League game with Hibs was postponed, leaving Eddie Turnbull searching for a friendly game to fill the gap. The manager favoured a trip abroad, hoping that a few days in the sun might give his players a lift, and contact was made with Belenenses, Sporting Lisbon and Porto, but it was found that their financial guarantees did not match expectations. Valencia had given their players a few days off, while Real Betis replied that they would have jumped at the chance but had already committed to another game. Tom Hart, realising that Atletico Madrid were due in London to play Chelsea, quickly contacted the Spanish club to ask if they might play in Edinburgh first, but the Spaniards were looking for a guarantee of more than £20,000, which was excessive to say the least. Hibs offered £14,000, knowing that a crowd of around 20,000 would cover that and leave a little bit left over. They felt that this was a reasonable offer, given that the Spaniards had won only two of their 11 League games to date, but a deal could not be struck anywhere abroad and so Hibs stayed in Scotland.

Such friendly games were useful in that they brought no pressure and allowed the manager to experiment a bit, which he duly did when trialist Yugoslavian goalkeeper Milo Nizetic was given a start in a hastily arranged game against Kilmarnock at Rugby Park. Twenty-seven-year-old Nizetic played for Hibs' old UEFA Cup adversaries, Hajduk Split, and was hoping to win a contract at Easter Road and become the first Yugoslav to play in Scottish football. The poor guy must surely have been having second thoughts as Killie rattled four goals past him, the marksmen being Houston, McDicken and Welsh. It's not clear what the attendance was that day, but George Best did play, and he was sure to have attracted a decent crowd.

Two days later, Hibs welcomed Jock Wallace's Leicester side to Edinburgh after the manager had met Eddie Turnbull at a function in Glasgow. The Foxes had a number of good players in their side, including goalkeeper Mark Wallington, defender Dennis Rofe, midfielder and ex-Hibee Bobby Smith, and a talented young attacker named Gary Lineker, who played alongside a former Rangers man and one-time Hibs loan player, Martin Henderson. The game ended at 3-2 to Hibs, with McLeod scoring a brilliant hat-trick, the first goal being the one that would stick in the mind as he was set up by some wizardry on the left wing by George Best. City scored through Larry May and Scotsman Derek Strickland, while Bobby Smith was given a warm welcome back to his old haunt. Milo Nizetic played in that game and had a good 90 minutes, but unfortunately for the big keeper he broke a bone in his hand in that game and had to return home to Split, his trial with Hibs now over.

It was back to competitive football on the Saturday as Hibs visited Morton at Cappielow. With George Best declared as absent due to injury, young Derek Rodier was drafted into the starting XI and scorned a couple of early chances, probably due to nerves as much as anything else. The game, on a very muddy pitch, seemed to be heading for a 0-0 scoreline until late in the proceedings, when Andy Ritchie and Jim Tolmie struck for the home side and left Hibs once again without any points from the encounter. During the game, the Hibs goalkeeper Jim McArthur was struck in the eye by a glass phial thrown from behind the goal. Thankfully, it did no damage, although referee Tommy Muirhead spotted the incident and later advised he would be reporting it to the SFA. There had been a spate of throwing incidents across the game in Scotland and the authorities were determined to take action in order to stamp it out. At Easter Road on the same day, Joe Ward, back from injury, finally got his first goal in Hibs colours – but unfortunately it was in a 3-2 defeat for the reserves, with Davie Whyte getting the other goal for Hibs.

Third-placed Rangers provided Hibs with their next test when they arrived at Easter Road for a League match the Saturday before Christmas. Sitting behind Celtic and Morton, the Ibrox club had played two games more than those clubs and so knew the importance of getting a win against the basement boys in Leith. The Hibs record at that time made dismal reading: from the 17 games played only two had resulted in wins and three in draws. They were the lowest-scoring team in the League, with just 15 goals, and second only to Dundee in the matter of most goals conceded at 33. There seemed little hope of a rare win for the Greens, and when Tommy McLean gave Rangers the lead there was a feeling of 'here we go again' among the home support. That feeling persisted until George Best tore Sandy Jardine apart out on the left before delivering the perfect pass for Higgins to fire home an equaliser. Hibs had their tails up now and were playing with a spirit and determination that had been lacking in many games previously. Would another draw have to suffice? It looked like it until Colin Campbell popped up in the Rangers box to score the goal that gave Hibs a 2-1 win. It was a super performance by Hibs, and it looked as though it could maybe provide a turning point with the fixtures coming thick and fast over the holiday period.

Just when things seemed to be looking up, Mother Nature took a hand and caused the next two fixtures to be postponed. Firstly, Pittodrie fell victim to a heavy snowstorm and a deep frost and then the New Year's Day game at Easter Road, where Dundee were the intended visitors, fell victim to the conditions. Eddie Turnbull had been desperate for that game to go ahead and the club had called on willing volunteers from the Supporters' Association to help cover the playing surface with a protective layer of straw, but it was all to no avail.

Hibs finally got back on the competitive trail when they visited Kilmarnock early in January. This would be the fourth meeting of the season at that venue, where a League game, a League Cup game and a friendly all ended up in victory for the home side. In another story of missed opportunities, Hibs once again lost at Rugby Park, this time 3-1. The Greens had much of the play in the first half, but failed to capitalise on it, even missing a penalty when McLeod's shot came back off the post. Best then had a net-bound volley cleared off the line. Meanwhile, Killie leftwinger Bobby Street scored two smart goals to put his side ahead before Campbell headed the ball home to give Hibs a lifeline. It would be Killie and Bobby Street who scored the only other goal, prompting the sports editors in the Sunday newspapers to come up with headlines such as 'Killie finish Streets ahead'.

League leaders Celtic rolled into town on Saturday, 12 January 1980, and nobody heading to the game that day would have given Hibs a chance against a side who had scored 39 goals in 19 games, more than twice the 18 managed by Hibs. An injury to Arthur Duncan meant that his left-back jersey would be taken by Duncan Lambie, who turned in a sterling display while helping his side to a very creditable 1-1 draw. The roar from the home fans that greeted George Best's opening goal on 23 minutes was deafening. Picking up a pass from Campbell on the right side of the Celtic penalty area, Best wrong-footed Alan Sneddon before unleashing a rocket shot which Peter Latchford touched but could not keep out. The home side were giving as good as they got but, as ever, spurned further chances to score, allowing Roy Aitken to snatch an equaliser. It was sickening not to win, but the home fans were at least encouraged that Hibs had managed to push the League leaders all the way.

In the week following that 1-1 draw, Hibs learned that the Scottish Cup would see them facing either Meadowbank Thistle or Stranraer in the third round. Also during that week, Eddie Turnbull took his players south for a return friendly with Leicester City at Filbert Street. The appearance of George Best ensured a decent turnout, and Hibs won away from home for the first time in a long while. What a pity it wasn't a League game! After more than three seasons in the jersey, Jackie McNamara finally managed to get his first goal for the club and Tony Higgins added a second with a strong header to make the final score 2-0. It was good to see Hibs keeping a clean sheet, with Jim McArthur, protected well by the young central defensive partnership of Gordon Rae and Craig Paterson, in fine form.

A cold snap kept Hibs out of action until the last Saturday of January when they played their third-round Scottish Cup tie against Meadowbank Thistle, who had disposed of Stranraer with some ease in round two. Being a home tie for Thistle, there was some thought that the game might be moved to Easter Road, as on the previous occasion when the clubs clashed, but the SFA ordered that the game be played at neutral Tynecastle. With Rae suspended, George Stewart returned to play his first game for three months following a lengthy spell out due to injury. His troublesome knee stood up to the test as he marshalled the Hibs back four into achieving a clean sheet. At the other end, a cross from Higgins was headed home by Callachan for the only goal of the game, setting up a home tie against Ayr United in round four.

Further bad weather meant Hibs did not play again until 9 February when they faced a good-going Morton side at Easter Road. The Greenock outfit had been a bit of a surprise package so far and they remained the main challengers to Celtic at the top of the table. As the fans settled themselves in, there was a shock as the line-ups were announced, with the Hibs No.11 being named as Willie Murray. No George Best in the side would surely make the task of getting two vital points all the harder, but Hibs thrilled their support with a great display and a winning scoreline. McLeod got two, taking him into double figures for the season and man of the match Murray scored the winner after Morton had fought back with goals from Joe McLaughlin and Bobby Thomson. That had been Willie Murray's first League goal for two years and it could not have come at a more opportune time for the League's basement club. The result also had the distinction of providing Hibs' first Premier League win against the men from Greenock, the six previous games between the two having resulted in four draws and two wins for Morton.

When it became known after the game that George Best was not injured but had just not turned up in Edinburgh on the Saturday morning, the newspapers were quick to speculate as to the reasons for his non-appearance. It was an open secret that George had been battling with the bottle, and many an editor concluded that his absence must have been down to his problems with alcohol. As it turned out, George had been instantly suspended by Tom Hart, who paid no heed to Best's reputation and treated him like any player. Non-appearance without any contact or explanation, regardless of the reasons, meant Hart considered the player to be in breach of contract and so he implemented that suspension. It became clear during the days that followed that Best had flown into Edinburgh on the Sunday to apologise to the chairman. He trained on the Monday with the players and then sorted the situation out over lunch with Hart, and the suspension was duly lifted.

Around this time there was other news coming out of the club. Firstly, Hibs declared a genuine interest in having an undersoil heating system installed at Easter Road. Coventry City had pioneered this new technology in England and their chairman, Jimmy Hill, hosted a visit by a large number of chairmen from English clubs plus representatives from both Hibs and Rangers in Scotland. The Hibs men were directors Jimmy Kerr and Alan Hart, and their report back to Hart was on a very positive note. Although the system would cost around £50,000 to install, Hibs were inclined to make the investment as the number of postponed home games had become a cause for concern. The number of midweek matches needed to clear the backlog meant an inevitable drop in revenue as crowd sizes were always smaller than they would be on a Saturday.

Counting the win at Leicester, Hibs had gone three games without defeat when First Division pacesetters Ayr United arrived at Easter Road for the Scottish Cup fourth-round tie, the game having been moved to the Sunday to avoid clashing with Saturday's rugby international at Murrayfield and a home tie for Hearts at Tynecastle. New manager Willie McLean had turned the League season around for Ayr, who had been struggling near the foot of the table when he took over but were now in second place and had a number of decent players in their ranks. Newest signing Derek Frye, a £12,000 buy from Dundee United, was the son of former Easter Road favourite Johnny Frye and had shown excellent form since his move from Tannadice. In the game itself, Hibs had to work hard to break down a very well organised defence and they had to do so without the help of George Best, whose jersey had gone to Willie Murray and whose absence was again shrouded in mystery. Eventually, Hibs wore their opponents down and goals from Lambie and McLeod ensured safe passage into the next round, where they would face Berwick Rangers away.

After the game it was revealed that George Best had turned up at the stadium on time, but that he had been 'unfit' for the Cup tie and immediately placed on the transfer list. Although the actual words never formed part of any official club statement, it was pretty widely understood that Best had been drinking before reporting for the game. After another apology and an agreement to seek treatment, Best was taken off the transfer list and given another chance at the club.

The opportunity to extend the unbeaten run from four games to five came when Hibs visited Tannadice in the latter part of February. In a very close game, Hibs fell to a single goal scored by Willie Pettigrew. The fact that Jim McArthur was voted man of the match indicates that the margin might have been wider but for the keeper's heroics. This match would be McNamara's last in a Hibs jersey for three games, as the result of a suspension kicking in, but the talented defender had been selected by Jock Stein, along with Ally McLeod, to represent the Scottish League against the League of Ireland, and so that offered the chance of some match practice during his enforced absence. It was a trip that many players did not fancy for some reason, and each of those named was given the option to withdraw, but the two Hibs men were happy to be recognised by their country and gladly agreed to travel.

Still adrift at the foot of the League and looking racing certainties to make the drop, Hibs travelled to Ibrox on the first day of March knowing that in their 11 previous away League games they had failed to win even one, and indeed had only scored four times in those matches. Once again, the announced results would include the words 'Hibs nil' as Rangers took the points with a solitary goal from the head of Derek Johnstone. It's not as though Hibs didn't have chances, as they finished the stronger side, but missed efforts from Higgins and McLeod meant yet another defeat on the road.

At the beginning of the following week, two new 'old' faces appeared in the dressing room after the club secured the services of Peter Cormack, brought back to Scotland from Bristol City, and Willie Ormond, who was installed as a coach after parting company with Hearts. In his time away from Leith, Cormack had won two championships, an FA Cup winners' and two UEFA Cup medals while plying his trade down south. Peter, who arrived on a two-year deal, had made his debut for Hibs back in November 1962 and at the time of leaving the club to join Nottingham Forest had scored 119 goals, a trend everyone hoped would continue given the precarious position Hibs found themselves in. Willie Ormond, the only member of the Famous Five who had cost a transfer fee when he was bought from Stenhousemuir, had managed St Johnstone, Scotland and Hearts before returning to his spiritual home.

The Scottish Cup tie took Hibs just over the border into England to face Berwick Rangers at Shielfield, and it was a tense affair as Cormack made his first appearance and wore the No.5 jersey, carrying on his tradition after having worn that number many times for Liverpool. Even with the promptings of the new boy and with Best on the wing, the Premier League side could not break their hosts down and had to settle for a 0-0 draw and a replay in the following midweek. As Hibs had shown their best form at home and were facing a lower-league outfit, it was assumed that the Easter Road side would breeze past Berwick into a semi-final tie with Celtic, but the Greens, without Best in the starting line-up, made really heavy weather of winning the match and did so by the narrowest of margins when McLeod finally found a way past goalkeeper Keith Davidson.

A day before meeting Dundee at Dens Park in the League, Hibs dipped into the transfer market with one player coming in and another departing. The new face belonged to 21-year-old Bobby Torrance, purchased from St Mirren. The forward had been in Eddie Turnbull's thoughts for some weeks and the manager was delighted when the player became available, moving quickly to secure his signature. Leaving the club was big Tony Higgins, who joined Partick Thistle. Tony had been a firm favourite with the fans and many were sad to see him go.

At Dundee, Hibs gave a debut to Torrance and early in the game he struck the post with a vicious curling shot that had keeper Ally Donaldson beaten all ends up. Another debutant was Lawrence Tierney, a midfielder picked up after being released by Hearts, and the youngster gave a good account of himself despite the end result. Dundee opened the scoring through Eric Sinclair before Hibs proceeded to pound the Dee defence, but that old failing of missing the target reared its head time after time, so that when Dundee scored again it was effectively game over for the Greens. That second goal, scored by Jim Shirra, was followed by a third from Ian Ferguson to make the final score 3-0.

Ten days later, Hibs met Dundee again, only this time it was at Easter Road. The game marked Peter Cormack's 300th appearance for the club and witnessed the return from suspension of Jackie McNamara. Jackie, along with Ally McLeod, had turned out for the Scottish League in Ireland and so was not too match rusty for his return to business with Hibs. In a first half during which George Best can only be described as having been quite wonderful, Hibs took a two-goal lead, Best himself getting the first and then laying on a second for Murray. In many games this season Hibs had failed to take advantage when in command, but this would not be one of them as McNamara inspired his defensive colleagues into recording a clean sheet. The win brought with it two very valuable points, and though many had already written Hibs off as relegation certainties, Eddie Turnbull would not hear of such talk. In the programme that night was word of an invitation for Hibs to tour Scandinavia in the summer, but the club turned this down as it was not financially viable.

A trip to Parkhead to face championship favourites Celtic would certainly test Eddie Turnbull's faith in his players in the extreme. In a first half that produced no goals, Hibs certainly held their own and might have snatched a lead but for a fine save by Peter Latchford to deny Bobby Torrance his first goal for the club. The second half, however, was a much different story. A penalty, when Brazil was adjudged to have handled in the box, gave Bobby Lennox the chance to put Celtic ahead from the spot and he duly obliged. Hibs then lost McNamara to injury and the home side capitalised against a weakened defence by scoring three more goals through Frank McGarvey, Johnny Doyle and Roddy McDonald. It was a crushing blow and cast Hibs adrift by ten points at the foot of the table, although they had a game in hand over Dundee United, the Tannadice side sitting in the safe third-bottom spot.

By chance it was Dundee United who offered Hibs the next opportunity to close the gap at the bottom when they arrived at Easter Road on the first Wednesday in April. In his programme notes, Eddie Turnbull emphasised the absolute need to make home advantage count against those sides still in the relegation mix and pointed out what many felt to be the case in saying that relegating two teams from ten merely led to negative tactics in most Premier League games. After 90 minutes of extreme tension and an absence of any flowing moves, Hibs found themselves on the wrong end of a 2-0 scoreline after Billy Dodds and Willie Pettigrew slotted goals past Jim McArthur. Also in the programme that night was an article advising that Hibs were once again going to be pacesetters in Scottish football by being the first club to install undersoil heating, work being planned for the coming close season.

The following weekend, Hibs were in Paisley for a meeting with St Mirren, who had fared well in the League and were among the chasing pack behind leaders Celtic. It would be another case of 'if only' for the Greens as early chances were spurned and the ultimate penalty paid when Alan Logan and Lex Richardson struck to win the game 2-0 for the hosts.

Their recent League form was hardly a source of inspiration for either the players or the travelling fans when Hibs headed west to play Celtic in the semi-final of the Scottish Cup on 5 April 1980. Around 33,000 fans were in the stadium to watch Hibs lose a goal to Bobby Lennox, come within inches of equalising through Gordon Rae and then fold completely to eventually lose the game 5-0. Celtic and not Hibs would now go forward to meet Rangers in the final, while the Easter Road men had to aim all their concentration on improving their League status.

Any attempted escape from the relegation spot would have to begin at Pittodrie, but 24 hours before that Wednesday night tie with Aberdeen, drama was unfolding at Easter Road, where Eddie Turnbull relinquished his post as manager of Hibernian after having been in charge for eight years and nine months. During Turnbull's tenure, Hibs had won a League Cup and two Drybrough Cups while reaching the final twice in the Scottish Cup and once in the League Cup. Add to that a couple of seasons when Hibs had pushed Celtic hard for the championship and it is evident the positive impact Eddie had made on the only club that he had ever played for. With no manager in place, Hibs moved quickly to put Willie Ormond in charge of the team, and he would certainly have his work cut out with Hibs facing no fewer than seven League games in 17 days.

In an encouraging start to his tenure at Easter Road, Ormond steered Hibs to a 1-1 draw against high-flying Aberdeen, the first away point the club had won in a very long time. Gordon Rae was the Hibs marksman, Andy Watson netting for the Dons. McArthur had a fine game in goal and Best, who was attracting covetous eyes from clubs in America, showed bursts of sparkling form from his left midfield position.

On the following Saturday, Dundee United arrived at Easter Road for the second time in two and a half weeks and once again they left with both points in a 2-0 win. Willie Pettigrew was again on target and United's second goal came from Edinburgh-born youngster Eamonn Bannon, who had been signed from Links Boys' Club. That game was the last Best would play for the club, as he was allowed to leave to take up an offer from San Jose Earthquakes in the US. George left saying he had thoroughly enjoyed his time with Hibs, was genuinely grateful to chairman Tom Hart, who had been more than fair, and would do his utmost to control his now very public drinking problem. The love affair between the Hibs support and Best had been short, but it would be enduring.

Relegation was basically a certainty for Hibs now, but they still had to fulfil their League commitments in this hectic period. Two days after losing to Dundee United, Hibs were back at Easter Road to face Kilmarnock, who now had no relegation worries. With that pressure removed, the Rugby Park men played relaxed football and took the points with a 2-1 win. An Ally McLeod penalty took his tally for the season to 13, with Houston getting two for Killie.

Forty-eight hours later, a very weary Hibs took to the field again in an away match with Partick Thistle. On the day, the game could have gone either way, but was eventually settled by a Colin McAdam header which kept the points in Glasgow.

Saturday 26 April gave Hibs their final chance to actually win an away game when they took on Morton at Cappielow. Manager Willie Ormond handed a first-team debut to schoolboy goalkeeper Dave Huggins, and the youngster had reason to be thrilled with his performance, especially as he had dislocated a finger during the first half and had to have it put back in place, which must have been painful. Huggins could do nothing to prevent the Morton goal, which came from the penalty spot and was converted by Andy Ritchie, but likewise Roy Baines in the Morton goal was left helpless as Ralph Callachan pounced on his mishandling of a Cormack shot to equalise with just two minutes left to play. A draw it was, and it meant that Hibs had failed to win a single away game in their League campaign, surely the main factor in their ultimate relegation. Worth a mention here is that Davie Reid came off the bench to replace Derek Rodier for the second half and became Hibs' second debutant of the day.

The first team still had three matches to play before this abysmal season could come to a close and all three were at home. The first brought St Mirren to Easter Road, and when Doug Somner converted an early penalty things looked grim to say the least, but Hibs fought back and Rae scored a spectacular equaliser when he volleyed home from just inside the box before substitute Torrance popped up to score his first for Hibs and a winning goal at that. Torrance had replaced Bobby Hutchinson, playing his last game for the club after being released from his contract. Bobby suffered facial injuries that required a good number of stitches and after receiving hospital treatment he was taken home to Monifieth in a car laid on by the club.

The last two games of the season rather summed up the whole campaign. Attendances at both were small, and those who did go should have been awarded medals as they watched their heroes lose 5-0 to Aberdeen, the Dons lifting the League title in the process, and 1-0 to Partick Thistle.

First Division football beckoned for Hibs. As luck would have it, their oldest rivals had clawed their way back into the Premier League and so it would be another season without a competitive derby match to look forward to.

Chapter Fourteen

1980/81

STRAIGHT BACK UP

Not having been involved in anything other than Premier League football since the last League reconstruction had occurred, belonging to a 14-club First Division meant breaking new ground for Hibs. Instead of meeting four times each, the teams met on only three occasions, which resulted in some opponents only visiting Easter Road once and others twice. The way the fixtures worked out for the Greens meant that they would have to travel twice to play Dundee, Motherwell, Ayr United and Dumbarton, while those named would only come to Edinburgh once. After the poor away form shown in the previous season, this caused a little concern for the supporters, but the fact that the opposition did not include the likes of Rangers and Celtic compensated a little.

Money would be tighter than ever in this campaign and it was unlikely that Hibs would be making any expensive purchases, relying instead on those already at the club and a new batch of youngsters brought in at youth level. Among those called up were Stuart Rae, Colin Kelly, Stephen Marney, Martin Munro, Jim Doig, Ian Black, Tom Aitchison, Brian Rice, Andy Clarke, Hugh Hamil, Carlo Crolla, Alan Irvine and Gordon Byrne. Bobby Hutchinson had, of course, left the club and no new purchases had been made in the close season, so the 18-man party that embarked on a short pre-season tour of the Highlands consisted of the first-team pool and a few promising youngsters from the reserves.

First up was a game against Brora Rangers, Hibs running out convincing 4-0 winners. Goals from Torrance (2), McLeod and Callachan put Hibs on easy street and manager Ormond took the chance to hand a first-team debut to three youngsters who all came off the bench during the game. Martin Munro, Carlo Crolla and Stuart Rae were the players involved, the last named being still a schoolboy and only 15 years old. What a way to spend the school holidays for young Stuart!

From Brora, Hibs moved on to Elgin, making that their base for the remainder of the tour. Elgin City kindly allowed the club to use their ground for training, even though the sides were not due to meet each other.

Keith provided the next test and Hibs won 1-0 with a goal from Cormack in a freak rainstorm that had the pitch virtually waterlogged long before the match finished. Had that been a League game it would surely have been abandoned, but the sides agreed to play to a finish.

The final tour match saw Hibs in Inverness taking on Thistle and beating them 2-1 with goals from McLeod and Brazil. It could have been a wider winning margin as McLeod missed a penalty when the keeper pushed his shot to the side, and Ralph Callachan sliced wide with the goal gaping. But the goal from Brazil proved to be the last in the game, which saw Jim McArthur play the first half and Dave Huggins the second. All 18 players had managed some game time in a successful Highland foray.

It was back to Edinburgh now for one more friendly game before getting down to League business. Hibs had invited John Toshack's Swansea City to Easter Road on Tuesday, 5 August 1980. The Second Division side had assembled a strong squad for their forthcoming tilt at gaining promotion to England's top division and fielded their strongest XI, which included the likes of Leighton James, Robbie James, Leighton Phillips and Scotsmen Dave Stewart in goal and Tommy Craig in midfield. All of this was not enough to entice the fans along, and just over 3,000 were in attendance to watch the sides draw 1-1. In a move the club was set to embrace in future games, the terracing was closed off to spectators with only the stand and enclosure being used. This led to a very poor atmosphere and looked really odd into the bargain. Leighton James had opened the scoring and Swansea looked as though they might complete their Scottish tour with three wins out of three, having already beaten Dunfermline and Raith Rovers, but a tactical switch by Willie Ormond late in the game saw Arthur Duncan grab an equaliser. Astonishingly, that was Arthur's first goal for 18 months, and it was a relief to him to score it. Having been a regular marksman in the past, he was distressed at his lack of goals, but to be fair to him he had played almost exclusively in defence for most of that 18-month fallow period. During the game, Ormond made a substitution, giving young Jim Doig the chance to come off the bench for his first-team debut.

This first home game of the season saw the appearance of a new-look match programme. Now costing 20p, it was quite different from what had gone before with the club deciding that all the text would be printed in green ink, giving it a most unusual look. As to the content, it had the usual offering of manager's comments, visiting team notes, information on forthcoming games and, of course, adverts. The last of those included a full-page offering from the West End Health Club asking the question: 'Fat? Unfit? Get in shape with us!' Other advertisers included Leith Glazing, Derek Gilchrist Insurance, George Stewart's Chesser Inn, Sloan Volkswagen, Jimmy O'Rourke's Corstorphine Inn, Thornton's Sports, Silver Fox Coaches, The Royal Nip and the Bank of Scotland. Missing this year was the Bukta advert, as the club had ended their sponsorship deal with the company and the players were now wearing an Umbro kit without any sponsor named on the front.

That game against Swansea was not only the first home game of the season but also the first game played on a pitch which now had undersoil heating, installed in the close season and expected to last for at least 50 years. There was no need for it in August, of course, but it would come into its own in the winter months that lay ahead.

During the following week, former chairman William P. Harrower sadly passed away. His tenure as chairman began in 1963, when he took over from Harry Swan, and ended in 1970, when he handed over to Tom Hart.

At last the season was getting under way, and Hibs began their quest to gain promotion back to the Premier League with a home game against Raith Rovers. Manager Gordon Wallace had seen his side beaten by Swansea in their pre-season build-up, but they had also beaten Chelsea, and so winning the two points on offer would mean Hibs would have to be at their best. One familiar face in the Rovers line-up was Pat Carroll, who had joined them from Hibs last season, and the smile on his face at full-time told the story as the visitors took both points with a 1-0 win, thanks to a goal from Ian Ballantyne in the final minute of the game. It was a bitter blow, but perhaps served as a wake-up call in terms of the players realising that promotion could not be achieved without a lot of hard work.

The League Cup, sponsored this season by Bell's, matched Hibs up with Alloa in the first round at Recreation Park, but that tie was not due to be played until the end of August and the Easter Road men had two League games and the delayed final of last season's East of Scotland Shield to address first. When the players set out for Stirling to play the first of those three games they did so in the knowledge that Hibs had not won a League away game for 17 months, but that unenviable record was soon ended as the visitors cruised to an easy 2-0 win with goals from Cormack, a rasping shot that went in off the underside of the bar, and Rae from an Arthur Duncan cross. Meanwhile, the reserves were winning 3-1 at Easter Road, with Derek Rodier netting a fine hat-trick. The centre, at just 21 years of age, was the 'veteran' in a very young Hibs side that also included Colin Kelly, Stephen Marley, Hugh Hamil, Willie Jamieson, Brian Rice and Ross McGinn, all of whom would make their first-team debuts in the coming midweek against Hearts in that delayed East of Scotland Shield final at Tynecastle. Down 2-0 and looking out of it, the young Hibs side came storming back when a 25-yard thunderbolt from Rice flew past Ian Westwater in the home goal and Gordon Rae then headed the equaliser that would take the match to a penalty shoot-out. All five Hibs penalties were converted, thanks to Jim Brown, Jackie McNamara, Ralph Callachan, Ross McGinn and Gordon Rae, while Hearts missed one of theirs and so the Greens took the trophy. McGinn had been attached to Manchester City before joining Hibs and came to Scotland on the recommendation of Bobby Johnstone, who lived in the Manchester area.

The last game before that League Cup tie with Alloa brought Berwick Rangers to Easter Road and player/manager Dave Smith must surely have prepared his side by stressing how well they had done in eliminating Hearts from this season's East of Scotland Shield at the semi-final stage. That game had ended at 0-0, with Berwick edging the penalty shoot-out 4-3, suggesting that the Gorgie club and penalty shoot-outs were not meant for each other. But Berwick were vulnerable – they had opened their league campaign with a 9-0 defeat from Hamilton – and on the day Hibs won easily enough by a 3-0 scoreline. Perhaps they should have scored more, with Berwick down to ten men for the final half hour, but a double from McLeod, one from the penalty spot, and a single from Craig Paterson, his first ever League goal for Hibs, won the day and made the debut of Hugh Hamil a happy occasion to remember.

Around this time it became known that George Best's stint with San Jose Earthquakes was nearing its end and that the Northern Irishman, still a registered Hibs player, might well be back in Edinburgh soon until his future was determined. It was not beyond the bounds of possibility that he would turn out for Hibs again, but the club were making no commitment and merely acknowledged that some other club might pay an agreed fee for his services. George had cost Hibs £50,000, and it seemed only fair that a fee be obtained if he were to move on from Easter Road.

Hibs' next two fixtures would be against Alloa in the League Cup, the first of those at Recreation Park on Wednesday, 27 August. Manager Alex Totten had the home side well organised at the back and it took Hibs a little while to break them down, but in the end goals from McLeod and Rae provided a handy lead to take into the second leg – which was perhaps just as well, as Alloa held Hibs 1-1 at Easter Road, with Hugh Hamil's first goal for the club carrying Hibs into a third-round tie with Clyde. Hamil was delighted with his goal: the Dumbarton-based lad was still only part-time with Hibs. This match also saw Andy Clarke being rewarded for impressing in reserve team outings with a place on the first-team bench and a debut appearance after he replaced Cormack during the second half.

September was going to be a very busy month for Hibs, with eight games scheduled – six League and two League Cup matches. The first of those was in round three of the Bell's League Cup against Clyde at Shawfield. Ahead of that game, Hibs had secured the signature of ex-St Johnstone, Everton, Birmingham City and Newcastle forward John Connolly. The 29-year-old had been a Willie Ormond signing in Perth and had scored twice in his last game for Newcastle prior to joining Hibs. Having twice broken a leg in the past, he was given a thorough examination by the Hibs medical team. He passed with flying colours and made his debut against Clyde in a game won 2-0 by Hibs, with McLeod and Rae repeating the goalscoring performance they'd made in the last round at Alloa. Connolly played in midfield alongside young Ross McGinn, who had been drafted in to replace the unavailable Hugh Hamil.

Three days later, Hibs faced up to Motherwell at Easter Road in the knowledge that the Lanarkshire side were among the few fancied to be vying with Hibs for promotion that season. They had not made the best of starts, however, and had won only one of their three League games, although they were still in the League Cup and had smashed six goals past Stenhousemuir in their last outing. With McLeod missing, Hibs drafted young Willie Jamieson into the attack for his League debut. Willie's only previous first-team appearance had been against Hearts in the East of Scotland Shield, but he made the most of his latest outing by scoring the only goal of the game. It was a mere tap-in after Derek Rodier's shot had only been partially stopped, but Willie didn't care as his strike won both points for Hibs and kept them up with the leading pack.

Three days later, Hibs were at Dens Park to face Dundee, who were struggling at the foot of the table. George Stewart, who had been told just days earlier that the club would allow him to leave if he could find a club, was drafted in to replace Craig Paterson, who was away with the Scotland Under-21 side. Stewart was immense against his old club and helped Hibs to a fine 2-1 win, with that deadly combination of McLeod and Rae on target for Hibs while Brian Scrimgeour scored for Dundee. Hugely surprising that night was the return of George Best to first-team action. Back from the United States, George had been asked to fly up from London to appear in the game and had agreed immediately, making his presence felt by laying on the winning goal for Rae. George took the opportunity to discuss his future in a meeting with Tom Hart, and the club agreed that although he was not on the transfer list, if a suitable offer came in they would not stand in the way of the player.

When Hibs travelled to Somerset Park for their next game they met an Ayr side who were in good spirits following a win at Tynecastle in the League Cup. Confidence was high among the home players and they took the game to Hibs from the off, opening the scoring through Eric Morris. But Hibs hung on in and scored three goals in the final 15 minutes through McLeod, Jamieson and Rae, securing the points that took Willie Ormond's men to the top of the table, despite losing Hugh Hamil during the game to a hairline fracture in his leg.

Impressive going forward, Hibs would be a handful for any of their rivals, but special mention must be made of a defence that had conceded only two goals in five League outings. Craig Paterson, freshly back from being voted man of the match in an Under-21 game in Sweden during the week, was in outstanding form and looked every bit a Premier League quality player, benefiting from playing alongside the more experienced and influential Jackie McNamara. Incidentally, victory at Ayr was achieved without Best in the line-up as he had been given permission to go to Belfast to fulfil a previously agreed commitment.

East Stirling had gained promotion from the Second Division, and were holding their own in the First, when they arrived at Easter Road in the middle of September. Notably, the Falkirk team's away form had contributed largely to their second-place finish, and they had started this season in the same vein by earning four out of their five points on the road. With no household names in their line-up, they still managed to hold the Division leaders to a very creditable 2-2 draw, thanks to a double from centre-forward Alex Grant. At the other end, Jamieson also managed a double not only to maintain his impressive recent scoring record but also to earn himself a call-up to the Scotland Under-18 squad.

Douglas Park was Hibs' next port of call to face Hamilton, who were just two points behind them. This was the first visit for Hibs since the mid-Sixties, and they scored a goal to remember in securing a 1-1 draw when John Connolly went on a mazy solo run before hammering the ball past Rikki Ferguson in the home goal. George Best was back in the line-up and played well enough, as did Jamieson, who was unlucky not to keep his scoring run going when he hit the post with a snap shot from the edge of the box.

The second leg tie of the Bell's League Cup game with Clyde brought the Bully Wee to Leith on Wednesday, 24 September. Leading 2-0 from the first game, Hibs were favourites to progress into the last eight, and it was a great pity that there wasn't a larger attendance on the night that George Best arguably gave his best performance to date in a Hibs jersey. He was in brilliant form, spraying passes left and right, with the number not reaching their intended target easily counted on the fingers of one hand. Young and old in the crowd marvelled at his craft, and it was no surprise when he laid on both goals for Willie Jamieson in a 2-1 win, Brian Ahern getting the Clyde goal from the penalty spot. Those goals took Jamieson's tally to six in seven first-team games, impressive by any standards and just reward for the 17-year-old, who worked hard at his game. That win took Hibs through 4-1 on aggregate and into a quarter-final tie with Ayr United, the Somerset Park men having knocked out Premier League opposition in Hearts and Morton to reach that stage.

The day after that Cup win, Hibs moved once more into the transfer market to secure the services of utility man Terry Wilson from Arbroath. Terry was out of contract with the Gayfield Park club, and a transfer tribunal would be needed to decide how much Hibs would have to pay for him. Wilson, now 20, was a Fife-born Hibs supporter who had started his career at Dunfermline before moving on to Aston Villa at just 16 years of age. He had two years at Villa Park before joining Arbroath and could play in either midfield or up front.

An extremely busy September fixture list came to a close when Clydebank arrived at Easter Road determined to close the gap between themselves and their hosts. Under the guidance of Willie Munro, they were staying in touch with the leading pack, but their promotion aspirations took a severe dent when Hibs turned them over 4-1. A debut goal from Terry Wilson endeared him to the fans, while Connolly, Rae and McLeod also found the target, Jim Fallon striking for the Bankies.

That good run of form in September had Hibs sitting nicely at the top of the table, but October started with them being brought down to earth with a bump at Dumbarton. Missing a host of first-half chances proved costly to the visitors when the Boghead side notched two without reply in the second. John Gallagher and Mike Rankin sent the home fans away happy and caused Willie Ormond to say of his team that any form of casual play would be punished as that's exactly how Hibs had conceded the goals that lost them the game.

An early chance to make amends came just three days later when Hibs were at East End Park to face Dunfermline. At least half of the crowd of 5,600 were Hibs fans and they enjoyed their outing as, inspired once again by George Best, their team took both points with a double from McLeod in a 2-0 win. Those goals took Ally to the top of the First Division scoring charts, which until then had been led by Hamilton's Jamie Fairlie. It was fantastic that Best played, because he had already booked flights to California for the previous weekend but decided to cancel them so that he could turn out for Hibs in this important fixture. It was now known, of course, that George was to be transferred to San Jose and would play only two more games for the Greens before leaving. Despite his ups and downs, he had been a breath of fresh air in Scottish football, drawing crowds wherever he played.

The saga surrounding Terry Wilson's value was still ongoing as Hibs offered £15,000, which they thought was a reasonable sum, but Arbroath felt the figure should be closer to £50,000. Given that the last occasion on which Hibs paid £50,000 for a player they had signed George Best, you would be forgiven for assuming that the Angus club were being unrealistic in their valuation.

At this point in the season Hibs lost another player when George Stewart moved on from the club after four years and 181 appearances for the team he had supported since a boy. Stewart had been a good servant and captain, and everyone at the club wished him well.

A midweek match at Ayr followed with the sides clashing in the first leg of their League Cup quarter-final tie. In a tense, exciting game, Derek Frye gave the hosts the lead, only for Terry Wilson to equalise. Then Jim McArthur was hurt in a heavy clash with Ayr's Ian Cashmore, causing the Hibs keeper to play for the remainder of the game with a knee heavily bandaged. George Best, playing in borrowed boots after his bag had gone missing at Glasgow Airport, set up McLeod to fire Hibs ahead, but Ayr came storming back and a second goal from Frye earned his side a deserved 2-2 draw. Another player who limped through a large part of a tousy game was Jackie McNamara, but the Hibs man was made of stern stuff and would not give in to his injury, seeing out the 90 minutes.

Saturday, 11 October 1980, would be a landmark day at Easter Road, featuring as it did the final appearance in a Hibs jersey of George Best. More than 7,000 fans, well above the anticipated attendance, flocked to Easter Road to offer their farewells. Captain-for-the-day Best did not let them down, leading his team to a 2-0 win over Falkirk. Goals from Connolly and Jamieson kept Hibs at the top of the table – and meant that George had not played in a losing Hibs team this season.

The first third of the First Division programme would end with Hibs taking on St Johnstone at Muirton Park in mid-October. Jim Docherty put the home side in front and Hibs were struggling to get level until late in the game. With 15 minutes left and both McNamara and Callachan off injured, Willie Jamieson equalised from a Wilson cross and McLeod clinched the points with a long-range effort in the dying moments. That win made it 11 points from a possible 14 in away matches and was a huge improvement on the form shown in the previous season. Those injuries to Jackie and Ralph would mean physio Tam McNiven would be a busy man in the days ahead, but if anyone could get those guys back fit and playing it was McNiven, a tremendous physio and one of the unsung backroom heroes at the club.

The prize of a League Cup semi-final appearance awaited the winners of the second-leg quarter-final between Hibs and Ayr United at Easter Road. Locked together at 2-2, there would have to be a winner in this game even if it meant going to a penalty shoot-out, but as it turned out the visitors won the game 2-0. Unbeaten away from home, Ayr were able to match Hibs in every area of the park and the home side certainly missed their injured pair, Jim McArthur and Jackie McNamara. The game actually was poised at 0-0 at the end of normal time, but extra-time goals from Eric Morris and Derek Frye carried the visitors through. In the Ayr team that night was left-back Steve Nicol, who would go on to star many times for Liverpool and Scotland in the years ahead.

By a quirk of fate, the same opponents arrived at Easter Road just three days later to take Hibs on. In his programme notes, Willie Ormond expressed his disappointment at the League Cup exit but reaffirmed his belief that the only competition that really mattered to his side was the First

Division, with promotion the number one priority. It was again a tight affair, but this time Hibs came out on top, winning 1-0 with a goal from Brazil. Colin Kelly retained his place in goal as Jim McArthur was still out injured, but there was no starting place for Terry Wilson. Hibs had now been told that they would have to pay Arbroath £35,000 for Wilson's transfer. That seemed to most to be an excessive sum, but Hibs had no choice but to hand over the money once the tribunal had made its determination.

With winter frost causing some problems with the fixture card, Hibs were happy that their investment in an undersoil heating system would soon be paying dividends, although their next match was actually an away fixture against Motherwell. Once again, Colin Kelly started in goal and the youngster had a decent game, faultless for the goals that Motherwell scored in winning 2-0. The Motherwell goalscorers that day were Albert Kidd (pen), a man who would in years to come write his name into Hibernian folklore in a most unusual way, and Willie Irvine. Those dropped points made the top of the Division look somewhat tighter, with both Raith Rovers and Ayr United breathing down the necks of pacemakers Hibs.

An unsavoury incident during the next match, against East Stirling, spoiled the good reputation that Hibs' large travelling support had earned in the Division. A linesman was struck on the head by an unopened beer can, and the club would be punished as a result. Chairman Tom Hart urged fans to report the culprits in such instances and vowed that once identified they would be barred from Easter Road. The offender was actually caught that day and would appear in court for his mindless actions. As to the game itself, East Stirling did extremely well to hold a strong Hibs team to a 1-1 draw. Ian Robertson scored for the home side and Jamieson for the visitors, but that dropped point cost Hibs the lead in the Division as Raith Rovers moved into top spot. Jim McArthur had returned from injury and played well, while Willie Ormond handed a debut to Jim Brown, the second player of the same name to be on Hibs' books at the same time. This Brown, listed as 'Jas.' in the programme, with the other Brown just plain old 'J.', had been the 'experienced trialist' who had turned out for the reserves in their recent defeat by Aberdeen and had seen previous service with Aston Villa, Portsmouth and in Greek football. After the game, and by way of encouraging the players to give their all in pursuit of the title, Tom Hart promised the squad a holiday-plus-games trip to California, but only if they won the First Division. One of the sides Hibs hoped to face if the trip came off were George Best's San Jose Earthquakes, who had paid the Easter Road side £30,000 for the Northern Irishman.

There had been a concern for some time regarding the health of manager Willie Ormond, but the former member of the Famous Five had battled on bravely in his quest to see the club restored to the top flight. Sadly, however, Willie was forced to heed the advice of the medical experts and relinquish his post as manager. His final game in charge came on Saturday, 15 November, when Hamilton visited Easter Road. The Douglas Park side, handily placed in sixth position and arriving on the back of a good win over third-placed Ayr United, pushed Hibs all the way in a six-goal thriller. McLeod scored twice, the first from the penalty spot, and Rae added a third, but the visitors scored through Bobby Graham, Brian Wright and Neil Howie to share the spoils.

It was unthinkable that Hibs should go any length of time without a manager as the race to regain Premier League status could not be allowed to falter, and so Tom Hart moved swiftly to appoint a successor to Willie Ormond. The chosen man was Bertie Auld, who was managing Partick Thistle in the top division but was not on a contract and jumped at the chance to manage a club of such stature. Auld brought with him his right-hand man at Firhill, Pat Quinn, meaning that the new management team was once again made up of former players. With Quinn coming as part of the deal, both John Fraser and Stan Vincent left the club after 26 and ten years' service respectively.

The new manager soon made his views on the game known to the Hibs support and it was music to their ears to hear him talking of playing attractive football in order to get the club back where they belonged in the top flight of Scottish football, competing for the title, challenging in the cups and qualifying for Europe. These were brave words indeed from Auld, who had moved from managing part-time Partick to full-time Hibs with a promise that he would give every player the chance to impress but would also be instructing the scouting staff to be on the look out for potential signings.

Auld's first game in charge saw him taking Hibs to Kilbowie Park to face Clydebank, where honours were even until late in the game when full-back Jim Brown set up new signing Jas Brown to fire Hibs ahead. Two points looked safe until, in the dying seconds, the Bankies' substitute Blair Miller squeezed home an equaliser. Based on that one game, Bertie Auld announced that there was clearly a lot of work to be done and he promptly put in motion his intention to hold a number of midweek games to allow him to assess the whole playing staff. One of those would be against Meadowbank Thistle in the East of Scotland Shield semi-final, while others would be closed-doors bounce games. That draw at Kilbowie meant Hibs had now gone four games without a win, but they still held on to second place behind Raith Rovers. One thing on the horizon that would not help Hibs' cause was a four-game suspension for Jackie McNamara after he was booked for the fourth time this season in that match at Kilbowie.

The new managerial partnership took control of their first home game when Dunfermline arrived in Leith at the end of November. Struggling in the bottom half of the table, Harry Melrose's team had been boosted by the fact that a bid by Airdrie for top scorer Sandy McNaughton had been rejected by the club's board, meaning that he would continue to assist the team in their efforts to climb up the Division. The Pars had two former Hibs men in their starting XI, Hugh Whyte in goal and John Salton at the heart of their defence, and both men played their part in restricting Hibs to a 1-0 win, thanks to a goal from McLeod. It wasn't particularly pretty to watch, but it got Hibs back on the winning trail and that alone was a good sign with Raith Rovers looking as though they would be difficult to budge at the top. That goal was Ally McLeod's 14th of the season and the likeable forward was already looking favourite to top the scoring charts at the club yet again.

Partick Thistle, having lost their manager to Hibs, decided on his replacement that weekend, and who should it be but Peter Cormack, who left Easter Road to take up the post. It was quite a surprise appointment. Cormack was still on the playing staff at Easter Road and although he combined his playing duties with coaching some of the younger players, he had no managerial experience. And yet here he was, joining a team in the top flight. Hibs were not too pleased, because Cormack was only six months into his two-year contract, prompting the Easter Road side to forward a compensation claim for £19,000 to the Jags. Cormack was an innocent party in all of this and left with best wishes from all at the club.

With McNamara about to start his four-game suspension, Bertie Auld signed Billy McLaren from Morton. McLaren, like McNamara, was versatile and could play in a number of positions. Auld stated that the player would cover for Jackie and then be deployed elsewhere when the suspension had been served. Hibs would be McLaren's sixth club, after spells with Dunfermline, Raith Rovers, East Fife, Queen of the South and Morton, and he would remain part-time while continuing his job with the civil service.

He made his debut in the side that travelled to Brockville to face Falkirk on the first Saturday of December. It would be a happy occasion for the big defender as he was made captain for the day and his new side won 2-0, with goals from McLeod and Rae. McLeod missed a penalty, but the goal he did score was a peach as he fired home from a tight angle. Gordon Rae's goal came early in the second half when he slotted home a pass from Callachan to put Hibs back on top of the First Division.

The Meadowbank Thistle game came next and the winners would face Berwick Rangers in the final after the Shielfield Park side had eliminated Hearts in the semi. It was bitterly cold on the night and but for the effectiveness of the undersoil heating the game might not have taken place. Hibs gave Paul McGlinchey and Stevie Brown a start in the match and both gave a good account of themselves. After 90 minutes the teams were locked at 0-0 and a penalty shoot-out was required to establish a winner. It reached the stage of three goals each when Jas Brown missed from the spot, allowing Thistle to go 4-3 ahead when Roddy Georgeson converted. Gordon Rae needed to score to keep Hibs in it. He missed, and Thistle went through to the final.

With the festive period and its normal glut of fixtures approaching fast, Hibs welcomed St Johnstone to Easter Road on First Division business. Astonishingly, the Saints, lying just six points behind Hibs, arrived as one of only two teams in the whole of the UK who had not been beaten away from home, the other team being Rangers. They had conceded only three goals on their travels, and so a difficult encounter surely lay ahead. Playing at left-back for the Saints that day was ex-Hibee Rab Kilgour, while the attack was led by a young striker named Ally McCoist. In football, records are made to be broken and St Johnstone's proud away record was shattered by a rampant Hibs side, who cruised to a 4-0 win. Somewhat bizarrely, Hibs were awarded three penalties during the game as referee Mike Delaney punished the Saints defenders for some rough play in the area. McLeod stepped forward to take the first one and promptly missed, his second miss in two games. When penalties two and three came along, Callachan took responsibility and duly converted both. The other two goals came from Rae, who had an impressive game marred only by his booking, which would mean a three-match suspension in the weeks ahead. With the points safely in the bag, Bertie Auld brought Gordon Byrne off the bench to make his first-team debut when he replaced John Connolly.

Five days before Christmas, Hibs headed to Dens Park and gave their hosts a very early gift in conceding a first-minute goal to Eric Sinclair. Hibs then pounded the Dundee defence, but found keeper Bobby Geddes in brilliant form and could not find a way past him. It looked like curtains for the visitors when Dundee were awarded a penalty, but Jim McArthur superbly saved the spot kick taken by Jim Shirra. Try as they might, Hibs could not get level and the points stayed on Tayside, although many felt that they had been unlucky on two occasions not to be awarded a penalty by referee Stewart of Glasgow. On both occasions, Ralph Callachan was toppled in the box and certainly the TV footage shown that night backed up the strong claims made at the time. After the game, Bertie Auld, who had flown to Leicester during the previous week to check out possible signing targets, offered the view that if Hibs continued to play the way they did at Dundee, they would win the First Division. I'm sure everyone knew what he meant, but they had actually lost the match, and so they needed to play as they had against Dundee but with the added ingredient of winning goals.

The weather between Christmas and New Year was not at its best, but that didn't stop Hibs hosting lowly Stirling Albion on the 27th. Arriving for the game that day, Hibs fans read with interest in the programme that the club had decided to enter a team in the Under-18 League because Bertie Auld felt that many of the reserves were too inexperienced to make the jump to first-team level and would benefit by dropping down to this newly created team. Of course, that meant that Hibs would need to increase their playing staff a bit to fill in the gaps the reserves would now have, and Auld would be busy doing that in the weeks ahead.

Jackie McNamara was back in the starting line-up against Stirling Albion having served his suspension, but as he returned, Gordon Rae dropped out to serve a similar sentence. The visitors packed their defence and the Greens had to work hard to break it down. The pressure paid off in the end as McLeod grabbed a double and Connolly a cracking single to win the day 3-0 and maintain top spot in the Division.

Elsewhere in Scotland there was news that would interest Hibs fans: Pat Stanton, having left his assistant manager post at Aberdeen to take charge of Cowdenbeath, had so impressed in his five months at Central Park that he had been chosen to fill the vacancy created when Harry Melrose left Dunfermline.

On New Year's Day 1981 it was a case of top v bottom when Hibs visited Shielfield Park to take on Berwick Rangers. It was certainly a happy holiday period for the Greens as they followed up that 3-0 victory over Stirling Albion with a 2-0 win in this match. McLeod once again found the target and Duncan added another in a game where the home side rarely threatened Jim McArthur's goal. Making his debut that day was Gary Murray, newly signed by Bertie Auld from Montrose. The 21-year-old centre-forward had scored 14 goals for his previous club and turned full-time after signing his Hibernian contract.

Two days later, Hibs were back at Easter Road to take on a Dumbarton side who had bettered them in their last encounter. It was to be a day to remember for Gary Murray as he scored the only goal of the game to endear himself instantly to the home support. A big, strong lad, he was full of running and made a very good impression during those 90 minutes. That day saw the conclusion of the second round of the Scottish Cup and when the draw for the third was made it paired Hibs at home with Pat Stanton's Dunfermline.

During the following week, manager Auld made transfer offers for three players, but only two of those proved successful. Celtic agreed to sell full-back Alan Sneddon to the Easter Road outfit, and at 22 years of age Sneddon had many years ahead of him in the game. He thought nothing of dropping down from the Premier League to join Hibs, convinced that he would be back in it next season anyway. The second player to join was 21-year-old midfielder Ian Hendry, who had seen service with Aston Villa, Hereford and Cambridge before joining Hibs on a contract until the end of the season. The player Hibs missed out on was Jim Morton of St Johnstone, as the clubs could not agree a deal. Specific fees were not known, but Auld did say that Hibs had spent a six-figure sum in securing the signatures of his new players, adding that he hoped for a decent Cup run to bring some cash back into the club.

Having met and beaten the bottom clubs in their last two matches, Hibs then faced a tough fixture at Stark's Park, Kirkcaldy. Raith Rovers had suffered a couple of postponements due to the weather and so had two games in hand when the sides met, but were only three points behind going into the game. A large travelling support saw Alan Sneddon making his debut, but unfortunately for the new boy he gave away a penalty, which Allan Forsyth converted to put the home side two up after Derek Steel had opened the scoring. Both Gary Murray and Ally McLeod hit the woodwork, but there would be no more goals as Raith secured a 2-0 win and made life at the top of the Division very tense indeed.

Having lost out at Stark's Park, Hibs next faced a home tie with a fast-improving Falkirk side who had taken nine points out of a possible ten in the last five games. Manager John Hagart had known that newly promoted sides would always find the step up in class a major hurdle, and his players had taken some persuading that they were good enough to be in the First Division, but the message seemed to be getting through after that recent sequence of results. Back in the Hibs side was Gordon Rae, his suspension over, and there was a starting place in the No.11 jersey for young Paul McGlinchey following a string of good performances in the reserves. Thanks to the undersoil heating, the match was one of only two in Scotland to survive the appalling weather, when around five inches of snow blanketed the country. It was a tense affair as Falkirk brought every man behind the ball when Hibs were in possession, but a way through was finally found when Craig Paterson struck the only goal of the game. The big defender was up for a free kick and was the quickest to react when Jamieson headed the ball across goal, knocking his shot past the unprotected George Watson in the Falkirk goal. An interested spectator in the stand that day was Pat Stanton, checking out his club's Scottish Cup opponents.

Twenty-four hours later Hibs welcomed Inverness Thistle to Easter Road for a friendly match. The Highland outfit had played Hibs when the Easter Road side were on a pre-season tour and wanted this game to prepare them for their upcoming Scottish Cup tie against East Stirling. With manager Auld watching on from the stand, Hugh Hamil had a cracking game, laying on goals from both Willie Jamieson and Derek Rodier in Hibs' 2-1 win. Rodier's goal earned praise from Auld, who described it as 'a dream of a goal'. New boy Ian Hendry was given a run in the game and gave a good account of himself in central midfield.

In the week leading up to the Scottish Cup tie with Dunfermline, Hibs released four players from their contracts in an effort to trim the wage bill. Neil McNeil, Andy Clarke, Jim Doig and Colin Tomassi all received compensation and good luck wishes in their search for a new club.

Although Dunfermline were struggling in the League, they very nearly pulled off a shock result to ditch Hibs out of the Cup. Pat Stanton's men were leading until late in the game, thanks to a goal from Mike Leonard, and the Pars will have felt aggrieved at losing a very late equaliser to McLeod. However, Hibs had created a host of chances and were well worth a second bite at the cherry in visiting East End Park for the replay. With Hugh Hamil drafted into the side for that game, Hibs had a more solid look to their midfield and the youngster certainly played his part in assisting the Greens to a 2-1 win after extra time. Rae had headed a brilliant opening goal for Hibs, who looked to be heading for the next round until the same player conceded a penalty in the 90th minute, which Sandy McNaughton converted to take the tie into extra time. Both Rae and Hamil were involved in the move that created the match-winning goal for Callachan, a goal that set up a round-four meeting with Falkirk at Easter Road.

Three days later, on the last day of January 1981, Hibs were at Shielfield to face basement boys Berwick Rangers. Manager Auld decided to give Ian Hendry his debut, but the 21-year-old made the match memorable for all the wrong reasons. Just 20 seconds into the game, he went into a tackle and suffered a compound double leg fracture when his shin guard splintered. Ian was taken to Berwick Royal Infirmary and then transferred to Edinburgh Royal Infirmary, but it would be many months before he regained anything like full fitness. Whether it was that horrific accident or a matter of tiredness following their gruelling extra time match at Dunfermline, or indeed a combination of both, we will never know, but Hibs couldn't find a goal in the game. Thankfully, they didn't concede one either and their 0-0 draw was made more palatable when news filtered through that closest rivals Raith Rovers and Dundee drew and lost respectively, meaning no ground was gained or lost.

When Dundee visited Easter Road on Saturday, 7 February, they had slipped to fifth place, some 11 points behind leaders Hibs but with three games in hand. Their recent form had caused them to slip in the race and had cost them in the Scottish Cup, too, after Hibs' opponents in round four, Falkirk, had eliminated them at Brockville, but they stood up to the test against the Greens and secured a valuable point in a 0-0 draw. Defensively, the home side never looked threatened, with Jim Brown in for the suspended McLaren, but the forwards couldn't find a way past stand-in Dundee keeper Alan Blair, who had replaced the injured Bobby Geddes.

In the match programme for the Dundee game, supporters were told of a new initiative to be brought in by the club. The League Management

Committee had ruled that from next season the home side would retain all of the gate money taken at games. In view of that, Hibs would introduce a 'family ticket' for the South part of the main stand. This would be in the form of a season ticket which would admit one adult and one child or, for a slightly higher price, one adult and two children. In the same programme it was intimated that goalkeeper Jim McArthur had been voted the 1980 player of the year by the Supporters' Association. In a relegation year, that was quite some achievement.

Twenty-four hours after that Dundee game, Bertie Auld flew to Dublin, taking in the match between St Patrick's and Shelbourne. He was following up on a tip-off about a forward, and although the player in question failed to impress, Auld felt the exercise worthwhile in order to keep an eye open for players who might interest him. Back at Easter Road, secretary Cecil Graham was in negotiations to take Hibs on a pre-season tour of Germany. Bearing in mind that Tom Hart had promised the squad a trip to California if they clinched promotion, there was plenty of incentive for Hibs to keep playing well and aiming for the title.

Round four of the Scottish Cup brought Falkirk to Easter Road on Valentine's Day, but there would be no massacre on this occasion as Hibs scrambled a 1-0 win with a goal from the penalty spot by Callachan. The visitors had packed their defence in the first half and Hibs felt aggrieved when what looked like a valid claim for a penalty was waved aside by referee Jim Renton, but he was more accommodating in the second period when a shot from Rae was netbound and Alan Mackin punched it off the line. Callachan sent keeper George Watson the wrong way, but try as they might Hibs could not grab a second and so nerves were evident right up to the end. Ally McLeod was dismissed two minutes from time for lashing out when a Falkirk defender took a wild lunge at him. That was the first dismissal of the season for Hibs and meant an automatic one-match suspension for McLeod.

After the match, the draw for the fifth round was conducted in the Hibs boardroom, with two legends of the game doing the business. Lawrie Reilly had first pick out of the bag and withdrew the ball signifying St Johnstone or Rangers. The former Ibrox centre-half, Willie Woodburn, then pulled out Hibernian. During the tie between St Johnstone and Rangers at Muirton, the Perth side had been ahead until the dying seconds, when Rangers equalised. The replay would determine which side had home advantage for the tie with Hibs on 7 March.

Hibs would now play their third home game in a row after drawing with Dundee in the Division and beating Falkirk in the Cup. Hamilton had been going along steadily in the top half of the table, but a run of four consecutive defeats had seen any slim hope of promotion evaporate. Hibs did nothing to help their cause by coasting to a handsome 4-0 win after

Jamieson, in for the suspended McLeod, nabbed two while Connolly and an own-goal from right-back John Brown completed a miserable afternoon for the Accies keeper, Rikki Ferguson. Still leading the Division, Hibs now had nine games left to play, five at home and four away. The chasing pack was led by Raith Rovers, who were three points behind but with three games in hand, while Ayr United and St Johnstone trailed Hibs by seven points, but with just one game each in hand.

Two players who had endured long injury absences would turn out for the reserves during the following week when Dundee United sent their second string to Easter Road. Ally Brazil and Terry Wilson were in the starting XI, along with Billy McLaren, Gary Murray and three trialists, but United were too strong for Hibs and ran out comfortable 4-0 winners.

One month after taking two games to dispose of Dunfermline in the Scottish Cup, Hibs travelled to East End Park and recorded their biggest away win in League competition for eight years by hammering the Pars 5-0. Both Callachan and McLeod were missing from the Hibs team, but Jamieson and Connolly made good use of their chance to shine as each grabbed a double, Rae getting the other from the penalty spot. Connolly in particular had an outstanding game, almost single-handedly destroying the home defence, while Jamieson scored twice for the fourth time this season.

The stunning win over Dunfermline set Hibs up nicely for their visit to Ibrox on Cup duty to face Rangers. Unfortunately, they had to make do without the services of the injured Callachan, a cup-tied Gary Murray and Ally McLeod, whose father had died in the days leading up to the game. If nothing else, this match would give Bertie Auld the chance to gauge the gulf between his First Division squad and that of Premier League Rangers, and in the first 20 minutes it has to be said the gulf looked as wide as the Grand Canyon as Rangers tore into the Hibs rearguard and scored twice through Bobby Russell and Colin McAdam, but Hibs bucked up their ideas after that and pulled a goal back, thanks to Jackie McNamara. From then on, Hibs gave as good as they got, but in pursuing an equaliser they left room at the back for John MacDonald to score a third and take Rangers into the semi-final draw. It was a spirited performance from the Greens and there was much to take from the game in a positive sense, especially the top-notch performance of goalkeeper Jim McArthur, who'd had quite a week as it turned out. On the Tuesday, he was named as runner-up to Alan Rough as Mackinlay's Personality of the Month and then on the Thursday his wife gave birth to their daughter, Nicola Dawn, which made his display at Ibrox all the more admirable.

Out of the Cup, Hibs could now concentrate on securing promotion and their next challenge in that regard came when St Johnstone visited Easter Road. The Saints boss Alex Rennie still harboured hopes that his side might clinch one of the promotion places, and his players must surely have bought into that as they defeated Hibs 2-1 in a closely fought contest. Ironically, McNamara was once again the Hibs marksman when he could hardly be considered a prolific scorer, but the Saints struck twice through John Brogan and Jim Docherty to dent Hibs' promotion hopes. The fact that Brogan scored one of the goals was made all the more painful by the fact that he had been the subject of a £120,000 transfer offer by Bertie Auld and the Perth club had refused to sell him.

Three days later, Hibs had a chance to make amends when they travelled to Boghead to face Dumbarton, whom they had beaten 1-0 at Easter Road early in January. The winning goal that day was notched by Gary Murray, and he clearly enjoyed playing against the Sons of the Rock as he scored twice in a 4-1 win for Hibs. The other two Hibs goals came from Rae, while John Docherty scored for the home side to salvage some pride.

With games running out fast, it really was nip and tuck at the top of the First Division. From a Hibs perspective, there was good news in that the main challengers had failed to fully capitalise on their games in hand and were actually two points behind the Easter Road side, with the same number of games played, when Hibs made the tricky visit to Somerset Park to face Ayr United, who had slipped out of the promotion race in recent weeks. With a sizeable travelling support cheering them on, Hibs took the game by the narrowest of margins when Jamieson scored the only goal on the stroke of half-time, his twelfth in the League – a pretty decent contribution from a 17-year-old. Ally McLeod was restricted to watching from the stand, having twisted his stomach muscles in training, and although he felt he could take part the manager decided not to risk him.

Hibs were really looking good for that promotion spot now, but what had not actually been decided at this point was whether the ten-club Premier League, with two relegation places, would continue. The 38 League clubs had already made it clear they wanted change before this season even got under way, but as they had been unable to agree on a better format than the current one, no changes had yet been made. Hibs had thrown their hat into the ring in support of two leagues, with 16 teams in the top league and 22 in the other. The top league would then consist of 30 games, each side facing the others just once at home and once away. The 'shortfall' in fixtures would be made up by the restoration of the League Cup to a sectional basis and would mean, excluding the Scottish Cup, that each team in the top league would play a minimum of 37 games. It was unclear at this point just exactly what changes if any would be made, but it's unlikely that any of the clubs realised that changes to the league format would be talked about on a regular basis for the next 20 years and more!

The chance to secure another two points towards promotion came with a visit from Stirling Albion to Easter Road on Saturday, 4 April. Manager Alex Smith had made his team a difficult one to break down, but it was their inability to score goals that had kept them in the bottom three for most of the season. Indeed, they had failed to score in their previous nine League games, and that number was increased to ten by the time the final whistle blew. Unfortunately, Hibs also failed to score that day, and it is little wonder that the visitors were far happier with the point gained than Hibs were. But it wasn't all bad news. It was Jim McArthur's 18th shut-out of the First Division season, and while Hibs were dropping a point so, too, were their nearest rivals, which meant that the damage was limited.

With just four League games remaining, Hibs knew when they hosted East Stirling on 11 April that three more points would guarantee Premier League football next season. The Firs Park side had already ensured their survival in the First Division and so were playing with a deal of confidence, relaxed in the knowledge that they had nothing to lose, but Hibs played with a purpose and determination and took both points with a 2-0 win. Fittingly, the man of the match was Arthur Duncan – whose forthcoming testimonial game was fully merited given his sterling service to the club – but the goalscorers on the day were Callachan and Connolly, while Ally McLeod came on as a late substitute for Willie Jamieson to get himself back into action after an eight-week absence due to injury. After the game, it became known that results elsewhere meant Hibs were now guaranteed promotion, and they could now focus on trying to secure the League title.

Wednesday, 15 April 1981, became a landmark day in the history of Hibernian FC when, in front of their own fans at Easter Road, the Greens won the First Division championship in style with a crushing 3-0 win over Clydebank. In a blistering first 45 minutes, Gordon Rae struck two sweet volleys and Craig Paterson bulleted home with his head from close range to demoralise the visitors. The second half was really party time for the fans as Hibs just coasted to their three-goal win and resultant championship medals, no doubt further elated by the fact that, come 8 May, they would be on their way to the US to play Fresno, San Diego, San Jose and two matches in Haiti. It has to be said that the players fully deserved this trip, paid for by a joyous Tom Hart, who was over the moon to see his club back in the top division, as their efforts throughout the season had demonstrated to all how determined they were to take Hibs back to where they rightfully belonged. A special mention for Willie Ormond, who set them on the right path before illness caused him to have to leave the club, and to Bertie Auld, who finished the job so well.

There remained one more objective for the Hibs players before they departed on that trip as they had still to face Raith Rovers in the second last game of the campaign. The Greens had taken points from every other side in the division except the men from Kirkcaldy and they were determined to put that to rights. Rovers were still hoping for the other promotion place, but they had both St Johnstone and Dundee breathing down their necks and so could ill afford to slip up when they visited Easter Road. In a fast, exciting 90 minutes the visitors found Jim McArthur in breathtaking form and failed to find a way past him, while Murray McDermott at the other end had to pick the ball out of the net twice as both Callachan and Murray found the target. It was a crushing blow to the Fifers, as Dundee won and St Johnstone drew on that same day, which nudged the Kirkcaldy team down to third place.

A long and often entertaining season finally came to a close when Hibs took on Motherwell at Fir Park towards the end of April. Neither side really had much to play for and although the home side scored first, Gary Murray equalised to make the final score 1-1.

One final task awaited and that was the staging of a testimonial match for long-time loyal servant Arthur Duncan. The game was billed as Hibs v International Select, but unfortunately the weather was atrocious and only 5,000 fans turned up to watch. The Select side scored through Charlie Nicholas (2), Mark McGhee and Tony Higgins, and Hibs responded through Ally McLeod, Gordon Rae and Alan Sneddon. Making his Hibs debut that day was 19-year-old Stuart Turnbull, signed from Dundee.

Chapter Fifteen

1981/82

DEATH OF AN INSTITUTION

It was a busy close season for everyone connected to Hibs. The club first had an American tour in May and, after a few weeks' break, followed their recent practice of touring the Scottish Highlands in preparation for the competitive games that lay ahead.

The opening US tour match took Hibs to Fresno, where Gordon Rae, Gary Murray, Ally McLeod and Arthur Duncan shared the goals in a 4-2 win, and two of those players shared the goals when Hibs defeated George Best's San Jose Earthquakes 4-2, with Rae firing a hat-trick while Murray got just the one. After that second game, Hibs invited San Jose to visit Scotland for a return friendly, and the American side were only too delighted to accept as they would be the first from the US National League to make such a trip.

From California, Hibs travelled on to Haiti, where the weather was hot but the reception was hotter. In the first game, which ended 0-0, the Hibs players were hacked to the ground at every opportunity. Both Tom Hart and Bertie Auld stated clearly that if similar treatment was meted out in the second game their players would be promptly taken from the field, thereby ending the match. The warning went unheeded, and when Arthur Duncan was hacked down twice in a row and Ally McLeod was knocked out in a shocking challenge, Bertie Auld had seen enough and called his players off. The game, which had been level at 0-0, was never completed.

After a few weeks of rest back in Scotland, the players assembled at Easter Road for pre-season training in the middle of July. The first-team squad from last season remained intact and was added to when Hibs signed 25-year-old, Dalkeith-born Bobby Flavell from the Swedish side Vastar Haninge. Flavell had reached the end of his contract with the Swedes and had asked Hibs for training facilities. Bertie Auld liked what he saw and so offered the player a contract, paying the Swedish club a nominal fee to secure his transfer. The player was absolutely delighted to be given this chance – he had been born and raised a Hibs supporter. Another player joining the club was the very experienced goalkeeper Ally Donaldson, who had been with Dundee for many years but had latterly been in dispute with the Dens Park club. With 20 years of first-team football behind him, Ally was a good player to have around the club as his influence with the young goalkeepers on the staff could only be beneficial.

Further down the pecking order a few young lads had been called up, including Ricky Haddow, a forward from Coatbridge YM; Norrie Innes, a midfielder from Gartcosh United; Tom Kelly, a midfielder also from Gartcosh; Robin Rae, a goalkeeper from Musselburgh Windsor; Mike Korotkich, a midfielder also from Musselburgh, and Alan Samuel, a midfielder from Salvesen Boys' Club. Jimmy O'Rourke, apparently, would be busy running his public house in Corstorphine and so would spend much less time at the club. In view of that, the ex-Motherwell and Hibs man Willie Hunter was brought in to look after the reserve and Under-18 sides.

The Highland tour started with a game in Dingwall against Ross County, where Hibs ran out comfortable 4-0 winners and Rae got another hat-trick, Callachan notching the other. Two days later, Hibs were in Inverness taking on Caley and a 2-0 win was recorded, with McLeod and Rae the marksmen. Just 24 hours later, Hibs were back in Edinburgh and facing up to Sunderland at Easter Road. Arthur Duncan was in sparkling form down the left and had a hand in all three goals scored by Callachan, McLeod and Rodier.

As an experiment, manager Bertie Auld played Willie Jamieson in central defence in a friendly down at Coldstream which Hibs won 2-0, with Jamieson and Rodier getting the goals.

The competitive season would kick off with the League Cup having been reinstated as a tournament where teams would play in groups with each group winner progressing to the quarter-finals. In the Hibs group were St Johnstone, St Mirren and Celtic, and so a tough start to the season was guaranteed.

On 8 August, Hibs fans made their way to Easter Road for the first of those League Cup games, against First Division St Johnstone. It's worth mentioning the programme for that day, if only to say that it had departed from that horrific green text of the previous season! As always, the chairman had a few words for the support, asking especially the younger ones to be on their best behaviour but praising them in general and asking for patience while the team did their best during their first season back in the top flight. Of course, Hibs were the only Edinburgh side in the Premier League that season because Hearts were now back in the First Division.

The Perth side had been the last to beat Hibs, away back in March of this year, and they were to repeat that feat by the same scoreline of 2-1. Gary Murray struck for Hibs, but his goal was not enough to prevent them starting their League Cup campaign with a damaging defeat against a side who had two marksmen who were drawing admiring glances from Premier League clubs. The players in question were Ally McCoist and John Brogan, and each would score their fair share of goals in the years ahead. With Jim McArthur in a contractual disagreement with the club, Hibs called on the experienced Ally Donaldson to step into his shoes and he could not be blamed for either of St Johnstone's goals, turning in a very decent performance, as did debutant Bobby Flavell in an unfamiliar right-back role.

St Mirren provided the next challenge and they would be in confident mood after defeating Celtic in their opening tie. Donaldson had three excellent saves during the game to deny the Buddies, while Hibs had perhaps the best chance to score when Callachan should have done better from an Arthur Duncan cross. In the end, the midweek game finished at 0-0, with manager Auld singling out McNamara, Flavell and Donaldson for praise.

Parkhead beckoned in game three of the League Cup section and Hibs went into the encounter without both McArthur and Callachan, the latter having joined the keeper in a contractual dispute. The first half of the game was a nightmare and Celtic swept into a three-goal lead before Arthur Duncan pulled one back. The second half was better after Bertie Auld changed the formation, but there would be only one more goal scored and it went to the home side, winning them the match 4-1. Amazingly, this gave Celtic their first points in the competition. St Mirren led the group, from which Hibs would struggle to qualify.

Off the field, there were some interesting goings-on at Easter Road as the club called an extraordinary general meeting of the shareholders to discuss a change in share capital of the company from £2,000 to £500,000. The additional cash, should the proposal be approved, would be used towards ground improvements. Rather intriguingly, the official statement calling the EGM stated: 'The reasons for this step will not be revealed until the meeting when 498,000 new shares will be created.' Other off-field news included the fact that manager Auld was trying hard to bring some new faces to Easter Road. Already the club had made two unsuccessful attempts to lure Erich Schaedler back from Dundee, and the Irish League was also an area that Auld felt might produce the kind of players he was looking for. Finally, Alan Sneddon was appointed club captain, taking over from Jackie McNamara.

With just one point from their opening three League Cup ties, Hibs hoped to improve when they entertained unbeaten St Mirren at Easter Road, but it proved to be a bad night for the club in losing 1-0 after Frank McDougall notched the only goal of the game. To add to Hibs' misery, both Stuart Turnbull and Willie Jamieson limped off with what seemed to be ankle ligament damage, while McArthur and Callachan watched from the stand as their disputes with the club were still unresolved.

The match programme that night offered the details behind that increased share capital issue and removed the mystery surrounding its purpose. With the influx of cash, the club had purchased the ground from Edinburgh District Council and planned to erect a covered enclosure opposite the main stand. The project would cost close to £400,000, but the Grounds Improvement Trust would donate up to half of that money to make it a more viable proposition. Work on the covered area would begin in 1982 and would involve a reduction in the height of the terracing on that side of the ground. The club intended, in time, to install seating in that area. As to the new shares and who purchased them, it was intimated that of the 498,000 available, Tom Hart had purchased 373,000, taking his share in the club to 75 per cent, while the remaining 123,000 were available for sale. As Hibernian FC was a private company, the club would invite one or more interested parties to purchase those remaining shares, which would provide additional finance. One other matter from that EGM was the appointment of a new director, named as Tom Hart junior. He resided in Jersey and probably wouldn't be seen at or around the stadium too often, but he hoped to get to as many games as possible using his newly purchased Cessna aircraft to bring him north from the Channel Islands.

Muirton Park, Perth, was the next stop for Hibs, who were looking for revenge after the opening-day defeat at the hands of St Johnstone. Manager Bertie Auld was not present as he was at the Carlisle v Preston game watching potential signings. Pat Quinn took charge of the team and steered them to a fine 2-1 win, both of Hibs' goals providing 'firsts' for their scorers. Flavell struck his first goal for his new club and Rodier got his first senior goal. McDonald scored for the home side. Jackie McNamara was injured in the first half and had to have an X-ray on his heel. Thankfully, there was no damage to the bone. His replacement from the bench was young Peter Docherty, who had been doing well in the Under-18 side and didn't let himself down after being given this unexpected opportunity to show what he could do. The 2-1 scoreline makes it look like a close game, but Hibs were in command throughout and could have scored more, both Rae and Murray hitting the woodwork. Back in the team was Ralph Callachan, who, along with Jim McArthur, had signed a 28-day deal while negotiations on longer-term contracts went on. McArthur did not feature in this game, though, Ally Donaldson retaining the keeper's jersey.

The final League Cup section match brought Celtic to Easter Road for the first time in 20 months, the last clash having ended at 1-1 when George Best scored a stunning goal for Hibs. After a poor start to the season, the Parkhead men were beginning to get up a head of steam and after 90 very entertaining minutes they went home with the two points on offer after winning the match 4-1. Just as the Perth scoreline had not told the whole story neither did the 4-1 from this game as Hibs were much more involved in the game than the result would suggest. Certainly, Celtic scored through Frank McGarvey (2), Dom Sullivan and Murdo MacLeod, but Hibs, who scored through a Craig Paterson header, were denied time and again by Pat Bonnar in the Celtic goal. The big Irishman had two quite magnificent saves to deny both Rodier and Rae (who finished the game with a black eye after an accidental clash of heads with Davie Moyes). Young Peter Docherty had retained his starting place with McNamara still out injured and he did well before tiring later in the game and being replaced by McLeod. Another who came off the substitutes' bench was Ian Hendry, the player who had suffered a double leg break in his debut match at Berwick and who had now completed his long road to recovery.

The match programme for the Celtic game contained a fascinating article about an Irish player by the name of Vincent Furey. It seems that the *Sunday Mail* newspaper had carried a story which criticised Hibs in their treatment of the player and Tom Hart was incensed by this blatant misrepresentation of the facts, so much so that he decided to explain what really had happened, as opposed to what the newspaper had reported as happening. In effect, Hibs had received a letter from the chairman of Gweedore Football Club in the Irish Republic. The letter referred to Vincent Furey, a player at the club, who was very anxious to become a professional footballer and could not imagine himself playing for anyone other than Hibernian. The letter went on to say that Vincent would be in Edinburgh in July, travelling to Scotland at his own expense and hoping to be given a trial with Hibs. He was described as a very good footballer of around 17/18 years of age and would surely be an asset to whichever club signed him. Pat Quinn replied to that letter, saying Hibs would be happy to give the lad a trial but making no promises other than that. In time, Vincent had his trial, failed to impress and was not taken on. The newspaper suggested that Hibs had acted improperly – Tom Hart had now set the record straight.

Although Hibs had not fared that well in their League Cup section they were still in favour of the format reintroduced this season. Other clubs felt that the knock-out system was better, but Hibs would certainly vote in favour of the sections format should the subject be raised again in future.

Saturday, 29 August, marked Hibs' official return to the Premier League as this was their first League match in the current campaign, marked by the parading of the First Division flag prior to kick-off. It had been 29 years since Hibs had enjoyed a similar unfurling of a League flag when they were celebrating their third championship in five years. It was to be a joyous day all round as Hibs dominated their match with fellow new boys Dundee and won 2-0, after goals from Murray and Rae in the space of just five minutes. Both McArthur and Callachan featured positively in this game and the fans were hoping that those much-admired players could soon settle their disputes with the club. Three other players from that match are worthy of mention. Hibs youngster Peter Docherty played the full 90 minutes and looked very accomplished alongside Craig Paterson. Meanwhile, Erich Schaedler, at left-back for Dundee, was 'serenaded' throughout the game by the Hibs choir, who wanted the likeable defender to return to Easter Road at the earliest opportunity. The third player wore No.11 for Dundee that day and was fairly anonymous throughout, but he would have a major part to play in the minds of Hibs supporters in the years ahead – Albert Kidd.

It was good to win the opening day League fixture and Hibs hoped to continue that form as they visited Ibrox early in September. Rangers would be a whole different challenge to Dundee, but Bertie Auld was confident that his players had nothing to fear from the Glasgow club, and his confidence was rewarded with an excellent 2-2 draw in a game that Hibs really could have and should have won. McLeod, who had missed the opening win over Dundee, was back in the fold as was McNamara, recovered from injury and preferred at such a tough venue to teenager Peter Docherty. Rangers started the better and scored first when Jim Bett beat McArthur with a low drive, but McLeod's lung-bursting run to get on the end of Callachan's pass was rewarded as he steered the ball past Peter McCloy from close range. Hibs then had a couple of chances to take the lead but failed to take them and were duly punished when Davie Cooper scored a second for Rangers. Hibs went looking for an equaliser and left themselves exposed at the back, resulting in a penalty against them when Bobby Russell was toppled in the box. Tommy McLean took the spot kick, but Jim McArthur saved magnificently and Hibs were still in the game. With time running out, Rae pounced on a loose ball to fire past McCloy and level the match. In the very last minute, McCloy pulled off a great save to deny Gary Murray a winning goal.

Hibs and Airdrie had yet to clash in a Premier League game as the Lanarkshire side had won their first placing in the top League the season before last, when Hibs were relegated. In fact the last time the teams had met on League duty was in April 1975 at Easter Road and Hibs had triumphed 6-1 that day, with Arthur Duncan one of the scorers. Only Duncan and McArthur of the current squad had played that day and both would have a prominent part to play this time around, too. Manager Bobby Watson was anxious that the Diamonds get something from this game as they had won no points as yet, having lost to Celtic and St Mirren in their opening fixtures. He would be looking to one-time Hibs target Sandy Clark to open up the Hibs defence. At the other end, Tranent-born John Martin would try to keep the Hibs attack out. On the day, Martin was the busier goalkeeper and could do nothing to stop Flavell cracking the ball home from a superb Duncan pass to give Hibs the lead. Try as they might, however, Hibs could not get a second. Two great saves from McArthur denied Sandy Clark, but late in the game the visitors equalised through Brian McKeown, making the final score 1-1.

A win and two draws meant an undefeated start to the season, but that run ended in their next game when they lost 1-0 at Pittodrie to a Neil Simpson goal. Hibs had never really troubled Jim Leighton in the home goal, and the same could be said about the Dons in relation to Jim McArthur. Late in the game, however, a momentary lapse of concentration let Simpson in and the points were lost. One bright note was that Erich Schaedler, who had rejoined the club from Dundee, came on as a second-half substitute and looked to have lost none of the athleticism and commitment that were part and parcel of his game. It had taken two months of negotiating to bring Erich back and the Hibs supporters were delighted to be reacquainted with one of their favourites.

Surprise packages St Mirren provided the next League challenge when the sides clashed at Love Street in late September. The Buddies were hot on the heels of leaders Celtic at this early stage and were soon putting Hibs under pressure, but the visitors held firm and had a chance or two to take the lead without converting either. With just five minutes of the game remaining and with Hibs looking comfortable at the back, a driven shot from Doug Somner hit McNamara on the arm and, incredibly, referee McKenzie pointed to the penalty spot. Even the St Mirren players had the decency to look stunned at the award as the ball had clearly played the man, but they were not about to look a gift-horse in the mouth and Billy Stark sent McArthur the wrong way to record the only goal of the game. The press reports after the game were scathing in their criticism of Mr McKenzie but the fact remained that Hibs had now lost two games in succession, both of which they might easily have won if the chances they created had been taken.

Hibs had now slipped into a mid-table position, already six points behind leaders Celtic. The Greens were locked on four points with three other sides, including Dundee United, who would provide the next League challenge at Easter Road. The Arabs had lost two of their first five League games, but they had enjoyed some remarkable success in cup competitions, most notably the UEFA Cup, travelling to France and sticking five goals past Monaco! In the League Cup, they had strolled their section and then defeated Hamilton in the quarter-finals to set up a semi-final appearance against Aberdeen. They were in good form when they arrived at Easter Road that day and soon took the lead through Davie Dodds, but Hibs were in determined mood and deserved the equaliser when it came along, thanks to Arthur Duncan. That was the first point since March 1979 that Hibs had taken from Dundee United, who had become something of a hoodoo side for Bertie Auld's men. Arthur's goal was his first in the Premier League since January 1979, and you could say that both the goal and the point won had been a long time coming.

On Monday, 5 October 1981, George Best returned to play at Easter Road, but on this occasion he would be wearing the strip of his latest club, San Jose Earthquakes, who had arrived in Leith to play that return friendly arranged during Hibs' close-season trip to California. The game allowed Hibs fans to once again witness the magic of a true superstar while it also allowed Bertie Auld to try a couple of things he would not dream of doing in a League game. One of Bertie's decisions was to play 17-year-old Robin Rae in goals and it was a gamble that paid off, the youngster having an excellent game in front of a crowd that was double the number of that for the Dundee United League match just 48 hours earlier. Clearly, even at 35, Best was still a big hit with fans the world over and he showed flashes of his genius throughout this game, but those were not enough to inspire his team-mates as Hibs ran out 3-1 winners. Derek Rodier, who had been impressing in the reserves, led the attack and scored two fine goals, but the strike of the night belonged to Erich Schaedler, who belted home a goal from all of 30 yards, his fourth for the club. The Earthquakes, with Dundonian Mike Hewitt in goals, got their consolation through Italian-born centre-forward Tony Crescitelli. The match programme for that game held some interesting data on Hibs' record in friendlies, noting that the Greens had played 108 such matches, winning 58, drawing 22 and losing 28, scoring 315 goals and conceding 149. Random results of interest included a 6-1 away win over Bayern Munich in 1950, a 3-2 away win over Marseilles in 1956, a 2-0 home win over Torino in 1961 and a 2-0 home win over Real Madrid in 1964.

Hibs were back at Easter Road the following Saturday to play Morton in a League match. The visitors had won three and lost three of their six matches to date and manager Benny Rooney was doing a fine job, despite losing two of his top players when Jim Tolmie joined Belgian side Lokeren and forward Bobby Thomson departed to Middlesbrough for £200,000. With ex-Hibs goalie Roy Baines, ex-Hearts man Drew Busby and the irrepressible Andy Ritchie in their starting XI, they might have expected to cause the home side some problems, but an upbeat Hibernian won the game at a canter by 4-0. Gary Murray opened the scoring and might have had a hat-trick if later shots had hit the net instead of the bar, while Flavell, McLeod and Callachan added their contributions towards making it a miserable return to Easter Road for Baines. It was a bit of a miserable afternoon for Jackie McNamara, too, as he accidentally clashed heads with Erich Schaedler and ended up being carted off to hospital with concussion.

A significant development around this time was the addition of two new directors to the board. Two Kennys, Waugh and McLean, had snapped up the majority of shares that had become available, Kenny Waugh buying the larger stake in the club. Aged 44, he had a number of business interests in Edinburgh, including a string of betting shops. It was revealed that by May 1983 he would be installed as chairman, with Tom Hart adopting the role of president. Hart felt that the time had come for a younger man to take the reins, but he would remain involved and work closely with the new chairman. The other Kenny, McLean, a 53-year-old businessman and high-profile Hibs fan with a number of business interests in the city, had purchased a number of shares for himself but also for his son – another Kenny – and a number of other prominent Hibs men, including Douglas Cromb and Tom O'Malley, both of whom would have roles to play in the years ahead. There was a degree of negative reaction among some elements of the support concerning the sale of shares to Kenny Waugh, who had attempted and failed to buy a majority shareholding in Hearts just a few months earlier, but Tom Hart was not phased by that and declared that 'Hearts' loss is Hibs' gain', and that the new man was known to be a long-time supporter of the Easter Road club.

Prior to Hibs playing their next League game, an away tie at Firhill against Partick Thistle, news filtered out that goalkeeper Jim McArthur had signed a deal to the end of the season, thereby ending the month-to-month arrangement that had been in place. The keeper was undoubtedly an important part of the team and could not be faulted for trying to win the best contract available to him. Other more general news involved the fact that the 38 League clubs had met to discuss the League format for the coming seasons. The proposal put forward was for two divisions of 16 and 22, with a three-up, three-down arrangement, but the vote was split 19 for and 19 against and so no changes would be made. Hibs had been strongly in favour of change, arguing that the current set-up of a ten-team Premier League with two clubs relegated was stifling the game, making it far too negative and, most importantly, driving the fans away. Even among the ten there was a 5/5 split in relation to the vote for change, and that had been a major disappointment for the Hibs representatives present on the day.

As to the game against Thistle, Hibs once again lost by the narrowest of margins while on the road, with only Kenny Watson's second-half penalty goal separating the sides. It was genuine bad luck again for Hibs when most present agreed that a draw would have been a fairer result.

Of the eight League games played to date, Hibs had won just two with three draws and three defeats, leaving them with seven points. Those three defeats had been suffered away from home and all by a single goal. That kind of form was hardly inspiring when Celtic were the next side to be faced. The game was at Easter Road, where Hibs' form had been reasonable if not great, but the Glasgow side arrived undefeated with only one draw spoiling an otherwise perfect record. They had scored 20 goals for the loss of only seven, while Hibs had conceded the same number but only scored ten. Everything seemed set for an away victory, but the Hibs players had other ideas. It looked grim when referee Galloway awarded Celtic a penalty, but McArthur brilliantly parried Charlie Nicholas's spot kick and then bounced up from the ground to save the rebound try from Frank McGarvey. With McNamara and Paterson holding firm in front of McArthur, Hibs gradually got more and more into the game until late in the second half Mr. Galloway once again pointed to the spot. Thankfully, the award this time was given to Hibs when Roy Aitken toppled Gordon Rae in the box, and Ally MacLeod swept the ball low into the net under the flailing arms of keeper Pat Bonnar. Hibs had inflicted the first defeat of the season on Celtic and the home support left the stadium that night feeling happier.

A win against the League leaders was surely the tonic needed to go into the East of Scotland Shield semi-final match against Hearts at Easter Road the following Tuesday. After all, the Gorgie side were in the First Division and not having the best of times there, but it didn't stop them spoiling the fun for Hibs as they ran out 2-1 winners. Roddy McDonald had given Hearts the lead and then Hibs started to pepper Henry Smith's goal but found the big keeper in sparkling form. Eventually, late in the game, substitute Derek Rodier found a way past Smith and it looked as though a penalty shoot-out was on the cards. Jumping for a headed challenge with Derek O'Connor, Craig Paterson got a nasty cut above his eye. While he was off having six stitches put in the wound, Hearts pressed forward and Gordon Rae, in trying to head the ball clear, only succeeded in knocking it past a bemused Jim McArthur to give Hearts victory.

The following Saturday, Hibs were on the road again when they travelled to Dens Park to face Dundee. The Dark Blues had come up with Hibs, but were finding life in the Premier League quite tough and were sitting joint bottom of the table with Airdrie. After three successive 1-0 defeats on the road, Hibs were looking to buck that trend against a defence that had conceded 23 goals, but the Greens could not find a way through, despite dominating for virtually the entire game, and had to be satisfied with a 0-0 draw. A point was better than nothing, but Hibs had created enough chances to win several games and so it was disappointing to only draw. They were not alone in not having won away from home, however, with five of the ten clubs still to do so, perhaps highlighting the negative 'do not lose' mindset that was stifling the game in this cut-throat League.

Having defeated one half of the Old Firm a couple of weeks earlier, Hibs next hosted Rangers at Easter Road. The Ibrox club had suffered a shock home defeat by Partick Thistle the week before, but so far during this campaign they had not lost away from home. Already in the League Cup final, they had not fared so well in the European Cup Winners' Cup, having gone out in the first round to crack Czech outfit Dukla Prague. At Easter Road, they had enough in the tank to win by 2-1 through goals by Jim Bett, one from the penalty spot. Gordon Rae was the Hibs scorer.

On that same afternoon, the reserves were involved in a bizarre 1-1 draw with Dundee at Dens Park. After half an hour, goalkeeper Robin Rae made a great save from a full-blooded close-range shot and then was quick to make it a double save when a Dundee forward tried to pounce on the rebound. Sadly for Robin, he dislocated a finger in the incident and had to quit five minutes later. Hibs put outfield player Willie Jamieson in goals, and he did very well. At half-time, unused substitute Gordon Byrne volunteered to go in goal and Jamieson returned to the outfield. Although Byrne played well, he was beaten by a good free kick, but young Ricky Haddow salvaged a point when he capitalised on a late error in the Dundee defence. It was a point well won, considering the need to play three different players in goals during the 90 minutes.

Back on the road again the following Saturday, Hibs were expected to record their first away win of the season against a very poor and struggling Airdrie, but the Diamonds shocked them, and probably even their own fans, by winning the match 3-1. Sandy Clark had opened the scoring, but Rae soon equalised, only for John Flood to put the home side in front again. McLeod had a great chance to draw Hibs level again, but the usually cool and calm forward somehow sliced the ball wide with the goal gaping. Airdrie took heart from that and went on to score again through Jim Rodger. The match had been Jackie McNamara's 250th for Hibs, but it was not a milestone game he would recall with any great affection.

During the week following that defeat at Airdrie, John Connolly left the club as a free agent at his own request. The former Scotland winger was with Hibs for 15 months and was one short of a half-century in appearances when he decided that first-team football was not on the cards at Easter Road and that he needed to look elsewhere.

One draw and two defeats in the last three League matches had left Hibs sitting in mid-table with just 11 points from 13 starts when Aberdeen visited Easter Road towards the end of November. The Dons, tucked in behind Celtic at the top of the League, arrived in Leith in good form and it was no surprise that Scotland manager Jock Stein had named five from Pittodrie in his squad for the forthcoming World Cup qualifier in Portugal. They had also been going very well in the UEFA Cup, having disposed of holders Ipswich in the first round and then Arges Pitesti of Romania in the second. Those successes had set up a third-round clash with Hibs' old adversaries, Hamburg, and certainly you had to hope that the Dons would have better luck against the German outfit than Hibs had had. As to the League clash on that day, Neil Simpson gave Aberdeen a 1-0 lead, but a superb equaliser from Ralph Callachan earned Hibs a well-deserved draw.

The Hibs goal came when Duncan floated a lovely cross in from the left that drifted over the Aberdeen defenders and was met by Callachan's head as the midfield player made a late run into the box. Outstanding for Hibs that afternoon was Craig Paterson, who did not have the injured McNamara alongside him for once but dovetailed well with replacement Ally Brazil to stifle the Dons forwards throughout the game.

Robin Rae, having recovered from both a dislocated finger and a shoulder injury sustained in a motorcycle accident, was back between the sticks for Hibs reserves when St Johnstone came to Easter Road. The game finished at 2-2, with Brian Rice getting both Hibs goals, but the main talking point among the home fans surrounded the trialist wearing the No.7 jersey. In time, we would learn that this was Ricky Hill, a 19-year-old forward who came from Bermuda and had been recommended to the club by Denis McQuade, who had played under Bertie Auld when the manager was with Partick Thistle. Ricky Hill was black, and up until that time very few black players had played in Scotland, but he had shown enough when Alan Hart and Pat Quinn had flown out to see him. They liked what they saw and brought him back with them for a trial with Hibs.

The following day, Hibs director Tommy Younger was taken to hospital having suffered a heart attack. He was placed in intensive care, but the 51-year-old vice-president of the SFA made a good recovery and was soon allowed home.

As November neared its end, Hibs were back on the home trail when St Mirren faced them at Easter Road. The sides had already met three times this season, having been drawn in the same League Cup section, and Hibs had yet to score against the Buddies. Having scored against both sides of the Old Firm as well as Aberdeen on their own pitch, Hibs were confident that their lack of success against St Mirren would come to an end that afternoon, but that confidence was misplaced as the sides fought out a 0-0 draw. Even the former Saints man Ally McLeod, who was making his 300th appearance for Hibs, could not find a way past a packed defence, and it was a disgruntled Hibs support that left the stadium that night, once again convinced that the ten-club Premier League was not throwing up attractive fixtures and was instead encouraging clubs to be more concerned with not losing than winning. It had been a pretty miserable November for Hibs, but the fans were used to that – in the previous six Novembers, Hibs had won only one match, a defeat of Dunfermline during last season's spell in the First Division.

Hibs were still without a win on the road when they began December with a visit to Tannadice. The home side boasted the best defensive record in the League, with Richard Gough and Paul Hegarty at the centre of the defence and the ever-dependable Hamish McAlpine in goal. From the off, Hibs went on the attack and totally dominated the first half without being able to score. Arthur Duncan, celebrating his 34th birthday and playing further forward now that Schaedler had returned to the left-back spot, was particularly unlucky when he twice beat McAlpine, only to see the ball strike the woodwork and then be cleared. In the second half, Hibs still had the balance of play and should have scored through Murray and Rae, but they would pay for their failure to take a lead as United won a soft penalty from referee Mike Delaney, which Eamonn Bannon duly slotted home for the only goal of the game. Odd-goal defeats were becoming an unwelcome norm, as were penalties conceded late in games, this latest one being the sixth of the season so far.

Back at Easter Road, the reserves were going down 2-1 to United, with Ricky Haddow getting the Hibs goal from a good pass by Ricky Hill. The player from Bermuda was really suffering in the cold December weather and had taken to wearing three jerseys and three pairs of socks when he turned out for Hibs.

The cold snap hit the fixture list the following weekend and among the casualties was the Morton v Hibs tie scheduled to be played at Cappielow. Hibs actually 'lost' that game as the sitting Pools Panel deemed it to be a home win. Given the away form the Easter Road men had been displaying, it's perhaps no surprise that the panel voted that way. The idle Saturday suited both McNamara and Flavell, both of whom were struggling with injuries and would now have an extra week to recover.

On the Saturday before Christmas there had been a snowfall in Edinburgh, but the newly installed undersoil heating enabled the match between Hibs and Partick Thistle to go ahead. There was evidence of snow on the pitch and an orange ball was used as the home side recorded a comfortable 3-0 win over their Glasgow opponents. This was only Hibs' fourth League win of the season and it was significant that Ally McLeod was among the scorers, as he'd done just that in each of the other victories. Ally struck twice against the Jags and Gordon Rae scored the other. In good form for the Greens that day were not only the two scorers but also Arthur Duncan and Ralph Callachan, the latter having ended his monthly contracts by signing on until the end of the season.

The programme for that Partick Thistle match carried a plea from Tom Hart for an element of the support to behave or stay away from Easter Road. His concern revolved around the fact that following the Rangers game, windows of both private homes and the buses of the visiting fans had been smashed, and Hart made it very clear that such behaviour was not acceptable. Indeed, he pointed out that the club had paid out a massive £5,000 in policing costs for the Rangers game alone and such costs simply meant the club could not spend the cash elsewhere. Of course, he was absolutely right to castigate the 'fans' who brought the good name of the club into disrepute, although Hibs were by no means the only club with such a problem as their supporters had often had their buses stoned when visiting away grounds, especially at Ibrox.

When Siberian-like weather took a grip in Scotland over the Christmas and New Year period, Hibs found their scheduled League matches postponed and took the unusual step of inviting Manchester United up to Easter Road on Boxing Day 1981. United brought their full squad of very talented players and the pitch allowed for a decent game of football to evolve. Hibs took the lead when substitute Willie Jamieson fired a shot past Gary Bailey from close range, but the visitors equalised when Frank Stapleton headed home a Brian Robson cross. The game finished at 1-1, which was a very creditable result for Hibs given the quality of the opposition. It was a good result for the visitors, too, because the last time they had played at Easter Road, in 1952 for Gordon Smith's testimonial game, they had lost 7-3! One player not at that game was Ricky Hill, who was back home in Bermuda, the club having promised him a trip home for Christmas. Indeed, the club suggested that he should not return until the spring, when the weather would be warmer.

The Greens were back in competitive action on 2 January 1982 as Dundee arrived at Easter Road having had a reasonable sequence of recent results, lifting themselves out of the relegation places in the process. They had scored 27 goals so far, and that was ten more than Hibs. On the other hand, they had leaked far too many at the other end of the park, with 38 conceded in comparison to just 14 by Hibs. The first half was relatively even, with both sides creating chances but failing to take them, but with almost the last kick of the half, Eric Sinclair fired the visitors ahead. A half-time pep talk from Bertie Auld soon resulted in Hibs laying siege to the Dundee goal, and it wasn't long before Jamieson volleyed home an equaliser. A winning goal looked on the cards and it was duly delivered by McLeod in rather strange circumstances. Hibs had been awarded a direct free kick around 20 yards out, and Ally coolly slotted the ball into the top corner, only for referee Galloway to incense the home crowd by disallowing it because a Dundee player had breached the ten-yard rule. It seemed as though Hibs were to be punished for the actions of an opposition player, but Ally wasn't perturbed in the least as he took the kick again and popped the ball into the opposite corner from the first!

Two good points were won at a time when other teams were inactive, Hibs once again benefiting from the installation of undersoil heating. In fact, the weather was so bad all across the country that the club was inundated with inquiries from both sides of the border to host friendlies at Easter Road, but it was just not feasible to accommodate these requests.

An away game at Pittodrie, scheduled for the following Saturday, was called off late due to a frozen playing surface and so Hibs quickly arranged a home friendly against First Division leaders Motherwell, but even that game was in doubt when overnight snow on the Friday threatened to scupper Bertie Auld's plans to keep his players in action. Saturday morning saw an army of reserve players and fans willing to help to clear the pitch and the game went ahead, Hibs winning 2-0 after Callachan and Rodier had found the target. One huge plus point out of this game was the long-awaited return of Jackie McNamara to the starting line-up after the defender had spent weeks out due to a stress fracture in his leg. Jackie had a super game and didn't look as though he had ever been missing. Interested spectators at Easter Road that day were two directors from Rangers, who wanted to see how the pitch held up with its undersoil heating. They were sufficiently impressed to return to Ibrox to recommend that Rangers should follow the path taken by Hibs.

The next scheduled match brought Airdrie to Easter Road. The Diamonds had not played a competitive fixture for five weeks due to the big freeze. Hibs were looking for revenge for their earlier League defeat at Broomfield, but the Airdrie players, noted for their 'robust' style of play, were quick to challenge any Hibs man with the ball. Gordon Rae had to retire with a broken nose and bruised cheekbone after jumping in a challenge with Airdrie keeper John Martin, while Craig Paterson took a few knocks in rough-and-tumble challenges with Sandy Clark. Redressing the balance somewhat was Erich Schaedler, who would not allow anyone to bully either him or any of his team-mates, and 'Shades' made a few meaty challenges to ensure that Airdrie didn't have it all their own way in the physical battle. It wasn't pretty to watch, but Hibs must have realised that goals win games, not brawn, and when Jamieson headed a Callachan cross back into the six-yard box McLeod was there to score the only goal of the game. That victory took Hibs up to fourth, and while they had played more games than the clubs around them it was always better to have the points on the board rather than games in hand.

That win came at the end of a week in which chairman Tom Hart celebrated his 60th birthday, and he welcomed the victory by saying it was a great birthday present, won in difficult circumstances by the men on his side, who had played football – which, I suppose, was a back-handed way of saying Airdrie had not intended to do the same! The points were also won in front of a whole host of managers from other teams who watched from the stands after their own games had fallen foul of the weather. Those in a packed directors' box included Peter Cormack (Partick Thistle), Ricky MacFarlane (St Mirren), Donald Mackay (Dundee), Benny Rooney (Morton) and John Hagart of Falkirk, who brought his entire first-team squad with him.

The Scottish Cup was now the focus of attention as Hibs set off in their attempts to win that coveted trophy for the first time in 80 years. The third-round draw had paired Hibs with John Hagart's Falkirk, and that explained his club's keen interest in the Airdrie game. The Bairns were in the top half of the First Division and going quite well in their chase for promotion, but the Premier League side were too good for them on the day as Rodier and Duncan gave Hibs a 2-0 win and took the Greens into the fourth-round draw.

Late January brought an end to the terrible weather conditions and meant that Hibs would now face two consecutive away games, at Ibrox and Parkhead, over the space of four days. Rangers had won the corresponding fixture at Easter Road, but they would not take both points on this occasion as Bobby Flavell scored a second-half equaliser after Derek Johnstone had given the Gers a 1-0 lead at the interval. It was Flavell's fourth goal of the season and, interestingly, Hibs had not lost in any of the games in which he scored.

On the Tuesday night following that well-deserved point at Ibrox, Hibs were back in the west to face League leaders Celtic at Parkhead. The Glasgow giants were clear leaders and had lost only twice in 18 starts, but significantly one of those defeats had come at the hands of Hibs at Easter Road, where the home side won 1-0. After 90 minutes of entertaining football the sides could not be separated, and the game ended without a goal being scored. Manager Bertie Auld was delighted with his players, but was fiercely critical of the Scottish sporting press that had roundly condemned Auld's tactics of playing for a draw. The manager took exception because both sides had lined up with a 4-4-2 formation and Hibs had created as many chances as Celtic, if not more. A similar scenario had unfolded at Ibrox a few days earlier, but the press, much of which was based in the west, chose to criticise rather than acknowledge that Hibs had matched both Glasgow clubs and had taken two points from two very difficult away games. The press, though, would pay no heed and would carry on throughout the years ahead, reporting in a negative way about any side that dared set out its stall to win points in Glasgow.

Off the field, it was reported that Kenny Waugh had represented Hibs when delegates of all 38 League clubs had met in Dunblane to discuss various aspects of Scottish football. A number of ideas were discussed, although any changes to the rules would have to go before the AGM of the Scottish League. One idea was that an extra League point should be awarded if a team scored three or more goals in a game. Another idea put forward involved awarding three points for a win and still only one for a draw. Hibs did not support this and suggested instead that it be three points for a win, two points for a scoring draw and one point for a 0-0 draw. At the end of the day, all of these ideas were left as just that, with no decision to raise them at the next AGM.

Also off the field but player-related was the announcement by Hibs that they had signed teenage goalkeeper Ian Spalding from Armadale Thistle.

The youngster was brought to the attention of Bertie Auld, who then watched him play and was impressed. Although now on the books, Ian would remain with Armadale in the meantime.

The points won at Ibrox and Parkhead should have provided a platform from which Hibs could continue their good form, but when they next played, against Dundee United at Easter Road, there was a distinct feeling of déjà vu among the home fans on the terracing. Last time out, United had won 1-0 thanks to an Eamonn Bannon penalty and they repeated that this time around when the same player got the only goal of the game from the spot after a handling offence in the Hibs 18-yard box. It was a huge disappointment for the home support to witness United continuing their incredible run against Hibs, as the Greens had now failed to beat the Tannadice men for almost three years. In the stand watching that day was Dusan Nenkovic, manager of United's next European rivals, Radnicki Nis, and he was said to be impressed both by United's display and the very friendly welcome extended to him by Hibernian.

As fate would have it, Hibs' opponents in the fourth round of the Scottish Cup would be Dundee United, the Arabs having home advantage. Given the dismal record Hibs had in this fixture in recent years, few gave them much hope of success on Tayside, but that didn't stop a sizeable support heading north to cheer the Greens on. Even before the game kicked off there would be tragic news following an accident on the approach to Perth. A double-decker bus, packed with Hibs fans, toppled over after being hit by a severe gust of wind. There were 74 fans aboard, and 18-year-old Mark McGhee lost his life while a number of others were injured. Tom Hart and Bertie Auld immediately issued a statement saying how everyone at the club was devastated and that they would both attend Mark's funeral to pay their respects.

Most of that was unknown to the Hibs fans at the game, and they sang and chanted their way through a match that ended 1-1, John Holt being on target for United and Gordon Rae levelling the tie with 25 minutes left. Hibs, with Flavell playing an unfamiliar left-back role in place of the injured Schaedler, had looked down and out until Rae held off two challenges to fire home, and that goal gave the visitors a lift for the remainder of the game, when Hibs looked the more likely to score a winner.

The following midweek brought United to Easter Road for the Cup replay, with the sides knowing that an away trip to St Mirren awaited the victors. A fast-flowing game unfolded, and Hibs took the lead thanks to Craig Paterson, possibly boosted by the news that he had been selected to play for the Scotland Under-21 side in the European Championship quarter-final first-leg tie against Italy in Catanzaro later in the month. Chances to extend the lead came and went, but with the referee about to blow for full time Billy Kirkwood scrambled home an equaliser to take the game into extra time. No further goals were forthcoming and so a second replay would be required, with Hibs winning the toss to decide the venue. Sadly for Paterson, that draw meant he had to pull out of the Under-21s' trip to Italy.

Off the field, the Hibs Supporters' Association announced its intention to elect chairman Tom Hart as honorary president in recognition and appreciation of his efforts over the years on behalf of the club. This was a very popular move with the support and the association hoped to invite Scotland and former Hibs manager Jock Stein along to present the award. Hart was a Hibs man through and through, who had recently arrived at Tannadice with a Hibs scarf around his neck because he wanted to wear 'the colours for the cup'. While Tom senior was being recognised in this way, Tom junior tendered his resignation from the board, saying that as he resided in Jersey he did not feel able to contribute much to the running of the club.

Ahead of that second replay, Hibs travelled to Love Street to face second-placed St Mirren and gained a very creditable 2-2 draw with Gordon Rae bagging both goals for the visitors and Frank McAvennie and Frank McDougal on target for the Buddies. Rae's goals took him to the top of the scoring charts for Hibs and ended Buddies goalkeeper Billy Thomson's run of four consecutive games against Hibs without conceding a goal.

The second replay against Dundee United drew a crowd in excess of 15,000 to Easter Road on Monday, 22 February, but the vast majority of them would go home disappointed as United took the lead through John Holt late in the first half and then punished Hibs with two more goals in the second as the Easter Road men chased the game. Those goals came from Davie Dodds and Eamonn Bannon, who once again converted a penalty against the Greens. So ended 300 minutes of gruelling Cup football when United could have won it in the first meeting and Hibs should have won it in the second.

With the Scottish Cup disappointment behind them, Hibs welcomed champions-elect Celtic to Easter Road on the last Saturday in February. With a five-point lead at the top over St Mirren, Billy McNeill's side looked certs to take the League flag, but they were facing a side they had not beaten this season, having lost 1-0 at Easter Road and drawn 0-0 at Parkhead in the two meetings so far. In a pulsating 90 minutes, Hibs dominated their opponents and should have won the game by more than Gordon Rae's solitary goal. Celtic were never at the races. For Hibs, this win made it five points out of a possible six against them, and perhaps even more impressively it gave Jim McArthur and his defensive colleagues three clean sheets against a team who had scored 42 goals in 20 games. A stand out in this match was Gary Murray, who had suffered an up and down season due to injuries but who terrorised the Celtic left flank throughout the 90 minutes.

Saturday 6 March was the day upon which Hibs finally won their first away game of the season, beating Partick Thistle 2-1 at Firhill. It had been a long time coming, but it was worth the wait as Rae and Paterson found a way past Alan Rough in the home goal. Ironically, it was Tony Higgins who scored for Partick and he had been in the last Hibs side to win an away Premier League match, when the Greens defeated Hearts at Tynecastle on 28 March 1979. Tony had just returned to the Thistle side after recovering from injury and he took his goal well. After his recent goalscoring exploits, Gordon Rae had deservedly been picked as the Mackinlay's Scotch Whisky Scottish Footballer of the Month for February 1982 and would receive a cheque for £100 and a gallon bottle of whisky as his prize.

Now that the hoodoo over away wins had been broken, a second chance to win on the road came along in the following midweek when Hibs went to Pittodrie. Once again, Gordon Rae found the target for the Greens, but the Dons won the game 3-1 with goals from Neale Cooper, Drew Jarvie and a Gordon Strachan penalty.

Being a Wednesday night, only a few hundred Hibs fans had made the journey north to cheer on their team, and while the Greens were going down 3-1 and the visiting fans were trying to lift their favourites, tragedy was unfolding in the stand. Chairman Tom Hart collapsed and was rushed to hospital, where he died in the early hours of the morning of Thursday, 11 March 1982, of a brain haemorrhage, never having regained consciousness. This was devastating news not only for his family but for everyone connected with Hibernian Football Club and the game in Scotland itself. Hart had been a fearless innovator, a strong and positive presence within the club and a man who had not been afraid to put large amounts of his own money into the game. His stewardship had lasted for 11 years and embraced the Turnbull's Tornadoes era, the signing of George Best and the winning of the First Division title – although Hart was on record as saying he never wanted to win that particular title again. The impending award to make him honorary president of the Hibs Supporters' Association and the intended handing over of the chairman's role to Kenny Waugh would not now be possible as the man who had every right to be known as 'Mr Hibs' had sadly passed away.

In the days that followed, tributes poured in. Alex Fletcher, Scottish minister for sport and a regular at Easter Road said: 'Tom was the most important man in Scottish football for some years. He was an outstanding man; one who would rather give than take. It's a tragic loss for Hibs in particular and Scottish football in general.' Hearts' vice-chairman, Wallace Mercer, said: 'What he has achieved in the game is considerable. It's very sad for football. During my short time in the game he always extended a warm welcome to all of us at Tynecastle.' Former player Jimmy O'Rourke added: 'I owed a great deal to him. He was a father figure to me throughout our days together with Hibs and like many others I'll miss his cheery welcome and sound advice.' And finally, club legend Pat Stanton had these words to say: 'A terrible shock. He had a tremendous influence on Hibs' fortunes and did so much for the club. We'll all miss him very much.'

After the devastating loss of Tom Hart, life had to go on at Easter Road and that started with a visit from Benny Rooney's Morton to the capital. Good home form had kept Morton out of the relegation dogfight, but they had gained only four points while on the road and that record looked likely to remain with Hibs leading 2-1 going into the final minute of the game. Yet another goal from Rae and a second by Murray had only been responded to by a John McNeill strike. Then Andy Ritchie equalised with almost the last kick of the ball. It was a poor point to lose in a match that Hibs had dominated, but there was certainly a subdued atmosphere at Easter Road that day as the Hibs fans came together for the first time since the death of Tom Hart.

When the funeral of Tom Hart took place at Warriston on 15 March, a huge crowd attended and there were representatives from every Scottish club, many travelling long distances to be present. Former players were in evidence, too, and those included John Brownlie, who had journeyed up from Newcastle. The chapel was full to capacity, with many more people outside, as fans of all ages swelled the numbers to pay their own tribute to the man that had been so good for the football club they all supported and loved.

Hibs had seven games left to play now, and the first of those was against Dundee at Dens Park in the middle of March. Leading at the interval through an Iain Ferguson goal, the home side were stunned in the second half by two magnificent goals from Ralph Callachan. The first was outstanding: Ralph went on a 50-yard run, exchanging a couple of passes with team-mates before sliding the ball past Bobby Geddes. The second came from a brave, close-in header. Callachan was injured in the process and had to be carried off. The game was all but over with Hibs leading 2-1 when that late lapse struck again and Ray Stephen scored to level the match in the last minute. Callachan, after that accidental clash with Danny Cameron, was later treated at Edinburgh Royal Infirmary and found to have a depressed fracture of the cheekbone. Surgery was required, and Ralph would be out for several games while he recovered.

The last Saturday in March brought Rangers to Easter Road. John Greig's men were trailing Celtic and Aberdeen in the League race, and while their League performance may not have been up to their usual high standards they already had the League Cup in the bag and faced lowly Forfar in the Scottish Cup semi-final, with every prospect of having the chance to add a second cup to the trophy cabinet. On the day Rangers arrived, Hibs announced that Kenny Waugh had now been formally installed as chairman of the club and he was in the directors' box to witness a tense 0-0 draw, with neither side enjoying lengthy periods of dominance. Chances were made by both sides, Murray, McLeod and Flavell having the best of them for Hibs, while Ian Redford and Bobby Russell kept Jim McArthur busy at the other end.

Struggling Airdrie provided Hibs with their next challenge as April began with a visit to Broomfield. A typical battling encounter ensued, but Hibs refused to be intimidated and Willie Jamieson, in only his fifth League appearance of the season, bagged a brace to win the game 2-0 for Hibs. The youngster clearly liked that venue – back in October, he had notched a double for the reserves there. The win over Airdrie gave Hibs back-to-back clean sheets and took them on to the 30-point mark in the League. European qualification was out of their reach, but equally they had steered clear of the relegation zone. One player not at Broomfield was Ralph Callachan, who had received permission from the club to take a short break with his wife in Majorca. The club felt the rest and the climate would aid the player's recovery as he was still unable to eat solid foods, but Hibs were hopeful he would be fit to join the club on a confirmed visit to Malta immediately after the last game of the season against Morton. The Easter Road club had been invited to play against Malta Hibs to celebrate the islanders' 50th birthday.

Aberdeen had been on a bit of a charge in pursuit of leaders Celtic when they visited Easter Road on 10 April. The Dons were seven points adrift, but had two games in hand, so they had everything to play for against Bertie Auld's men. A first-half injury to McNamara, which resulted in the Hibs man going off suffering from concussion, seemed to disrupt the defence and Aberdeen took full advantage, scoring three times without reply. Those goals, scored by Gordon Strachan, Mark McGhee and Drew Jarvie, gave Hibs their biggest defeat to date in that season's League campaign.

A midweek trip to Cappielow followed, and it would end in defeat again for Hibs. Roddy Hutchison and John McNeill scored for Morton, with Jamieson getting a consolation goal for the visitors. Robin Rae made his full debut that night and it was tough on the youngster to be on the losing side. He had the satisfaction, though, of knowing that he had played well and could not be blamed for either of the goals conceded.

Hibs had just three fixtures left to fulfil and that sequence of games started with a visit to Tannadice. Football, as the saying goes, is a funny old game, and it was ironic that Hibs gave their poorest performance of the seven against United this season and yet managed to win the game 1-0. Jim McArthur was back in goals, but he didn't have a lot to do as both sets of players looked as if they were wishing the close season was already with them. The one bright spot for Hibs was the move that led to the winning goal. There was clever play by Rodier, who raced down the wing and evaded a number of tackles before sending a searching cross into the box, which Stuart Turnbull duly headed past the stranded Hamish McAlpine. The points were not significant in terms of League positions, but that long barren run against United had finally come to an end.

The second-last home game of the season brought St Mirren to Easter Road for what would be the sixth meeting between the clubs. With three draws and two defeats, Hibs were looking to reverse the trend by winning the game and that's exactly what they did after Jamieson gave them the lead. Billy Stark levelled from the spot, but then Hibs, too, were awarded a penalty. Regular taker Ralph Callachan was still out injured and McLeod was on the bench, so for a few moments there was indecision as to who should take the kick. Gary Murray then stepped forward and lashed the ball past Billy Thomson to secure a 2-1 win on the day.

May 1982 started off badly as Hibs went to Parkhead, having taken five points out of six and conceded no goals in the previous three encounters, only to crash and burn 6-0 against a side feeling the hot breath of Aberdeen down their necks in a frantic, exciting finish to the League championship. Bertie Auld, safe in the knowledge that Hibs would finish sixth regardless of results in the remaining games, had taken his family to Spain for an end-of-season holiday and so Pat Quinn was in charge of the team at Parkhead. The Easter Road men were never at the races and deserved the hiding they got, but even that crushing defeat didn't stop Hibs having the best record of all the other Premier League clubs against Celtic.

When Partick Thistle arrived in Leith on 8 May they knew they had to win the game to keep alive their hopes of avoiding relegation, but Peter Cormack's men could only manage a 1-1 draw after Gary Murray equalised Alex O'Hara's opening goal. The programme notes for this game carried the news that Hibs' intended visit to Malta had been cancelled because Malta Hibs had failed to forward any air tickets, and that had been part of the deal for the Easter Road men to travel there.

Twenty-four hours later, the Hibs Under-18 side that had been funnelling young players into the reserves while still maintaining a challenge for their own League title met Celtic at Easter Road. The clubs were separated by just two points, with the Glasgow outfit having a slightly better goal difference. A draw would suit Hibs, but Celtic needed to win, and a decent crowd turned up to watch the young Hibees lift the youth crown, a real feather in their cap in what was their first season competing at this level.

With the season rapidly reaching its conclusion, Hibs announced a new initiative in the shape of Hibs Kids, a club for children aged between nine and 16. Already around 500 application forms had found their way to Easter Road and each youngster would receive a monthly newsletter, a membership card entitling them to a discount on goods bought in the club shop and free tickets to certain games in the coming season. This was a fine initiative by the club, and the Hibs Kids membership would thrive for many years to come.

One game remained and it took the Greens back to Cappielow, where they fought out a dull 0-0 draw, the point won ensuring that the final tally in the League would be 36 points from 36 games. Alan Sneddon had accumulated the most appearances, 52 in all, while Gordon Rae finished top scorer with 16 strikes on target.

It had been a long and sometimes difficult season for Hibs, but the main thing was that they retained their Premier League status while nearest neighbours and oldest rivals Hearts had missed out on promotion by one point and would remain in the First Division for another season, having been beaten on the final day by champions Motherwell.

Chapter Sixteen

1982/83

A LEGEND RETURNS

A new season invariably brings new faces at a football club and Hibs were no different than any other side in that regard. Craig Paterson, who would have been able to leave under freedom of contract, was sold to Rangers for a fee reported as being £200,000, and while chairman Kenny Waugh admitted he would have liked to keep the player he stated that to do so Hibs would have had to almost double Craig's salary, which their budget could not sustain. Paterson had been voted Player of the Year by the Hibs Supporters' Association and would return in due course to receive his reward.

From the monies coming in, Bertie Auld secured the signatures of Bobby Thomson from Middlesbrough and Peter Welsh from Leicester City. Thomson had gone south from Morton, and although he had spent only ten months at Ayresome Park he was their top scorer after only 18 League appearances. Coatbridge-born Welsh was with Leicester for six seasons. He could play in either defence or midfield, and Auld was happy to have a utility player with good experience in his squad.

As ever, Hibs headed north as part of their pre-season training and competed in three games in the Highlands. The opener was against Brora Rangers and Hibs were more than a little ring rusty, managing only a 3-3 draw, with a last-minute goal needed to salvage the pride. Willie Jamieson scored either side of new boy Bobby Thomson, who was making his debut along with Peter Welsh. A few of the younger players made the trip, and both Brian Rice and Kevin Hoggan came off the bench during that Brora game.

Two days later, Hibs were in Dingwall to face Ross County and once again Thomson was on target, although he took a late knock and had to be replaced. Willie Jamieson took his personal tally to three in two games and young Kevin Hoggan scored a peach of a goal in Hibs' 3-1 win. The last tour match brought Hibs up against Inverness Caley and they triumphed by 3-1, all three goals coming from Gary Murray, who was replacing the rested Thomson.

Travelling home from Inverness immediately after the Caley game gave Hibs around 24 hours to recover and prepare themselves for a home match against First Division Hearts. The clubs had agreed to compete for the Tom Hart Memorial Trophy, a cup purchased personally by new chairman Kenny Waugh in recognition of the late chairman's contribution to both Hibs and Scottish football. It would be the first chance for Hibs fans to see Thomson and Welsh in action, while Hearts fans would get their own first look at Sandy Jardine, transferred from Rangers. After a fairly entertaining 89 minutes with the sides evenly matched and the game looking like it would go to a penalty shoot-out, Jackie McNamara beat Hearts keeper Henry Smith in the jump to head home the winning goal and ensure that it would be Hibs captain Alan Sneddon who would step forward to receive the trophy from the Scotland manager, Jock Stein.

The 30p programme for the first home game of the season contained a full-page advert from Cotters World Travel of Lothian Road urging readers to consult them if they were considering foreign travel. They were, after all, the official travel agents for the club and the fervent hope from those reading that advert must have been that Cotters would be busy in the future, with Hibs having qualified for Europe! Fans were being urged to consider buying a season ticket, special rates being available for pensioners and children. It must have caught the eye, because we were informed that the previous season's sales had already been surpassed. On the football front, Hibs could look forward to a League Cup section with holders Rangers, Clydebank and Airdrie, while the New Year's Day game, traditionally derby day but not when the clubs were in differing divisions, meant a trip north to Aberdeen. Finally, in recognition of his long service to the club, Jim McArthur was to be awarded a testimonial match, and already a committee had been formed to organise the event. McArthur had joined from Cowdenbeath ten years previously and had played around 300 games for the club.

The competitive season began with a visit from Rangers in the League Cup, and the match programme that day carried a stern warning from the Hibs board. The matter related to the behaviour of fans after the match against Hearts, when 'a trail of broken windows was left between Easter Road and Princes Street' by hooligans who were 'killing the game'. Attendances throughout the game were dropping and the board had no doubts that hooligan behaviour by fans was one of the main contributing factors. The statement said that 'from all accounts Hibs supporters were not the main culprits', but any Hibs fans involved were asked to stay away from the club. There is no doubt that hooliganism affected attendances, which had also suffered from the cut-throat, negative nature of the Premier League.

In the game itself, Rangers took an early lead through John MacDonald, but right on the stroke of half-time Gordon Rae equalised with a low drive that beat keeper Jim Stewart at his left-hand post. The visitors had Craig Paterson in their line-up alongside two other new boys, Dave McKinnon from Partick Thistle and Robert Prytz from the Swedish club Malmo. From a Hibs perspective, both Ally Brazil and Derek Rodier, who had been stalling over new contracts during the close season, had put pen to paper and started the game against Rangers.

Another who played in that 1-1 draw with Rangers was Ralph Callachan, who had also had problems with a new contract but who had ultimately signed a three-year deal, much to the satisfaction of manager Bertie Auld, who rated the former Hearts player highly. Callachan had sat out the last part of last season due to injury and must have been pleased that Hibs were among the first clubs in Scotland to put all their staff on a BUPA scheme, which ensured prompt and private medical treatment.

Off the field, around that time Hibs appointed Kenny McLean as vice-chairman to replace Alan Hart. Like Kenny Waugh, McLean had various business interests in Edinburgh, but both men spent long hours at Easter Road, working hard to ensure that the club moved forward. One of their main projects was to secure sponsors, and they were delighted to announce a deal with Fisher's Garage which would see the club having the name of the Alfa Romeo dealers on their shirt fronts. The club would also get the use of eight Alfa Romeo cars, and the deal was estimated to be worth £100,000.

Clydebank, having won their opening game against Airdrie, topped the group when Hibs arrived the following midweek. The Kilbowie side made life difficult for a Hibs team who seemed to play only in fits and starts, but eventually the visitors took the points with a 2-0 win. Gary Murray had put Hibs ahead fairly early in the game, but the second goal, courtesy of Gordon Rae, did not arrive until the final minute. Jackie McNamara, who had taken an ankle knock in the first half, refused to let the injury hamper him as he inspired Hibs to victory from a midfield role. Once the second goal went in, Jackie relented and left the field, to be replaced by 16-year-old Derek McWilliams, whose first-team debut lasted all of 60 seconds. Another who played well that night was Ally Brazil, who slotted in well alongside Peter Welsh at the heart of the defence. It had been a busy week for Brazil: between those games against Rangers and Clydebank, his wife had given birth to a baby son.

On the following Tuesday night, the reserves got their own League Cup campaign under way with a narrow 1-0 win over Raith Rovers at Easter Road. Ten of the players who took part in the game were still eligible to turn out for the Under-18s, but the starting XI had their average age boosted somewhat by the inclusion of both Arthur Duncan and Bobby Flavell, each returning from injury and getting much-needed match practice. The only goal of the game was scored by a newcomer to the club, Pat McCurdy.

Game three of six brought Airdrie to Easter Road, the Lanarkshire side now in the First Division having suffered relegation. Changes had occurred at Broomfield, too, with the club selling its top scorer and long-time Hibs target, Sandy Clark, to West Ham and replacing him with Blair Miller, who had been top scorer with Clydebank. Having stuttered in beating Clydebank, Hibs floundered totally against the Diamonds and Bertie Auld later said he felt that this had been the worst performance from his side since taking over some two years before. Trailing 1-0 after Schaedler had put through his own goal, Hibs scored a last-gasp equaliser when Welsh opened his account for the Greens, heading home a cross from Callachan. It really was dismal stuff from Hibs, who were giving their fans the first sight of the famous green and white jersey with the new sponsor's name emblazoned on the front.

There was yet another statement from the board in the match programme that day. Under a heading of 'Stop this foul practice', fans were urged to behave or the good name of the club would be seriously threatened. Prompting the statement was the behaviour of a number of fans in the standing enclosure behind the visitors' dugout during the game against Rangers, whose officials had complained that they had been spat upon and had pies and other objects thrown at them. Frankly, this was deplorable behaviour and the Hibs management were totally correct in calling for an end to it. Additional policing around that area might have helped, but would have involved substantial additional costs.

The loss of a home point to Airdrie had handed Rangers the advantage in the League Cup section, so it was imperative that Hibs made home advantage count in their next game, which brought Clydebank to Leith. The Bankies had proved to be stuffy opponents in the Kilbowie encounter and they were much the same in this meeting, which finished at 1-1. Not for the first time, Hibs seemed totally disjointed and as they struggled the fans became more and more restless as they watched the visitors control large parts of the game. Eventually, Rodier managed to find a way through to score for Hibs, but Jim Given soon equalised, effectively ending Hibs' interest in the competition, even though they still had two games to play in the section. The Bankies' two forward players that day, both promoted from a successful Under-18 side, were Bobby Williamson and Tommy Coyne. Not to be outdone, Hibs had given Derek McWilliams the whole of the second half when he came on the park to replace the injured Murray.

The attendance at that Clydebank game was poor, although it was indicative of attendances over the whole competition. The format of the competition was under scrutiny as many clubs felt that mixing Premier League and First Division clubs in the same group made for unattractive fixtures. Given the Airdrie and Clydebank results, Hibs had a case in point.

The next challenge took Hibs to Ibrox to face Rangers and they would have to do so without the services of Brazil, Welsh and Murray, all injured in the draw with Clydebank. Willie Jamieson, who had played centre-half in the pre-season game against Brora Rangers, found himself wearing the No.5 jersey and McWilliams was again pitched in from the bench when he replaced Rodier during the second half. It was by necessity a backs-to-the wall display by Hibs, and they did extremely well to hold a full-strength Rangers team to a 0-0 draw.

The last day of August saw the reserves defeat Cowdenbeath 2-1 at Easter Road, a result which ensured they had won their League Cup section, dropping only one point along the way. Gary Murray, returning to fitness, scored both goals and it was a real triumph for a side that contained mostly Under-18 players. Interestingly, one Under-18 who did not play that day but would soon make his breakthrough into first the reserves and then the first team was Paul Kane.

The final League Cup section match for the senior team took them to Broomfield to face Airdrie and the game was an unmitigated disaster for Bertie Auld's men, who were played off the park by their First Division opponents and lost the game 3-1. Rae scored for Hibs, while Campbell, Faulds and Miller scored for the Diamonds, who might have had many more but for the heroics of Jim McArthur. There was not a huge travelling support, but those who did make the journey were not slow to make their feelings known as they booed the team off the pitch.

At this point, Hibs were in turmoil, but change would occur far more rapidly than the fans might have dreamt possible. The day after that humbling defeat at Broomfield, Bertie Auld, Pat Quinn and John Lambie severed their connections with the club, and left Hibs without a manager, first-team coach and youth coach. The board moved swiftly and, amazingly, before the day was out a new management team was in place. It was one which met with huge approval from the fans. The new manager was none other than Pat Stanton, and his assistants were George Stewart and Jimmy O'Rourke. It was the dream team from a fan's perspective as all three were known to be staunch Hibs men and all three had, of course, played for the club.

Since leaving Hibs as a player to join Celtic, Pat had cut his teeth in a coaching sense by accepting the post of assistant manager to Alex Ferguson at Aberdeen before venturing into management on his own with Cowdenbeath and then Dunfermline, where he teamed up with George Stewart. The Hibs board expressed heartfelt gratitude to the board of Dunfermline for allowing Stanton and Stewart this chance to step up a division, while Jimmy would be returning to the fold after having been out of football for a few months. The manager's post was, of course, full-time, but Stewart and

O'Rourke were happy to accept part-time contracts as that would allow them to combine their football commitments with those of running their businesses.

The general consensus among the support was that the new appointments would surely see Hibs returning to passing and attacking football. Many felt that under Bertie Auld the whole approach was too negative and revolved around not losing. Hibs fans wanted to see their side go out and try to win matches, and they felt that the new appointments would see those traditions return.

Two days into their new jobs, the management team had to send out a side to play St Mirren at Easter Road in the first Premier League game of the season. The date was Saturday, 4 September 1982, and it was a landmark day not just for the management team but also for the members of the Hibs Kids club. Around 750 of them were invited along for the first time under this initiative, and each would receive a club badge and a copy of the first ever Hibs Kids newsletter. The youngsters certainly enjoyed themselves as Hibs went after St Mirren from the off and but for the brilliance of Billy Thomson in the visiting goal the home side would have surely won the game, which ended at 0-0.

One good piece of news that weekend was that Alex Cropley was back in town and training with Hibs. He was a free agent, having finished his contract with Portsmouth and the new management team was only too happy to offer him facilities with an eye to returning to the club on a permanent basis.

Pat Stanton was quick to bring the fans up to speed with some of his ideas. He felt the club could benefit from a couple of new faces and was scouring the transfer market while also very conscious that Hibs had benefited greatly in the past by keeping tags on youth and boys' club football. That being so, he would personally get in touch with officials at such clubs to establish contact and make them aware he was willing to run the rule over any player each club might think promising.

The next match for Hibs took them to Rugby Park, a ground where the Greens had not had the best of fortunes for some time, although the manner in which they took control of the game seemed to belie the fact that they were actually playing away from home. Jamieson gave Hibs a deserved lead and Flavell might have doubled it had his shot not come back off the post, but a late lapse in defence allowed Paul Clarke to equalise and Hibs had to be content with just the one point. Playing at centre-half for Hibs that day was Gordon Rae, who was immense throughout and added weight to the argument of those who felt it was his best position, Pat Stanton seemingly among that number.

On the following Monday evening, the reserves entertained Kilmarnock at Easter Road and fought out an entertaining 2-2 draw, part-timer Pat

McCurdy and a trialist getting the home goals. McCurdy lived in the west and actually trained with Morton, but Hibs were confident they had a promising player on their hands and were quick to emphasise that training with the Cappielow club was just an arrangement to cut down on Pat's travelling.

Two points from two games could and should have been four, but Hibs just couldn't kill teams off, and Stanton was stepping up his search for a forward as a result. In the previous season, Hibs and Dundee United had met on no fewer than seven occasions, and the next home game in this campaign brought the Tannadice club to Easter Road. United had won all of their League Cup games and had not lost in the League. Indeed, they hadn't even conceded a goal in the League. Very well organised defensively and creative in midfield, United had taken the bold step of signing ex-Arsenal and England star Charlie George on a short-term contract. Fans making their way to the game that day must have hoped to see George, but he did not feature as the teams battled out a 0-0 draw. Jackie McNamara won the sponsors' man of the match award and Hibs once again had chances to take the points but couldn't convert them.

Twenty-four hours earlier, the reserves had crashed to a 4-0 defeat at Tannadice, even with Arthur Duncan and Alex Cropley in the side. Two early goals were conceded and that forced Hibs to chase the game, meaning gaps at the back were exploited and another two were conceded. Aside from Duncan and Cropley, this was a very young Hibs team and from that point of view the consistency element was one that would be lacking as coach Jimmy O'Rourke tried different combinations and occasionally introduced trialists into the game.

Indeed, the reserves were in action again the following Thursday evening when they hosted Celtic at Easter Road and Jimmy O'Rourke made several changes to the side beaten at Tannadice, including the introduction at right-back of a young lad named Kevin McKee. A bigger than average crowd turned up to see 'Sodjer' back in the green and white of Hibernian and Cropley had a fantastic first half, spraying passes left, right and centre and setting up a goal for Pat McCurdy. Cropley's lack of match fitness caught up with him in the second half as George McCluskey stole the limelight with a hat-trick to give the visitors a 3-1 win.

Two days later, the first teams clashed at Parkhead, and it is safe to say that little went right for the Easter Road men. It was a daunting task taking on a team who had started the season with three straight wins, scoring 11 and conceding only one in the process. By contrast, Hibs had started with three draws, scoring only one goal and conceding only one. In the opening minutes of this game, the defence failed miserably to clear the ball and Murdo MacLeod stepped in to snatch a goal which had been gifted on a plate. Midway through the first half, Erich Schaedler had to quit with a heel injury that would later see him put in plaster, while Brazil also had to limp off with a knee knock. They were replaced by Stuart Turnbull and Arthur Duncan, but the new boys could not save Hibs from conceding the second and final goal of the game, scored by Paul McStay.

During the following week, Pat Stanton tried very hard to bring a couple of new faces to the club, but negotiations were not going smoothly, leaving him frustrated as he knew exactly who he wanted. At the eleventh hour, he finally got one of his men, Willie Irvine, a 26-year-old striker from Motherwell, who was a new face in the side for the visit of Morton. In fact, a few 'old' faces were missing, too, as Schaedler, Brazil and Welsh all missed the game due to injury. Bobby Thomson got Hibs off to a good start against his old club when he opened the scoring, but Hibs could not get a second and the visitors grabbed two late goals through Andy Ritchie and Eddie McNab to steal the points. Irvine had a quiet debut, although he showed a few nice touches and gave cause for optimism that goals would come once he had settled in.

On 9 October, Hibs were at Dens Park to face Dundee, who had started the season somewhat better than the Greens. Although playing at centre-half, Gordon Rae opened the scoring for the visitors when he came forward for a corner taken by young Brian Rice. Hibs then went looking for a second, but the old failing of missing chances caught up with them when Jim Smith equalised. Still, Hibs looked the more likely side to go on and win the game until referee Joe Timmons took a hand in proceedings. A rash rather than reckless challenge by Thomson earned him what most observers thought was a very harsh booking. Minutes later, Thomson went in for another challenge, and to the surprise of just about everyone present the referee brandished a second yellow card, meaning that Thomson was sent off. Even the Dundee players tried to get the referee to change his mind, and after the game it was shown that Thomson had made only three tackles in the whole game, none of which had really seemed like bookable offences. The Hibs man's problem was that he had a bit of a reputation, and many neutral observers felt that it had cost him dear. Reduced to ten men, Hibs found that Thomson's dismissal had given their hosts a boost and it was disappointing if not surprising that Dundee went on to score again through Iain Ferguson to win the game 2-1.

On the Monday following that game, Hibs moved to sign 25-year-old midfielder Mike Conroy, and the new man went straight into the reserve side that faced Dundee at Easter Road. It would be a scoring start for the new man and Kevin Hoggan also found the target, but the visitors scored three, which meant another defeat for the reserves. They had fielded a trialist in the No.11 jersey who turned out to be the former Raith Rovers, Hearts and Ayr United winger Malcolm Robertson. The 'trialist' did so well that he was immediately offered a three-month deal and added to the first-team squad.

Pat Stanton was getting quite concerned that with Hibs trying to run three teams, many of those in the Under-18s would also turn out for the reserves, meaning that they quite often played two games a week, a heavy workload for youngsters.

Four days later, the reserves were in action again, meeting Motherwell at Easter Road and drawing the game 3-3. Hibs' scorers were Derek Rodier, Ricky Haddow and Alex Cropley. Watching from the stand was Pat Stanton, and it was this game as much as anything else that persuaded him to approach the board and say he wanted to scrap the Under-18 side, citing the fact that a number of the youngsters in the Motherwell game had looked dead on their feet as they had played far too much football. The board sanctioned the move, Hibs reverted to running just two teams, and Jimmy O'Rourke would have a fresher bunch of players to work with.

Only Motherwell were behind Hibs in the League now, and they faced Hibs in the next match at Easter Road. New boys Willie Irvine, Mike Conroy and Malcolm Robertson were all in the Hibs starting XI, while Motherwell, fresh from defeating mid-table St Mirren, included ex-Ayr United keeper Hugh Sproat, former Celtic man Johannes Edvaldsson and ex-Hibee Bobby Flavell, who had moved there in the past couple of weeks. Still absent for Hibs were Brazil and Welsh, who joined Schaedler in having to have injured legs put in plaster. Welsh also required a cartilage operation and would be out for some time. All of those players were defenders, which meant that Hibs had to go with a back four of Alan Sneddon, Jackie McNamara, Gordon Rae and Arthur Duncan. At the end of 90 tense minutes, Hibs took the points after Rae scored the only goal of the game.

The following Tuesday night, Hibs fielded a strong XI against Meadowbank Thistle in the East of Scotland Shield. Sitting top of the Second Division, Thistle gave Hibs a real test on the night and the Greens barely scraped home 2-1 with both goals coming from Bobby Thomson. After the game, the Hibs players were very complimentary about their opponents and tipped them to win promotion into the First Division. Unlucky not to feature that night was Pat McCurdy, who had now moved house to Edinburgh after having been made redundant from his job as a painter with just one year of his apprenticeship left. Delighted to have him, Pat Stanton pledged that the club would help him find a job and predicted that as he could now train with his own team-mates his game would surely improve.

Rangers were in hot pursuit of Celtic at the top of the League when Hibs visited Ibrox towards the end of October, and but for a huge slice of bad luck the Easter Road men might well have taken a deserved point from the game. Rangers opened the scoring against the run of play when a defensive lapse allowed Derek Johnstone to steer the ball past McArthur, but Hibs fought back and Murray squeezed home a fine equaliser from inside the six-yard box. Then Sneddon took a knock on his already heavily strapped ankle and that injury impeded his free movement, allowing Rangers to capitalise on it whenever the opportunity arose. Hibs had the ball in the net again for what could have been a 2-1 lead, but the referee disallowed it for offside and then McNamara put through his own goal to give the hosts the lead. Hibs then missed a penalty, but shrugged that off and Murray levelled the game, the first time Hibs had scored more than one goal in a League match this season. To make life even tougher for Hibs, goalkeeper McArthur then suffered a mild concussion and had to go off, which meant that Arthur Duncan had to take over in goal. Almost immediately, Derek Johnstone restored Rangers' lead, but they would not score again as Duncan performed well between the sticks and his team-mates gave him plenty of protection. An unlucky 3-2 loss, but a loss just the same, keeping Hibs at the wrong end of the table with only Kilmarnock and Motherwell below them.

At Easter Road, Alex Ferguson's Aberdeen side arrived in fine form, lying only two points behind leaders Celtic in the League table. They were also going very well in Europe, sitting on the brink of a quarter-final place in the Cup Winners' Cup, having disposed of Swiss side Sion and Dinamo Tirana of Albania, and holding a 2-0 lead in their match with Lech Poznan of Poland. A tough task for Hibs, then, and it was made all the tougher when Peter Weir put the visitors ahead. To their credit, Hibs stuck in and gradually fought their way back into the game, but it took a last-gasp equaliser from Murray to salvage a very welcome point.

November 1982 started with Hibs going to Love Street to face St Mirren and there was a surprise inclusion in the squad when former Hibee Bobby Smith was named among the substitutes. It had been four years since 'Smudger' left Easter Road to join Leicester City and his return, at least initially, was in the form of a one-month loan arrangement. Just what Smith thought of Hibs that day only he could say, but it wasn't pretty for him watching from the bench. In 45 appalling first-half minutes, Hibs had McNamara sent off for two bookable offences and they conceded three goals just to rub salt in the wounds. Smith joined the fray in the second half when he replaced Thomson, and Hibs moved Conroy to sweeper, where he commanded his area and stopped the rot or the home side might have scored a good few more. McNamara's dismissal meant he would miss the next match, but the points accrued would also lead to a further three-game ban, and so Conroy might have found himself wondering if sweeper was a role he would have to play again.

In his programme notes for the next home game, which brought Kilmarnock to Easter Road, Pat Stanton offered the view that the results the team had been getting were, with the exception of the drubbing at Love Street, not an accurate reflection of his team's performances. It was hard to argue with him, as Hibs had suffered some bad luck, but things needed to be turned around fast as it was easy to slip towards the foot of the table and hard to get away from there once you'd arrived. Having just been promoted to the Premier League, Killie were finding it difficult to put together any kind of run of results. They had won only one League game, just like their hosts. Ian Bryson gave the visitors the best start with an early goal, but Hibs fought back and Thomson soon equalised. Stanton had given Bobby Smith the No.8 jersey that day and his decision to do so was more than vindicated when the Leicester City loan man scored a cracking goal to put Hibs 2-1 up. Sadly, nerves then kicked in for the home side and Derrick McDicken equalised to salvage his side a point.

During the following week, speculation was rife that Hibs were trying to sign Alan Rough from Partick Thistle and there was certainly an enthusiastic response to those stories from the majority of Hibs fans. To be fair to Jim McArthur, who must have heard the rumours too, Hibs' plight could hardly be blamed on him as he had turned in many fine performances during his side's run of poor results. In fact, McArthur was very much in the spotlight when Hibs lost their next League outing 3-0 at Tannadice. Early in the game, the keeper dived bravely at the feet of Paul Sturrock, but the United man's momentum carried him on to a clash with McArthur's leg, resulting in a gaping wound appearing below the keeper's knee. It looked a bad one, and Tom McNiven at first thought the keeper should come off, but McArthur asked that the wound be stitched so that he could carry on. Stitches were duly applied and Arthur Duncan heaved a sigh of relief, as he would have been the player to take over in goal if McArthur had gone off injured. Right on half-time, Willie Irvine went over on his ankle and had to be replaced by Jamieson. To make matters worse, Rae then suffered a thigh strain, which restricted his movement. On top of all that, McNamara was absent due to suspension, and so it is hardly surprising that Hibs lost three goals, Eamonn Bannon, John Reilly and Davie Dodds finding the target.

This run of bad luck and injuries would have been very unwelcome at any time in the League campaign, but doubly so going into the next match against League leaders Celtic at Easter Road. The comparison of each team's record with the other was scary, to say the least: Celtic had ten wins, 34 goals for and 21 points, while Hibs had one win, nine goals for and just seven points. Hibs could certainly have done with a goalscorer of the calibre of Celtic's new young sensation, Charlie Nicholas, and the fans on the terracing were often heard bemoaning the fact that Ally MacLeod, a regular scorer, had been allowed to leave Easter Road earlier in the season. On the day, Nicholas didn't find the net, but Frank McGarvey (2) and Celtic's other young and exciting player, Paul McStay, got another, while Hibs countered with a double from Murray. It was tough luck on the Hibs man to score two against a normally rock-solid defence and yet still finish on the losing side.

Much more importantly that day was the fact that Hibs had 'got their man'. Pat Stanton had persuaded Scotland goalkeeper Alan Rough to leave Partick Thistle after 13 years with the Jags and join Hibs. It was a major coup for the club, and although Rough was on the losing side and conceded three goals, he was cheered off the park at the end by a home support thrilled with his signing. Aged 31, Rough had 51 caps to his name and there was no reason to think he would not go on to get many more.

Though at Parkhead, the reserves were struggling and down 4-0 when they suddenly found a bit of form and managed to pull a couple of goals back through Kevin McKee and Kevin Hoggan. Once again, there were a number of trialists and for the first time a Hibs team sheet named Michael Weir among the starting XI. The youngster had impressed when given trial outings with the second string. In fact, Hibs had been pruning the staff a bit as Stanton attempted to reduce the wage bill and bring on board some of the younger players. Gone from Easter Road were Derek Rodier, who was sold to Dunfermline, Tony Duffy, Norrie Innes, Ricky Haddow, Colin Morton, Alan Samuel, Derek McWilliams and Warren Marshall.

With the number of injured players at Easter Road slowly reducing in number, it was a shock when trainer Tam McNiven was rushed into hospital and straight into intensive care having suffered a heart attack. Tam was a hugely important member of the backroom team as well as being massively popular with players and fans alike, and there was a collective sigh of relief when it was reported that he had reacted positively to treatment and would soon be back on his feet.

Having played four games in November and managed to accrue just one point in the process, Hibs hoped to start December with a win at fellow-strugglers Morton. With McNamara serving the last game of his suspension, Hibs went with a very young central defensive partnership of Jamieson and Rae, both of whom were outstanding, as was Alan Rough, who made a string of excellent saves to deny the home side a goal. This was the first occasion during this campaign that the Greens had not conceded when away from home, although they could not find the net either. The 0-0 draw saw Hibs firmly rooted at the bottom of the table. That game also heralded the end of Bobby Smith's loan period with the club, as he set off back to Leicester City. He would be missed, as he had performed well during his short return to the club.

It was imperative that Hibs start adding some points to their dismal total of just eight from 14, and Pat Stanton hoped that the return of McNamara from suspension, coupled with having Rough in goals, would help the defence to concede fewer. At the same time, the forwards had to score more than they had in order to win games. Dundee presented Hibs with their next challenge when they arrived at Easter Road in mid-December. The Dark Blues were in a mid-table position and had been idle the week before as their fixture was postponed due to their opponents being involved in the League Cup final. Manager Donald Mackay, himself once a goalkeeper, had been having problems signing a keeper he felt would improve the team, and so there was a certain amount of irony that the man he chose was Colin Kelly, a keeper who had been with Hibs but never really got beyond the reserve team. As it was, Kelly had a great game and stopped Hibs from scoring more than the one goal they did get after Rae beat him with a close-range shot. Rae had been pushed forward from that central defensive role and the move paid off, but the pity was that his goal was only an equaliser as the visitors were already ahead through a goal from Peter Mackie. A 1-1 draw was not going to do Hibs any favours in their efforts to climb off the bottom, but a point was better than none and provided some sort of foundation upon which to build.

The reserves had taken to playing on Monday evenings, and their latest game saw them lose 3-2 at Dens Park. The Hibs goals were scored by Willie Irvine and one of two trialists in the starting XI. What was not obvious from the scorer details was that the trialist who scored was none other than Ally McLeod, who had been released by Dundee United and who was training with Hibs again while he sought out a new club. As he was not a signed player, Hibs had to play him as a trialist, which was bizarre given the number of times he had found the net when a regular in the first team.

The last match before Christmas took Hibs to Fir Park to face Motherwell, who were struggling near the foot of the table. Classy football was in short supply during the 90 minutes, although young Brian Rice, drafted into a midfield starting spot due to injury and suspensions, always tried to put his foot on the ball and make a telling pass. The game had 0-0 written all over it until Murray popped up to fire a shot past Hugh Sproat which ensured that the two points were heading back to Edinburgh. Other results that day meant that the Hibs win shot them up to eighth in the table, proving just what a tight situation existed in the bottom half.

The win at Motherwell represented a good start to the busy holiday period, when four games would be played. The second of these brought Rangers to Easter Road on the Monday between Christmas and New Year. Trailing leaders Celtic by a massive ten points, the Gers had not been having the best of seasons and had lost out in the League Cup final to their Old Firm rivals. They started the game the better of the two sides, but Hibs were resolute in defence and slowly began to come into their own. Chances were made and missed by both sides, and keepers Jim Stewart and Alan Rough had the broadest smiles at the final whistle as neither had been beaten.

In 'normal' circumstances, the New Year's Day game would see Hibs either at home or at Gorgie to face Hearts, but the latter were currently in the First Division and so Hibs had to travel all the way to Aberdeen instead. It was a long way to go to get beaten, but Hibs managed just that in going down 2-0 after a double from Mark McGhee. Both Turnbull and Callachan failed to finish the match due to injury and they were replaced on the day by Bobby Thomson and Gordon Byrne, so full marks to Pat Stanton for trying to win the game by introducing an extra forward into the fray.

The fourth and final game of the festive period brought St Mirren to Easter Road to first-foot Hibs. In his programme notes, the manager repeated what he had said when he first arrived: he saw the season as one for consolidation rather than a time for chasing a League title or even a place in Europe. Hibs had already had a season in the First Division in the recent past, and they did not want to suffer the same fate as Hearts. The Buddies were just above Hibs in the League and a home win would have allowed the Greens to leapfrog them. On the day, Hibs scored twice, but one of those was an own-goal when Sneddon tried to steer the ball wide for a corner but only succeeded in putting it into his own net. The Hibs goal came from Arthur Duncan, who had a great 90 minutes, giving his all as usual despite suffering from flu. Indeed, he looked none too well at the final whistle. Arthur really was a marvellous servant to Hibs, even though his team-mates were always ribbing him about being the last to turn up for training every day. He had no excuses, if that were true, as he lived literally five minutes' drive away from Easter Road!

After that hectic holiday schedule, the players enjoyed a couple of days off before heading down to Rugby Park to play a Kilmarnock side who had hit a poor run of form and were now propping up the rest of the League. The record books showed that Hibs had enjoyed less success at that venue than at any other since the late Fifties, and they had not even beaten Kilmarnock home or away since March 1977. All of the statistics were forgotten when Hibs won 2-0 in a game they dominated for almost the entire 90 minutes. Conroy got the opener, his first for the club, and Thomson, playing in a deeper midfield role, scored the second. Hibs could have had more but hit the woodwork twice, while at the other end Alan Rough was rarely troubled. Someone not at the game that day was Tommy Younger, who, in his capacity as SFA vice-president, was at Ibrox to assist with the draw for the third round of the Scottish Cup. Tommy drew out the home teams and Hibs were among those, but their opponents for that tie were Aberdeen, promising an exciting but very difficult match in the near future.

The signing of Alan Rough brought a real upturn in Hibs' fortunes and the clean sheet he had against Killie was his fourth in seven games. Eight points had been gained over that period, and that meant that Hibs were up to sixth, six points ahead of bottom club Kilmarnock. Rough's heroics rightly won him the Mackinlay's Scotch Whisky Football Personality of the Month for December – as well as winning him the adulation of the Easter Road support.

During the following week, a mixed side of reserve and first-team players tackled Edinburgh City in a friendly and won 5-0, the goals coming from Thomson and Turnbull, who each got two, and Brian Rice. Trialist Graham Harvey played for 45 minutes and did well.

Mid-January brought a good-going Dundee United to Easter Road, although the Arabs had not done their championship hopes much good in losing to both Aberdeen and Rangers in recent weeks. Even with those defeats, Jim McLean's men were still in third spot and handily placed should the teams above them have slips of their own. In addition, United had reached the quarter-finals of the UEFA Cup by eliminating Isak Refvik's club, Viking Stavanger, as well as PSV Eindhoven and Werder Bremen to set up a tie with Bohemians of Prague.

A stern challenge was anticipated at Easter Road that day and a stern challenge is exactly what Hibs got, but it was not all United as the home side gave as good as it got. Murray actually had the ball in the net having shrugged off a challenge from David Narey, but referee Ferguson didn't play the advantage rule and called play back to award Hibs a free kick just outside the box. Then Rae missed a penalty by diverting from his normal style of smashing the ball towards goal. Instead, he tried to place it and Hamish McAlpine guessed right to make a fine save. United also had their chances, but found Rough in good form. In the end, a 0-0 draw was about right as both sides would have been unhappy not to gain at least one point from the game. Man of the match was youngster Brian Rice, who had a superb game on the left of the midfield four.

During the following week, Pat Stanton beat Rangers to the signature of a young striker plying his trade with the East Lothian side Ormiston Primrose. Twenty-year-old Graham Harvey was a Prestonpans lad and joined the club on a full-time basis after impressing the manager when playing as a trialist in the reserves, scoring two goals against Dundee in one of those outings which took place at Dens Park and which saw the wee Hibs lose 5-3. While Harvey was arriving, others were leaving. Malcolm Robertson reached the end of his three-month trial period and youngsters Stuart Rae and Kevin Hoggan did not have their contracts renewed.

Only one game remained before that eagerly awaited Scottish Cup clash with Aberdeen and that was at Parkhead against Celtic, who were still leading the League. Both Thomson and Callachan missed the match through illness and injury respectively, while the Celtic team was at full strength. The game was barely started when Frank McGarvey put the home side ahead and Charlie Nicholas soon added a second. With half-time fast approaching, Hibs got one back when Tom McAdam put through his own goal, but any confidence gained from that soon disappeared as Celtic scored again early in the second half through McGarvey. George McCluskey got another to make the final score 4-1, but those Hibs fans present on the day agreed with Pat Stanton's post-match assessment that Hibs were never three goals worse than Celtic. The visitors had created numerous chances throughout the game, but had failed to take them and paid the price.

The final game in January 1983 would be that Scottish Cup confrontation with Aberdeen. The Dons were not only holders of that trophy but also genuine title challengers and quarter-finalists in the European Cup Winners' Cup, where they would face Bayern Munich. Manager Alex Ferguson had blended together a side containing both young and experienced players and they were certainly doing him proud. Goalkeeper Jim Leighton was a rock at the back, as were the central defensive partnership of Alex McLeish and Willie Miller, while the guile and craft of midfield players such as Gordon Strachan and Neil Simpson ensured that forwards Mark McGhee and Eric Black got plenty of service. For Hibs, there was both good and bad team news. The good news was that after a lengthy absence and just one hour of playing in his reserve team comeback, iron man Erich Schaedler was back in the No.3 shirt. 'Shades' really was a fit boy and he went on to have a good 90 minutes in this Cup tie. The bad news was that Murray and McNamara had heavy strapping on their right legs, as they were both less than 100 per cent fit, while Welsh had protective padding over a head wound that had needed eight stitches and Callachan, just back after an injury absence, could not move freely enough and would be replaced at half-time by Irvine.

The high-flying Dons against the walking wounded was always going to spell disaster for Hibs and disaster it was as the visitors recorded a 4-1 win. Peter Weir, Neil Simpson, Andy Watson and Mark McGhee all found the target, while Rae struck for Hibs. When Rae scored, the Dons were pegged back to 2-1 and looked edgy for a spell, but after both Welsh and Irvine had missed good chances to draw Hibs level the visitors regained their confidence and pulled away. Poor Alan Rough had now conceded four goals in each of his last two games and yet he had not played badly in either. It must have been galling for him to lose the four against Aberdeen, knowing that Leighton, his biggest rival for the Scotland No.1 jersey, was at the other end of the park having a reasonably easy afternoon.

With the winter weather starting to have an effect on fixtures, Hibs once more felt the benefit of having undersoil heating when Morton visited Easter Road on 5 February 1983. It was a day to remember for hundreds of youngsters as the club made it an occasion for Hibs Kids members to swell the crowd. Those youngsters certainly enjoyed themselves, as did 21-year-old Graham Harvey, who made his first-team debut and found the net to put Hibs one up. Goals had come easily for Harvey when he played in the Juniors, having scored around 90 for Ormiston Primrose in a little over two years, but he was a full-time professional now and playing against the likes of Morton's big Joe McLaughlin and ex-Celt Jim Duffy, neither of whom could stop him opening his account. A second goal on the day, with Rae the marksman, wrapped up a welcome two points against a club who were just one point adrift of Hibs when the game kicked off.

That fierce February weather took a real grip of the country during the following week, with heavy snowfalls in just about every part of Scotland. In Dundee, where Hibs were next due to play, efforts to clear the Dens Park pitch were thwarted after some stubborn patches of ice would not thaw in time for the match to go ahead. The late Saturday afternoon postponement didn't stop Hibs from arranging a friendly for the following day, when Alan Durban brought his Sunderland side north to make use of Hibs' playable surface. Graham Harvey kept his starting jersey and during the game 16-year-old Kevin McKee came off the bench to make his first-team debut, while another teenager, Brian Rice, wore the No.8 jersey. The Black Cats had a number of very good players, including Scots Iain Munro, Ally McCoist (newly transferred in from St Johnstone) and Gordon Chisholm. It was the Scots who found the target, McCoist putting the visitors ahead and Chisholm getting the winner after Thomson had fired Hibs level.

With another blank Saturday looming, Hibs organised a friendly with Swansea City at Easter Road on Friday, 18 February. Incredible as it may seem, the visitors could name 11 full internationalists, with players from Yugoslavia, England and Wales on their books. Perhaps best known to the fans at the game would be keeper Dai Davies, midfielders Ray Kennedy and Robbie James and strikers Bob Latchford and John Mahoney. For their part, Hibs named 16-year-old Paul Kane as a substitute and the youngster came on to replace Peter Welsh, thereby earning his first-team debut. The final score in the game was 1-0 to Hibs, thanks to another first when Willie Irvine scored, and it could have been more as Gordon Rae had what looked like a good goal chalked off, while Dai Davies pulled off at least three wonderful saves.

The players may have been idle the following day, but Pat Stanton, George Stewart and chairman Kenny Waugh headed north to watch Aberdeen take on Hibs' next opponents, Dundee, in the Scottish Cup. Meanwhile, at Easter Road, the reserves didn't do themselves justice in only drawing 1-1 with Arbroath, although it was a significant day for Ally Brazil, who made his comeback after being out for some time with a cracked ankle bone.

Dens Park was declared playable on the Tuesday night and Hibs went there knowing a win would take them level on points with the home side as well as drawing them away from the lower reaches of the League. Rae took to the field with a black eye suffered in the game against Swansea, but the big defender-cum-striker had a fine game, as did his team-mates, who scored a goal in the second minute through Rice and never looked like conceding at any point. Rice's goal was his first for the senior team and once again the red-headed youngster played with a maturity way beyond his years. Erich Schaedler limped off just after half-time with a thigh strain, but he was such a quick healer that everyone was confident he'd be back in the No.3 jersey by that weekend.

Strugglers Motherwell brought a bitterly cold February to a close when they visited Easter Road and included their latest three signings in their starting XI. All three had an Aberdeen connection, Andy Dornan and Andy Harrow having played for the Dons, while goalkeeper Nicky Walker had been born there. Another who appeared for the Steelmen that day was young Brian McClair, who had scored a hat-trick against Rangers and the winner against Celtic, making him worth the watching. Hibs were without Schaedler and had to switch Duncan to left-back, which meant less penetration down the right side of the visiting defence. In fact, Arthur was just back from Hong Kong, having been invited over there to make a guest appearance for Hong Kong Rangers. The speedy winger made the long trip, but missed out on the actual game because torrential rain made the pitch unplayable. It was disappointing for the Hibs man, but at least he had enjoyed a break away from the Scottish winter. The game with Motherwell finished at 1-1, the goals coming from Willie Irvine, his first in the League, and Andy Harrow.

By their own standards, Rangers were having a very poor League season and sat just fourth in the League, no fewer than 16 points behind leaders Dundee United. Arriving at Ibrox on the first Saturday in March, Hibs were just eight points behind Rangers and lying in sixth place. Jamieson and Rae again played in the centre of defence and the youngsters performed brilliantly throughout the 90 minutes. Jamieson actually put Hibs ahead, and for a long time it looked as though his goal would win the points, but Gordon Dalziel equalised to save Rangers a point. It was a good point to collect, but a bitter taste was left in the mouth when the home side's official publication, the *Rangers News*, carried an article in which Hibs were accused of 'brutal' tackling. The Hibs board were incensed and complained officially to the SFA, who in turn wrote to Rangers asking for an explanation of those comments. The irony of this situation was not lost on the Hibs fans who were at Ibrox that day and witnessed any number of heavy tackles on Hibs players going unpunished by referee David Syme. Nor was the irony lost on those same fans whose buses had to run a gauntlet of flying bricks and bottles as they tried to get away from the stadium.

Aberdeen were scheduled to be the next opponents for Hibs, but the fixture was cancelled as the Dons would be playing in the Scottish Cup that day. The Easter Road side tried to fill the blank weekend by inviting Liverpool to travel north for a friendly, but the English side declined the offer and so the Hibs players had a weekend off.

The break allowed some who had been nursing injuries to set about improving their fitness, although Schaedler was the one player unlikely to recover quickly from a niggling heel injury. Callachan did make good use of that non-playing time to get his fitness back, so much so that he was able to turn out for Hibs' next match, against St Mirren at Love Street. After a first half in which both sides had chances to go ahead, Hibs suffered a sucker punch early in the second when a move from a corner allowed Mark Fulton to open the scoring for the Buddies. Manager Pat Stanton was angry at his defence for losing that goal, as it came from a rehearsed move that the manager had warned his players to look out for. Shortly after that, Rae thought he had equalised, but referee Kenny Hope disallowed the goal, much to the puzzlement of Rae and his team-mates. The same player then hit the post with another effort, but St Mirren swept up the field and scored a second through Doug Somner. Willie Irvine missed a good chance to pull one back, but a third goal, scored by Alan Logan late in the match, secured the points for the home side.

Hibs were still close enough to the second-bottom spot in the League to make the fans at least, if not the players, nervous about visiting Dundee United, who were still well in the hunt for the League title. Only leaders Aberdeen had conceded fewer League goals, as the likes of Maurice Malpas, Richard Gough, Paul Hegarty and David Narey stopped opposing forwards getting too close to Hamish McAlpine's goal. The Greens opened the scoring through Rae, but were punished for defensive lapses when Davie Dodds, Ian Britton and Richard Gough all scored first-half goals to put the Arabs 3-1 ahead at the interval. If the first half had belonged to the hosts then the second firmly belonged to the Hibees, as they scored twice through Irvine and Rice to level the game and then peppered the United goal for the last ten minutes of the match without further success. The game ended 3-3, and the pick of the goals was the one scored by Rice, who struck a beautiful left-footed volley high into the net. It was a great way for him to celebrate the fact that he had just signed a new three-year deal with Hibs. Running Rice close for the goal of the game was centre-half Gordon Rae, who had thundered his one in from all of 40 yards.

During the previous week, a much-loved face was seen once again around the stadium as trainer Tam McNiven returned to work after his heart scare. Tam was only in the door five minutes when he started working on Schaedler, who showed remarkable progress thanks to McNiven's ministrations and very nearly made the team for Tannadice.

Three days after the first team had won that point at Tannadice, the reserve sides of both clubs met at Easter Road. The visitors topped the reserve League and had been unbeaten until that night, when two goals from Pat McCurdy kept the points in Leith. It was a marvellous result, given that Hibs included two trialists in their team. One of those was later offered a contract by the club. Callum Milne, a 17-year-old right-back, came from Salvesen's Boys' Club and immediately showed his promise with a solid game against a United reserve side containing six players with first-team experience.

Poor Kilmarnock had found the step up to Premier League football just a little too hot to handle and were firmly rooted at the bottom of the table when they visited Easter Road on 2 April 1983. With only three wins and eight draws from 28 starts, Jim Clunie's men were rapidly running out of games in their efforts to stay up. Hibs did absolutely nothing to boost their hopes by turning on the style and hammering them 8-1 in front of a small but highly excited crowd. Going into the game, Hibs had been one of the lowest-scoring sides in the table, but you'd never have thought so on the evidence of this display.

Kilmarnock were quite literally destroyed by a team on the top of their form. No fewer than six players shared the eight goals, although Graham Harvey, who did not score, had as good a game as any of his team-mates and did not look like a player who had been in the junior ranks just a few short weeks before. Thomson scored twice, though one of those was from the penalty spot, while Irvine also notched a double and there were singles from Duncan, Rae, McNamara and substitute Pat McCurdy, who had only 20 minutes on the park but managed that goal and saw another effort strike the outside of the post. Kilmarnock's goal came from their top scorer, Brian Gallagher, but that was the only blip on an afternoon when hundreds of Hibs Kids were in the crowd. There's no doubt that the youngsters would have enjoyed their day, with some perhaps asking if Hibs played like that all the time!

That 8-1 win was a record score in the Premier League and the biggest total in a championship match since Ayr United had lost 8-1 in December 1972 – to Hibs. There was almost another record in that win over Killie, as three of the back four scored. Sneddon, the odd man out, professed later that he was happy to concentrate on his defending and let others chase the goals.

Celtic were next in line to visit Easter Road and nobody who went along that day had any thoughts of another eight goals for the home team. The Glasgow side had opened up a three-point gap at the top of the table and were determined to maintain that lead. It turned out to be a bad day for Hibs and for McNamara in particular, as the ex-Celt was ordered off and Hibs lost the match 3-0. On-fire Charlie Nicholas scored twice and Davie Provan added another as the home side struggled to contain a strong Celtic XI.

Games were running out now, and Hibs were still not mathematically safe from relegation when they made the trip through to Cappielow to face Morton, themselves in the thick of the relegation battle. At the end of the 90 minutes, Hibs looked to have achieved League safety, but the home side would have to battle on. A single goal decided the tie when Thomson fired past Roy Baines, but Hibs should have scored more and even missed a penalty when Callachan blasted his shot over the bar after Thomson had been upended by Joe McLaughlin. With McNamara out suspended after his red card against Celtic, the captain's armband was handed to Gordon Rae, who was delighted to skipper the side to victory but dismayed that he suffered an injury in doing so. Although he played the full 90 minutes, Rae limped off and a later X-ray revealed a fractured bone in his foot. It was bad luck on the big guy as he had been in great form but would now miss several matches. It was as well that Ally Brazil was fit and back in the team as McNamara was scheduled to miss four games in total, while Rae looked as though he might be out for at least three. To add to the injury woe, Erich Schaedler made his comeback as a second-half substitute and suffered an injury to his ankle that saw a strip of skin ripped off. Brian Rice, now a first-team regular, celebrated that win in the knowledge that he had been selected to represent Scotland at Under-19 level for a forthcoming trip to Mexico.

When Dundee visited Easter Road on 23 April both sides knew that they were safe from relegation. The problem was that neither side really had anything to play for, and that was probably reflected in the fact that they fought out a pretty insipid 0-0 draw. It could have been all so different had Hibs converted even one of the three gilt-edged chances they had in the opening five minutes, but they couldn't and the game just deteriorated from that point forward.

April ended with a defeat at the hands of Motherwell at Fir Park. The Steelmen needed the points to stave off rivals Morton, who were one place below them in the second relegation spot, and they deservedly took those valuable points thanks to a double from Andy Harrow. It was true that Hibs had dominated the second half when they were trailing only 1-0, but as they pushed more and more players forward looking for an equaliser they conceded a second in the dying moments. A surprising absentee from that match was Hibs manager Pat Stanton, who had been unhappy for some time that the board were not willing to invest in new players. Stanton felt that if Hibs were to be a force again he would need to have fresh faces for the coming season and was disappointed at the response when he broached the subject. Thankfully, there would be clear-the-air talks and he would stay on to take Hibs forward.

Just three games remained now and two of those were against Aberdeen, one at home. Although the Greens were safe, the manager wanted full effort from his players so as to finish the season on a high note. The first of the Aberdeen games was at Easter Road and it marked the first-team debut of 16-year-old Kevin McKee, who had a fine 90 minutes up against Peter Weir and was only beaten to the man of the match award by a man more than twice his age! At 35, Arthur Duncan was still giving everything for Hibs and he had a sparkling display against the Dons, almost scoring late in the game. The visitors had been awarded a penalty, but Rough saved Gordon Strachan's effort and that inspired the Greens to go for a winner. It didn't arrive and the game finished at 0-0, but it was an entertaining encounter thoroughly enjoyed by the fans. Amazingly, Aberdeen would be playing Real Madrid in that European final before they next met Hibs and Pat Stanton was most probably not the only Hibs fan who wished them well.

Rangers arrived at Easter Road on 7 May for the sixth and final meeting with Hibs this season. They held the edge with one win, the other four games being drawn and they would hold the edge this time, too, as they took the points with a 2-1 win after Davy Cooper struck twice and Callachan scored for the hosts. In the programme that day was an article stating that Hibs were disappointed not to be allowed to accept an invitation to play in a four-team tournament in Spain towards the end of the coming August. Apparently, the club had been offered £10,000 appearance money and an all-expenses-paid trip to Cadiz to join in the tournament with the host club, Athletic Bilbao, the newly crowned champions of Spain, and an as yet unnamed team from Yugoslavia. No reason is given as to why permission was refused, but it is likely that the block came from the SFA, as the Scottish domestic season would be in full swing at that time.

The final League game of the season took Hibs to Pittodrie to face the Aberdeen side who had done Scottish football proud by defeating Real Madrid to win the European Cup Winners' Cup. Needless to say, Pittodrie was packed and the Dons were on a high, thrashing an overwhelmed Hibs side 5-0.

Long-serving Jim McArthur brought Hearts to Easter Road for his testimonial game, and despite the pouring rain around 5,000 fans turned out to watch Hibs win 4-2. The goals came from Jamieson and Murray, who each struck twice for the home side, while Hearts counted through a Brownlie own-goal and Cammy Fraser.

And so the season closed. It had been a long and difficult one and the club had lost a devoted Hibs man in Tom Hart, but on the plus side the management team were all Hibs men who wanted to nurture local talent, and already there were signs that a number of the reserves would go on to make the grade.

Chapter Seventeen

1983/84

YOUNGSTERS GIVEN THEIR CHANCE

Stornoway on the Isle of Lewis provided the venue for Hibs' first pre-season game, in which they faced a Stornoway Select and breezed home by 4-0, with Kane, Thomson, Murray and Jamieson the scorers. The match held a special significance for Erich Schaedler as the tough-tackling left-back was returning to action after spending large parts of the previous season on the treatment table. An ankle injury required two separate operations at the Princess Margaret Rose Hospital, but he came through the Stornoway match without any ill effects and was ready to face the challenge of this new season.

Having 'Shades' back was a real bonus and the Hibs support was delighted for the popular defender while being equally delighted at the appointment of a new assistant manager. That post went to a former Hibee stalwart, John Blackley, who returned to the club that had given him his start in senior football. 'Sloop' had 12 years with Hibs as a player before moving on to Newcastle and thereafter to Preston North End before returning north to Hamilton, where he was player/coach. Interestingly, Blackley had maintained his registration as a player, although he was quick to point out that at 35 he anticipated only ever turning out for the reserves to help the young lads in developing their game.

While on the subject of the reserves, it is worth pointing out that Pat Stanton had high hopes for a number of the youngsters starting out at Hibs. Already Brian Rice had tasted first-team football and Paul Kane had scored for the first team in Stornoway, while Kevin McKee was another who caught the manager's eye.

The first match scheduled for Easter Road that season was a friendly fixture against Queen's Park Rangers and the programme for the game contained some very interesting information regarding development of the stadium. Chairman Kenny Waugh explained that the high terracing opposite the main stand was in the process of being demolished at a cost of around £120,000 and the future plan was to cover the remaining part of the terrace before eventually covering the 'Dunbar' End to create an all-covered stadium capable of housing around 30,000 spectators. Another feature of the new season would be an electronic scoreboard, situated on the roof of the covered area behind the goal at the Albion Road end of the ground, and it was anticipated that the scoreboard would 'pay for itself' via the revenues secured from companies wishing to advertise on it.

As for the QPR game, Hibs played well enough, but early injuries to Schaedler and McNamara seemed to upset the balance of the side. The injury setbacks, added to the fact that Rough had an uncharacteristic off day, might explain why the hosts lost 3-2. The Hibs goals came from Thomson and Murray, but the talking point after the game was the booking of Mike Conroy by referee Andrew Waddell. Hibs had been awarded a penalty, which Thomson converted only for Mr Waddell to order a re-take as Conroy had encroached into the area. The Hibs man tried to point out that he had actually been pushed into the area by an opponent, but the referee was having none of it and booked him. After all of that, Thomson's re-take was saved by keeper Hucker.

Before the big kick-off, Hibs had another pre-season test when Swansea City visited Easter Road on 10 August, and although the Welsh side had been newly relegated from the top flight in England they still had a number of players capable of living with the best. Manager John Toshack could call upon the likes of John Mahoney, Colin Irwin, Bob Latchford, Alan Curtis and Chris Marustik, but as it happened they were not good enough on the day as goals from Brian Rice and Gary Murray saw Hibs home. That game's match programme contained a message from the chairman encouraging fans to invest in a season ticket with the promise that as well as the monies being spent on stadium redevelopment there was also a commitment to improving the playing staff. Season tickets could be purchased for: Centre Stand – Adult £60; Junior/OAP £40; North Stand – Adult £50; Junior/OAP £35; North Enclosure – Adult £35; Junior/OAP £25 and Main Terracing – Adult £32; Junior/OAP £22.

On the following Monday evening, Hibs faced Brechin City at Glebe Park and had to rely on a last-minute goal for a share of the spoils. Robin Rae kept goal for Hibs but got poor protection from his defence, and it took a double from Irvine and a single from Murray to secure a 3-3 draw.

Two days later, the pre-season games came to an end when Meadowbank Thistle visited Easter Road in a game somewhat overshadowed by the fact that Thistle's David Connolly broke his leg in a challenge with Paul Kane. There is no doubt the clash was accidental, a fact quickly agreed to after the game by boss Terry Christie, and everyone connected with Hibs wished the player a speedy and full recovery. In the game, ex-Hibee Colin Tomassi scored for the visitors, but Hibs won the day with goals from Willie Irvine and Brian Rice.

Celtic provided the opposition for the opening League game of the season at Easter Road. The Parkhead club arrived under the new management team of Davie Hay and Frank Connor, who had spiced up their squad during the close season by enticing Brian McClair away from Motherwell for £75,000 after Charlie Nicholas had left to join Arsenal. With around 15,000 fans in the ground, Hibs more than held their own in the first half, but a poor five-minute spell early in the second saw them concede two soft goals and thereby give up the points on offer. It was a travesty really, as Hibs were well worth a point, but those lapses at the back cost them dear. Incidentally, the new electronic scoreboard that was to have featured for the first time failed to operate and remained blank throughout the 90 minutes.

Just prior to that opening game, Pat Stanton was delighted to announce the latest recruit to the Hibs ground staff. Gordon Hunter, a teenaged centre-half, had put pen to paper and become the latest Hibs-supporting local lad to join the club. Spotted while playing for Musselburgh Grammar, he was initially snapped up on an 'S' form but had shown sufficient promise to earn a place on the ground staff. He got off to a good start by scoring two goals in the final of the John White Memorial Trophy Five-a-Side competition, won by Hibs and prompting Gordon to say: 'It's unusual for me to score goals, but I've always wanted to be a professional footballer and I used to stand on the terracing here and wonder if I'd ever sign for a club.'

On the reserves front, the second string were at Celtic Park that afternoon and were within seconds of achieving what would have been a very worthy point. Leading thanks to a Graham Harvey goal, they were pegged back by a Brian McClair equaliser and the same player added another well into the second half. Within five minutes, however, Hibs were level again when Pat McCurdy smashed home from 12 yards, but right on the stroke of time the home side scored a third and winning goal. Picked out by John Blackley as Hibs' most composed player on the day was Gordon Hunter, who was obviously into the thick of things while the ink on his contract was still trying to dry out!

On the Wednesday evening following that home defeat by Celtic, Hibs opened their League Cup campaign with a home match against Dumbarton in the first leg of a second-round tie. Although they were a First Division and part-time club, Dumbarton could not be taken lightly. Under manager Billy Lamont they had shown good pre-season form, including a 1-0 victory over a Celtic XI. But they had lost two of their better players in the close season after John Donnelly had joined Leeds and Graeme Sinclair had been snapped up by Celtic. The League Cup fixture did not catch the imagination of the Hibs support, a crowd of only 3,500 turning up, but it was those who stayed away who would be kicking themselves as the home side ran out 5-0 winners. Goal hero on the night was Willie Irvine, who struck a hat-trick. The first of the three came in 17 minutes when Alan

Rough threw the ball out to Bobby Thomson, who went on a run before hitting a low cross into the Dumbarton box. Gary Murray cleverly stepped over the ball to fool the defence and leave Irvine to shoot home the opener. The second was less graceful, with Irvine first to react to a loose ball in the box, and the third came late in the game when keeper Tom Carson failed to clear his lines and Irvine lobbed it over him into the empty net. A fine treble for the striker was added to by Bobby Thomson and an own-goal from Mark Clougharty. In an odd change to the competition rules, there were two rounds played on a knock-out basis, with Hibs getting a bye in the first round, and then the 16 remaining clubs would be split into four sections of four with each side meeting home and away and the section winners going into two semi-finals. Nice to see the authorities keeping the competition rules simple!

In order to qualify for those section matches Hibs had to complete their tie with Dumbarton and so travelled on the Saturday to Boghead, where they won 2-1 on the day and 7-1 on aggregate. With manager Pat Stanton choosing to stay in Edinburgh to 'spy' on Hearts with the upcoming League fixture in mind, the team facing Dumbarton were looked after by John Blackley, who reported back that although Hibs had not played all that well they had still managed to win the game, with Conroy and Irvine on target. Dumbarton's score came from an Erich Schaedler own-goal. Winning that tie took Hibs into a section alongside Kilmarnock, Airdrie and Celtic, and the ties would be interspersed with League fixtures in the weeks ahead.

In fact, Hibs' very next fixture was the first in the League Cup section and brought Kilmarnock to Easter Road on the last day of August 1983. In front of a paltry crowd of around just 3,000, Hibs took the points with a 2-0 win after Rice and Irvine beat Alan McCulloch in the visitors' goals. Fans attending that night and buying a programme were 'introduced' to teenager Stuart Jacobs, who had been born in New Zealand but who lived in Kirkcaldy and travelled from there to Easter Road each day for training. Stuart owed much to the fundraising efforts of nine stalwarts who supported the Manawatu club in NZ, and in particular to the efforts of goalkeeper George Dunning and his brother Danny, who were intent on giving the youngster a chance to make the grade with Hibs and had even arranged for him to stay with their Scottish auntie while in this country. Two reserve games had already shown the Hibs coaching staff that the lad had talent, and so he had settled pretty well in his new home.

It was derby day next and Hibs faced their oldest rivals in front of 19,206 fans at Tynecastle. Hibs twice took the lead and yet lost 3-2. In a fairly even first half, Hibs took advantage of a defensive lapse and Ralph Callachan scored against his old club to send the Greens' fans in the crowd wild, but just 12 minutes into the second period a promising young striker named

John Robertson levelled from close range. I doubt if anyone present that day would have thought for one minute that Robertson would go on to haunt Hibernian in the years ahead. Willie Irvine, in fine scoring form, put Hibs in front again on 65 minutes, but the lead lasted just five minutes before Robertson struck again. Seven minutes later, his strike partner, Jimmy Bone, scored the winner.

Another League Cup fixture was played during the following midweek when Hibs went to Parkhead and crashed 5-1 in a game that saw Celtic in blistering form after their weekend win over Rangers and Hibs a shadow of the side who had pushed Hearts so close. For once, Irvine could not find the target with the Hibs goal coming from former Celt Mike Conroy.

A second consecutive away match in the League took Hibs to Tannadice with no points yet on the board and a twitchy support starting to worry even at this early stage about relegation. Just how many of the 5,900 fans were wearing green and white scarves is unclear, but it is an absolute certainty that they would not have enjoyed watching Hibs lose five goals for the second game in succession without managing to find the target at the other end. Hibs were a shambles that day, and an angry Pat Stanton later declared that he would not tolerate performances like that from players in Hibernian jerseys.

Having played Celtic, Hearts and Dundee United, Hibs took the field for their fourth League match when St Mirren visited Easter Road in front of 4,762 fans. The Buddies arrived in Leith with a solid team, including the likes of Billy Thomson in goals, Mark Fulton, Lex Richardson, Tony Fitzpatrick, Billy Abercromby and Frank McAvennie. However, they found Hibs in much better form after a hard week on the training pitch with Pat Stanton getting his message across that he expected the best from every player in green and white. A winning score of 3-1 brought the smile back to his face. Conroy, Irvine and substitute Graham Harvey were the marksmen.

The match programme for the St Mirren game offered an update on the progress of Easter Road's development. Director Alan Hart, who was masterminding the project, explained that covering the terracing opposite the main stand would cost around £100,000, although the club hoped to get £60,000 from the Football Trust towards those costs. It was hoped that any loan taken out for the £40,000 balance would be paid off in three years, and Hart was examining ways in which the club could meet the costs of the loan and its associated interest. Various organisations had been approached, including the Supporters' Association, which had reacted immediately by approving an initial £1,000 donation with a commitment to look at ways in which the fans could help further. On the subject of the Supporters' Association, the club revealed that a request had been received from Oman for permission to set up a branch there for a number of ex-pat workers from the Edinburgh area. Clearly, Hibs had fans far and wide even in those days.

A second consecutive home League match gave Hibs the chance to show their fans that the win over St Mirren was no flash in the pan, and they took that chance as around 4,000 watched them win 2-1 against Motherwell, with goals from Irvine and substitute Brian Rice, who scored from the penalty spot. The victory was hard-fought and pleased Pat Stanton, who had been in the manager's chair for just over a year now and felt that the youngsters coming through were providing the basis for a strong Hibs side in the future. Citing Brian Rice, Paul Kane and Kevin McKee as ideal examples, Pat also suggested that there were more kids pushing for a first-team start, including Pat McCurdy, who had impressed in the reserve side. Of course all of these youngsters would be brought on at the right pace because pushing them all into the first team on a regular basis might well work against them, but Stanton's general philosophy was: 'If you are good enough, then you are old enough.' All in all, Stanton felt that Hibs were moving in the right direction and the last two results seemed to reinforce that view.

While the first team were busy getting back on the winning trail the reserves were also in action, drawing 2-2 at Love Street, where a trialist centre-forward got both goals and was unlucky not to get a hat-trick. At the back, Gordon Hunter had another outstanding game alongside John Blackley, who was full of praise for the Musselburgh youngster. At Fir Park, it was once again a share of the spoils in a 1-1 draw, Pat McCurdy being the goalscorer. With Erich Schaedler playing sweeper and no fewer than four trialists in the team, a 1-1 result was a very creditable outcome on a rain-soaked pitch.

In between those games, the second string had taken part in a four-team tournament at Stirling University, and the outcome was a good one for a side who had goalkeeper Robin Rae playing at centre-forward! Young Kevin Wilson, who had just signed a one-year deal with the club, kept goal, and so Robin volunteered to turn out in attack. Indeed, he scored one of the goals in the 3-2 semi-final win over the host town's university side, McCurdy and Jim McMenamin getting the others. In the final, they met Scottish Universities and drew 2-2, the Hibs goals coming from McCurdy and Kevin McKee. The game went to a penalty shoot-out. Kane, McKee and Rae netted for Hibs, while McCurdy struck the bar, but Kevin Wilson saved twice and another effort went wide to ensure that Hibs won the tournament.

The first team's next test came with a visit to Muirton Park to face St Johnstone, who were firmly rooted to the bottom of the table without a single point to their name. After 90 minutes in which Hibs enjoyed long periods of possession, the points were won in a 3-0 victory, with goals by

Brazil, Irvine and Thomson. One player missing from the Hibs line-up at this time was Gordon Rae, whose place in central defence had been filled by Willie Jamieson. A niggling knee injury had kept Rae on the sidelines, but hospital scans had revealed no serious damage and the big fellow was working hard under the guidance of Tam McNiven to regain his fitness. This would come as good news to those who sat near him in the stand at Easter Road as Gordon himself confessed he could not keep quiet as he watched his team-mates on the field of play.

The first Wednesday in October brought Airdrie to Easter Road for a League Cup tie with Hibs trailing leaders Celtic in their section but hoping to get the win that would keep their qualification hopes alive. It was a dismal night with less than 2,000 fans watching as the sides contested a mind-numbingly boring 0-0 draw that effectively spoiled any chance that either side might have had to catch Celtic.

Around 21,500 fans attended Hibs' next game when the Greens travelled to Ibrox and had a shock in store for both their own fans and the Rangers players. Mike Conroy was struggling with an injury and as the players were on the coach heading for Glasgow, Pat Stanton announced that he was going to play John Blackley in defence. When Sloop rejoined Hibs he had never thought he would play in such a high profile match again but Stanton had every faith in him and he proved Pat right by turning in a five-star display. The hosts had the better of the first half and took the lead but in the second Hibs were by far the better team and created five clear-cut chances but sadly failed to make any of them count and so lost the match to that first-half strike.

That defeat at Ibrox left Hibs in sixth place in the Premier League with a record of three wins and four defeats while their next opponents, Aberdeen, were second behind Dundee United having won five and drawn one of their seven games to date. The Dons were a strong outfit and had won the last time they were in the capital when Hearts lost out at Tynecastle and they always presented a stern test with a rock solid defence, a creative midfield and a striking pair that knew the way to goal. It was the visitors that struck first but Hibs were not going to let the loss of that goal set them back and with an enthusiastic home support cheering them on they scored twice through Irvine to win the game 2-1 and collect two well deserved points. Those goals won Irvine the sponsors' man of the match award and took him to 13 for the season, including that earlier hat-trick against Dumbarton. Normally, wife Katrina would be cheering him on from the stand but she missed the game due to a touch of flu and so no doubt Willie would have enjoyed explaining to her that the first goal came from an Arthur Duncan cross that Irvine reached just ahead of Alex McLeish and that the second arrived when a long throw from Erich Schaedler was touched to him and his shot fairly flew past Jim Leighton in the Aberdeen goal.

A second consecutive home match brought Dundee to Easter Road with the visitors just a point behind their hosts. Interestingly, one team was sandwiched between Hibs and Dundee and that was Rangers who were already five points behind joint leaders Dundee United, Celtic and Hearts and occupying a very unfamiliar sixth place. The Dark Blues arrived in Leith on the back of a couple of good results and in Walker McCall and Iain Ferguson they carried a real goal threat but on the day Hibs edged it 2-1 with goals from an Irvine penalty and a cracker from Duncan.

The following midweek brought Celtic to Easter Road on League Cup duty with the home side anxious to make amends for that earlier 5-1 thumping in the same competition at Parkhead but there was never any chance of that as Stanton's men played out an uneventful 0-0 draw. A few days later they met again in the League at Parkhead where Hibs were out-thought and outplayed for the entire 90 minutes and once again crashed 5-1 with only Bobby Thomson's goal and some excellent play from Willie Jamieson cheering up the Hibs fans in the 13,777 crowd. One other item of note from that game was that it was Ally Brazil's 200th senior start for the club. Signed in 1976, it took the former Currie Hearts player around a season to make his breakthrough from the reserves but once he'd done that he had been a regular starter for the Greens.

During the following week Hibs travelled to Shielfield to face Berwick Rangers in the final of the East of Scotland Shield and Pat Stanton decided to give a few youngsters a starting place in the XI. After just five minutes O'Hara fired the hosts ahead only for 17-year-old Callum Milne to equalise with his first goal for the club. Marshall restored Berwick's lead but once again Hibs fought back when Marshall was unlucky in putting through his own goal. Rather than extra time the game went to a penalty shoot-out which Hibs won after ex-player Lindsay Muir missed his effort for Berwick.

Good as it was to win at Berwick, a thrashing from Celtic was hardly ideal preparation for what came next as Hearts were the visitors at Easter Road on the first Saturday in November. This would be the second derby of the season with the first having gone to Hearts after Hibs had twice led but then lost out to the odd goal in five. Around 21,000 streamed down Easter Road to witness an excellent game that both sides had the chance to win, but in the end each had to settle for a point in a 1-1 draw, with Robertson scoring for Hearts and Thomson for Hibs who were without the injured Jackie McNamara causing John Blackley to step in once more.

With all hopes of League Cup qualification now virtually extinguished, Pat Stanton decided to give 17-year-old Gordon Hunter his debut against Kilmarnock at Rugby Park and he was joined in the starting XI by Kevin McKee and Graham Harvey. Such games were ideal for fielding young players keen on gaining first-team experience and although Hibs lost

3-1 the third Killie goal did not come until very late in the game and Hibs might have had a point with a little more composure in front of goal. As it was the Hibs goal came from a very unlikely source in the shape of Erich Schaedler.

It was back to League business in the next game and with McNamara still sidelined Blackley took his place in the centre of the Hibs defence alongside Brazil when the Greens visited Love Street to face St Mirren. The first half was a bit of a disaster as the hosts snatched two goals and gave Hibs a mountain to climb in trying to get back into it. A half-time pep talk from Pat Stanton brought an improved performance from his men and Irvine pulled a goal back but try as they might they could not get an equaliser and so once again points were lost due to a sloppy start to a game.

A chance to get back to winning ways came with the visit of basement boys St Johnstone to Easter Road in mid-November. Hibs had already beaten them at Muirton and as the Perth side had managed only two wins in twelve starts, there were high hopes among the home support that two points could be gained. Kevin McKee got a start in the number eight jersey and young Paul Kane was on the bench as the home side strolled it with a convincing 4-1 win. At the end of the match Willie Irvine was able to claim the match ball for the second time this season after scoring a hat-trick while Arthur Duncan weighed in with the other.

Another side struggling that season was Motherwell and it was they that provided the next challenge when Hibs took them on at Fir Park. McNamara's knee injury was taking somewhat longer than he had hoped to clear up and so he was once again missing from a Hibs XI that had Brian Rice in midfield. The game marked the 100th senior appearance for Alan Sneddon and he celebrated by scoring his first goal for Hibs with a smart angled drive from 20 yards. Callachan added another and Hibs won 2-1 although it could have been 5-1 with the usual batch of chances missed in front of goal. Watching on that day was Gordon Rae, recovering from a fifth operation on a troublesome knee and still some way off in terms of making a comeback.

November ended with a midweek fixture at Broomfield where Hibs and Airdrie met in the final match in their section and once again Pat Stanton gave youth a chance with Robin Rae in goals, Kevin McKee and Gordon Hunter in defence, Mickey Weir, Brian Rice and Paul Kane in midfield and Pat McCurdy up front with Callum Milne and Kevin Wilson on the bench. Despite the inexperience of the vast majority of the starting XI Hibs ran out 3-1 winners with goals from Murray and Harvey, who got a double. Such a result, against a strong Airdrie and with so many youngsters in the side, prompted great optimism that better days may lie ahead for Hibs and their promising group of up-and-coming players.

It was back to as full strength as injuries would allow the following

Saturday when high-flying Dundee United visited Easter Road. The first meeting between the sides had Hibs crashing 5-0 at Tannadice when the gulf between the teams was painfully apparent and although the Arabs didn't manage five this time around they still had enough skill to secure a 2-0 victory in front of around, 7,000 fans. Hibs were so poor in spells that day it was amusing to watch many of the younger fans focusing their attention on the electronic scoreboard as opposed to the 'action' on the park!

Only two League matches had been won away from home when Hibs next hit the road for a trip to Dens Park, Dundee but that figure was soon increased to three as the visitors dominated their hosts throughout and easily took the points with a 3-0 win. Irvine with two and Thomson were the marksmen while Jamieson was outstanding at the back alongside Brazil.

Seven days later Hibs were on their travels again and this time it was to Pittodrie to face League leaders and European Cup Winners' Cup holders Aberdeen. The Dons had a fantastic record at home and in fact had lost only ten goals in 18 games and so the task set for Hibs was a difficult one, but they played very well on the day and were unlucky to go down 2-1. Irvine scored the Hibs goal while Jim Leighton and Alan Rough were both outstanding for their respective teams.

Tough fixtures were coming thick and fast as the Christmas and New Year holiday schedule got into full swing and Rangers were the latest to provide League opposition on the Tuesday between the two holidays. Although struggling in mid-table and two places behind their hosts, the visitors took the points with a 2-0 victory in front of more than 18,000 fans. It was a sad day all round for Hibs as the club announced via the programme the death of former stalwart Archie Buchanan. Joining Hibs from Edinburgh Thistle in the mid-1940s along with Lawrie Reilly, Archie was a key member of the half-back line from which Hibs launched their championship-winning side and even after he had stopped playing Archie, who was only 55 at the time of his death, maintained a connection with the club as chief scout. Some of Archie's team-mates were Tommy Younger, Sammy Kean and Bobby Combe and he would be a real loss to the football club.

Just four days after losing at home to Rangers, Hibs welcomed the other half of the Old Firm to Easter Road with Celtic desperate for the points that would keep them in touch with Aberdeen in the race for the League title. It was the last day of 1983 and it was bitterly cold as the 11,234 fans watched Hibs throw everything but the kitchen sink at their rivals and yet still fail to find the net. Celtic meanwhile hit the target once and took the points thanks to that 1-0 win. The match programme that day carried a message from chairman Kenny Waugh that began with the sentence, 'Much has been done and much remains to be done.' Essentially Waugh was remarking not just on the performances on the park but also the ongoing alterations to the stadium with the high terracing opposite the main stand now gone and plans in place to cover the remaining area just as soon as the finance to do so was available.

January began as most Januarys had before, with an Edinburgh derby, and the venue on this occasion was Tynecastle in front of a bumper holiday crowd of 23,499. On a tricky playing surface Hearts started the better and Rough was the busier of the two goalkeepers as he denied the home forwards throughout the first half. Within seconds of the restart, however, Donald Park latched on to a long clearance from his own defence and slotted the ball home to put the hosts ahead. Undaunted, Hibs pressed forward looking for an equaliser and it came when Callachan clipped a low ball into the penalty box and Irvine nipped in ahead of Craig Levein to slam the ball into the net and earn Hibs a point they fully deserved.

With the holiday fixtures now complete, Hibs resumed their Saturday afternoon football with a visit by St Mirren, who like their hosts were sitting mid-table with one eye on climbing into a European qualification spot. There is little doubt that visiting goalkeeper Billy Thomson was the busiest man on the park as he pulled off save after save to deny Hibs and his efforts were duly rewarded when his side secured a point in a 1-1 draw with Harvey being the only Hibee to find a way past the inspired goalie.

A quite fierce cold snap descended upon Scotland during the next week and it caused a number of postponements across the country with the St Johnstone v Hibs game among the casualties. With a blank Saturday on the cards, Hibs arranged to take a 20-strong party down to North Berwick and while there were a couple of training stints on the beach, the break was more about letting the players enjoy some free time playing golf and relaxing at their base, the Marine Hotel. Whether Pat Stanton relaxed is open to conjecture as he had appeared before the SFA, charged with making remarks to referee Bob Valentine after the League Cup clash with Celtic at Easter Road. Pat had felt that a number of key decisions had gone against his side and so voiced his opinion to Valentine but in doing so he earned himself a £200 fine and a warning about his future conduct.

During the following week there was huge sadness around Easter Road following the death of director Tommy Younger. Big Tom joined Hibs in 1947 from Hutchison Vale and soon made the number one jersey his own, as between 1949 and 1956 he racked up more than 200 appearances before his transfer to Liverpool with a fee of £9,000 going to Hibs. He played for and managed Falkirk for a while but was soon back at Easter Road when Tom Hart invited him to join the board. An Office Bearer with the SFA, Tom was a great ambassador for both Hibs and Scottish football in general and his death marked the passing of a truly great Hibee.

Little has been mentioned thus far on the progress of the reserves and that is due to the fact that coverage of their games was sparse in detail this season in the match programme, but news was provided of a stunning 6-1 win over Aberdeen in the Second XI Cup that took Hibs forward into a mouth-watering tie against Hearts at Easter Road. Both sides fielded a couple of first-team regulars but it was the return of long-time absentee Gordon Rae that had the home fans in good cheer as they watched him star in a fine 3-1 win. Pat McCurdy opened the scoring only for Gerry McCoy to equalise before McCurdy struck again and Gordon Rae rounded off a good night with a third some three minutes from time. Although only a reserve tie it was obvious that both sides were desperate to win, and the referee was a very busy man booking Callum Milne, Mike Conroy and Paul Kane of Hibs with McCoy and Irvine of Hearts also seeing yellow while player/manager Alex McDonald was sent off in the dying moments of the game.

Postponements hit again the following Saturday and most unusually Hibs lost their intended home fixture against Motherwell to the weather. A heavy snowfall on the morning of the match was too much for the undersoil heating and so the Greens found themselves having a second consecutive blank weekend. The draw for the Scottish Cup third round had been made around this time and it brought Second Division East Fife to Easter Road at the end of January. Arriving with a five game unbeaten run under their belts, the Fifers set out their stall to frustrate Hibs and it worked to perfection with the game ending at 0-0 and a replay at Methil that would bring in some much needed finance to the Bayview club. One of the main reasons East Fife secured that replay was the outstanding performance of young Gordon Marshall in goals and he was determined to emulate the feat of his father, also Gordon, who had kept goal for Arbroath in March 1977 when Hibs had tumbled out in an Easter Road replay.

As any Hibs fan knows, the Scottish Cup often turns out to be a graveyard for Hibs as opposed to a happy hunting ground and season 1983/84 proved no different. A huge travelling support and a higher than normal turnout by the home fans provided a crowd of around 6,000 to witness Hibs being harried and hassled throughout the game with their central defence being run ragged by an 18-year-old striker with electrifying pace and a real eye for goal. His name was Gordon Durie and he would go on to have a long and exciting career both north and south of the border, but his whole attention on that particular night was focused upon helping his team-mates record a 2-0 win to send Hibs crashing once again. That defeat was costly in more than one sense as Alan Rough picked up an injury that would keep him out of the side for several weeks with his ankle in plaster.

A trip to Tannadice was always going to be difficult but it was made more so by the fact that Rough was missing and Hibs were still without long-term absentee Jackie McNamara, coaching the reserves for the moment following the departure of Jimmy Thomson to Alloa, which meant that Jamieson would continue to partner Blackley at the heart of the defence. Further injuries and suspensions brought Paul Kane into the Hibs midfield and while youngsters Robin Rae and Kane gave a good account of themselves, the home side was too strong on the day and won the match 2-0. Rae could feel slightly aggrieved at the outcome because he had played that well, making notable saves from Ralph Milne and Paul Sturrock, he had been named man of the match by one or two of the sports journalists reporting on the game.

An opportunity to get back to winning ways presented itself in Hibs' next match as it took them to Muirton Park to face a St Johnstone side that was struggling near the foot of the table. In front of a poor crowd of just 2,416, both sides struggled to play any form of passing football and the match was won by the home side with a late strike bringing the only goal of the game. This was poor fare indeed from a Hibs side very obviously low in confidence and things would get worse before they got better in the weeks ahead.

In an effort to solve the lack of goals being scored, Pat Stanton dipped into the transfer market to bring 18-year-old Edinburgh-born John McGachie to Easter Road from Aberdeen, where the youngster had excelled in the reserves but had been unable to dislodge Mark McGhee, John Hewitt or Eric Black from the first XI. Raised in Gilmerton, John had joined the Dons from Salvesen Boys' Club and was delighted to get the chance to play football in his home town.

By chance it would be Aberdeen that Hibs next faced when the sides clashed at Easter Road late in February. Once again chances were created and not taken by the home side while the visitors struck twice to take the points home to Pittodrie. Young McGachie was actually given his debut that day when he came off the bench in the second half to replace the injured Graham Harvey.

Four consecutive defeats for the first team, including the Cup replay loss to East Fife, did not deter more than 9,000 fans turning out on Wednesday 29 February and their loyalty was rewarded with a fine 3-1 win against Dundee. Of course cynics might say Hibs attracted such a gate because the club gave fans free entry after the original game between the two had fallen victim to thick fog, but regardless of why so many were in the ground they must surely have enjoyed what they were seeing on the park. It was more like the Hibs of old as the chances were taken on this occasion and as soon as the first goal went in you could almost see the players relaxing into the game. On target that day were Paul Kane, Willie Jamieson and Willie Irvine from the penalty spot while Robin Rae had another solid game in goals and had no chance with the Dundee goal.

It's amazing what a win can do for the confidence as just three days later Hibs were at Ibrox thoroughly deserving the point gained from a 0-0 draw. It's true the home side had the bulk of possession but the Hibs defence, superbly marshalled by Gordon Rae, never looked as though it would be breached while at the other end both Irvine and Duncan were unlucky to see shots hitting the woodwork and bouncing clear.

Unfortunately the feel-good factor generated by those last two results was somewhat lost when Hibs put in a poor show in their next match against Motherwell at Easter Road and went down to a late winner in a 2-1 defeat. On the day a draw would have been a fairer result but the home side could not add to Irvine's penalty goal and paid the ultimate price for failing to take any one of a number of good chances.

With Hearts at home on Cup duty the following weekend, Hibs moved their Easter Road tie against a resurgent St Johnstone to the Sunday and with cash turnstiles back in operation the game drew a crowd of only 4,000. McNamara made his long-awaited return and McCurdy was given the number 11 jersey as Duncan was injured and young Pat had found the way to goal in the reserve side to earn his chance in the first XI. Alas it was not to be a good day for Hibs as they lost 2-1 in a game they always seemed to be chasing, but could only find the target once through Brian Rice. If it was a bad day for Hibs as a club it was an even worse day for Jackie McNamara as a player when he suffered a compressed fracture of the cheekbone and would as a consequence miss the rest of the season.

The match programme for the St Johnstone game contained some items of interest that are worth mentioning here. Bobby Thomson, serving a six-month ban after being sent off for pushing a linesman, was earning his wage by 'spying' on upcoming opposition, a job that manager Pat Stanton said the banned Hibs man excelled at. Plans were in place for a close season tour that would take Hibs to the Middle East and specifically to Jordan where touring teams often drew in crowds of over 20,000 fans. It would be another first for Hibs with many other parts of the globe having been toured at one time or another.

The last ten days of March had Hibs in action three times and on each occasion they were away from home, with the first trip involving a visit to Love Street. The Buddies had proved a tough nut to crack this season and would remain so by defeating the visitors 3-1 with Callachan getting the Hibs goal. It was another Jekyll and Hyde performance from the Easter Road men, who dominated periods of the game but failed to make possession count while making unforced errors at the back that ultimately cost them the points.

In the following midweek Fir Park was the venue for an exciting tussle with Motherwell and this time Hibs did take their chances in winning the game 3-2. Defensive frailties were still evident but at least the forwards found the net this time with Jamieson, Irvine and Rice all getting their names on the scoresheet.

A trip to Dens Park completed the trio of away games and once again Hibs managed to lift the points with a well earned 2-1 win thanks to goals from Irvine and Jamieson. Making a comeback that day was goalkeeper Alan Rough, who had now fully recovered from his injury, and without being disrespectful to Robin Rae who had played remarkably well when covering for Roughy, the big Scotland keeper gave a solid look to the Hibs rearguard. In fact Rough had readied himself for his comeback by playing for the reserves 48 hours earlier and had been outstanding in a 2-0 win with the Hibs goals coming from a trialist number eight and Graham Harvey.

It was around this time that Pat McCurdy, a prolific goalscorer with the reserves, was transferred to Hamilton where he hoped to get regular first-team football. Pat Stanton confirmed that McCurdy was a promising player but that he didn't fit into his plans and so the move was agreed to suit all parties and Pat left with the best wishes of all at Easter Road.

Following two good wins on the road Hibs opened their April account with a visit from Dundee United, a side riding high in the League and looking good for at least a qualification spot in the race for European football in the season ahead. With Paul Hegarty, Richard Gough, David Narey and Maurice Malpas in their rearguard the Arabs were always a difficult side to break down but Hibs managed it at least once with Jamieson scoring a lovely goal after being put through by a slide rule pass from Brian Rice. Try as they might United could not find a way past Rough and so the points stayed in Leith.

On the Monday night following, the reserves carved out a fine 4-0 win over Motherwell at Easter Road in a match that witnessed the continuing return to form of young Graham Harvey. The striker had been struggling due to lack of confidence but as is always the case with strikers lost confidence soon returns when they find the back of the net. Two goals in this match had Graham smiling again and he even had a hand in the other two, scored by Graham Harvey and Gary Murray. Three days later the wee greens were in action again when St Mirren were defeated 4-1 and Harvey's grin grew even wider as he helped himself to a hat-trick. Paul Kane was the other marksman and there was further good news as Jackie McNamara's cracked cheekbone had healed more rapidly than was expected and he played the full 90 minutes in both reserve games.

With a blank Saturday due to Cup semi-finals being played, Hibs took an extra few days of rest but faced Meadowbank Thistle on the Monday evening in the East of Scotland Shield at Easter Road. It was a night that would long be remembered but not for any positive reasons. In the game itself Hibs took the lead in the first minute from a Jamieson header but Graeme Armstrong equalised on the half hour. Soon after, Arthur Duncan fell awkwardly and was carried off with what was diagnosed later as a broken collarbone. As he left the pitch to a customary round of applause it was to be the last time Hibs fans would have the opportunity to show their appreciation for a wonderful player and loyal club servant because the injury effectively ended his Hibs career after 14 great years. Back on the field, the sides ended the game at 1-1 and went to a penalty shoot-out with Meadowbank winning it 5-4 after Thistle keeper Jim McQueen saved Callachan's kick.

Hearts were among the teams fighting for a European spot when they visited Easter Road on 21 April with the match drawing a crowd of around 17,500. Both sides were virtually at full strength and on the day cancelled each other out with the spoils being shared in a 0-0 draw.

It was back on the road again for Hibs after that mind-numbingly boring derby stalemate and it was Parkhead to which they travelled. The home side were still in hot pursuit of League leaders Aberdeen and yet the match attracted only 14,500 fans which was extremely disappointing. The game itself was a cracker with play flowing from end to end and with five goals scored during the 90 minutes. Unfortunately, Celtic got three while Hibs countered through Callachan and Rice but fell just short of salvaging a point when a shot from John McGachie, wearing the number 11 jersey vacated by Arthur Duncan, struck the bar in the dying moments.

Scottish football and especially everyone linked to Hibernian Football Club was deeply saddened on Friday 4 May 1984 to hear of the death of Willie Ormond. The wee winger joined Hibs from Stenhousemuir in 1946 and became a component part of the 'Famous Five' side that won three League championships. His career at Easter Road spanned 15 years and during that time he also represented his country 15 times, including at the 1954 World Cup in Switzerland. When his playing days were over, Willie ventured into management with St Johnstone where he enjoyed much success and left an indelible mark on that club with a stand being named after him. From there he took the Scotland job and was the most successful manager to date with a record of played 38, won 18, drawn 8 and lost 12. Willie took Scotland to the World Cup in Germany in 1974 where they were unbeaten in their group and were unlucky not to qualify for the later stages. Awarded an OBE for his achievements, Willie then returned to club management with Hearts before leaving Tynecastle to join Hibs as assistant to Eddie Turnbull and then as manager in his own right before ill health forced him to retire from the game. A lovely and very friendly man, he was hugely respected by all in the game and his death marked the end of a long and happy life.

Having faced the chasers Hibs now faced the chased when they met Aberdeen at Pittodrie at the beginning of May. The game started well for the Greens as McGachie raced clear of the Dons defence to put his side one up, but the home side was not top of the League for nothing, and they hit back with two goals before Rice got Hibs level and earned a point into the bargain.

And so we came to the final game of the season with Rangers the visitors to Easter Road. With a number of youngsters in the team Hibs gave a good account of themselves against a fairly strong Rangers outfit, and although both sides had chances to score neither could take them and the match petered out to a 0-0 draw.

Chapter Eighteen

1984/85

'JUKE BOX' ARRIVES

Hibs had thought they would spend a part of their pre-season in the Middle East, but unfortunately last-minute hitches prevented them from travelling to Jordan and so pre-season would involve a mini 'tour' of Scotland, a couple of friendlies at Easter Road plus Jackie McNamara's testimonial game, with English clubs providing the opposition for the last three of those games.

Manager Pat Stanton had identified a couple of signing targets and had approval from the board to pursue both Tommy McQueen of Clyde and Jamie Doyle of Partick Thistle, but he was thwarted on both occasions as McQueen, a very promising defender, elected instead to join Aberdeen, where he replaced Chelsea-bound Doug Rougvie, while Doyle's move was scuppered when the clubs failed to agree method of payment for the strong-running midfielder.

With no new faces in the squad, Stanton would look to give youth its chance as Kevin McKee, Paul Kane and Brian Rice had already tasted first-team football and there were a number of other youngsters knocking on the door. Those kids would be working with a new coach, Gordon Neely having arrived from Tannadice to take up that position at Easter Road. Neely had spent four years with the Arabs working under Jim McLean and brought a wealth of experience with him to Edinburgh.

Alloa was the first port of call for Hibs and a good work out saw the players finding their playing legs in a 1-1 draw, with Irvine the scorer in a match that featured young Callum Milne in the starting line-up, his performance drawing praise from team-mates and manager alike. Next it was off to the Highlands for a game against Elgin City, where an early Harvey strike put the visitors ahead. Elgin levelled by half-time, but in the second half Hibs scored two more, Thomson grabbing both. This was Thomson's first match since 11 February following his six-month ban and he took full advantage of trying to impress the gaffer that he was back to his best. In the next match, against Keith, Pat Stanton used his whole squad in making numerous substitutions throughout that game, but it didn't seem to upset the rhythm as the Greens won 3-0, with goals from Callachan, Jamieson and Harvey.

On the way back 'down the road', Hibs stopped off to play Second Division champions Forfar and found themselves behind before a full minute had been played, but they recovered to win 2-1 after goals from Jamieson and Callachan.

First Easter Road opponents of the season were Manchester City, managed by former Celtic stalwart Billy McNeill, and they had a number of quality players in their squad such as Ray Ranson, Paul Power, Mick McCarthy, Derek Parlane, Kevin Bond and Gordon Dalziel, but the star of the show was undoubtedly goalkeeper Alex Williams, who had replaced the departing Joe Corrigan, and who denied Hibs a win with a string of fine saves. In that game a young lad was given his chance to impress and didn't let anyone down, Billy McNeill saying after the game that he thought the youngster could have a big future in the game. The lad in question was John Collins, who, that afternoon, had been sweeping out the stand as part of his ground-staff duties and had thought Pat Stanton was pulling his leg when he told him he would be playing against Manchester City that very night. Another interesting snippet from that game was that Hibs played in their usual tops but without any sponsor named on the front, after Fisher's had made a late decision not to continue their deal with the club.

Sunday, 5 August 1984, marked the occasion of Jackie McNamara's testimonial. Newcastle were the opponents, while Hibs gave a starting place to John Collins and had a certain George Best back in a green and white jersey for the occasion. Jackie had arrived at Easter Road as part of the deal that took Pat Stanton to Celtic, and after an initial period when the fans viewed him as somehow responsible for the departure of a club legend, he soon won them over with his stylish play, whether at the back alongside George Stewart or in midfield. Eight years with the club had earned him a well-deserved testimonial and it speaks volumes that players like Best were prepared to make the effort to travel to Edinburgh to play in that game.

It was a lovely, sunny afternoon with a clear blue sky and a sizeable crowd watching on, but Newcastle obviously hadn't read the script as they triumphed 3-0. In truth, if both sides had taken all their chances it might have finished 7-7, but with Chris Waddle in dazzling form Peter Beardsley scored first and the Magpies captain, Kenny Wharton, got a double.

The final pre-season game brought Middlesbrough to Easter Road and just like City they had a few decent players in their squad. David Currie, Irving Nattrass, David Mills and Heine Otto were joined by one Tony Mowbray, a skilful centre-half who would return in another capacity at a future date. Sadly, neither side seemed to be firing on all cylinders and the outcome was a tame 0-0 draw.

The season proper kicked off with a visit from Celtic on Premier League duty and a healthy crowd of around 16,000 witnessed an entertaining game that lacked only goals to make it a real classic. Hibs enjoyed the early pressure without reward for their efforts and Celtic finished the stronger, but the day ended with Alan Rough and Pat Bonnar each keeping a clean sheet as the sides settled for a point each.

Around this time it became known that the SFA were extremely unhappy that George Best had played for Hibs in Jackie McNamara's testimonial match. Apparently, upon hearing that Hibs intended to field him, the SFA had fired off a letter to Tom O'Malley, chairman of the Testimonial Committee, informing him that as Best was not registered with the association and that his contract with his last club, Tobermore in Ireland, had expired, he could not play in the match. The committee then decided to approach Hibs to see if the club would 'sign' Best especially for the occasion, and so an appropriate contract was drafted up and signed by the Northern Irishman, allowing him to play and satisfying the SFA rules to boot. Not so, it would seem, as the SFA reminded Hibs that a player requires to be registered *before* he can play and so the club would have to appear before the Executive Committee of the SFA to explain itself and to face a likely fine for a breach of rules. How ironic that Hibs would be punished for arranging that the Edinburgh public get another chance to see George play in a match to benefit a loyal club servant. George played in such games all over the world without any such hitch, and only the SFA could be so bureaucratic.

The first away game in the League campaign took Hibs north to Dens Park to face Dundee and a healthy number of Hibs fans helped to swell the crowd to almost 7,000. The journey was well worth it as Alan Rough had a second consecutive shut-out, while Thomson struck the only goal of the game to give Hibs a 1-0 win and take them on to three points from two starts, which was a pleasing way to open the season. Particularly encouraging that afternoon was the contribution made by Kevin McKee, who looked very assured at right-back; Paul Kane, who led the attack, and Brian Rice, who sprayed passes left, right and centre from his midfield berth alongside the experienced Ralph Callachan.

For some time, manager Pat Stanton had been an admirer of the St Johnstone front man John Brogan, and after a couple of attempts to lure him to Easter Road he finally persuaded the goalscorer to join Hibs, where it was hoped he would help to eradicate the side's tendency to make a lot more chances than they ever managed to convert.

The League Cup had once again been revamped, this time into a straight knock-out competition. Having had a bye in round one, Hibs were handed a home tie against East Fife, allowing Brogan to make his debut in front of the Hibs support. As ever, the Fifers were a stuffy bunch and their twin strikers, Stevie Kirk and Gordon Durie, kept the Hibs defence busy throughout, but the tie was settled by the scoring of just one goal, Callachan finding the net to take Hibs into the third round.

After the retirement from the board of Jimmy Kerr, chairman Kenny Waugh announced three new appointments to join him and Alan Hart in the boardroom. Alan Young, Gregor Cowan and John Douglas were all lifelong Hibs fans and each was given a remit by Waugh. Young was a managing director of two construction companies and so would oversee ground redevelopment; Cowan was senior partner in a chartered accountancy business and would liaise between the club and the Hibs Supporters' Association, while Douglas was a company director and publican who would ensure that the stadium's appearance was consistently maintained.

A win and a draw was a decent situation to be in when the first Edinburgh derby came around at the end of August, although Hearts had started well enough, too, and on the day the sides were pretty evenly matched after goals from Paul Kane and Craig Levein looked to have led to a 1-1 draw, but in the very final seconds of the game Derek O'Connor slotted the ball past Rough to win the game 2-1 for Hearts and send their supporters in the 16,724 crowd wild with delight. One worrying matter from the game, apart from the result, was the fact that Callachan had to leave the field showing all the signs of having a heart problem. Thankfully, after five days of intensive medical tests, he was advised it had only been a virus and that he was fit to play again.

On the youth front, Gordon Neely had been busy setting up training camps both in Edinburgh and three other venues in Lanarkshire and the west as the club endeavoured to unearth the best young talents in these areas. Already two youngsters had caught the eye, one of them being Whitburn lad Steven McIlhone. He was interesting a number of English clubs, including Arsenal, with whom he had spent a week in training. The other was Salvesen Under-15s central defender Charlie Kivlin. Neely believed both lads had a chance in the game if they worked hard and took on board the coaching offered.

Four days after that sickening last-minute defeat by Hearts, Hibs were in action again, against Meadowbank Thistle in the third round of the League Cup. The last time the sides met, Thistle won on penalties in an East of Scotland Shield semi-final, and that game had been recent enough for both sides to be aware of what was needed to win through. It seemed that Meadowbank had been paying more attention, as following a quite dismal performance from Hibs the lower league side triumphed 2-1 after extra time, with only Callachan's goal to comfort the Hibs fans in the 5,600 crowd.

Twenty-four hours later at Easter Road, it was the Graham Harvey show as the big striker scored all three goals for the reserves in a 3-1 win over

Aberdeen, a performance that earned him a call-up to the first-team pool for the upcoming game at Pittodrie.

In fact, when the Saturday arrived, Harvey was handed a starting place by Pat Stanton and together with his team-mates turned in an impressive first-half performance, even though once again good chances to score were missed. The second half was a different story as Hibs struggled to contain the Dons and when the final whistle blew it was 4-1 to the home side, with substitute Jamieson the man on target for Hibs. Going into the game it had been known that manager Pat Stanton was not happy with his lot in terms of support from the board and, of course, a number of poor performances from his players. Evidence of that unhappiness was there for all to see during the Aberdeen match as the normally 'quiet man' was sent to the stand by the referee for hotly disputing an offside decision.

Hard on the heels of that difficult away match against Aberdeen came an equally difficult trip to Ibrox. John Brogan, who had missed a couple of games due to injury, was back in the starting line-up, where firepower in front of goals would hopefully improve. It was not to be as Hibs made chance after chance, failed to take them and ended up losing the game 2-0.

Saturday, 15 September 1984, seemed like it would be just another Saturday with Hibs looking to win at home against struggling Dumbarton, but the Greens played poorly and even though they scored through Kane and Thomson they lost the match 3-2. Only 3,700 fans turned up that day and the vast majority filed out at the end thinking life as a Hibs supporter surely couldn't get any worse. But it did. A disillusioned Pat Stanton went to see chairman Kenny Waugh and handed in his resignation. In fact, Pat had resigned the previous April but had been persuaded by Waugh to return. This time, there would be no change of mind. The news shattered the Hibernian supporters, who, despite the poor results on the park, had been behind the manager and welcomed his philosophy of bringing through promising youngsters. Some time later, Pat would say in an interview: 'I did enjoy being the Hibs manager, although on reflection it was perhaps the wrong time for me to be in charge of the club. Looking back, I would say the club was undergoing a tremendous period of transition, but I was aware that the chance might never come along again and I was desperate to take it when offered. The one aspect I certainly did enjoy was seeing a crop of good youngsters coming through, of whom John Collins, Michael Weir and Gordon Hunter were outstanding examples.'

And so, for the second time in his life, Pat left the club he loved and still loves to this day. The fans were again distraught because legends only come along every so often and to 'lose' one in such a manner was bitterly disappointing.

It would be wrong to leave the Dumbarton game without highlighting a couple of interesting items in the programme. After almost 22 years of service, trainer-physio Tam McNiven had been awarded a testimonial, and there would not be one single person that had anything to do with Hibernian who would not agree this was long overdue. The SFA/George Best saga had finally rumbled along to a close. Unsurprisingly, Hibs were fined, although a conciliatory letter from the Testimonial Committee appeared to have been favourably received as the fine itself was a paltry £100. With club marketing a growing concern among all professional outfits, Hibs appointed a new marketing manager in 24-year-old Raymond Sparks, who had been formerly in charge of PR at Falkirk's Coasters Arena. His first task would be to find a sponsor and he set his sights high, saying: 'I'm looking for a company with a national identity as a club like Hibs should be aiming for that.'

With Pat Stanton now gone, Hibs moved quickly to appoint his successor and they didn't have to look far as the new gaffer was John Blackley, promoted from his coaching role into the hot seat in time for him to take charge of the side that visited Tannadice on League business. After a week on the training pitch, Blackley had instilled the view into his players that those not giving 100 per cent would be dropped, and certainly the attitude against Dundee United was spot-on even though the game was lost 2-1 with Thomson getting the Hibs goal.

In the days following that match, John Blackley tried to enter the transfer market after releasing John McGachie, who joined Hamilton, and making it known that offers would be considered for Graham Harvey, who had been attracting attention with his goalscoring in the reserves. Another effort was made to bring Jamie Doyle to the club and approaches were made for Jim Rooney, Jim Holmes and Brian Gallagher, but none was successful. Blackley therefore turned his attention to searching for what he called a 'touchline specialist', or a winger if you prefer! One player who did join the club around that time was David Fellenger, who arrived on an 'S' form from Hutchison Vale. Hibs had beaten both Hearts and East Fife to his signature and Gordon Neely had high hopes for the young striker.

After a promising start in the League campaign, things had somewhat gone downhill. Hibs were at the wrong end of the table, and so it was hoped that a win could be secured in the next game, against Morton at Easter Road. Pressure to open his account for Hibs had caused a dip in the form of John Brogan, and the centre had to be content with a seat on the bench as he watched his colleagues Irvine and Kane hit the net. Wearing eight that day was Mickey Weir, and as the youngster tired later in the game he was replaced by Brogan, who finally got the monkey off his back by scoring a third for Hibs in their 3-1 win.

John Blackley was hopeful that the win over Morton would go some way to restoring lost confidence among his squad. After all, Hibs had played some good stuff in a number of games without getting any reward.

Unfortunately, the next two games did little to ease the manager's concern as first a missed penalty at Love Street denied the Greens a chance to take the lead and then the heads went down as the Buddies cashed in to win the game 2-0. A week later, Parkhead was the venue and once again a penalty featured in the eventual outcome, only this time it was awarded to Celtic, and they slotted it home before going on to win the game 3-0. To add to the misery, Gordon Rae was booked in the Celtic match and as a result would miss the upcoming games against Hearts and Aberdeen.

Both of those matches witnessed chances created and missed by Hibs, and it seemed that the prolific scoring that John Brogan had enjoyed with St Johnstone had totally deserted him once he moved to his new club. Indeed, his form had dipped so much that he merited only a place on the bench at Love Street and Parkhead. In an effort to provide the club with more firepower, Blackley moved into the transfer market and paid around £70,000 to bring Gordon Durie in from East Fife. The 18-year-old had impressed against Hibs in previous matches and Blackley had watched him in action in other games and liked what he saw, making the decision to spend that sum of money an easy one to take. News of the player's arrival was well received by the Hibs support as 'Juke Box' – the nickname stemmed from the popular TV show *Juke Box Jury* – had impressed them, too, with his performances against the Greens.

In the lead-up to the next match it was made known that Hibs were in negotiation with Carlisle with a view to bringing their player/manager to Easter Road as assistant to John Blackley. The man in question was Tommy Craig, and after all the talking had been done a deal was struck and the former Aberdeen, Newcastle and Sheffield Wednesday midfielder arrived in Leith to take up his duties. Initially, Hibs had offered cash plus Graham Harvey, but the player was not keen on that deal and so a straight cash deal was required to bring Tommy back north of the border.

When Archie Knox brought Dundee to Easter Road in the second half of October, his side had won just three times in ten starts. Like Hibs, they felt that things could have been so much better if even half the chances made had been taken. It didn't help them that two of their brighter stars, Cammy Fraser and Iain Ferguson, had been sold to Rangers, but new signings John Brown from Hamilton, Bobby Connor from Ayr and Stuart Rafferty from Motherwell looked as though they would prove useful acquisitions once they had settled in. A crowd of over 5,000 turned up on the day to watch Gordon Durie make his debut, and they were not disappointed as the youngster gave his usual full-blooded display in causing the Dundee defence all sorts of problems. It was another youngster, however, who gained the headlines, Paul Kane scoring the only two goals of the game to secure the points on offer.

Having lost out to a very late Derek O'Connor goal at Easter Road in the first derby of the season, Hibs were bent on revenge when their next fixture took them to Tynecastle. Manager Blackley was without the suspended Gordon Rae and drafted Jamieson into defence, while Brazil dropped to the bench to make way for debutant Tommy Craig in midfield, where it was thought his experience would be of great value in what was sure to be a tense affair. Around 21,000 excited fans witnessed Hibs dominating the first half hour, but once again they failed to take advantage and allowed their hosts to hold the balance of play for the remainder of the game. As neither side could find the net, another 0-0 draw was added to the many that already existed in terms of Hibs–Hearts meetings.

As reigning League champions, Aberdeen were once again leading the way in Scotland, even although they had lost Mark McGhee to Hamburg, Gordon Strachan to Manchester United and Doug Rougvie to Chelsea. Many clubs would have suffered at losing three such talented players, but the Dons had invested wisely in bringing Frank McDougal from St Mirren and Tommy McQueen from Clyde, and both players had quickly showed that the money was well spent. Hibs once again started the game well, but managed to go in a goal behind at half-time. When they were awarded a penalty early in the second half, it looked as though they might be back in the game. Sadly, it was missed, and the Dons scored two more rapid-fire goals to win 3-0 and send the Hibs fans in the 6,000 crowd home disappointed.

When a team are struggling at the wrong end of the table every fixture they face is considered hard, and certainly there was no exception to that rule for Hibs as their next challenge brought Rangers to Easter Road. During the week preceding that game, John Blackley had been on a scouting mission and reported that he might make a move for the player being watched. Indeed, Blackley was already negotiating with a number of other clubs to bring players in, and so it seemed obvious that those already at Easter Road would have to buck up their ideas about remaining with the club. Facing Rangers gave the 11 on display that very chance and they grasped it with both hands in securing a 2-2 draw in a pulsating match watched by a crowd of around 14,000. Goal heroes for Hibs were Callachan and Irvine, while Gordon Durie was hugely unlucky not to open his Hibs account after a raking drive from the edge of the box struck the bar and bounced to safety. One peculiar thing about that game was that the ball boys at the end of the ground occupied by the visiting fans were decked out in Rangers tracksuits! This was something the club decided to try after ball boys at the home match with Hearts had been pelted with missiles.

Mid-November saw Hibs making the trip to Dumbarton to face the side whose 3-2 win earlier in the season at Easter Road had resulted in the resignation of Pat Stanton. The Sons of the Rock had a broadly similar record to Hibs going into the game, with both sides on nine points, but Dumbarton had a superior goals-against figure to put them just ahead in the table. Hibs started the game very poorly and soon paid the price when their hosts raced into a 2-0 lead, but Gordon Durie finally got the break his excellent play deserved and his double earned Hibs a point. Unfortunately, Hibs finished the game with just ten men after McNamara was ordered off. The red card would lead to a four-game ban. Little did we know at that time, but McNamara's absence was to coincide with a dreadful run of results.

One of the main challengers for the League title, Dundee United, provided Hibs with their next test when they arrived at Easter Road in late November. Considered by many to be the most technically gifted outfit in Scotland, Jim McLean's side were a fine blend of youth and experience, with the likes of established stars like Hamish McAlpine and Maurice Malpas being joined by John Clark and Eamonn Bannon. With McNamara suspended, John Blackley kept changes to a minimum by drafting Paul Kane into the side, and the youngster played his part in securing a point from a 0-0 draw.

Two points from their last two games meant that Hibs had slipped further down the table and now sat second-bottom with only Morton beneath them, four points adrift, so when the sides clashed at Cappielow it was imperative that the Greens took something from the game. On a cold and wet day on a very muddy pitch, the Hibs men were sadly out of touch and suffered a humiliating 4-0 defeat to pile the pressure on Blackley's shoulders, with the fans starting to get really worried about relegation.

Desperate efforts were being made to bring in new faces, but there always seemed to be some hitch in negotiations, and so Hibs faced a very busy December and festive period of fixtures during which points just had to be picked up to haul them up the table. A training-ground injury to Rough deprived Hibs of his services in their next game, which brought mid-table St Mirren to Easter Road. Robin Rae deputised for Rough and was badly at fault for the second goal in a 3-2 defeat in which Durie once again found the net, the other goal coming off a St Mirren defender. Ralph Callachan was substituted in the match and his place was taken by young Michael McManus – the only first-team appearance he would ever make.

A second consecutive home game meant that Hibs next faced Celtic in what would be their last Easter Road fixture of the calendar year. The Glasgow club were chasing leaders Aberdeen and did themselves a massive favour by defeating a lacklustre Hibs side 1-0 to take the points home to Parkhead. Disappointingly, only 9,000 fans attended the game.

Bad weather took its toll on the fixture card and Hibs were not in action again until 29 December 1984 when they travelled to Dens Park to face mid-table Dundee. Once again, the performance from the Greens was less than satisfactory and Dundee were worthy 2-0 winners, leaving John Blackley scratching his head in trying to figure out just why his players were so much below par. Of course, one or two new faces in the line-up might have helped, but the board had made it clear there was no finance available and the manager had to rely on the players at his disposal. Part of the difficulty regarding insufficient finance stemmed from poor Easter Road attendances, but it was a catch-22 situation as the fans were failing to turn up to watch poor displays, and so income from gate money was down.

Another calendar year over and Hibs moved into 1985 with a home fixture on New Year's Day against Hearts. The Gorgie club had not won a Ne'er Day fixture since 1966, but they soon rectified that by taking the points in a 2-1 win. Gary Mackay and Sandy Clark did the damage and only Jamieson's strike gave the Hibs fans in the 18,925 crowd anything to cheer about. The New Year also brought a new-look match programme, with the price increasing from 30p to 40p, although the content varied little from what had gone before. Certainly, the programme was now a bigger size but didn't have any more pages than the 30p version, and so it was difficult to understand why the change had been made in the first place.

Things were becoming pretty desperate for Hibs now as only Morton sat below them in the Premier League, and so they faced a daunting task as they headed to Aberdeen for their next game. It was very nearly a top-versus-bottom clash, and the result was what might be expected in such circumstances, the Dons winning 2-0. It has to be said that Hibs gave a good account of themselves and on another day might well have taken a point from the game. Making his debut in that game was Colin Harris, a striker signed from Dundee in a swap deal that took Graham Harvey to Dens Park, and 'Bomber' was unlucky not to find the net on his first appearance in green and white when a downward header came off a post and was swept clear by a defender.

Hard on the heels of that visit to Pittodrie was another away fixture, the opposition this time being Rangers at Ibrox. Fifteen points separated the teams as they kicked off but 90 minutes later the gap was reduced to 13 as Rice and substitute Harris scored the Hibs goals in an excellent 2-1 win. Harris had replaced Durie with ten minutes left and scored what proved to be the winning goal in the 86th minute, earning his new side two points they could scarcely have believed they would get.

With that great win at Ibrox behind them, Hibs now met Dumbarton at Easter Road in what was effectively a 'four-pointer' as the Sons of the Rock were one place and three points above their hosts. Beating Rangers certainly had a positive effect on the attendance for this match, with around 8,200 fans there to witness a good 3-1 win for Hibs. Alan Sneddon scored a rare goal, while Durie and an own-goal ensured two valuable points for Hibs.

A bitterly cold spell of weather then disrupted the fixture calendar again, but with the benefit of undersoil heating Hibs managed to arrange a friendly against Celtic on 26 January. It was a day that one player in particular would never forget. The fans, too, would have happy memories of a 6-3 win and a 'Benny' Brazil hat-trick. Granted, Celtic had been out of action for a couple of weeks and it was only a friendly, but one look at Mickey Weir's shins after the match would give a fair indication of just how 'friendly' the match was. As a player who suffered more criticism than he enjoyed praise from the Hibs support, Benny was very popular both with his team-mates and the managers he played under. Not exactly the most graceful of players, he made up for that with his determination and non-stop running. It was a cracking hat-trick, involving a sweet half-volley from the edge of the box, a flashing header as he stooped to a low cross and a penalty that sent the keeper the wrong way. Also on target for Hibs that day were Durie, Jamieson and Rice, while Celtic scored through Mo Johnston, Paul McStay and Brian McClair.

During the following week, John Blackley added to his squad when Joe McBride signed from Oldham on an 18-month contract in a deal brokered personally by chairman Kenny Waugh. McBride, whose father, Joe, had also starred for Hibs in years gone by, had gone south at just 16 years of age to join Everton and had four good seasons at Goodison Park before moving on to Rotherham. His spell with the Yorkshire side was not a good one and lasted only a year before he signed up with Oldham. Unfortunately, and after playing some of his best football at Boundary Park, manager Joe Royle inexplicably dropped him from the starting XI in a move that confused even the fans of the club, but which seemed to indicate to Joe that he might be better moving once more. The 24-year-old left-sided forward or midfielder jumped at the chance of coming home to Scotland and it was reported at the time that his dad felt that Joe junior couldn't have picked a better club to join.

League football resumed for Hibs with a meeting on 2 February at Tannadice against Dundee United. McBride was listed as a substitute, but didn't get on to the field as he watched his new team-mates losing 2-0. By chance, it was United at Tannadice again just three days later – on this occasion in the third round of the Scottish Cup. Sadly, the outcome was the same, although United went one better in winning 3-0.

A week later, it was basement boys Morton at Easter Road and McBride was given his full debut, wearing the No.11 jersey. The last time the sides had met at Cappielow, Morton had blown Hibs away with a 4-0 pasting, but the boot was on the other foot this time as the Greens hammered their visitors 5-1. Durie, who had been finding it a little difficult adjusting to the pace of the Premier League, scored a stunning hat-trick, the other goals coming from Sneddon and substitute Harris. Joe McBride had an excellent debut and was involved in three of the five goals. The only real negative in the game was the sloppy defending for the Morton goal.

Bad weather struck again in what was proving to be the coldest winter in many years. It affected the whole of the UK, which prompted Coventry City to get in touch to propose a visit to Easter Road, but Hibs decided instead to have a Friday night fixture against the touring Moscow Dynamo. Although not a competitive game, it was thought by John Blackley and Tommy Craig that the young Hibs squad could learn a lot from playing against such a good side. With the pressure off, Hibs relaxed into a good, free-flowing game, winning 2-0 after a double from the in-form Gordon Durie.

A fortnight later, thanks to a let-up in the frosty weather, Hibs visited Love Street, a ground where they never seemed to find their form, and it was no different on this occasion as they lost 2-1, Brazil getting the goal. Blackley was less than happy with the seeming lack of character in his side and was resolved to do something about that before the League position worsened. Certainly, the Greens seemed happy to allow their hosts to set the pace – a dangerous road to follow. One player who did not feature that afternoon was Bobby Thomson, whose dramatic dip in form had seen the goals totally drying up. With the thought in mind that a change of scenery might do him some good, Hibs loaned Thomson out to his former club, Morton, for the remainder of the season.

It is interesting to note some of the names popping up in Gordon Neely's programme notes on the fortunes of the various youth teams. David Fellinger, Paul McGovern, Danny Lennon and Alan Peters had all caught Neely's eye and he had high hopes for their future with the club. Incidentally, after a poor start, the new match programme was now definitely improving and had plenty of good reading to fill the time before kick-off and the half-time interval.

A visit by Dundee on the first Saturday in March did little to fire the imagination of the Hibs supporting public, with barely 5,000 in attendance to watch a dismal display and a 1-0 defeat. In fairness, the visitors were no better than Hibs, but cashed in on a defensive mistake when John Brown fired home the only goal, giving Rough no chance. It was a worried support that left the stadium, all too aware that two clubs would be relegated at the end of the season and Hibs were too close for comfort to that second-bottom spot.

Another enforced break meant that Hibs were not in action again until the middle of the month, when they faced a very tricky tie against Celtic at Parkhead. The hosts had been in great form, but Hibs defended superbly, Rough giving the kind of display that had earned him a recall to the Scotland squad. It was a tight game throughout and for the second time in succession only one goal was scored. Thankfully, it came from Paul Kane as

Hibs bust a few pools coupons by taking the much-needed points back to Edinburgh.

During the following week, Hibs brought a former player back to Easter Road when they signed Iain Munro from Dundee United. The Tannadice side had initially suggested a loan deal, but Hibs were keen to have the player on their books and so a deal was struck to bring him to Easter Road permanently. Munro, who had originally joined Hibs from St Mirren, had left Easter Road ten years earlier to join Rangers and had enjoyed spells with both Stoke City and Sunderland before returning north of the border.

The new man had a place on the bench for the next Hibs game, against League leaders Aberdeen at Easter Road, and he must have wondered just what he'd let himself in for as the Dons recorded a 5-0 win in a stormy, bad-tempered match. Frustration among the Hibs players manifested itself in the shape of a number of bookings for rash challenges, while on the terraces the home supporters were totally dismayed at what they were watching and made their displeasure heard loud and clear. Quite honestly, Hibs were atrocious that day and it was obvious from very early in the game that the visitors were streets ahead in skill and application.

Only six League games now remained, and Dumbarton still posed the biggest threat to Hibs' Premier League survival, making the upcoming match at Boghead a do-or-die game for both clubs. Ahead of that, however, Hibs had the small matter of an Edinburgh derby at Tynecastle to consider. Hearts were in a comfortable mid-table position and from the off in this encounter they took the game to Hibs, scoring twice through John Robertson and Sandy Clark. Hibs, however, would not give up and when substitute Joe McBride came off the bench to score two goals in the last six minutes of the game those Hibs fans in the 17,814 crowd who were still hanging on hoping for a miracle must have been praying mighty hard! Joe's second goal, from a stunning free kick, sent the Hibs fans into raptures, while debutant Iain Munro must have decided that maybe coming back to Hibs was not such a bad thing after all.

A personal memory from that derby involves me passing a Hibs supporters' bus in Westfield Road as I made my way back to my car after the game. The bus looked about three-quarters full and every face at every window looked as glum as glum can be. As I started to pass the bus, wearing a grin as wide as the road itself, a Hibby jumped off and asked me why I was looking so 'bleeping' happy. I told him of McBride's late double and he shot back on to the bus to tell all. As I looked back, the bus was literally rocking at the roadside and the singing was rising in volume as more and more of the passengers realised that we'd grabbed a vital point.

The point earned at Tynecastle had helped open up a little bit of a gap over Dumbarton, who had lost that day, but the next match involved the two sides clashing and was a 'must win' for the Greens to take the pressure off a predominantly young team. The club, realising the importance of this fixture, laid on buses and around 1,800 Hibs fans joined the 'armada' of coaches, together with countless cars, vans and motorbikes, as the attendance reached 6,200, most of whom were wearing green and white. The atmosphere in the ground was electric and the Hibs players responded magnificently as Willie Irvine rediscovered his scoring touch with the opening goal and Brian Rice volleyed a second to give the visitors a 2-0 half-time lead. They had little difficulty in protecting the scoreline until a final whistle that triggered joyous scenes among the huge travelling support. The win opened up a three-point gap on Dumbarton in the second relegation spot and certainly helped ease the pressure, although John Blackley was quick to point out that there were still eight points available from the games remaining. As it turned out, Dumbarton never gained a single point from their remaining matches, but Hibs didn't know that would happen and so had to keep looking to gain points themselves from the last four fixtures.

Dundee United visited Easter Road in mid-April virtually assured of European football next season because of their League placing, but they met a Hibs side intent on building on the good work following that vital win over Dumbarton. Hibs managed to compete for the full 90 minutes and probably finished the stronger team, but they had to be content with a 1-1 draw, Gordon Durie getting the goal.

Another home game followed seven days later against St Mirren, who were also chasing a European qualification spot. Under manager Alex Miller, the Buddies had narrowly lost out the previous season and were vying with Hearts and Dundee for the final European place. Reference to John Blackley's post-match comments will indicate what sort of day his team had. 'One of the worst displays of the season,' said the manager, and few would disagree as the Greens crashed 4-0 and never really threatened Campbell Money's goal throughout the entire 90 minutes. It was as well that Dumbarton had hit a losing streak, as form like that smacked of relegation and the home support was less than enamoured with the players after the final whistle sounded.

The penultimate League match of the season took Hibs to Cappielow to meet a Morton side already facing relegation, due mainly to a very leaky defence that had lost almost 100 goals in the 34 games played. Hibs didn't do them any favours by adding another two into the goals-against column, but it took a while to secure a 2-1 win with the players once again looking somewhat lacklustre. Youth had its day for the Hibees as Kane and Rice got their names on the scoresheet.

A long and often trying season finally came to an end with a visit from Rangers, who had won the League Cup and qualified for the UEFA Cup – although it must be said that this amounted to a poor season by their standards. Despite the final scoreline of only 1-0, courtesy of a Paul Kane strike, it has to be said that Hibs were by far the better side that day. They were solid at the back, and with Weir and Callachan pulling the strings in midfield the visitors were a pretty sorry lot by the time the game ended. On a personal note, it was a great day for my son, Kevin, whose birthday it was and he was the Hibs Kids mascot, which made the win all the sweeter.

Chapter Nineteen

1985/86

'JUKE BOX' DEPARTS AGAIN!

As Scottish football prepared itself for another season it did so in the wake of both the Heysel and Bradford disasters, incidents which brought football from the back pages of the newspapers to the front for all the wrong reasons. Just 18 days after the last season had finished for Hibs with a 1-0 win over Rangers, the European Cup final between Liverpool and Juventus took place at the Heysel Stadium in Brussels, where more than 60,000 fans crammed into an arena that clearly wasn't up to safely accommodating that number. The atmosphere was hostile from the off and around an hour before kick-off trouble flared between the rival fans, who charged at each other across the terracing and easily broke through the pathetically sparse cordon of police officers. The upshot was that a retaining wall collapsed towards the area occupied by Juventus fans. Once the situation had finally been brought under control, the scale of the tragedy became clear: 39 Italian and Belgian fans killed and hundreds more injured. In time, this would cause UEFA to ban English clubs from all European competition for five years.

All of that came in the wake of the Bradford disaster, which actually occurred on the day Hibs beat Rangers. A massive fire broke out in one of Bradford City's wooden stands, causing mass panic among the City supporters, who were out in huge numbers to celebrate the fact that their club had secured the Third Division championship. The fire broke out around 3.40pm and spectators and stewards requested extinguishers be provided, but it was like a tinder-box as the hot spring and early summer weather had dried out the structure. Within a very short space of time, the wooden stand was ablaze and though the police worked hard to evacuate the area the exits could not cope with the crush as fans panicked. Sadly, no fewer than 56 supporters lost their lives and a further 256 were injured. The incident had been captured on camera by the television companies and made harrowing viewing on that evening's news bulletins.

Against that background, chairman Kenny Waugh was quick to point out that although the main stand at Easter Road was of wooden construction, measures had been taken to ensure a similar fate would not befall Hibernian.

On the playing front, Hibs started their pre-season with a short two-match visit to Ireland, where they defeated Shelbourne 5-1 and Waterford 1-0. Unfortunately, the trip was made without Brian Rice, who had been transferred to Nottingham Forest for a fee that would need to be set by a tribunal after the two clubs had failed to agree a figure. The transfer of Rice, it is fair to say, did not go down well with the Hibs support, but the youngster fancied trying his luck in England and no-one could really blame him for wanting to take that chance.

Back in Scotland, Hibs faced two more friendlies, the first of those at Glebe Park against Brechin City. Their manager, Ian Stewart, had moulded his side into a useful outfit and they gave the Greens a stiff test in a match that ended 0-0, with most present reflecting upon that as a fair result. Three days later, Hibs met Alloa at Recreation Park, but on the morning of that game they moved into the transfer market to secure the signature of 22-year-old Steve Cowan from Aberdeen. At £45,000, Cowan would prove to be a sound investment and he started his career well by heading a goal during the 3-1 win over Alloa. The other Hibs goals came from Joe McBride, and it's worth noting that Durie left the field at half-time to be replaced by young John Collins, who had an excellent 45 minutes.

An opening-day fixture against Aberdeen at Pittodrie was as tough as it gets, but Hibs played a lot better than the 3-0 defeat might indicate. The starting XI contained four teenagers, and manager Blackley was particularly pleased with the contribution of young John Collins in the Hibs midfield. Speaking after the game, Blackley said: 'We've a number of very talented youngsters here and we are looking for them to push for regular starts in the first team. A good example is John Collins, whom we have always felt was good enough to make the grade, and his performance at Pittodrie bodes well for the future. I am looking for the experienced guys in our side to help bring the youngsters on and if they all play to their potential on a regular basis we will improve on last season's poor finishing place in the League.'

Another difficult game soon followed as Hibs met Rangers at Easter Road in mid-August, but the home side had reason to be optimistic because, despite the lowly finish in the previous season, they had taken five points out of a possible eight against the Ibrox club. There would be some drama before the game even kicked off, however, as Rangers fans arriving late at the stadium and seeing huge queues at the turnstiles decided to use other areas of the ground to gain admission and that was clearly a recipe for disaster as 16,500 people tried to squeeze into a ground still under development in certain areas. In hindsight, it might have been better to have made the game all-ticket, and the club learned from the experience.

As it was, the match kicked off 28 minutes late and Hibs gave a debut to another new signing in Mark Fulton, who had joined the club from St Mirren in a £50,000 deal. It was also Steve Cowan's home debut and the new boys were unlucky to find themselves in a losing team as the visitors won the game 3-1, with substitute Gordon Durie the Hibs goalscorer.

The match programme for that opening game was as good as ever, having improved vastly from its first few issues, although the price had gone up 10p to 50p. If there was one niggle to collectors it was that there was no detail offered of the pre-season matches in respect of goalscorers, etc, and as many fans, especially the younger ones, were thirsty for such detail it was a pity it had not been included.

The League Cup, sponsored by Skol, kicked off for Hibs with a visit from Cowdenbeath, and John Blackley made sure his players knew they would have to be at their best to beat the lower-league outfit. Cowdenbeath had beaten St Mirren in last season's competition and had won the right to face Hibs this time around by disposing of Berwick Rangers in the first round, a game watched by Blackley, who was impressed with what he saw. Barely 4,000 fans turned up to watch, and it was the stay-away brigade who lost out as a rampant Hibs crushed the visitors by 6-0. Alan Rough, newly voted Player of the Year by the Supporters' Association, could have popped out for a cup of tea he was that under-employed, whereas Ray Allan in the Cowdenbeath goal had a very busy night indeed. New boy Cowan endeared himself to the home support by grabbing a hat-trick, while Durie got two and Brazil the other. Cowan, described by Blackley as a utility player who could be deployed either in midfield or up front, soon formed what would prove to be a formidable partnership with Gordon Durie in a two-pronged attack. An interesting snippet from the programme that night was a picture of 13-year-old Salvesen Boys' Club centre-half Steven Tweed signing an 'S' form with the club.

In the League, it had been two games and two defeats when St Mirren came to Easter Road on 24 August and that became three in three as the visitors capitalised on a series of defensive blunders to win the game 3-2. It was a real pity that these mistakes occurred as going forward Hibs looked really good, but Kane's penalty conversion and a McBride strike counted for nothing in the end.

It was League Cup time again in the following midweek when Motherwell visited Easter Road. In the previous round, Steve Cowan had won the sponsors' man of the match award after scoring a hat-trick and that had earned him a nice silver tankard and a cheque representing a share of the £350 Skol had agreed to pay to any player getting three goals in a match. It was tough luck on Steve that his feat was matched by Mike Larnach of Clydebank and Bobby Williamson of Rangers. In this third round, the sponsors had put up a £700 prize to be shared by any players who could manage a hat-trick, and clearly Cowan had his eye on the loot, but he could only manage two. There was, however, a Hibs hat-trick – from Gordon Durie. A single from McBride ensured that Hibs won easily by 6-1 and the majority of the 6,000 fans present went home happy, if somewhat mystified as to why their team could strike such good form in the League Cup but not in the League.

On the day following that match, Hibs received word that the transfer tribunal had set the fee for the sale of Brian Rice to Nottingham Forest at £175,000, which was a huge £100,000 more than Forest boss Brian Clough had originally offered. Of course, Hibs had already spent £95,000 bringing Cowan and Fulton to the club and so that £175,000 already had a sizeable dent in it.

Tough League games were coming thick and fast, and Hibs' next challenge lay at Tynecastle. Last time in Gorgie, Hibs had needed two goals in the last six minutes from substitute Joe McBride to secure a point, and they looked as though they might have managed a share of the spoils this time, too, after Durie had equalised an early goal from John Colquhoun. But Sandy Clark had other ideas, popping up nine minutes from time to win the game for Hearts and send the majority of the 17,457 crowd into raptures. A derby loss is bad enough to stomach at the best of times, but it was the fourth defeat out of four League games, and it left Hibs firmly rooted to the bottom of the table, with both Motherwell and Dundee two points above them. Further bad news emerged after the game when it became known that Paul Kane had fractured his cheekbone and would be out for several weeks as a result.

On the Monday following the derby defeat, John Blackley was active again in the transfer market. The new arrivals were 29-year-old goalkeeper Dave McKellar, signed from Carlisle on Tommy Craig's recommendation after the Hibs man had persuaded Blackley of the former Derby, Brentford and Ipswich man's suitability as back-up to Alan Rough, and 19-year-old Joe Tortolano, who hailed from the Stirling area but joined Hibs on a free transfer from West Bromwich Albion.

Two days later, Hibs clashed with Celtic at Easter Road in the first game of a rapid double-header against the Parkhead club, firstly in the quarter-final of the League Cup. In Steve Cowan and Gordon Durie, Hibs had the joint top scorers in the competition, with both players on five goals, while Celtic's Mo Johnston and Rangers man Bobby Williamson were sitting on four.

Hibs had been showing really good form in the League Cup and that form continued in an eight-goal thriller settled eventually by a penalty shoot-out as the sides finished the game locked together at 4-4. With construction of a covered enclosure under way on the main East terracing, the home support among the 15,770 crowd was crammed into the cowshed behind the goals, the enclosure and the main stand, and it's a safe bet to suggest that not a soul left the ground until the drama was complete.

With two minutes on the clock, Maurice Johnston fired the Celts ahead as his 25-yard shot struck Brazil to wrong-foot Alan Rough. With thirty minutes on the clock, Cowan headed home a Durie cross to equalise, and eight minutes later Durie himself scored with the head from an Alan Sneddon cross. Half-time was fast approaching, but Davie Provan fired Celtic level. Fifty-seven minutes in, Colin Harris came off the bench to replace John Collins. Harris had been on the park for only three minutes when he put Hibs 3-2 up after rounding keeper Pat Bonner and rolling the ball into an empty net. Hibs were still patting themselves on the back when Johnston made it 3-3 to take the game into extra time. Eight minutes into extra time, Roy Aitken went on a run that took him past four defenders before he shot low past Rough to make it 4-3, but three minutes after that a Durie shot struck McGrain and flew past Bonner to make it all-square at 4-4.

A penalty shoot-out was needed, and it took place in front of the packed cowshed. First up was Iain Munro, who scored, and then Roy Aitken watched Rough brilliantly save his penalty. Durie made it 2-0 and Rough was the hero again as he pushed Peter Grant's spot kick away, but then Rae missed and Paul McStay scored to make it 2-1 to Hibs after three penalties each. Mark Fulton scored for Hibs as did Brian McClair for Celtic, meaning that Brazil could win the tie with the fifth Hibs penalty in the shoot-out. Poor Benny made a hash of it, and Tommy Burns scored to take the tie to sudden-death. Up stepped Steve Cowan for Hibs and he coolly fired home to put the Greens ahead. Celtic central defender Pierce O'Leary, brother of Arsenal's David, blazed his penalty high over the bar to send Hibs into the semi-finals after what was truly an epic battle.

Stunned by that League Cup defeat, Celtic took their revenge big style in the League match on the Saturday by hammering hapless Hibs 5-0, thus ensuring that the Easter Road men remained at the bottom of the League.

With the arrival of McKellar and Tortolano, it was perhaps inevitable that players might leave and that's exactly what happened as young goalkeeper Robin Rae was released by the club, being promptly snapped up by Morton, and Bobby Thomson signed for Blackpool for a nominal fee. Other news involved word of Alan Rough's call-up to the Scotland squad for the crucial World Cup qualifying match against Wales at Anfield. Rough's inclusion, despite Hibs shipping goals so easily, was a measure of the faith shown in him by Scotland boss Jock Stein and, believe it or not, a reflection of his current good form – but for Rough's fine goalkeeping, Hibs would surely have lost even more goals.

The Scotland match against Wales, mentioned above, would be remembered for years to come for both happy and sad reasons. Happily, Scotland drew the match and as a result progressed to a play-off game against

Australia. But there was a shocking postscript to that victory – the death of Jock Stein, who collapsed just as the final whistle sounded. A man who lived and loved football, Stein had steered Celtic to European Cup glory in 1967 and had managed Hibs for a spell before that. The stunning news of his death, a huge loss to Scottish football, brought mourning not only throughout the nation but beyond it, too.

With Kane out injured, manager John Blackley promoted young Eddie May from the reserves for a visit to Dens Park on League business, and although the midfielder gave a good account of himself he was on the losing side as the hosts scraped it 1-0. That defeat left Hibs with a record of played six, lost six, goals for four, goals against 17, and, of course, no points. Above them at the bottom end of the League were Motherwell on two points and Hearts and Clydebank on five. Needless to say, the Hibs supporters were less than happy with their lot and had it not been for the excellent results in the League Cup John Blackley might well have been feeling the pressure from the terracing. Hibs had to start picking up points, and fast, but it seemed that fate was conspiring against them after their scheduled home game with fellow strugglers Clydebank was postponed after torrential rain in Edinburgh caused the park to be waterlogged.

Around this time, word reached the club of the death of former player Tommy D'Arcy, who had been snapped up in 1952 from Armadale Thistle after having played only four games for the West Lothian outfit. A striker, Tommy was in the reserves when the Famous Five were thrilling crowds everywhere, but he got his first-team chance when Lawrie Reilly was in dispute with the club and he gave his all while wearing the Hibernian colours. Opportunities were at a premium for the player, so he decided to move on and subsequently played for Southend, where he failed to settle. He returned briefly to Hibs before joining Queen of the South, where he ended his playing career and returned to his trade as a plumber. Just 52 when he died, Tommy deserves his place in Hibernian's history as one of the hundreds of players down through the ages who were proud to wear the green and white.

The next action for the Hibees would be to face Rangers at Easter Road in the League Cup semi-final first leg, and just ahead of that fixture another new face was introduced into the first-team dressing room when Gordon Chisholm was brought in from Sunderland, having played more than 250 games for the Roker Park side. Thrust straight into the starting XI, Chisholm won instant popularity by scoring against Rangers, who lost the match 2-0 as Durie added a second and Rough brilliantly saved a penalty. It was a good lead to take to Ibrox for the second leg, but before that would happen, Hibs finally got their first League points on the board by beating Motherwell 1-0 at Easter Road, the goal coming from Benny Brazil.

The following midweek saw Clydebank at Easter Road to fulfil the

League fixture postponed earlier due to adverse weather conditions, and Hibs extended their winning streak to three with a classy 5-0 demolition of the visitors. Kane was back in the fold and had a telling contribution to make, being involved in three of the five goals. Cowan bagged a hat-trick and Durie got the other two.

The recent good League form had lifted Hibs out of bottom spot in the table, and their 2-2 result at Tannadice ensured that Motherwell would remain below them. The draw with the Arabs marked the return to action of long-term injury absentee Ralph Callachan, and the experience he brought to the midfield certainly helped a great deal in securing the point. In-form Steve Cowan got one of the goals and right-back Alan Sneddon the other.

A huge travelling support, boosted greatly in number thanks to the special buses arranged by the club, wound its way along the M8 to Ibrox for the second leg of the League Cup semi-final. A crowd of 38,000 was entertained throughout and the Hibs support was in fine voice at the end because, although the Greens lost 1-0 to a Davy Cooper goal, the aggregate score of 2-1 carried the club into a Hampden final against Aberdeen.

Back to League business on the Saturday, Hibs welcomed second-top Aberdeen to Easter Road in what many were classing as a Skol Cup final rehearsal. Hibs had not won in their last five League encounters with the Dons and had in fact scored only one goal in those games, as against the 17 racked up by Alex Ferguson's men. It was gratifying, therefore, to watch a Hibs side playing well and earning a 1-1 draw, with Cowan scoring against his former club.

Ahead of the Skol Cup final, Hibs had another date in Glasgow when they travelled to Ibrox for a Premier League match and defeated their hosts 2-1, thanks to an own-goal and a winner from substitute Colin Harris. Winning at that venue is as delightful as it is rare, and although far fewer Hibs fans made the trip this time, those who did left the ground sporting mile-wide grins because the points took Hibs out of the relegation places in the League.

Reaching any cup final is an achievement, and for Hibs to reach the Skol League Cup final at Hampden on Sunday, 27 October 1985, was an achievement and a half, bearing in mind that they had been showing abysmal form in the League and had needed to dispose of both Celtic and Rangers for the right to face Aberdeen. Some 40,061 fans attended the game, with the Hibs contingent shading it in terms of majority. The opening exchanges saw Cowan bring out the best in Jim Leighton, but it was not long before John Hewitt started to make a huge impression on the game as his perfect cross was headed home by Eric Black after just nine minutes. Three minutes later, Hewitt was at it again, only this time it was Billy Stark whose head connected to make it 2-0. Try as they might, and they did try, Hibs could not force a way through the Dons defence, brilliantly marshalled by Willie Miller, and so when Black got his second and Aberdeen's third, the Cup dream was over for the Hibees. A late flurry saw Leighton brilliantly save a 30-yard piledriver from Paul Kane after substitute John Collins set him up, but it was too little too late and the silverware was Pittodrie bound.

One consolation for Gordon Durie, other than his runners-up medal, was that he finished top scorer in the tournament and won a holiday to the value of £1,400 for his efforts.

On the reserve front, new signing Joe Tortolano had been making an impression, scoring twice in a 2-2 draw at Pittodrie, and he got one in a 2-1 win at Ibrox to make his mark early for the club. John Collins had appeared in those games, too, and was greatly impressing coach Gordon Neely, who said of the Galashiels lad: 'When I was with Dundee United we looked at him a few times but decided against signing him, and in a way I'm glad because he's now at Hibs and I foresee a very bright future for him in the game.'

The Cup final disappointment now behind them, Hibs got back down to League business when they met Clydebank at Kilbowie on the last Saturday of October. Tortolano earned a place on the bench but was an unused substitute as the visitors carved out a fine 4-2 victory. On target for the Greens were Brazil, Kane and Cowan (2). The points gained meant that both Clydebank and Motherwell remained below them in the table.

Much was being made at this time of the fact that Hibs were nearing the 5,000 mark in terms of League goals scored, although abandoned games and matches played in the Regional or Southern Leagues during times of war were excluded. Going into their next match, against Dundee, Hibs were nine short of that magic figure, and they duly reduced it to seven by defeating the Dark Blues 2-1 with goals from Kane and Durie. Open for the first time that afternoon, albeit only partially, was the new covered East terracing, and with winter showers almost the norm in November it couldn't have been completed to better timing. The intention was that the full area would be open for Hibs' next home game, against Hearts at Easter Road.

With those seven goals needed to reach 5,000, there would have been more than one Hibs fan in the crowd of 19,776 hoping for a repeat of the January 1973 scoreline, but the only thing that got anywhere near seven was the number of yellow cards, each side earning three during the 90 minutes. A 0-0 share of the spoils was just about right on the day, but few present could have imagined what the loss of that one point might mean to Hearts come the last day of the season.

Love Street was the next venue and Hibs went there knowing they could draw level in the middle of the table if they could get both points. The

Greens started the game very well, scored early and built on that to win the match 3-1, with full-back Sneddon getting one of his occasional goals and Kane and Cowan also finding the back of the Buddies' net. The match marked the first-team debut of Joe Tortolano and the youngster played his part in winning two good points from an away game.

Back on the road the following week, an increasingly confident Hibs side were at Parkhead to face title-chasing Celtic in front of 21,500 fans, a fair proportion of them wearing emerald green as opposed to the bottle-green colour favoured by their hosts. A cracking first 45 minutes and some stout defending towards the end of the game earned Hibs a well-deserved point. Gordon Chisholm, enjoying the midfield role handed to him by John Blackley, got the goal in a 1-1 draw.

Due to an earlier postponement, a third consecutive away game should have taken Hibs to Motherwell on the last day of November, but a severe overnight frost caused the game to be postponed for a second time. Hibs were more fortunate than most because they had a game arranged for 3 December, when Dunfermline would provide the opposition in the Tom Hart Cup. The Pars, managed by Jim Leishman, were going along well in the Second Division and put out a side close to full strength, while John Blackley promoted a few reserves to the first XI to reward them for their efforts over the previous months. In a very entertaining game, the Greens won 5-3, the goals coming from Fulton, Chisholm, Durie, May and a Paul Kane penalty. New recruit John Ramage, a goalkeeper brought in from Penicuik after Dave McKellar had failed to settle and had returned south, played the full 90 minutes, making a number of good saves.

The continuing bad weather kept Hibs out of competitive action, but on Tuesday, 10 December, they welcomed the crack Dutch outfit Feyenoord to Easter Road for a friendly. Although the visitors were the reigning Dutch champions, fewer than 5,000 fans braved a very cold evening. They enjoyed the spectacle, with Hibs running out 4-2 winners. Cowan bagged two while Kane scored from a penalty and May also found the target.

Friendly matches were all very well, but Hibs had to keep focusing on their recent good League form so as not to get dragged into the developing relegation struggle with St Mirren, Clydebank and Motherwell. Unfortunately, they did their cause no good whatsoever in their next outing at Pittodrie, when they crashed to a 4-0 defeat and had Durie sent off as the players somewhat lost their discipline, much to the annoyance of John Blackley. Durie's dismissal would prove costly for both the player and the club, as he would now miss four matches at a time when there was a pile-up of fixtures and every first-team player would be needed.

Anxious to put that poor showing behind them, Hibs regrouped for the next challenge that brought Jock Wallace's Rangers to Easter Road on the Saturday before Christmas. The Gers had shown inconsistent form in their recent games, losing the feelgood factor generated by a 3-0 win over Celtic by slumping to a 3-0 defeat against an ever-improving Hearts at Tynecastle. On this occasion, they were worth the point they gained in a 1-1 draw, the Hibs goal coming from Joe Tortolano, his first for the club.

On 27 December 1985, Hibernian fans were stunned and deeply saddened to hear of the death of Erich Schaedler. Initially, it was unclear as to the circumstances of his death, but as the days ticked by the whole very distressing story came out. It was said that in late November Erich and his wife had divorced, and this event had a profound effect on the usually chirpy Schaedler, who had left Hibs some time earlier to join Dumbarton. His team-mate at Boghead, Gordon Arthur, later intimated that 'Shades' had seemed very down, but like everyone else the Dumbarton man was devastated when the details of Erich's death emerged. On Christmas Eve, Erich, a huge enthusiast of 12-bore shotgun hunting, had gone on a shooting trip, alone as per normal. That night, he failed to collect his dogs from a neighbour who'd been asked to look after them, and so the police were called and a search arranged. On the 27th his body was discovered in his car in remote woods and it became known that Erich had taken his own life. Just 36 when he died, Erich was enormously popular wherever he played and the author's own memory of the man is that he was a down-to-earth bloke with no airs or graces who played his football with passion and commitment but who always had time to chat with fans, whether it be after a game or even during some chance meeting.

With a very heavy heart, the players, officials and supporters of Hibernian Football Club had to face the prospect of a New Year's Day battle with Hearts at Tynecastle, as the game had survived a heavy frost. At the end of the 90 minutes, the Hibs fans present in the 25,605 crowd probably wished that it hadn't as the hosts won 3-1 and cemented their place at the top of the Premier League, although they had played more games than their closest rivals. Hearts scored midway through the first half, when Ian Jardine took advantage of some slack marking, and then, with 19 minutes of the game remaining, John Robertson scored to double the lead. Within a minute, Harris had pulled one back and to their credit Hibs went hunting for an equaliser. As often happens in such circumstances, space was left at the back and Sandy Clark ended the scoring with Hearts' third just two minutes after Harris had offered a glimmer of hope.

4 January 1986 brought Clydebank to Easter Road, and for the crowd of just over 6,000 it would be a day to remember for a few but a day best forgotten by most. The Bankies had not been out of the bottom two all season, and in fact occupied second-bottom place, but they seemed to find some good form against a Hibs side seemingly still hung over from the derby defeat and took both points by defeating their hosts 3-2. The 'few' mentioned were the Clydebank players and officials and their handful of

spectators, but the many were those of an emerald green persuasion, unmoved by the fact that Cowan had found the target as had May, who had added his name to the following list, having scored Hibs' 5,000th League goal.

Goal 1,000 – Bobby Reid v Aberdeen on 21 March 1914
Goal 2,000 – Jimmy Dobson v King's Park on 21 November 1931
Goal 3,000 – Bobby Combe v Raith Rovers on 10 January 1953
Goal 4,000 – Jim Scott v Kilmarnock on 4 February 1967
Goal 5,000 – Eddie May v Clydebank on 4 January 1986

With the disappointment of two consecutive League defeats still in their minds, Hibs next travelled to Dens Park, where they met a side just two places and three points above them in the table, but it was to prove to be another dismal afternoon for the Hibs fans present as they watched their favourites go down tamely in a 3-1 defeat, with only a goal from Callachan offering any kind of consolation.

One item of good news at this point was that Gordon Durie had now served his suspension and could resume his place in attack alongside strike partner Steve Cowan as Celtic arrived in Leith. Hibs had missed the bustling striker and his return was a major contribution to Hibs stopping the rot by securing a 2-2 draw with their title-chasing opponents as he nabbed one of the goals while Cowan got the other. The encouraging thing about this result was that it was achieved with no fewer than five teenagers in the starting line-up, and it was achieved after having gone two goals behind. Outstanding in the No.11 jersey that afternoon was John Collins, a lad of slight build but who was deceptively strong and had a real eye for a pass. His work rate was phenomenal, and together with his developing skills it was plain for all to see that this was a lad who could go a long way in the game.

January was nearing its end and as is always the case that brought round three of the Scottish Cup, in which Hibs had been matched up against Dunfermline at Easter Road. The Pars had visited earlier in the season and had lost 5-3, although two of their goals had come in the dying moments, but Hibs knew they'd have to be at their best to progress. On a run of 19 games unbeaten in Division Two, Jim Leishman's men pushed Hibs all the way but could not prevent goals from May and Cowan easing the Greens into round four, where they would face Ayr United at Easter Road. One highly encouraging fact regarding that game was that although it was played on a Sunday it attracted 15,500 fans, with the Pars accounting for about 3,000 of that number.

The following weekend, barely 5,000 turned up to watch Hibs take on the bottom club, Motherwell, and it was somewhat puzzling to the board that so many had chosen to watch the Cup game and yet had turned their backs on a vital League match. As it was, Hibs turned in a dazzling display to hammer the Steelmen 4-0. Two goals from Cowan, taking him to 19 for the season, an own-goal and a first for the club by Collins sent the fans home happy and, importantly, put additional space between Hibs and the relegation spots in the League.

A week later and the lift from that 4-0 win was cancelled out by a 4-0 defeat at the hands of Dundee United at Tannadice. Quite simply, Hibs were outplayed in every area of the park and but for Rough the defeat might have been even more embarrassing. True, United were second in the table and had lost only 20 goals in 23 games, but Hibs never looked like altering that statistic and John Blackley had to accept that with so many youngsters in his side there were always going to be inconsistencies in level of performance.

The players had an early chance to put things right again as their next match brought First Division Ayr United to Easter Road. Former Scotland boss Ally MacLeod was back in charge at Somerset Park, but had been finding the going quite difficult with his side sitting second-bottom in the table, but they defended exceptionally well in this Cup tie and only a single strike by Eddie May separated the teams at the final whistle. It had looked as though it might go to a replay, with Hibs not helping their cause any by missing a penalty, but they kept going and were rewarded with May's injury-time winner. By way of consolation, Hibs were not the only Premier League club to struggle against lower-league opposition that day as Aberdeen and Celtic defeated Arbroath and Queen's Park by the narrowest of margins, while Dundee United were forced into a replay with First Division Kilmarnock.

That narrow win in the Cup earned Hibs a plum quarter-final tie at home against Celtic, but ahead of that were a few very difficult League fixtures, the first of those bringing Aberdeen to Easter Road. The Dons were genuine title contenders, sitting second in the table some four points behind leaders Hearts, but with a game in hand. They had a very strong defensive unit, with Jim Leighton protected in goal by the central defensive partnership of Alex McLeish and Willie Miller, and so it was no surprise that Hibs could not find a way through while conceding a single goal at the other end and thereby losing the points on offer.

There were a couple of interesting items in the match programme that day. Firstly, it was 25 years ago to the day that 54,000 fans had packed into Easter Road to watch the Greens defeat Barcelona 3-2 in a second-round, second-leg tie of the Fairs Cup, the first leg in Spain having finished at 4-4. Bobby Kinloch scored the important third goal that night from the penalty spot and triggered some of the most despicable scenes ever witnessed in Scottish football when the Barca players completely lost the plot and pursued the German referee all over the park, at one point knocking him to the ground. To his credit, the official refused to give in to their tantrums and so a piece of Hibernian history was made. Also in the programme that day was a picture of five of the Hibs Under-14 side who had been invited to Denmark in the coming summer to compete in a tournament. The five were David Nicholls, Steven Dunn, Chris Reid, Lee Baillie and Ian Sieger, and at least two of that number would go on to make appearances in the first XI.

When teams are sitting too close to the bottom of the table for comfort there are never any easy games, but poor Hibs had found that in their previous two League encounters they had faced and lost to championship contenders. There would be no respite as the next fixture brought Dundee United to Easter Road, and the Tannadice club had conceded fewer goals than any other side in the division. Four points behind Hearts and with three games in hand, they did their challenge the world of good by defeating Hibs 1-0, although it was a scrappy goal that took the points to Tannadice. Bizarrely, despite being third-bottom, Hibs were just nine points behind Rangers, with three games in hand, and so a winning run of a few games would launch them into contention for a European spot. Conversely, of course, a run of a few more defeats would have the Greens fighting a relegation battle.

With their Scottish Cup quarter-final tie against Celtic on the horizon, Hibs had one more League fixture to play and that took them to Ibrox, where a crowd of around 16,500 saw the Light Blues secure a 3-1 win to send Hibs home pointless once again, only Cowan finding the net. In his after-match press conference, manager John Blackley expressed his disappointment at the defeat, citing a couple of occasions when Hibs might have scored had Durie elected to pass rather than shoot. He excused his striker by saying all goalscorers have to have that kind of arrogance to succeed in the game. Imagine Blackley's surprise the following Monday morning when a certain national newspaper led the Hibs story with the headline 'Big-Head!' and a narrative suggesting that Blackley had referred to Durie as having a big head and of being too selfish. The club was up in arms about this and issued a statement to the effect that the manager had said no such thing, adding that anyone who knew the player would realise that nothing could be further from the truth. Headlines sell papers, even when those headlines grossly misrepresent what has been said, and Hibs were not alone in having to put up with the kind of tactics some sports hacks still employ to this day.

In their last five outings, Hibs had won only once and that was the narrow defeat of Ayr United in the Cup. The four League games yielded no points and saw nine goals conceded and only one scored. All of this was hardly ideal preparation for the visit of a strong Celtic side on Saturday,

8 March 1986. Hibs had, of course, enjoyed relative success in the other Cup competition by reaching the final, even though their League form had been poor at the time, and had beaten Celtic on penalties after a match that had finished 4-4 after extra time. So, just maybe, they could do it again. In front of a 20,000 crowd, Hibs started brightly and matched the visitors for most of the first half until Brian McClair finally broke the deadlock in the 43rd minute. Six minutes into the second half, Hibs were level when a Tortolano free kick found Cowan in the box and the striker gleefully shot home past Latchford. After that the Celts then went 2-1 up, but 17 minutes from time John Blackley made what would be a telling double substitution, replacing Brazil and a limping John Collins with Colin Harris and Eddie May. The new men had only been on the park for two minutes when Chisholm headed Hibs level from a corner and then, with seven minutes left, Hibs won a penalty that Cowan converted. The atmosphere in the ground was now white-hot, and the visiting fans were relieved when McClair converted a late penalty. But the scoring wasn't over yet. With the referee looking pointedly at his watch, young Eddie May got on the end of a Harris cross to head the winner and send the home support into raptures. Once again, with the odds stacked high against them, this young Hibernian team had confounded the Scottish footballing public by winning a game they had absolutely no right to expect to be able to win.

It would be fair to say that the stunning win over Celtic gave everyone connected with Hibernian a huge boost at a very important time, as League games were running out and Premier League safety was of the utmost importance. In mid-March and on a Wednesday night, St Mirren, one place and two points ahead of the Greens, came to Easter Road to play a match postponed earlier in the season. That League-table deficit was soon eradicated. With the rain teeming down, Cowan helped himself to a wonderful hat-trick, sending the Hibs fans in the 7,000 crowd home in good spirits. Cowan was immense that night, but he was not alone as the youngsters in the side all played their part, Callum Milne proving the pick of the bunch.

The next weekend took Hibs to Kilbowie to face Clydebank, who were staring relegation in the face, and the Greens did little to relieve their hosts' concerns by winning the match 3-1 in front of a very disappointing attendance of around 2,000. Goals from Chisholm and a double from the in-form Tortolano saw Hibs home safely and secured another two valuable points.

In the days that followed, Hibs were delighted to hear that Scotland manager Alex Ferguson had included Alan Rough in his initial pool of 29 for the World Cup in Mexico, and few could argue with the big keeper's selection as he had been in fine form throughout the League campaign. Leaving the club that week, albeit on loan, was Willie Irvine, who joined

Falkirk until the end of the season. The striker had been top scorer for Hibs two seasons ago, but had found a starting place difficult to achieve with Cowan and Durie the automatic first choices. That meant Willie had played most of his games for the reserves in recent months, and he hoped that this fresh challenge might kick-start his career.

Three days after winning at Clydebank, Hibs were on the road again when they visited second-bottom Motherwell. Manager John Blackley chose to give a starting place to Mickey Weir, his first since September as he had been dogged by injuries, and although the diminutive playmaker had a decent 45 minutes before being replaced by Collins, he could do little to stop the Greens going down 2-0 against a club fighting for Premier League survival.

While one half of Edinburgh was 'enjoying' the ups and downs of League football with decent runs in the cups helping to keep the spirits up, the other half had been quietly going about the business of making a very genuine attempt at winning the League title. Hearts had gone 21 Premier League games without defeat when they arrived at Easter Road for the fourth and final derby of the season. That run had taken them to top spot, with 39 points from 29 games, and yet they had scored only three more goals than Hibs, who had played only one game more. The big difference lay in the goals-against column, as Hearts had conceded just 28 to Hibs' 54. Hot on the heels of the Tynecastle outfit were Dundee United on 36 points, with one game fewer played; Aberdeen with 35 points, with again one fewer game played, and Celtic on 33 points, with two games fewer played. It is safe to say that Hearts undoubtedly went into the game as favourites and after 90 minutes that tag was found to be justified as they took both points in a 2-1 win in front of 20,756 fans. It was a typical feisty derby, with six bookings and plenty of meaty challenges, but it could have been so different if the Greens had held on to their equalising goal for a little longer. Sandy Clark had given Hearts a half-time lead, but Cowan equalised in the 64th minute, only for Hearts to be given a penalty just two minutes later. The scourge of Hibernian, John Robertson, converted it to give his club a new Premier League record of 22 games in a row without defeat.

The Scottish Cup semi-final meeting with Aberdeen was looming large, but ahead of that Hibs travelled to Love Street to face St Mirren and turned in a good 90 minutes to win 2-0, thanks to goals from Kane, who was later sent off, and Gordon Rae. Missing from the starting line-up was Gordon Durie, who had suffered an injury in the Hearts game and now looked extremely doubtful for the Cup semi-final.

Off the field, it became known that League reconstruction in Scotland would mean no relegation at the end of this season, a fact that no doubt resulted in huge sighs of relief at both Fir Park and Kilbowie, as it meant that though Motherwell and Clydebank looked certain to finish in the 'relegation' spots, they would not go down. Instead, the Premier League would be increased to 12 clubs, each playing the other home and away twice. Of course, that meant that it would be a 44-game League programme and likely to stretch most clubs in terms of the depth of their player pools.

Ahead of all of that, the Cup semi-final took place at Dens Park, Dundee, the SFA having taken the sensible view that asking fans of two east-coast clubs to travel to Glasgow was pretty unreasonable. On the night in question, a huge travelling support headed north from Edinburgh, with traffic jams causing chaos for those trying to get to the stadium on time. At one point there was a tailback from the Dens area all the way down through Dundee and on to the Tay Bridge, where traffic was virtually at a standstill. So it was that fans streaming into the ground after the game had already started were both stunned and delighted to see Gordon Durie in the No.10 jersey, but it was to be a gamble that backfired on John Blackley as 'Juke Box' was clearly struggling from the off and in time had to be replaced by Harris. It was too much to ask of this young team to find another unexpected Cup victory, and the Dons ran out relatively easy winners by a 3-0 scoreline.

Effectively, that was the season over for Hibs as they no longer had an interest in the Cup, and League reconstruction had removed any thoughts of relegation, although the Greens would probably have been safe had relegation still been in place. Imagine if you will, then, the sort of bragging Hibs fans had to endure from the fans of their oldest rivals as Hearts still held top spot in the League and had reached the Cup final, where they would face Aberdeen. Those of a maroon persuasion were taking every opportunity to boast of their team's achievements and declare themselves proud to be Hearts fans, but, as we shall see, the old saying 'pride comes before a fall' could have been written for our nearest neighbours.

Hibs had four League games left, and the first of those brought Dundee to Easter Road on a damp Saturday afternoon in mid-April. A pretty dull 90 minutes saw Hibs scrape through by 1-0. The strike came from defender Gordon Rae, who showed Hibs' punchless attack, with Durie still out injured, the way to goal. On that same afternoon, Hearts won 3-0 at Tannadice and the bragging noise went up by a few decibels.

A week later, Hibs were at Parkhead to face Celtic, who had narrowed the gap on Hearts at the top of the table and were determined to fight until the last whistle on the last day for the League flag. With the majority of the 16,000 crowd getting loudly behind the home side, Hibs made two critical defensive errors that led to goals and to defeat at the hands of the Hoops. On the same day, Hearts dropped a home point to Aberdeen in a 1-1 draw, scoring their equaliser through John Colquhoun with just three minutes left on the clock.

The penultimate game of the season for Hibs involved another away game, this time at Motherwell where 2,400 utterly bored but dyed-in-the-wool fans watched the Steelmen win 3-1, the Hibs goal coming from Cowan. On the same day, Hearts scraped home 1-0 at Tynecastle with a goal from Gary Mackay. The strain of trying to hold off Celtic was showing, but the Hearts players were still hanging in there, and this result meant that everything would go down to the results on the last game of the season.

When Gordon Durie limped off at Dens Park in that Cup semi-final a few weeks earlier, no-one in the crowd that day would have known that it was to be his last appearance in a Hibs jersey. A number of English clubs had been showing more than a passing interest in the goalscorer, and when Chelsea made an offer reported as being very close to £400,000, Hibs felt they could not refuse. So 'Juke Box' said his farewells and headed off to Stamford Bridge, with the Hibs board pledging to use the funds to strengthen the squad for the coming season.

There was still one game left to play in the current season, and that brought Dundee United to Easter Road. The crowd size that afternoon was pretty moderate, as most Hibs fans had presumably booked themselves on long overseas holidays to get away from the inevitable gloating of their Hearts-supporting friends and neighbours. After all, Hearts needed just a point from the away game with Dundee to secure the League title. Given their long unbeaten run, that was surely a formality. Even if Hearts lost, then Celtic would need to defeat St Mirren by five clear goals to steal the League flag away. In the Hibs crowd that day a number of fans had brought transistor radios, in a kind of morbid fascination over the League outcome, but as the clock was winding down to 90 minutes having been played and Hibs found themselves 2-1 down, Cowan being the Hibs scorer, there was suddenly an almighty shout as news came in from Dens Park that, with seven minutes left to play, Hearts had gone a goal down. By now there was more interest in gathering around those with transistors than there was in the action on the field in front of them, and I will never forget the look on the face of United's Maurice Malpas as he successfully appealed for a throw-in, only to be deafened by a mighty roar from those close to him on the east terracing as news came through that Dundee had scored a second in the 89th minute. Perhaps now the reader will understand my sudden interest in the Hearts results for these last few games!

The fans watching those games in 1986 did not have the benefit of instant news from the internet. They had to rely on the BBC reporting over the radio waves, and it soon became known that not only had Hearts lost 2-0, but Celtic had beaten St Mirren 5-0 to steal the title on goal difference. That day, a certain Albert Kidd became a folk hero to every Hibernian fan on the planet, as it had been the perm-haired substitute who had come off the Dundee bench to grab those two goals and leave the huge Hearts travelling support's dreams in tatters. Cruel, perhaps, but had the boot been on the other foot I am 100 per cent certain that the Hearts fans would have reacted in exactly the same way.

Two days after that devastating result, Hearts visited Easter Road to play in the final of the East of Scotland Shield, both clubs fielding sides mixed with reserves. Billy McKay scored twice for Hearts, while Kane got a last-minute consolation for Hibs.

Little did Hearts know that they'd have to settle for that Shield as their only honour. On the following Saturday, they went to Hampden and were soundly thrashed 3-0 by Aberdeen in the final of the Scottish Cup.

INDEX

Abercromby, Billy 289
Aberdeen FC 1, 7, 11, 20, 23, 34, 40, 45–6, 55, 59, 60, 73–4, 86, 91–2, 101, 110, 127–8, 131, 138, 139, 145–6, 149, 150–51, 155, 163, 166, 168, 173–4, 181–2, 187, 188, 190, 195, 202, 207–8, 218, 219, 246, 250–51, 258, 260, 272, 275–6, 283–4, 291, 294, 297, 300–301, 306, 309, 311, 314, 318, 323, 328
AC Milan 57, 71
Adair, Gerry 94
Addison, Derek 160
ADO (Holland) 1
Ahern, Brian 108, 225
Aird, Kenny 14, 15, 85
Aird, Peter 115
Airdrie FC 6, 10, 17, 21, 30, 33, 43, 48–9, 56, 60–61, 69, 77–8, 109, 116, 118, 245–6, 250, 254, 260, 293
Aitchison, Tom 220
Aitken, Bobby 119, 134
Aitken, Fred 10, 15, 33, 37, 78
Aitken, Roy 213, 249, 321
Aitkenhead, Johnny 136
Allan, Ray 319
Allan, Thomson 2, 5, 6, 10, 20, 21, 22, 88, 99, 100, 120, 122, 134, 193
Alloa FC 302, 318
Altafini, Jose 105–6, 107
Anastasi, Pietro 105, 107
Ancell, Bobby 3
Anderson, Alan 74, 101
Anderson, Andy 165
Anderson, Bill 162
Anderson, Des 119
Anderson, Leif 181
Anderson, Stan 108
Anglo Scottish Cup 158, 200
Ayr United 158, 159–60
Blackburn Rovers (quarter-final) 161, 162

Bristol City (semi-final) 163, 164
St Mirren 200–201
Arbroath FC 19, 23, 72, 80, 94–5, 110, 117
Archibald, Steve 181, 196, 202
Armadale Thistle 322
Armstrong, Graeme 299
Arrol, John 6, 111
Arsenal 41, 109
Arthur, Gordon 326
Aston Villa 29
Atletico Madrid 96
Auckland FC 152
Auld, Bertie 51, 53, 54, 55, 62, 111, 165, 172, 229–30, 231–3, 235, 236–7, 238, 240, 241–2, 243, 245, 246–7, 251, 253–6, 255, 260–61, 263, 265–8
arrival at Easter Road as manager 229
Australia 152
Ayr United 27, 31, 41, 46, 54, 58, 73, 80–81, 85, 91, 108–9, 116, 118, 124, 129, 132, 137, 147, 149–50, 153, 155, 162–3, 166, 168, 170–71, 173, 224, 227–8, 237

Bailey, Gary 253
Baillie, Doug 15
Baillie, Lee 329
Baines, Roy 43, 51, 79, 89, 106, 196, 206, 219, 247, 283
Baker, Joe 45–6, 47, 48, 49, 50, 51, 52, 53, 59, 60, 61, 85, 99, 112, 165
Ball, Allan 65–6, 159, 160
Ballantyne, Ian 222
Banas, Jan 31
Bangerter, Hans 87
Bangu (Brazil) 1, 2
Banks, Gordon 133, 148–9
Bannon, Eamonn 174, 218, 252, 256, 257, 273, 310
Barcelona 39

Barclay, Bill 207
Barr, Les 125
Barry, Roy 6, 113, 114, 118, 120, 130, 135, 136, 168, 190
Bartram, Per 47
Bats, Joel 145
Bauld, Willie 154
Baxter, Bobby 150
Baxter, John 115
Bayern Munich 41
Beardsley, Peter 303
Beattie, Billy 30
Beattie, Frank 53
Beedie, Stewart 203
Belenenses, Lisbon 190
'Benny' *see* Brazil, Ally 133
Bermuda 49
Berwick Rangers 56, 113, 187, 223, 232, 234, 292
Besa FC 68–9, 70–71
Best, George 208–9, 210, 211, 212, 213, 214, 215, 216, 217, 218, 223, 224, 225, 226, 227, 228, 240, 243, 247, 258, 303, 304, 307
Bett, Jim 245, 250
Bettega, Roberto 105, 107
bigotry, Hart's harsh words about 204
Birch, Trevor 193
Birmingham City FC 14
Black, Eric 278, 297, 323, 324
Black, Gordon 115
Black, Ian 220
Black, Jim 10, 17, 26, 29, 36, 51, 60, 61, 66, 85, 94, 98, 100
Player of the Year 100
Blackley, John 'Sloop' 1, 11, 12, 15, 28, 32, 35, 36, 42, 44, 45, 48, 51, 56, 60, 61, 62, 66, 79–80, 85, 86, 91, 97, 99, 101–3, 107, 109, 120, 123, 125, 130, 132, 135–8, 142, 145, 147, 152–3, 158, 160, 162–4, 172, 285, 287–8, 290–93, 297

appointment to management 307
management skills 307–13, 315, 318–20, 322, 325, 328–32
Player of the Year 142
Blackpool FC 2, 13
Blair, Alan 234
Blair, Jim 27, 36, 43, 44, 46
Blyth, Jim 201
Boersma, Phil 44
Bohemians 119, 141
Bond, Kevin 303
Bone, Jimmy 61, 194, 201, 205, 289
Bo'Ness United 1
Bonnar, Pat 244, 249, 304
Bonner, Pat 321
Bonthrone, Jimmy 59, 73–4, 127, 131
Bosman ruling 90–91
Bourke, John 93, 109, 167, 206
Bradford City disaster 317
Bradshaw, Paul 161
Brand, Ralph 28
Brazil, Ally 'Benny' 133, 155, 159, 160, 167–8, 170, 173, 177, 192, 197, 198, 199, 200, 202, 217, 221, 228, 236, 251, 265, 267, 270, 271, 279, 283, 291, 293, 294, 309, 312, 313, 319, 321, 322, 324, 330
Brechin City 286, 318
Bremner, Billy 87, 121
Bremner, Des 72, 76, 77, 83–4, 85, 89, 92, 94, 95, 99, 101, 108, 109, 110, 111, 112, 114, 116–17, 123–4, 126, 127, 128, 129, 137, 139, 141, 143, 147, 151, 155, 157–60, 163–6, 170, 172, 175–6, 179–81, 183, 189–93, 197, 205
Player of the Year 121–2
sale to Aston Villa, fans' anger about 205
transfer to Aston Villa 205
Britton, Ian 281
Brogan, John 237, 242, 304, 306, 307, 308
Brora Rangers 161, 220, 263
Brotherston, Noel 161
Brough, John 191, 193
Brown, Ally 65
Brown, Charlie 79
Brown, Gordon 150
Brown, Jas 228, 231
Brown, Jim 155, 200, 201, 222, 228, 229, 234
Brown, Jock 150
Brown, John 236, 308, 313
Brown, Peter 150

Brown, Steven 177
Brown, Stevie 187, 194, 195, 197, 198, 230–31
Brown, Tony 65
Brownlie, John 36, 37, 49, 51, 52, 53, 58, 60, 63, 66, 68, 69, 70, 72, 76, 77, 86, 88, 91, 92, 94, 99, 102, 116, 117, 118, 119, 120, 122, 125, 128, 129, 130, 132, 134, 137, 139, 140, 141, 143–7, 150, 153, 160, 164, 172–4, 176, 178, 269, 284
Bruce, Sir John 97–8, 101
death of 131
Bryson, Ian 273
Buchan, Martin 60
Buchanan, Archie 294
Buchanan, Ken 54
Burns, Jim 56
Burns, Tommy 321
Busby, Drew 37, 48, 61, 69, 85, 122, 247
Busby, Matt 108, 150
Byrne, Gordon 220, 231, 250, 276

Cagliari 1, 2
Cairney, Joe 206
Caldwell, Alex 130
Caledonia, New Zealand 152
Calgary Kickers 175
Callachan, Ralph 128, 177, 178, 180, 181, 186, 197, 201, 210, 219, 221–2, 231, 243, 250, 252, 256, 259–61, 288, 293, 295, 298, 300, 303, 304, 305, 309, 310, 316, 323, 327
arrival at Easter Road 178
Callaghan, Jim 117
Cameron, Danny 259
Cameron, Jim 53
Cameron, Kenny 52, 54, 123, 203
Campbell, Colin 122, 177, 178, 182, 193, 194, 195, 197–8, 201, 212, 213
Campbell, Dick 179–80
Campbell, Jackie 206
Canada 169, 174, 175–6
Cant, Jimmy 101
Capello, Fabio 105
Carroll, Pat 97, 111, 112–13, 114, 117, 118, 119, 133, 138, 157, 160, 178, 191, 222
Carruthers, Peter 115
Carson, Tom 288
Cashmore, Ian 227
Celtic 5, 9, 19, 23, 28, 32, 39, 45, 55, 59, 64, 73, 81, 83, 86, 91, 92, 105, 114, 130–31,
135, 139, 146, 151, 154–5, 162, 172–3, 181, 186–7, 195, 197, 204, 213, 217, 248–9, 255, 257, 261, 269–70, 273–4, 277–8, 282, 286–7, 294–5, 300, 303–4, 308, 310, 312, 313–14, 321, 325, 327, 332
abandoned game after Celtic supporters' pitch invasion 127
replay of abandoned game 130
Cerro (Uruguay) 1
Channon, Mike 109
Chisholm, Gordon 279, 322, 325, 330
Christie, John 163
Christie, Terry 286
Clark, Bobby 38, 40, 45, 66, 110, 127, 133, 188, 202
Clark, John 310
Clark, Sandy 205, 207, 245–6, 250, 254, 266, 311, 320, 326, 331
Clark, Willie 67
Clarke, Andy 220, 223, 234
Clarke, Dave 168
Clarke, Paul 268
Clemence, Ray 44, 124, 125
Cleveland, Ohio 1
Clinging, Ian 183
Clough, Brian 73, 119, 320
Clougharty, Mark 288
Clunie, Jim 122, 180, 200, 282
Clyde 11, 12, 18, 22, 30, 34, 44, 49, 56, 60, 87, 95, 107–8, 115–16
Clydebank FC 160, 164, 167, 170, 174, 226, 229, 238, 322–3, 324, 326–7, 330
Coldstream FC 241
Coleraine FC 41
Collins, Bill 171–2
Collins, John 303, 306, 318, 321, 324, 327, 328, 330, 331
Colquhoun, John 320, 332
Combe, Bobby 136, 150, 294
Combe, Jim 327
Conn, Alfie 39, 48, 71, 86
Connolly, David 286
Connolly, John 29, 47, 117, 223–4, 225, 226, 231, 232, 236, 238, 250
Connor, Bobby 308
Connor, Frank 287
Conroy, Mike 173, 197, 204, 270, 271, 272, 286, 289, 291, 296
Cook, Jim 48
Cooper, Davie 160, 199, 202, 245, 284, 323
Cooper, Neale 258
Copland, Jackie 44, 67, 201

INDEX

Cork Hibs 63, 118
Cormack, Peter 1–7. 9–11, 13–25, 26–31, 33–5, 122, 124, 163, 215–16, 219, 221–3, 230, 254
Corrigan, Joe 303
Cousin, Alan 3, 10, 14, 19, 25
Coventry City 26, 41, 201–2
Cowan, Gregor 305
Cowan, Mark 37
Cowan, Steve 318, 319, 320, 321, 323, 324, 325, 327, 328, 330, 331, 333
Cowdenbeath 39, 45
Coyne, Tommy 266
Craig, Joe 69–70, 102, 111, 151, 155, 162
Craig, Tommy 137, 221, 308, 309, 313, 320
Cramond, Gordon 163
Crescitelli, Tony 247
Crolla, Carlo 220
Cromb, Douglas 248
Crooks, Garth 148–9
Cropley, Alex 14, 22, 23, 33–5, 39, 42, 46–9, 51–3, 55, 56–7, 59, 60, 63–4, 66–7, 70, 72–3, 75, 77–9, 83, 84, 85, 87, 89, 93, 94, 95, 101, 102–5, 108–9, 116, 120, 134, 166, 268–9, 271
Cruickshank, Jim 20, 38, 122, 128, 131, 136, 155
Crystal Palace 168
Cuccureddu, Antonello 105
Cup Winners' Cup 66, 67–8, 68–9, 70–71, 74, 77, 78, 79
Currie, David 303
Curtis, Alan 286
Cushley, John 49, 109
Cuthbertson, John 'Cubby' 115

Daily Record 65
Dalglish, Kenny 73, 92, 114, 135, 146, 172–3
Dallas 1
Dalziel, Gordon 280, 303
D'Arcy, Tommy 322
Davidson, Bobby 79–80, 101, 127
Davidson, Keith 216
Davidson, Kenny 39, 40, 41, 43, 45, 46, 47, 49, 60
Davidson, Vic 130, 159, 170
Davies, Dai 279
Davies, Wyn 14
Davis, Joe 1–7, 9–12, 13–14, 16–17, 19, 20, 22–3, 26, 30, 33, 115
Dawson, Ally 198
Deans, John 'Dixie' 3, 34, 53, 54, 59, 62, 92, 105, 106, 112, 114, 130, 131, 135
decimalisation 47

Delaney, Mike 231, 252
Demster, John 201
Derby County 96, 119–20
Deveronvale 117, 157
Dickson, Andy 79
Dickson, John 39
Dickson, Peter 159
Dinamo Bucharest 41
Djurgaardens 147
Dobson, Jimmy 327
Docherty, Gerry 108
Docherty, Jim 227
Docherty, John 237
Docherty, Peter 188, 200, 243, 244, 245
Docherty, Tommy 29, 195
Dodds, Billy 217
Dodds, Davie 246, 257, 273, 281
Doig, Jim 220, 221, 234
Domenech, Raymond 183
Donaldson, Ally 11, 17, 203, 216, 240–41, 242, 243
Donaldson, George 101
Donnelly, John 287
Dornan, Andy 280
Douglas, John 305
Doyle, Jamie 302, 307
Doyle, Johnny 58, 121, 129, 146, 217
Drogheda United 141
Dropsy, Dominique 183, 184
Drybrough Cup 63–4, 82–3, 97, 98, 202
Duchart, Alex 115
Duffy, Jim 279
Duffy, Tony 274
Dumbarton FC 70, 78, 93, 94, 109–10, 117, 226, 232, 237, 306, 309–10, 311, 314–15
Duncan, Arthur 'Nijinsky' 5, 9, 28, 31–2, 35, 36, 38, 40, 41, 42–6, 48, 53, 55, 56, 58, 59, 61, 63, 66–70, 72, 75, 77, 78, 81, 83, 85, 86, 88, 92, 93, 143, 147, 153, 155, 157–9, 162, 163, 166, 168, 172–6, 178, 181, 190, 192, 195, 197–9, 240–42, 245–6, 251–2, 255, 265, 269–73, 276, 280, 282, 284, 291–3, 292, 293, 298–300, 299, 300
in dominance over Hearts (season 1975/76) 119–27, 129, 131, 133–9
'Nijinsky' epithet 37
Player of the Year (1974/75) 126
relegation then bounce-back (season 1979/80) 206, 213, 221, 222, 232, 238–9
so near and yet so far (season 1974/75) 97, 99–105, 107–10, 113, 114, 116, 117

Duncan, Bobby 6, 7, 8, 9, 20, 21, 40, 43, 54, 85
Duncan, John 77, 93, 100
Dundalk FC 141
Dundee FC 6, 20, 31, 32, 34, 42, 47, 57, 61, 77, 88, 93, 94, 104, 112, 118, 126, 130, 134, 139, 168, 178, 203, 208, 216–17, 224, 231, 234, 244–5, 249, 253, 259, 270, 274–5, 279–80, 283, 292, 294, 297, 299, 304, 308, 310–11, 313, 322, 324, 327, 332
Dundee United 1, 4–5, 9, 18, 23, 30, 34, 38, 41, 44, 54, 58, 67, 76, 89, 91, 95, 102, 111, 123, 128, 137, 140, 144, 148, 150, 153, 160–61, 164–5, 165, 167, 171, 184, 189, 192–3, 207, 215, 217, 218, 246–7, 251–2, 256, 260–61, 269, 273, 277, 281, 289, 294, 296–7, 299, 310, 312, 315, 323, 328, 329, 333
Dunfermline FC 4, 5–6, 10–11, 20, 24–5, 30, 34–5, 44, 49, 56, 60, 94, 107, 115, 226, 229–30, 236, 325
Dunn, Lawrie 97, 98, 115
Dunn, Steven 329
Dunning, Danny 288
Dunning, George 288
Durban, Alan 279
Durie, Gordon 'Juke Box' 296, 304, 308–13, 309, 310, 311, 312, 313, 315, 318–25, 319, 320, 321, 322, 323, 324, 325, 327, 329, 331–3, 332, 333
Dynamo Dresden 41
Dynamo Kiev 148

East Fife 54, 58, 67, 76, 85, 89
East of Scotland Shield
1968 23
1969 24
1970 35
1971 41
1975 117
1978 167
1979 197–8
1980 222–3
1986 334
East Stirling 225, 228, 238
Easton, Jim 31, 66
Edina Hibs 22
Edinburgh City 277
Edinburgh Evening News 89
Edvaldsson, Johannes 131, 151, 162, 209, 271

Edwards, Alex 27, 55, 56, 57–62, 63–4, 65–6, 68–70, 74–8, 80, 84, 89, 91, 94
  Player of the Year (1977) 158
Eintracht Frankfurt 96
Elgin City 49, 157, 178, 220–21, 302
L'Équipe 73
Eusébio 73, 78
Evans, Alan 121
Ewing, Dave 43–4, 45, 48–50, 51
Eyemouth United 28

Fairbairns Off Licence 10
Fairlie, Brian 177, 190
Fairlie, Jamie 226
Falkirk FC 8, 12, 16, 20–21, 43, 48, 55, 59, 72, 80, 92, 104, 227, 230, 233
Fallis, Ian 114
Fallon, Jim 226
Famous Five 51, 52, 128, 166, 190, 216, 228, 300, 322
Farm, George 85
Farmer, Jim 177, 187, 197, 202, 206
Fazackerley, Derek 161
Fellenger, David 307, 313
Ferencvaros 41
Ferguson, Alex 48, 54, 59, 85, 161, 170, 180, 181, 207, 267, 272, 278, 330
Ferguson, Iain 216, 259, 270, 291, 308
Ferguson, Rikki 225, 236
Fernie, Willie 91, 114
Feyenoord 14, 325
Filippi, Joe 54, 85, 150
Finnigan, Willie 115
Fitzpatrick, Tony 161, 201, 289
Flavell, Bobby 240, 242, 243, 245, 247, 252, 255, 256, 260, 265, 268, 271
Fleming, George 16
Fleming, Ian 102, 138
Fleming, Jim 16
Fleming, Rikki 121, 137, 177, 179, 180, 183
Fletcher, Alex 258
Fletcher, John 153, 208
Flood, John 250
Flucker, Peter 115
Foote, Ian 128, 198
Ford, Bobby 69, 139
Ford, Donald 6, 74, 85, 89, 101
Forfar FC 303
Forrest, Jim 40
Forsyth, Alex 184
Forsyth, Allan 233
Forsyth, Tom 40, 71, 164
Forte, Joe 122, 133
Fraser, Cammy 284, 308
Fraser, John 122, 139, 180, 229

Fresno 240
Frye, Derek 215, 226–7, 227
Frye, Johnny 215
Fulton, Mark 281, 289, 319, 320, 321, 325
Furey, Vincent 244
Fyfe, Graham 39, 40, 71, 97, 98, 138, 139, 149

Gala Fairydean 28
Gallagher, Brian 282, 307
Gallagher, John 101, 226
Gardner, Pat 67
Garland, Kenny 74, 75, 101
Garner, Willie 138
Geddes, Bobby 231, 234, 259
Gemmrish, Albert 183
Gentile, Claudio 105
Geoghegan, Andy 150
George, Charlie 119, 269
Georgeson, Roddy 37
Ghana 13
Gibson, Ian 173
Gibson, Johnny 108
Gibson, Willie 154, 155, 193, 194, 201
Gillies, Don 163
Gilmour, John 48
Given, Jim 266
Glasgow Herald 65
Glavin, Ronnie 61, 111, 112, 151, 154, 162, 195
Glentoran 1, 2
Goldthorp, John 80
Goldthorpe, John 104
Gordon, Alan 34, 52, 53, 58, 59, 60, 61, 62, 63–71, 74, 75, 77–9, 81, 82, 84, 85, 86, 88, 89, 91–2, 94, 120, 122
  Player of the Year (1973) 83
  so near and yet so far (season 1974/75) 97–102, 104, 107, 111, 112, 114, 115
Gorgon, Jerzy 31
Gorman, Dave 125
Gornik Zabrze 31
Gough, Richard 251, 281, 299
Gould, Bobby 65
Gow, Gerry 163
Graham, Arthur 128
Graham, Bobby 104, 113, 136, 144, 149, 229
Graham, Cecil 185, 187, 235
Graham, Johnny 30–33, 35–9, 41–4, 47–9, 54, 91, 121
Grant, Alex 225
Grant, Colin 2, 3, 9, 26–7, 34
Grant, John 115
Grant, Peter 321
Grasshoppers Zurich 41
Gray, Andy 102, 128
Gray, Eddie 8

Greaves, Jimmy 56
Greig, John 3, 7, 22, 40, 47, 48, 86–7, 171, 178, 259
Guimaraes 41–2

Haddow, Ricky 241, 250, 252, 271, 274
Haffey, Frank 112
Hagart, John 119, 122, 136, 233, 254–5
Hagberg, Goran 147
Haiti 240
Hajduk Split 71, 77, 78, 79, 211
Hall, Henry 38, 68, 93, 134, 137
Hall, Ian 133
Hamburg FC 19, 20, 21, 96
Hamil, Hugh 220, 222, 223, 224, 233, 234
Hamilton, Johnny 27, 28, 34, 39, 40, 51, 52–6, 59, 64, 65, 78, 83
Hamilton, Ronnie 40
Hamilton, Willie 16, 99, 115, 148
Hamilton Academicals 225, 229, 235–6
Hancock, Jim 162
Hannigan, Ernie 47
Hansen, Alan 28, 111, 146, 165
Harper, Frank 45
Harper, Joe 23, 38, 40, 45, 59, 65, 66, 74, 91, 92, 93, 94, 95, 96–104, 106–10, 113, 115–16, 117, 149, 181, 187, 190, 202
  in dominance over Hearts 118–28, 132–4, 137–8
Harper, Willie 115
Harris, Colin 311, 312, 321, 323, 326, 330, 332
Harrow, Andy 280, 283
Harrower, William P. 4, 40, 222
Hart, Alan 157, 214, 251, 265, 289, 305
Hart, Sheila 77
Hart, Tom 40, 51, 87, 90, 94, 98, 108, 122, 142, 143, 145, 157, 164, 181, 193, 204, 209, 210–11, 214, 218, 222, 224, 228, 229, 235, 238, 240, 243, 244, 248, 254, 257, 284, 295
  birthday celebrations for 254
  funeral of 259
  sudden death of (and tributes to) 258–9
Hart Jr., Tom 243, 257
Hartford, Asa 65
Harvey, Graham 277, 278–9, 282, 287, 289, 292, 293, 295, 297, 299, 302, 305, 306, 307, 308, 311
Harvey, John 15–16, 154

INDEX

Hawick Royal Albert 28
Hay, David 112, 287
Hazel, John 46, 49, 52, 53, 57, 94
Hearts 6, 8, 12, 15–16, 20, 23, 28–9, 31, 33, 34, 38, 45, 53, 58, 66–7, 74–6, 85, 89, 101, 122–3, 128, 136–7, 147–8, 151, 153–4, 155, 174, 181, 184–5, 193–4, 201, 249, 264, 288–9, 292, 300, 305, 308–9, 320, 324, 331
  McBride's late double against 314
Hector, Kevin 119, 175
Hegarty, Kevin 106
Hegarty, Paul 251, 281, 299
Heggarty, Kevin 46
Heighway, Steve 44, 124–5
Hellberg, Gert 181
Henderson, Albert 80
Henderson, Martin 138, 163, 164, 211
Henderson, Willie 48
Hendry, Ian 232, 233, 234, 244
Henry, Jim 67
Hermiston, Jim 40
Herriot, Jim 14, 52–5, 58, 60, 61, 65–7, 70, 79, 82–3
Hewitt, John 297, 323
Hewitt, Mike 247
Heysel Stadium disaster 317
Hibs
  boardroom changes 40, 247–8, 265, 305
  botton of Premier League after defeat at Firhill 206
  'brilliance' praised by Billy Bremner 87
  Celtic, crushing 6-1 defeat in final by 62
  Centenary Dinner 128
  Centenary Year 119–20
  Civic Reception for 129
  defensive strength in First Division campaign 224–5
  dream team (Stanton, Stewart and O'Rourke) arrive at Easter Road 267–8
  Drybrough Cup success against Celtic 64–5
  Drybrough Cup success against Celtic (again) 83
  European qualification in third place (1969/70) 34–5
  First Division and breaking new ground 220
  First Division champions 238–9, 244
  5000th League goal (Eddie May v Clydebank) 237
  friendly games, problems with arrangements (and funding) 210–11

George Best signing 208–9
Hibs Kids 261–2, 268, 278–9, 282, 316
League Cup final, 6-3 loss to Celtic 106
League Cup victory over Celtic (2-1) 72–3
magnificient seven against Hearts 74–6
Norwegian amateurs at, trials and tribulations of 185–6, 187, 188–9, 191–2
Pat Stanton and dream team come in aid 267–8
postponements 8, 32, 42, 56, 76–7, 88, 110, 132, 146, 149, 150, 167–9, 187, 190–92, 194, 212, 213, 252–4, 279, 280–81, 295, 296, 310, 312, 313, 325
Premier League record 8-1 against Kilmarnock 282
Rangers in Cup Final (1979), two replays, extra time and a narrow defeat 198–9
ranking joint 5th in Europe (*L'Équipe*) 73
recording stars 77
share capital for ground improvements 242
squad for return to Premier Leage football 240–41
tragic fatal bus accident near Perth 256
transfer talk, Shankley's unhappiness about 27–8
Turnbull takes the reins 51–62
undersoil heating at Easter Road 214, 222, 233, 252, 253, 278–9, 312
young players called up for First Division season 220
young players influx of (1978) 177
Hibs Supporters' Association 14, 36, 83, 100, 126, 158, 159, 171–2, 210, 257, 258, 263, 305
Hickton, John 51, 52
Higgins, Hugh 115
Higgins, Tony 72, 77, 79, 80, 83, 84, 85, 86, 98, 111, 113, 114, 115, 116, 118, 146, 153, 160, 161, 162, 163, 168, 170, 171, 172–3, 175, 180, 181, 183, 187, 192, 193, 194, 195, 198, 201, 203, 204, 206–7, 212, 213, 215, 239, 258
transfer to Partick Thistle 216
Hill, Jimmy 214
Hill, Ricky 251, 252, 253
Hinton, Alan 175

Hinton, Kevin 119
Hlevnjak, Ivica 78, 79
Hogg, Davie 23
Hoggan, Kevin 263, 270, 274, 277
Hoggan, Wilson 48
Holmes, Jim 307
Holt, John 256, 257
Holton, Jim 201
Home Farm, Dublin 63
Hong Kong Rangers 152
Hood, Harry 59
Hopcroft, Bobby 46
Hope, Kenny 107, 160, 281
Houston, Bobby 161
Houston, Doug 83
Houston, Texas 1, 2
Howie, Neil 229
Howitt, Bobby 30
Huggins, Dave 177, 219, 221
Hughes, Emlyn 44, 124
Hughes, John 'Yogi' 9, 58
Hulston, Billy 26, 27
Humphries, Wilson 118–19, 121, 122, 139, 141
100 Years of Hibs (Docherty, G. and Thomson, P.) 108
Hunter, Ally 83
Hunter, Eddie 65
Hunter, Gordon 287, 290, 292, 306
Hunter, Ian 133
Hunter, Norman 8, 163
Hunter, Willie 23, 241
Hurlford United 112
Hutchinson, Bobby 99, 165, 166, 168, 170, 171, 178, 181, 183, 184, 186, 187, 188, 193, 195, 198, 201, 202, 203, 207, 208, 219, 220
  arrival at Esater Road 165
Hutchison, Roddy 206
Hvidovre 82

Ibrox, disaster at 45
IFK Norrkoping 180–81, 182
Innes, Norrie 241, 274
Inter-Cities Fairs Cup 26, 39, 40, 41–2, 43–4
  games during 1967/68 season 3, 5–6, 6–7, 8
  games during 1968/69 season 14, 16, 17, 18, 19, 20, 21
Inter Milan 41
Inverness Caley 241, 263
Inverness Thistle 140, 157, 178, 221, 233
Irvine, Alan 220
Irvine, Willie 228, 270, 271, 273, 275, 278, 279, 281, 282, 286, 287, 288, 289, 291, 293, 294, 295, 296, 297, 298, 299, 302, 307, 315, 330, 331

Irwin, Colin 286
Israel 190
Iversen, Odd 102, 103

Jacobs, Stuart 288
James, Leighton 221
James, Robbie 221, 279
Jamieson, Katrina 291
Jamieson, Willie 222, 224, 225, 227, 233, 236, 237, 238, 241, 242, 250, 253, 260, 263, 267, 268, 273, 274, 280, 284, 285, 291, 292, 294, 297, 299, 303, 309, 311, 312
Jardine, Ian 204, 326
Jardine, Sandy 86, 143, 164, 212, 264
Jarvie, Drew 61, 65, 66, 74, 128, 163, 181, 182, 258, 260
Jefferies, Jim 75, 193
Jeffries, Jim 123
Jensen, Bjarne 8
Johnston, Dave 57
Johnston, Harry 203
Johnston, Mo 312, 320, 321
Johnston, Willie 43
Johnstone, Andy 177
Johnstone, Bobby 136, 223
Johnstone, Derek 138, 142, 155, 178–9, 198, 215, 271–2
Johnstone, Jimmy 64, 105, 106
Johnstone, Willie 78
Jones, Mervyn 3, 54
Jonsson, Jan-Ake 181
Jonsson, Per 40
Jonsson, Sven 21
Jordan, Joe 137
Judge, George 16
'Juke Box' see Durie, Gordon
Juventus 105–6, 107

Kane, Paul 267, 279, 285, 286, 290, 293, 296, 297, 299, 302, 304, 305, 306, 307, 310, 313, 315, 316, 319, 320, 322, 323, 324, 325, 331, 334
Karlsen, Geir 115
Kean, Sammy 294
Keegan, Kevin 124–5
Keeley, Glen 161
Keflavik FC 85–6
Keith FC 221, 302–3
Kelly, Archie 136
Kelly, Colin 220, 222, 228, 275
Kelly, Tom 241
Kennedy, Ray 124, 279
Kennedy, Stewart 98, 181, 188
Kerr, Alex 110
Kerr, Jerry 52
Kerr, Jimmy 214, 305
Kidd, Albert 228, 245, 333

Kilgour, Rab 177, 179, 231
Kilmarnock FC 8, 12, 18, 22, 29, 34, 41, 43, 48, 56–7, 61, 79, 97, 103, 107, 114, 147, 152, 153, 156, 204, 208, 211, 212–13, 218, 268, 272–3, 276
destruction (8-1) of 282
Kindon, Steve 175
Kinloch, Bobby 4, 115, 328
Kinninmonth, Alex 107, 133
Kirk, Stevie 304
Kirkwood, Billy 160, 256–7
Kivlin, Charlie 305
Knox, Archie 308
Korotkich, Mike 241

Laidlaw, Joe 51, 52
Lamb, John 128
Lambie, Duncan 111, 126, 142, 190, 213, 215
Lambie, John 141, 166, 169, 267
Lamont, Billy 287
Larnach, Mike 183, 319
Larsson, Bo 40
Latchford, Bob 279, 286
Latchford, Peter 130, 172, 181, 204, 213, 217
Lazio 41
League Cup (later Skol Cup) ties 13–14, 63
Aberdeen FC 26, 27, 36, 37, 65, 66
Aberdeen FC (final, October 1985) 323–4
Airdrie FC 36, 266, 267, 291
Airdrie FC (quarter-final) 69, 70
Alloa Athletic FC 222, 223
Ayr United 83–4, 119, 121
Ayr United (quarter-final) 226–7
Brechin City 179–80
Celtic 242, 243–4, 289, 292
Celtic (and penalty shoot-out) 322
Celtic (final, and 6-2 loss) 23–4
Celtic (final, and 6-3 loss) 106
Celtic (final, and 2-1 victory) 72–3
Clyde 3–4, 26, 27, 223–4, 225
Clydebank 182, 183, 265, 266–7
competition rules, change in 288
Cowdenbeath FC 319
Dumbarton FC 84, 287–8
Dundee FC 3, 99, 100, 119, 120, 122
Dundee FC (sem-final) 17–18
Dundee United 52, 53, 66, 67, 68, 69, 178
Dunfermline FC 26–7, 119, 121, 122
East Fife 15, 16, 304–5

Falkirk FC 14, 15
Falkirk FC (quarter-final) 53–4
Falkirk FC (semi-final) 104
format changes 157–8
Kilmarnock FC 52–3, 205–6, 206–7, 288, 292–3
Kilmarnock FC (quarter-final) 101–2
knock-out revamp for 304
Montrose FC 141–2, 143, 203
Montrose (quarter-final) 123, 125
Morton 83
Morton (quarter-final) 185–6
Motherwell FC 3, 52, 53, 319–20
Queen of the South 65–6, 159, 160
Queen's Park 65, 66
Raith Rovers 14, 15
Raith Rovers (quarter-final) 85, 86
Rangers 99, 100–101, 142–3, 264–5, 267
Rangers (quarter-final) 39–40
Rangers (semi-final) 72, 87, 88, 320–21, 323
St Johnstone 14, 15, 36, 37, 99–100, 141–2, 143, 241–2, 243
St Mirren 242
League Management Committee 94, 98, 234–5
Lee, Francis 119
Leeds United 7, 8, 9, 12, 39, 41, 71, 86, 87, 122
Leicester City 211, 213
Leighton, Jim 181, 246, 278, 291, 294, 323, 324, 328
Leishman, Jim 88, 327
Leitch, Gordon 177, 189–90
Lennon, Danny 313
Lennox, Bobby 135, 204, 209, 217, 218
Leonard, Mike 191, 234
Levein, Craig 295, 305
Linderoth, Anders 147
Lineker, Gary 211
Lister, Ian 40, 46
Liverpool FC 41, 42, 43–4, 120, 122, 124–5, 126
Livingstone, Bobby 125, 203
Lloyd, Larry 44
Logan, Alan 217, 281
Lokomotive Leipzig 18, 19
Love, John 76
Lubanski, Wlodzimierz 31

Mabbutt, Kevin 163, 164
McAdam, Colin 93, 117, 130, 172, 206, 210, 219, 236
McAdam, Tom 70, 93, 128, 148, 277–8

INDEX

McAlpine, Hamish 52, 67, 111, 123, 135, 144, 148, 153, 167, 171, 207, 251–2, 261, 277, 281, 310
McAnespie, Alex 73
Macari, Lou 55, 62, 112
McArthur, Jim 70, 80, 83, 84, 89, 94, 101, 107, 108, 110, 113, 116, 121, 122, 123, 124, 125, 127, 128, 129, 130, 131, 132, 134, 192, 193, 195, 199, 201, 205, 206, 210, 211, 213, 215, 217, 218, 221, 227, 228, 231, 232, 236, 238, 239, 242, 243, 244, 245–6, 248–9, 257, 260, 267, 271–2, 273, 284
  Player of the Year (1980) 235
  testimonial game against Hearts 284
  testimonial match 264, 284
McAvennie, Frank 257, 289
McBride, Joe 18, 19, 20–41, 44, 49, 56, 312, 314, 318, 319, 320
McBride, Joe Jr. 312, 318, 319, 320
McCabe, Gerry 138
McCall, Walker 150, 153, 158, 159, 291
McCarthy, Mick 303
McCartney, Willie 147
McChesney, Iain 159
McClair, Brian 280, 287, 312, 321, 330
McClelland, Chic 181
McClellend, Joe 115
McCloy, Peter 48, 58, 72, 80, 138, 142, 145, 159, 171, 184, 193, 198, 245
McCluskey, George 172, 173, 269, 277–8
McCoist, Ally 231, 242, 279
McColl, Billy 164
McColl, Jimmy 52, 108, 170
McCormack, John 183
McCoy, Gerry 296
McCrae, Walter 53, 57
McCulloch, Alan 114, 288
McCulloch, Dave 109, 116, 171
McCulloch, Jim 48
McCulloch, Willie 160
McCurdy, Pat 203, 266, 268–9, 271, 282, 287, 290, 296, 298, 299
McDermott, Murray 239
McDicken, Derrick 107, 114, 273
McDonald, Alex 15, 40, 62, 98, 202, 207, 296
MacDonald, John 138, 179, 236, 264

McDonald, Mike 133–4, 135, 136, 138, 140, 142, 147, 155, 159, 162, 164, 167, 170, 172, 175, 179, 183, 184, 188, 189, 206, 210
McDonald, Roddy 114, 217, 249
McDougall, Frank 201, 205, 242, 257, 309
McEwan, Billy 59, 61, 63
McEwan, Willie 30, 38, 40
McFarland, Roy 119
MacFarlane, Ricky 254
McFarlane, Willie 28–9, 31–2, 36, 37, 38, 40, 43, 50
  Manager of the Month 30
McGachie, John 297, 300, 307
McGarr, Ernie 23, 45
McGarvey, Frank 161, 165, 172, 194, 195, 200–201, 217, 244, 249, 273, 277–8
McGhee, Alex 106, 133, 135, 139, 149, 150, 160, 166, 167, 168, 173, 177
McGhee, Mark 196, 239, 260, 276, 278, 297, 309
McGhee, Mark (fan who died in bus crash) 256
McGinlay, Brian 121, 130, 198
McGinn, Ross 222–3, 224
McGlinchey, Paul 160, 230–31, 233
McGovern, Paul 313
McGrain, Danny 197, 321
McGraw, Allan 1, 5, 6, 8, 10, 12, 14, 17, 21, 25
McGregor, Alex 82, 98
McIlhone, Steven 305
McIlmoyle, Hugh 84
McInally, Jackie 41, 59
McKay, Billy 334
Mackay, Dave 119
Mackay, Donald 254, 275
Mackay, Gary 311, 333
McKay, Jim 161, 162
McKee, Kevin 269, 274, 279, 284, 290, 292, 293, 302, 304
McKellar, Dave 320, 325
McKenzie, Roddy 17, 60–61, 69, 70, 84, 94
McKeown, Brian 246
Mackie, Peter 275
Mackin, Alan 235
McKinley, Columb 69
McKinnon, Dave 265
McLaren, Billy 230, 236
McLaughlin, Joe 214, 279, 283
McLaughlin, Sandy 18
McLean, Ally 141, 143, 151–5, 155, 157–73, 175–6, 178–80, 182–4, 187, 191–2, 194, 196, 198, 203–8, 210–11, 214–18, 220–21, 223–4,
226–7, 229–39, 240, 241, 244, 245, 247, 250–54, 260, 261, 275
McLean, George 3, 6, 25, 26, 80
McLean, Jim 3, 58, 102, 128, 165, 277, 302, 310
McLean, Kenny 247–8, 265
McLean, Tommy 8, 48, 53, 78, 79, 132, 143, 212, 245
McLean, Willie 214–15
McLeish, Alex 181, 278, 291, 328
McLeod, Ally 41, 54, 83, 85, 108, 109, 110, 113, 115, 116, 119, 120, 121, 126, 129, 130, 131, 132, 133, 134, 135, 138, 139, 328
McLeod, Johnny 112
McLeod, Murdo 186, 204, 244, 269
McManus, Michael 310
McMaster, John 131, 202
McMenamin, Jim 290
McMillan, Ian 116
McNab, Eddie 270
McNab, Neil 83
McNamara, Jackie 131, 143–4, 145, 153, 160, 166, 179, 183, 184, 185, 187, 189, 197, 200, 202, 207, 213, 215, 216–17, 222, 225, 227, 229, 232, 236, 237, 242, 243, 244, 245, 246, 247, 249, 251, 252, 254, 260, 264, 265, 269, 271, 272, 273, 274, 278, 282, 283, 286, 292, 293, 297, 298, 299, 302, 303, 304, 309, 310
  Player of the Year (1978) 180
  Player of the Year (1979) 210
  testimonial match 303
  250th goal for Hibs 250
McNamee, John 115
McNaughton, Sandy 230, 234
McNeil, Neil 234
McNeill, Billy 62, 64, 106, 204, 257, 303
McNeill, Dave 196
McNeill, John 259, 260
McNicol, Jim 46
McNicoll, Dave 123
McNiven, Tam 102–3, 129, 227, 273, 274, 281, 291, 307
McPheat, Billy 10
McPhee, Billy 54, 58
MacPherson, James 77
McQuade, Denis 152, 185, 251
McQueen, Tommy 302, 309
McSherry, Jim 137
McStay, Paul 270, 273, 312, 321
McVie, Willie 108, 130
McWilliams, Derek 265, 267, 274

Madsen, John 2, 10, 14, 19–21, 27, 30, 34
Mahoney, John 279, 286
Malmo FC 39, 40
Malpas, Maurice 281, 299, 310, 333
Malta Hibs 260
Manchester City 201, 303
Manchester United 253
Manitoba All Stars 175–6
Marine Hotel, North Berwick 295
Marinello, Peter 1, 9, 12, 13–16, 23–4, 26–31, 34–5, 135, 137, 139, 144, 159
Markie, John 80
Markland, Stuart 123
Marley, Stephen 220, 222
Marshall, Gordon 24, 30, 37, 38, 292, 296
Marshall, Warren 274
Martin, Bent 27
Martin, John 245, 254
Martin, Neil 2, 26
Marustik, Chris 286
Mason, Joe 71
Masterton, Danny 171
Mathie, Ross 57
Mathisen, Svein 185, 186, 188, 191, 192
Maxwell, George 208
Maxwell, Sam 57
May, Eddie 322, 325, 327, 328, 330
May, Larry 211
Meadowbank Thistle 162, 197–8, 202, 229, 230–31, 271, 286, 299–300, 305
Melrose, Harry 230, 232
Melrose, Jim 169, 197, 206
Mercer, Wallace 258
Middlesbrough FC 51, 52, 303
Millar, Peter 80, 208
Miller, Alex 142, 143, 199, 207, 315
Miller, Bertie 74
Miller, Blair 229, 266
Miller, Lord Provost John 129
Miller, Stewart 46
Miller, Willie 128, 181, 278, 324, 328
Mills, David 303
Milne, Callum 282, 292, 293, 296, 302, 330
Milne, Ralph 207, 297
Mitchell, Barrie 49
Mitchell, Doug 108
Mitchell, Ian 67
Moffat, Jim 203
Moller, Rene 16
Money, Campbell 315
Montrose FC 63
Moran, Doug 115

Morris, Eric 224, 227
Morrison, Eddie 70, 79, 91, 102, 103, 114
Morton 8, 11, 22–3, 29, 32, 42–3, 47, 57, 62, 71, 79, 89, 95, 106–7, 114–15, 182, 192, 196, 206, 211–12, 213–14, 219, 260, 262, 274, 283, 307, 310, 312–13, 315
Morton, Colin 274
Morton, Jim 232–3
Motherwell FC 8, 11, 12, 30, 34, 41, 46, 54, 58–9, 80, 88, 93, 94, 104, 113, 127, 130, 134, 138, 144, 149, 150, 154, 159, 164, 166–7, 170, 183, 187, 191, 196–7, 224, 228, 239, 253–4, 271, 275, 280, 283, 290, 293, 298–9, 322, 327–8, 331, 333
crunch League game for UEFA place 139
Mowbray, Tony 303
Moyes, Davie 244
Muir, Jim 41, 117
Muir, John 59, 93
Muir, Lindsay 113, 118, 119, 120, 133, 135, 136, 138, 139, 141, 143, 145, 169, 177, 292
Muirhead, Tommy 152, 172, 211
Mullen, Bill 60, 64
Müller, Gerd 73, 78
Munro, Bill 160
Munro, Iain 40, 82, 83, 88, 95, 97, 98, 102, 103, 104, 106, 107, 108, 110, 111, 115, 116, 119, 121, 122, 123, 124, 138, 142, 170, 279, 314, 321
Munro, Martin 188, 220
Munro, Willie 226
Murphy, John 3, 13, 26, 35, 79
Murray, Cameron 124
Murray, Don 122
Murray, Gary 203, 232, 233, 236, 239, 240, 241, 243, 244, 245, 247, 257, 259, 260, 261, 263, 265, 266, 267, 271–2, 273, 275, 278, 284, 285, 286, 288, 293, 299
Murray, George 127
Murray, Neil 106
Murray, Steve 65, 105, 106, 112
Murray, Willie 63, 72, 91, 97, 107, 109, 118, 133, 136, 138, 139, 166, 170, 171, 172, 175, 187, 191, 203, 214, 215, 217, 252
Musselburgh Athletic 113
MVV Maastricht 36, 49

Napoli 5–6, 6–7, 8, 12, 39
Narey, David 111, 150, 277, 281, 299
Nattrass, Irving 303
Neal, Phil 124
NEC Nijmegen 36, 98–9
Neely, Gordon 302, 305, 307, 313
Ne'er Day matches 8, 31, 45, 58, 74–5, 110, 131, 295, 311, 326
postponement of 150
Nelson, Denis 16, 60
Nenkovic, Dusan 256
Nesse Gutten FC, Levanger 97
New York 1
Newcastle United 14, 24, 26, 41, 146, 303
News of the World 73
Nicholas, Charlie 239, 248, 273, 277, 282, 287
Nicholls, David 329
Nicol, Steve 227
Nigeria 13
'Nijinsky' see Duncan, Arthur
Nizetic, Milo 211
North American Laegue 1
Nottingham Forest 24, 33
Nutley, Bobby 115

O'Brien, Gerry 174, 179, 189–90
O'Connor, Derek 185, 193, 249, 305, 308
Ogilvie, John 136, 190
O'Hara, Alex 165, 172, 173, 183, 197, 210, 261, 292
O'Hara, Tommy 159
Ohlsson, Par-Olof 181
Oldham Athletic 49
O'Leary, David 321
O'Leary, Pierce 321
Olek, Alfred 31
Olympia Ljubljana 14, 16, 17
O'Malley, Tom 248, 304
Ontario All Stars 175
O.P.E. Ostersund 82, 96
Ormiston Primrose 277
Ormond, Willie 61, 68, 136, 167, 174, 215–16, 218–19, 220–21, 223–4, 226, 227–8, 238, 300
death of 300
illness and managerial exit 228–9
medical advice to quit 228–9
O'Rourke, Jimmy 6, 7, 10, 11, 12, 14–17, 19–20, 23–5, 35, 98
coaching role for 180
Drybrough and League Cup (and 7-0 against Hearts at Tynecastle) 64, 65, 66, 67, 68, 69–75, 79, 80–81

INDEX

at Motherwell 111, 126, 149–50, 166–7
season 1970/71, management changes 41, 46–7, 49
season 1973/74, successes and failures of 88–9, 91–2
Turnbull Tornado 54, 56–62
Orr, Neil 186
Osborne, Billy 47, 115
Osgood, Peter 109
Osters Vaxjo 146–7, 148
Ottawa All Stars 99
Ottawa Tigers 175–6
Otto, Heine 303
Ozcan, Arkoc 21

Paisley, Bob 124
Park, Donald 74, 179, 197, 295
Parkes, Phil 175
Parlane, Derek 83, 98, 99, 125, 132, 142, 149, 155, 171, 179, 199, 303
Partick Thistle 5, 9, 17, 21, 28, 31–2, 57, 61, 69–70, 79, 84, 89, 102, 111, 118, 146, 149, 152, 161, 165, 172, 173, 183, 188–9, 197, 206, 210, 219, 230, 248, 252–3, 258, 261
  Sunday fixture at 151
Paterson, Craig 175, 176, 178, 201, 202, 203, 213, 223–4, 224, 225, 233, 238. 244–5, 249, 251, 254, 256, 263, 265
  Player of the Year (1981) 263
Paterson, Willie 139, 148, 157, 175, 191, 193
Payne, Graeme 123, 171, 184, 189
Pearson, Jim 47, 68, 92
Pecs Dozsa 41
Peebles Rovers 99
Pelé 106
Penman, Andy 32
Pepic, Mike 148
Peters, Alan 313
Peterson, Craig 166
Pettigrew, Willie 113, 127, 130, 135, 149, 154, 159, 166, 187, 207, 215, 217, 218
Phillips, Alan 116
Phillips, Gerry 121
Phillips, Leighton 221
Piasecki, Francis 183
Pintenat, Robert 145
Pirie, Billy 72, 101, 110
Plumb, Angus 115
Porterfield, Ian 4
Porto FC 3, 4, 5, 39
Power, Paul 303
Premier League 159, 179, 237, 331

creation of 118
discussions about 90–91
league reconstruction 331–2
Prentice, Bobby 148
Prentice, John 16, 86
Prentice, Rab 123
Preston, Tommy 67
Pringle, Alex 60
Printy, Ian 76
programme notes
  advertising revenues 120
  Archie Buchanan death announcement 294
  Australia tour discussed 151
  Barcelona, memories of 328–9
  Blackley's half-time with Boca Juniors 158
  Bobby Thomson's spying duties 298
  Bukta sponsorship deal 154
  Centenary Year celebrations 115
  change strip in purple, ge=reen and yellow (and black and white) 161
  change strip lettering controversy 161
  Cotters World Travel 264
  crown behaviour problems persist 266
  death of Willie Hamilton in Canada 148
  Des Bremner and trophies 121
  'family ticket,' introduction of 234–5
  fathers-and-sons, arrangements for 55
  foreign players, SFA and Employment Department recommendations 191–2
  Hart's plea on crown behaviour 252–3
  home advantage, counting on 217
  Jock Brown article 150
  Jock Weir pen picture 131–2
  John Madsen's return from Denmark 19–20
  League set-up, news of possible changes 89–90
  Motherwell Cup meetings 136
  new look for First Division 221–2
  Norwegian amateurs in sights of Hibs management 185
  opening game (1985) against Rangers 319
  optimism on Hibs' UEFA chances 123–4
  possible European rivals discussed 117
  Premier Reserve League introduced 158–9

presentation to Jimmy McColl 108
programme sales within stadium only 208
quaint ads in 42
record in friendlies 247
reserve football 91, 121–2
Scotland squad members 123
season 1974/75, news and ads in first programme 97–8
season ticket prices (1983), stadium redevelopment and 286
season ticket problems 188
seating damage 115
share capital for ground improvements 243
share capital issue and covered enclosure 243
stadium development 285–6
stadium development update 289–90
Tam McNiven testimonial 306–7
team results, Stanton's reflections on 272–3
Under-18 League participation 231–2
Under-14 side success 329
Vincent Fury affair 244
youth team performances 313
Provan, Davie 114, 186, 197, 282, 321
Pryce, Eddie 51, 52
Prytz, Robert 265
Purdie, Ian 101, 126

Queen's Park Rangers 285–6
Quilietti, Alan 177, 178
Quinn, Pat 4, 5, 7, 9, 15, 17, 21, 25, 54, 85, 229–30, 243, 244, 251, 261, 267

Rae, Gordon 159, 169, 175, 176, 179–81, 183–5, 193–9, 201, 203, 213, 218–19, 222–4, 226, 229–39, 240–41, 243–5, 249–50, 252, 254, 256–9, 262, 265, 267, 268, 270, 271, 273–5, 277, 279, 281–3, 291, 293, 296, 298, 308, 309, 331, 332
  Scottish Footballer of the Month (February, 1982) 258
Rae, Robin 241, 247, 250, 251, 260, 286, 290, 293, 297, 299, 310, 321
Rae, Stuart 220, 277
Rae, Tommy 84
Rafferty, Stuart 308
Raith Rovers 4, 9, 12, 16, 20, 28, 31, 222, 233, 238–9,

Ramage, John 325
Ramsay, Dougie 174
Rangers 11, 18, 22, 29, 32, 38–9, 41, 43, 46–7, 48, 57–8, 62, 63–4, 71–2, 79–80, 83, 86–7, 92, 97, 98, 108, 116, 125, 129, 132, 138, 145, 149, 152, 155, 159, 164, 167, 171, 178–9, 184, 195, 199, 202, 207, 212, 215, 245, 249–50, 255, 259–60, 271–2, 275, 280, 284, 291, 294, 298, 301, 306, 309, 311, 315–16, 318–19, 323, 325–6, 329
Rangers News 280
Rankin, Mike 226
Ranson, Ray 303
Rapid Bucharest 71
Real Mallorca 50
Red Star Belgrade 39
Redford, Ian 203, 260
Refvik, Isak 184, 185, 186, 188, 189, 190, 192, 277
Reid, Allan 133
Reid, Bobby 4, 165, 172, 327
Reid, Chris 329
Reid, David 200, 219
Reilly, John 273
Reilly, Lawrie 136, 235, 294, 322
Rennie, Alex 61, 236–7
Rennie, Stewart 54, 104, 134, 137, 139, 144, 166, 197
Renton, Jim 204, 235
reserve football 3, 14, 18, 22, 37, 39, 40, 72, 91, 98, 112–13, 121–2, 133, 138–9, 153, 158, 160, 166, 168–9, 189–90, 202, 212, 222, 236, 250, 252, 261, 285, 287, 290, 296, 299, 305–6, 324
  league set-up, changes in 178
  Stanton and the 1982/83 season 265–6, 267, 268–9, 270–71, 274, 275, 279, 281–2
  Stirling University four-team tournament 290
Revie, Don 87
Rice, Brian 220, 222, 251, 263, 275, 277, 279, 280, 283, 285, 286, 288, 290, 293, 298, 299, 300, 301, 302, 304, 311, 312, 315, 318, 320
Rice, Bruce 270
Richardson, Lex 217, 289
Rigo, Antonio 5, 7
Rioch, Bruce 119, 120
Ritchie, Andy 186, 196, 206, 211, 219, 247, 259, 270
Ritchie, Tom 164

Robb, Davie 37, 40, 60, 92, 128
Roberts, Phil 133
Robertson, Bobby 65, 70, 71
Robertson, Derek 100, 111, 133, 143
Robertson, Hugh 44, 49
Robertson, Ian 228
Robertson, John 289, 314, 326, 331
Robertson, Malcolm 132, 137, 154, 193, 270, 271, 277, 292
Robson, Brian 253
Rodger, Jim 250
Rodier, Derek 200, 204, 211, 219, 222, 224, 233, 241, 243, 244, 247, 249, 254, 255, 261, 265, 266, 267, 271, 274
Rodman, Brian 114
Rofe, Dennis 211
Rolland, Andy 52, 76
Roma 39
Rooney, Benny 182, 206, 247, 254, 259
Rooney, Jim 307
Rosenborg 82, 96, 99, 102, 103–4, 143
Ross, Brian 133
Ross, David 45
Ross County 241, 263
Rough, Alan 61, 79, 111, 146, 149, 165, 169, 172, 206, 210, 236, 258, 273, 275, 276–7, 278, 284, 287–8, 294, 295, 296, 299, 304, 305, 310, 313, 319, 320, 321, 322, 330
  arrival at Easter Road 274, 276–7
  transfer from Partick Thistle to Hibs 274
Rougvie, Doug 302, 309
Roxburgh, Andy 210
Royle, Joe 312
Ruddy, Dennis 117
Russell, Bobby 186, 196, 202, 236, 245, 260
Rylance, Derek 117

Salton, John 191, 230
Salvesen's Boys' Club 241, 282, 297, 305, 319
Samuel, Alan 241, 274
San Francisco 1
San Jose Earthquakes 218, 223, 228, 240, 247
Sauchie Thistle 114
Scanlon, Ian 174, 202
Schaedler, Erich 30–31, 49, 51, 82, 85, 87, 122, 130–32, 136, 145, 154–5, 159, 163, 208, 242, 245

  back from Dundee 246–7, 252, 254, 256, 266, 269–70, 271, 278, 280–81, 283, 285–6, 288, 290–91, 293
  death and distressing story of 326
  Drybrough and League Cup (and 7-0 against Hearts at Tynecastle) 66, 68, 74, 78, 79
  Jedburgh Hibs Supporters' Player of the Year 159
  League success so near in 1974/5 season 82, 85, 87, 97, 103, 107–9, 111, 117
  transfer to Dundee 165
  Turnbull's Tornado 53, 57, 59–60
Schalke 04 36, 52, 71
Scirea, Gaetano 105
Scotland 55, 85, 116, 137, 148, 321–2, 330–31
  Under-21 victories with Turnbull and McLeod outstanding 184, 187
Scott, Alex 4, 8, 13, 14, 17, 20, 24, 65, 99, 138–43, 144, 146, 148, 153–5, 157, 160, 182
Scott, Ally 65, 99, 138–9, 141–3, 146, 153–4, 157, 160, 182
Scott, Jim 2, 3, 14, 327
Scott, Jocky 88, 93, 94, 99, 100, 126, 128, 138
Scottish Cup (and Cup ties) 111, 190–91, 296
  Aberdeen FC 278
  Aberdeen FC (semi-final) 196, 332
  Airdrie FC 10, 59–60
  Arbroath FC 152–3
  Ayr United 214–15, 328
  Berwick Rangers 216
  Celtic 111–12
  Celtic (and boost of 4-3 victory over) 329–30
  Celtic (crushing 6-1 defeat in final by) 62
  Celtic (semi-final) 218
  Dundee FC 93
  Dundee United 134, 135, 256–7
  Dundee United (quarter-final) 47
  Dunfermline FC 132–3, 191, 233–4, 327
  East Fife 168, 296
  East Stirling 9–10
  Falkirk FC 235, 254–5
  Forfar Athletic 46
  Hearts 46
  Hearts (quarter-final) 193
  Kilmarnock FC 91

INDEX

Meadowbank Thistle 192, 213
Morton 77
Motherwell FC 135–6, 137
Partick Thistle 59, 169
Rangers 21–2, 32, 78, 236
Rangers (final) 198–9
Rangers (semi-final) 48, 61, 62
St Johnstone 92
Scottish Football Association (SFA) 17–18
Disciplinary Committee 77
disciplinary points and suspensions, rules on 200
fine and warning for Pat Stanton from 295
George Best controversy 304, 307
Referees' Committee 115, 134
Tommy Younger in line for Presidency 177
Tommy Younger re-elected at 98
Scottish Football League (SFL)
Dunblane discussions (and new ideas) 255
league format discussions 248
Scrimgeour, Brian 224
Seeler, Uwe 20
Seith, Bobby 58, 66, 101
Setterington, Alex 54
Shamrock Rovers 1, 2
Shankley, Bill 124
Shankley, Bob 3, 4, 6, 7, 9–10, 13, 18–19, 21, 24, 27
Shaw, Davie 115, 147, 150
Shaw, Graham 88, 115
Shaw, Hugh 134
Shaw, John 163
Sheffield Wednesday 13
Shelbourne 318
Shevlane, Chris 14, 19, 28, 37, 42, 51
Player of the Year (1969/70) 36
Shilton, Peter 133
Shirra, Jim 54, 216, 231
Sieger, Ian 329
Simpson, Billy 6, 11
Simpson, Neil 246, 250, 278
Sinclair, Colin 28
Sinclair, Eric 216, 231, 253
Sinclair, Graeme 287
Skol Festival Trophy 201–2
'Sloop' see Blackley, John
Smith, Alex 237–8
Smith, Bobby 72, 81, 83, 84, 85, 94, 97, 99, 100, 101, 107, 108, 111, 116, 117, 119, 120, 122, 128, 129, 133, 134, 139, 140, 145, 148, 152, 165, 190, 211, 272–4
Smith, Charlie 130
Smith, Colin 145

Smith, Dave 223
Smith, Doug 38, 52
Smith, Gordon 67, 114, 130, 136, 147, 150, 184, 207, 253
Smith, Henry 249, 264
Smith, Jim 270
Smith, Joe 163
Smith, Tommy 44
Smith, Walter 124
Sneddon, Alan 213, 232, 233, 239, 242, 262, 264, 271, 272, 282, 293, 311, 312, 321, 323, 325
Sneddon, Davie 204
Sochaux FC 142, 145, 146
Somner, Doug 59, 108, 149, 165, 197, 201, 210, 219, 246, 281
Sorensen, Erik 106
Southampton FC 109
Spalding, Derek 56, 72, 80–81, 92, 94, 102, 104, 109, 110, 113, 121, 131, 132, 135, 136, 153, 155
Spalding, Ian 255–6
Sparks, Raymond 307
Sparta Prague 41, 71
Sparta Rotterdam 41
Spartak Moscow 71
Sporting Lisbon 66, 67–8
Sproat, Hugh 116, 124, 132, 271, 275
St Etienne FC 142, 148
St Johnstone 6, 10, 12, 25, 29–30, 33, 42, 47, 57, 61, 68, 78, 93, 103, 111, 125–6, 129–30, 133–4, 139, 227, 231, 236–7, 251, 290–91, 293, 297, 298
St Mirren 21, 22, 27, 33, 40, 46, 82–3, 161, 165, 166, 169–70, 172, 180, 185, 194, 195, 204, 205, 209–10, 217–18, 246, 251, 257, 261, 268, 272, 276, 289, 293, 295, 298, 308, 313, 315, 319, 324–5, 330, 331
Stanton, Pat 2, 7, 11, 20, 35, 141, 166, 174, 181, 232–3, 259
captains armband for 26–33
dominance over Hearts in 1975/6 Centenary Season 118–119, 121–2, 124–6, 128–30, 133–4, 136
Drybrough and League Cup (and 7-0 against Hearts at Tynecastle) 63–7, 70–75, 77, 79, 82
League Cup final 1972, "Stantons' final" 73
League success so near in 1974/5 season 96–100, 102–5, 107–12, 114

management skills as legend returns 267–77, 279, 281, 283–4, 302–3, 304, 306
Player of the Year 14–16
resignation as manager 306–7, 309–10
resignation for 306
season 1970/71, management changes 36–8, 40–43, 45, 47–9, 51, 54–6, 58–62
season 1973/74, successes and failures of 85–9, 91–2, 94–5
SFA Disciplinary ban (14-days) 77
testimonial game for 174
transfer to Celtic 143–4, 154–5
youth given a chance 285, 287–93, 295, 297–9
Stapleton, Frank 253
Stark, Billy 161, 165, 195, 201, 246, 261, 323
Steedman, Davie 112
Steel, Derek 233
Steele, Jim 32, 149
Stein, Colin 1–12, 13–19, 22, 25, 32, 43, 62, 71, 116
Stein, Jock 72, 73, 81, 83, 112, 117, 215, 250, 257, 264, 321, 322
death of 322
Stephen, Ray 259
Stevens, Gregor 127, 164, 170
Stevenson, Eric 2–6, 8–11, 13, 16–17, 20, 24, 26, 28, 37–8, 46–8, 51–3, 55, 58
Stevenson, Jimmy 34
Stewart, Davie 54, 84, 221
Stewart, George 141, 145, 157, 158, 162, 165, 168, 176, 178, 183, 185, 192, 193, 195, 197, 201–2, 213, 224, 226, 267, 279, 303
arrival at Hibs 141
Stewart, Hal 29
Stewart, Ian 318
Stewart, Jim 107, 114, 265, 275
Stirling Albion 6, 10, 12, 28, 231–2, 237–8
Stoke City 1, 2, 148–9
Stornoway Select 285
Strachan, Gordon 120, 196, 258, 260, 278, 284, 309
Strasbourg 183, 184
Street, Bobby 212–13
Strickland, Derek 211
Stuart, Alex 123, 132, 149–50, 158
Sturm Graz 41
Sturrock, Paul 273, 297
Sullivan, Dom 49, 108, 181, 202, 244
Sunday Express 65
Sunday Mail 87, 244

Sunderland FC 1
Surjak, Ivo 79
Swan, Harry 177, 222
Swansea City 221–2, 279, 286
Sweeney, Gerry 47, 163, 164
Syiles, Bobby 51
Syme, David 207, 280

Tahiti 152
Tainton, Trevor 164
Tait, Bobby 163
Taylor, Ian 137
Taylor, Peter 119
Tel Aviv 190
Temperley, Willie 175, 176, 181, 187, 189, 191
Texaco Cup 48
Third, Brian 83
Thomson, Billy 180, 205, 257, 261, 268, 289, 291, 295
Thomson, Bobby 100, 185, 192, 196, 214, 247, 263–4, 270, 271, 272–3, 276, 279, 282, 283, 285, 286, 288, 292, 298, 302, 304, 306, 307, 313, 321
Thomson, Eddie 123
Thomson, Jimmy 115, 297
Thomson, Kenny 132–3
Thomson, Les 113
Thomson, Phil 108
Thunshelle, Arve 104
Tierney, Lawrence 216
Timmons, Joe 270
Todd, Colin 119
Tolmie, Jim 211, 247
Tom Hart Memorial Trophy 264, 325
Tom Martin, tailors 158–9
Tomassi, Colin 234, 286
Tomorrow's World (BBC TV) 144
Toronto 1–2, 169, 201
Torrance, Bobby 201, 216, 217, 219, 220
Tortolano, Joe 320, 321, 324, 325, 326, 330
Toshack, John 44, 124, 126, 221, 286
Totten, Alex 223
Townsend, Jim 106
Trondheim 82, 96, 99, 102, 103
Turnbull, Eddie 1, 7, 34, 38, 45, 82, 83, 84, 92, 94, 96, 98, 102, 103–4, 106, 107, 108, 109, 112, 113, 115, 116, 126, 135, 136, 139, 177–82, 184–90, 276, 300
  change and reconstruction (season 1977/78) 159–61, 163, 165–7, 169, 173–5

Cup campaign success and ultimate disappointment (1979) 190–97
defensive strengths but goal-scoring weaknesses in (season 1976/77) 141–5, 147, 149, 150, 154
eight years and nine months in charge, end of an era for 218
hospitalisation and major operations for 118–20
management skills, "seventh heaven" with 63–81
relegation, despite best efforts (saeaon 1979/80) 200, 203, 205–7, 209–13, 216–18
return to duty after illness 123–4
Turnbull's Tornadoes 17, 51–62, 66, 76–7, 91, 165, 178, 258
Turnbull, Stuart 239, 242, 261, 270
Turner, Brian 168
Tweed, Steven 319
Tynecastle Boys' Club 32

UEFA Cup 85–6, 87, 96, 99, 102, 103–4, 105–6, 107, 120, 124–5, 126, 142, 145, 146–7, 148, 173–4, 180–81, 182, 183, 184
United States 238, 240

Valencia 39
Valentine, Bob 171, 295
Vancouver 1, 2
Vancouver Island Vistas 175
Vancouver Whitecaps 175
Varga, Zoltan 74
Vincent, Stan 168, 178, 229

Waddell, Andrew 286
Waddle, Chris 303
Wagstaffe, David 161
Waldie, Sam 131
Walker, Nicky 280
Walker, Tommy 15
Wallace, Gordon 15, 42, 88, 126, 134, 144, 148, 222
Wallace, Jock 71, 83, 116, 142, 190, 211, 325
Wallace, Willie 70, 109
Wallington, Mark 211
Ward, Joe 108, 205, 206, 207–8, 210, 212
Waterford FC 63, 118–19, 318
Watson, Andy 208, 218, 278
Watson, Bobby 245
Watson, George 233, 235
Watson, Kenny 123, 248

Watson, Willie 113
Waugh, Kenny 247–8, 255, 258, 259–60, 263, 264, 265, 279, 285, 294, 295, 305, 306, 312, 317
Weir, Jock 131–2
Weir, Michael 'Mickey' 274, 293, 306, 307, 312, 316, 331
Weir, Peter 272, 278, 284
Welsh, Peter 263–4, 265, 266, 267, 270, 271, 278, 279
West Bromwich Albion 65
Wharton, Kenny 303
Wharton, Tom 'Tiny' 15
White, Davie 120
Whiteford, Derek 17, 56
Whittaker, Brian 210
Whyte, David 200, 202, 212
Whyte, Hugh 111, 112–13, 191, 230
Wigan Athletic 49
Wilkinson, Ian 27
Williams, Alex 303
Williams, Evan 64, 108
Williamson, Billy 131
Williamson, Bobby 266, 319, 320
Wilson, Billy 37
Wilson, Bob 55
Wilson, Bobby 47
Wilson, Jimmy 61–2, 93
Wilson, Kevin 290, 292, 293
Wilson, Mark 37
Wilson, Mike 129, 133, 138
Wilson, Paul 92, 106, 114, 135
Wilson, Sammy 3
Wilson, Terry 225–6, 228, 236
Wilson, Willie 7, 10, 23, 25, 61
Wolverhampton Wanderers 1
Woodburn, Willie 235
World Cup (1970) 29
Wright, Alex 109
Wright, Brian 229

Yorath, Terry 201
York FC 52
Young, Alan 305
Young, Quinton 27, 71, 129
Young, Tom 54
Young, Willie 55, 110
Younger, Tommy 40, 87, 96, 98, 122, 177, 193, 251, 276, 294, 295
  adeath of 295
Yule, Tommy 152, 153

Zoff, Dino 7, 105, 107
Zurich FC 10